D1592902

**Strategies in
Architectural Thinking**

Strategies in Architectural Thinking

Edited by
John Whiteman
Jeffrey Kipnis
Richard Burdett

Chicago Institute for
Architecture and Urbanism

The MIT Press
Cambridge, Massachusetts
London, England

© 1992, CIAU and the authors

Distributed by The MIT Press
Cambridge, Massachusetts and
London, England

Library of Congress Cataloging-
in-Publication Data

Strategies in Architectural
    Thinking/edited by
    John Whiteman,
    Jeffrey Kipnis and
    Richard Burdett
    256 pp. 173 cm x 258 cm.
        Selected and revised
    papers originally presented
    at a conference held on
    Sept. 9-11, 1988 at the
    Charnley House, Chicago.
        Includes bibliographical
    references
        ISBN 0-262-23159-X
    1. Architecture—Philosophy.
    I. Whiteman, John, 1954-
    II. Kipnis, Jeffrey.
    III. Burdett, Richard
    (Richard M.)
    IV. Chicago Institute for
    Architecture and Urbanism.
    NA2500. 583   1991
    720'. 1—dc20

                    90-26328
                    CIP

Acknowledgments
Ms. Elizabeth Diller and
Mr. Ricardo Scofidio, NY;
Ms. Florence B. Eichin,
Penguin USA, NY;
Mr. Richard Fleischner,
Providence, RI;
Ms. Dolores Gall, *Perspecta*,
New Haven, CT;
Mr. Paul Geuthner, Librarie
Orientaliste Paul Geuthner,
Paris; Ms. Mia Hipeli,
Alvar Aalto Foundation,
Helsinki; Ms. Patricia Johanson,
Buskirk, NY;
Ms. Paula Pergament,
Art Institute of Chicago;
Mme. Evelyne Trehin,
Le Corbusier Foundation, Paris;
Mr. Richard Tooke, MoMA;
Ms. Pia Vasama, Alvar Aalto
Museum, Jyvasklo, Finland;
Mr. Daniel Williams-Capone,
The Department of
Rare Books and Special
Collections, University of
Michigan, Ann Arbor;
Ms. Mary K. Woolever,
Ryerson and Burnham Libraries,
Art Institute of Chicago; Artists
Rights Society, Inc., NY; The
Reference Department Staff of
the Joseph Regenstein Library,
the University of Chicago

In September 1988 a conference on architectural theory was held in Chicago. The meeting was initiated by Jeffrey Kipnis who felt that it would be both constructive and informative to hold an extended working session on the ideas and writing of a loose group of individuals who were emerging at that time in the schools and journals. As director of the Chicago Institute for Architecture and Urbanism I placed the resources of the Institute at the group's disposal, and on the weekend of September 9-11, 1988, the conference was held at the Charnley House. Fifteen papers were presented to the assembled group together with selected responses. The papers in this volume are an edited selection of the subsequently revised papers, representing the most accomplished and provocative of the pieces.

More substantively, the papers reflect an emerging tendency to tie and untie architectural theory at the intersection of several issues at once cultural and architectural. Each paper included here has the virtue, perhaps the burden, of tracing a line of thought between issues primarily regarded as architectural, such as orthogonality or the relation between structure and ornament, and issues thought to be more cultural and therefore extrinsic and somehow irrelevant to architecture, such as gender, the structure of philosophical thought, or the textual strategy of a piece of literature. If there is one common thread to be found among this diverse set of writings, it is perhaps the idea that architecture and architectural thinking are inextricably cultural in construction and effect. Or, otherwise said, it is the idea that the once supposed autonomy of architecture is an illusion, at best a suspect quality, at worst a mask on a series of transactions and false stabilities that architecture ensures in a culture. The boundary of architecture, the line that demarcates that which is intrinsic and extrinsic to architecture is the most suspect gesture in architectural theory, and, while some may argue for its maintenance or for the impossibility of its erasure, none, I think, would argue that it is a gesture that goes without saying, that is somehow without trouble or difficulty.

The shadow concern behind the various issues of the individual papers and the strategies of their treatment is that of power, of the effects and constructions of power in and through architecture, and perhaps of the necessity if not the possibility of doing architecture within the close embrace of power. Each writer is intent on a certain depiction of the operations of power in architecture, and is writing back at architecture, aiming the line of a text against it or threading the written line through architecture. *John Whiteman*

Ann Bergren teaches Classics at the
University of California at Los Angeles.
She also teaches architectural theory at
Southern California Institute of Architecture.
She is currently working on a book entitled
Architecture Gender Philosophy.

Architecture
Gender
Philosophy

Ann Bergren

While Eve waited
inside of Adam
she was his
structure
her volume
filled him
his skin hung
on Eve's form
when God
released her
from Adam
Death rushed in
preventing collapse.
John Hejduk,
'Diary Constructions'[1]

Εἰς, δύο, τρεῖς
One, two, three.
Timaeus 17a1

I broach the topic of architecture and gender and philosophy first because of an exchange that took place in the fall of 1987 in Chicago. During the meeting of the ACSA forum on 'Architecture and Deconstruction' Peter Eisenman described something of Jacques Derrida's attitude toward architecture in the course of their collaboration to design a section of the Parc La Villette in Paris. As program for this collaboration – ultimately entitled *Choral Works* – Derrida supplied his essay on the *chôra* of Plato's *Timaeus*.[2]

In the *Timaeus* architecture and philosophy sign a contract of mutual translation.[3] The terms of its model of building and of aesthetic excellence found a tradition handed down via Vitruvius and Alberti as the 'Bible' of western architectural theory.[4] The mutual edification of philosophy and architecture in the *Timaeus* entails the construction of gender between them. Their 'ground-as-support' requires their complicity in the stabilization of

chôra. In deconstructing this cooperative 'choral work' resides the potential for the dislocation of Platonic ontology as formulated in the *Timaeus* and of Platonically informed architecture.

Meanwhile, back in Chicago (to imitate the constructive practice of the *Timaeus*), of Derrida's reaction to the architectural process, Eisenman claimed[5]:

> He wants architecture to stand still and be what he assumes it appropriately should be in order that philosophy can be free to move and speculate. In other words, that architecture is real, is grounded, is solid, doesn't move around – is precisely what Jacques wants. And so when I made the first crack at a project we were doing together – which was a public garden in Paris – he said things to me that filled me with horror like, 'How can it be a garden without plants?' or 'Where are the trees?' or 'Where are the benches for people to sit on?' This is what you philosophers want, you want to know where the benches are... [T]he minute architecture begins to move away from its traditional role as the symbolization of use, is where philosophy starts to shake. Because it starts to question its philosophical underpinnings and starts to move it around and suggest that what is under philosophy may be architecture and something that isn't so nice. In other words, it's not so solid, it's not so firm, it's not so constructed.[6]

According to Eisenman, philosophy needs for its own stability and freedom to move, an architecture that does not move, an architecture that stays put and symbolizes nothing other than its use.

At the same conference, Catherine Ingraham presented a paper exploring the 'rage' of architecture at the prospect of domination by language. She concluded:

> It seems to me interesting that the plan of domination supposedly exercised by language over architecture is actually resonating architecture's own plan of domination. I have no proposals for the horror of architecture for philosophy. [But] it could be that philosophy recognizes in architecture its own most frightening realization, which is that in some way architecture is the aestheticization of the pornography of power.

These two remarks, Eisenman's and Ingraham's, seemed to me to be related in reflecting a 'female' status of architecture vis-à-vis philosophy. I commented:

> Apropos 'architecture as the aestheticization of the pornography of power' I asked myself whether power is or could be a *pornê* (probably you all know that a *pornê* is a prostitute). And that reminded me of a thought I had in the morning when Peter was talking about the resistance of Derrida to the fact that your architecture won't stay put, once it is placed – that you want to move the idea of a garden. It reminds me of the whole problem of the female in general – that she must be mobile, she must be exchangeable in order for family and children and homes to take place. But the problem about her is that she is not a 'proper' wife for sure. Because by virtue of her movability, she also could move herself and she could be like a *pornê*. A *pornê* is the opposite of the proper wife – a *pornê* wouldn't stay put, once exchanged – this is Greek thinking about females. So the ambiguity with which architecture is treated is perhaps an essential and necessary one. Because you must be movable. Yet that is just what nobody can allow you – once you're placed, you have to stay put. I think it's the deconstructive activity that permits this kind of perception. So in a way deconstruction has made a contribution to you and you're perhaps the best example of it in that you show that architecture is a writing of power as a *pornê* – as a necessary, productive medium that must be mobile. And yet once put in place, the other can't allow the mobility. Plus, then, it also goes in the other direction. You seemed slightly angry at deconstruction for not providing a model and a foundation for you. So that there was a way in which you needed deconstruction and language to be a woman for you also.

II

After this comment in which I had, I thought, said something positive about Eisenman's dislocating architecture and about architecture as a *graphê* – which means both 'writing' and 'drawing' in Greek – a *graphê* of the power of the *pornê*, I was later complimented by an eminent architect present on having 'wiped up the floor' with Eisenman. This interpretation of the female as a category of blame coheres with a second impulse toward exploring the relation between architecture and gender and philosophy.

There has been relatively little treatment of gender in the theoretical discourse – the 'philosophy' – of architecture.[7] In architecture, gender has been studied mainly in the domains of history and form: what women have designed and built,[8] and what formal characteristics may be designated as intrinsically female.[9] But architectural theory does not meditate upon the gender of architectural activity itself. Architectural theory does not appear conscious of this issue as essential to its self-understanding – and thus germane to male or female, practitioner or theorist as well. This relative absence of theoretical reflection finds a practical counterpart in the male dominance – both ethical and statistical – among the stars of the profession. This practical presence and theoretical ignorance of the power of gender in architecture, together with the implication of gender in the remarks of Eisenman and Ingraham about architecture and philosophy, incite the present investigation. I begin by looking at gender in the mode of the symbolic, where it is constructed.

Psychoanalysis and anthropology have analyzed gender as the constellation of characteristics and values, the powers and the powerlessness, attached by a given social group to sexual difference.[10] As the sexes are different, the meaning of gender is differential. Gender is thus a machine for thinking the meaning of sexual difference. And, as if sexual difference were the very meaning of difference itself, gender functions universally as a machine for differentiation as such – the totem par excellence.[11]

Equally universal (so far) is the fact that gender difference is subjective in both senses of the term, and thereby rhetorical and political. The difference gender makes may be seen in a linguistic phenomenon of which gender is a chief example, if not the primary model and motivation. This is the phenomenon of marked versus unmarked categories.[12] It is the 'pervasive tendency in human thinking' to take one of the members of an opposition as unmarked so that it represents either the entire oppositional group (the 'zero-interpretation') or the opposite of the other, marked member (the 'minus-interpretation') – or in some contexts, even the marked category itself (the 'plus-interpretation').[13] The classic example of the procedure is gender terminology itself. For example, in English the marked term 'woman' indicates the presence of the 'marked' property 'female', while the unmarked term 'man' is used to indicate both the 'human being' in general (the 'zero-interpretation'), the absence of 'female' in the sense of 'male human being'[14] (the 'minus-interpretation'), and sometimes even 'female human being' (the 'plus-interpretation').[15] This mode of differentiation permeates both the linguistic and the non-linguistic spheres. For example, pants or trousers (in most Western cultures) are unmarked, skirts are marked. In logical symbolism, p is used ambiguously either as the proposition abstracted from its truth value or as the assertion of the truth of the proposition p. And it is the term 'truth value', itself, derived from the unmarked member, not 'falsity value', that designates the 'over-all category which has truth and falsity as members.'[16]

This marked versus unmarked categorization results from and expresses a privileged point of view. Ethnography records many instances in which the tribal name is also used as the term for 'human being' so that all other human groups become outside, 'marked' members, who can be designated only by phrases in which the base term bears an adjectival modifier, the mark of the group's 'something extra', its extra-normative condition.[17] The marked group has something excessive, something different – femininity or falsity, in the examples above – that makes it ambiguously more and less than human.[18]

Whether or not it is gender differentiation that provides the model for marked versus unmarked thought, gender differentiation universally (so far) takes the form of a marked versus unmarked distinction. By virtue of its subjectivity, however, this form of differentiation is not univocal. In the manner of linguistic shifters, a group may occupy both the marked and the unmarked condition, depending upon the other group with which it is being compared.[19] In English, for example, 'female' may be marked in relation to 'male', while 'nurse' is unmarked, requiring the adjectival supplement in 'male nurse' to designate a non-female.[20] Similarly, in the sphere of architecture – to turn back toward the subject at hand – architecture could be marked as 'female' in relation to philosophy (and again, I do not intend 'female' as a term of abuse or degradation), while architectural theory was marked in relation to practice, which in turn might function simultaneously as marked 'female' in relation to the economic and political power of the client and as unmarked 'male' in relation to the women working within the profession. And, moreover, there is nothing essentially (or 'ontologically') female about the biological sex to which the marked 'female' position is assigned. Even in the case of grammatical gender, an especially pervasive instance in which the twin tools of gender and the marked/unmarked opposition coincide, we find one counter-instance to the otherwise universally unmarked status of the masculine: in the Iroquoian languages it is the feminine gender that is unmarked.[21] What is not yet attested in human society is a gender differentiation that does not take the marked/unmarked form.

Is this model of gender at work between the architecture and the philosophy of the *Choral Works*?

To pursue this question I turn to what programs the program of the *Choral Works*, the female and the architect before philosophy and then in Platonic texts, culminating in the *chôra* of the *Timaeus*.

Female and Architect: Before Philosophy

The ancient Greek language records a culture dominated by the male. The term *anthrôpos* is unmarked, meaning both 'human being' (zero-interpretation), 'man' (minus-interpretation), and, with the addition of the female article, 'woman' (plus-interpretation). Outside of the poetry of Sappho, virtually no speech or writing by Greek women has been handed down. Corresponding to the unmarking of the male, Greek myth ascribes to the female a marked relation to knowledge, speech, and graphic creativity by virtue of a similarly marked social (dis)placement.[22] It ascribes this markedness to the architect, too. These 'para-philosophical' origins are critical to comprehending the gen(d)eric drama in the conceptual maneuvers of Platonic philosophy with regard to architecture and the female.

Early Greek epic attributes to the female in the figure of the Muses what will later become the object of philosophical desire – transcendent knowledge, grounded in presence and sight, that makes possible the speaking and the imitating of truth. The Muses are called upon to impart their truth to the male poet (*Iliad* 2.484-486):

Speak to me, Muses, with homes on Olympus, for you are
goddesses, you are present beside, you know ('have seen')
all things, but we hear only the report and know nothing.[23]

The Muses speak the truth, understood as the (re)presentation in its totality (here in *Iliad* 2, the total catalogue of Greek ships) of a past presence and sight in any present place. But because they know all, the Muses can speak not only the truth, but also falsehood, as they reveal in handing over the staff of inspiration to the male poet Hesiod (*Theogony* 27-28):

We know how to say many falsehoods (*pseudea*)
like (*homoia* 'like, same') to real things, and we know,
whenever we wish to, how to utter the truth (*alêtheia*).

By virtue of their transcendent knowledge of the truth, the Muses can imitate it perfectly. And since they can do so whenever they want to, who can tell whether even this very instance of their speech is a case of the truth or of its perfect imitation? Only those who know what the Muses 'wish' in this situation – *Was will das Weib?* – can know for sure. The rhetorical status of the Muses' speech cannot be determined by anyone outside themselves (or their intention), since it depends upon a position of epistemological mastery and individual desire that no man – not even the male 'author' of the text – can share.[24] This speech of the Muses remains an irresolvable ambiguity of truth and its figuration.

Greek myth derives this capacity to manipulate truth and imitation from the woman's power to determine legitimacy and illegitimacy – the proper and improper – in the area where it counts most in a system of 'father-rule', the reproduction of children. The woman can present a man with his own son or with a supposititious child. True paternity only the woman knows for sure. Rhea, the mother of Zeus, is a founding instance (Hesiod, *Theogony* 453-506). To her husband, the king Cronus, who had swallowed all of her previous children so that none could usurp his sovereign power, Rhea presents not the baby himself, but a *mêtis*. This term forms a crucial link between the architect and the female.[25]

Mêtis means the power and the product of 'transformative intelligence' – the mental and material process common to every *technê*, to the work of every artisan.[26] It embraces both mind and hand, both language and material. *Mêtis* thus integrates powers and activities separated in aesthetic traditions that draw a sharp line between the verbal and the visual, between the linguistic and the plastic, the written text and the building. It means continual shape-shifting, imitating the form of your enemy and defeating him with your trick at his own game.[27] It is the *dolos* 'trick, trap', the *kerdos* 'profit-gaining scheme', and the ability to seize the *kairos* 'opportunity'. Formally, *mêtis* is the *tropos* 'turning' that manifests itself in the complicity of putatively formal opposites. It is the reversal and the circle, each as the polymorphous double of the other.[28] It is thus weaving and twisting and knotting. It is every joint. It is every instance of 'the circular reciprocity between what is bound and what is binding.'[29] *Mêtis* is linked with builders and the builder's skills in the the *Homeric Hymn to Aphrodite* (12-15), where Athena, daughter of the goddess Metis, teaches the construction (*poiêsai*) of elaborate war chariots[30] to *tektonas andras* 'builder men' and weaving to *parthenikas* 'maidens'.[31]

Meanwhile, back in the myth of Rhea, she presents to her husband Cronus not a baby, but a *mêtis* in the form of a stone wrapped in swaddling, that is, 'swallowing' clothes – a morphological imitation of his desire for an inanimate child.[32] Cronus swallows the trick, literally (just as philosophy will later reappropriate the transcendental knowledge attributed to the Muses, and the creation by the Demiurge will surround the pre-cosmic *chôra* in the *Timaeus*). Later he is forced to vomit the stone, along with the rest of his children – forced by the true child, now grown into an avenger, the son he had thought dead within himself (just as Eisenman wants to expose the slippery architecture thought stable under philosophy).

This son is Zeus. As 'father of men and gods' and consummate CEO of the cosmos, Zeus pre-figures both the law-giver of the *Laws* and the Demiurge of the *Timaeus*. His policy in relation to *mêtis* becomes a paradigm – a sort of Form – in which later philosophy and politics attempt to participate.

Zeus' first act upon securing his kingship from his father is to turn the *mêtis* stone into a monument. In a 'classic' instance of political sovereignty as architectural trope and of architecture as political symbolization, Zeus 'sets up' the *mêtis* stone – the formal substitute for himself – 'to be a *sêma* 'sign' and *thauma* 'marvel' to mortals.'[33] The stone is a sign of Zeus and his rule as a working and work of *mêtis*, now fixed in the ground. His next move is to mirror that external fixation of *mêtis* by containing it within himself.

By an anachronism essential to the myth of valid sovereignty (one that is repeated in the institution of architecture in the *Timaeus*), Zeus now uses *mêtis* to acquire *mêtis* for the first time.[34] The *mêtis* he uses is marriage. For in early Greek *mêtis* is not just a word. She is a goddess, Metis, whom Zeus takes as his first wife. Their marriage is an architectural competition, pitting her *mêtis* against his in a contest of material and verbal transformation with her embodiment as the prize.[35]

They first struggle over entrance into her body. Although 'she turned into many forms to avoid being joined with him,'[36] Zeus manages to 'mix' with her in sexual intercourse (a union paralleled in the 'mixture' of the demiurgic intelligence and wandering necessity as causes in the *Timaeus*). Next they compete in body-making. Metis becomes pregnant, and it is foretold that she will bear a son who will supplant his father. But before she can give birth to a child, he 'seduces her wits by a trick of cunning words' and swallows her, 'so that the goddess will devise evil and good in his interest alone.' Having 'incorporated' the power necessary for the maintenance of his regime,[37] it is now Zeus himself who gives birth to her child – the goddess Athena – from his own head. On the divine level, at least, the unmarked 'male' is now able to bear the 'plus-interpretation' of a *mêtis*-man. This is the divine model, the Formal ideal. But the executives at the head of the human household cannot contain their protean property so successfully.

The female's *mêtis* – her control over legitimacy, propriety, ownership, and the 'own' itself – is a power of (dis)placement – a power of putting one child, both value and sign, in the place of the other. This power of place is gender determined. It derives from the capacity and the necessity to change places imposed upon the female by marriage exchange. In order for men to communicate with one another in systems of kinship and symbolic thought, they must prohibit incest, that is, they must move women from one *oikos* to another.[38] Once placed, however, the female is then (like a building and like Metis inside Zeus) supposed to stay put. She is supposed to become the sure foundation of the *oikos* of her husband. But as Greek myth obsessively repeats, the placement of the female is unstable: if the female is able to move, the stability of her construction is uncertain. The legitimate wife can turn *pornê* and, like Helen, reexchange or replace herself.[39] Diathetic ambiguity incarnate, 'speaking sign' that she is, the female can control her own place, by moving it or by allowing an alien to enter it. Female mobility is a *mêtis*, a *tropos* 'turning' that recoils like a drug: what makes marriage possible makes its certainty impossible.

The *pharmakon*-logic of female placement, like the ambiguity of the Muses' speech, is inherent as well in the graphic art of women – the work of *mêtis* par excellence, weaving.[40] So prevalent and definitive is the association of weaving and the female that Freud calls it the one contribution of women to civilization and an imitation, in fact, of their own anatomical destiny, the woven threads emulating the pubic veil over her lack of the penis.[41] And indeed, in Greek culture where women lack citizenship, the woman's web would seem to be supplemental, a silent substitute for (her lack of) phallo-political voice. But this is not a complete picture, for in Greek the utterance of poetry or prophecy – and in Plato, even the art of the statesman himself – is described as 'weaving'.[42] As Zeus appropriates *mêtis*, so Greek men call their product, in effect, a 'metaphorical web'. Weaving as figurative speech, and poetry, prophecy, and political philosophy as figurative web – each the 'original' of the other (we shall find the same relation between between architecture and philosophy in Plato).

Woman's weaving – her text – is thus a signal instance of the inebriated oscillation of truth and imitation, stability and mobility, sound and silence, speech and writing, and writing and drawing that constitutes for Greek the *graphê*.[43] The myth of Tereus, Procne, and Philomela is an eloquent example. When Tereus, husband of Procne, rapes her sister Philomela, he cuts out the woman's tongue to keep her silent – to keep her from telling her sister, his wife. Philomela responds with a *mêtis* that imitates her castrated voice. She 'wove *grammata* 'pictures/writing'[44] in a robe' that she sent to her sister.[45] In her power to defy physical constraints and to express what she knows through the silence of dumb material, the female remains the mistress of the graphic, of the constructed *mêtis*. This is the mark she shares with one Trophonius, mythological archetype of the architect.[46]

Trophonius occupies, along with other builders in Greek myth, an essentially marked, 'female' position both above and below the male norm – in particular, the normative status of a citizen with political rights.[47] This double status is expressed mythologically by a duplication of the architect himself. Architects worked in partnership then, too, Trophonius with his brother Agamedes, and Amphion, who raised the walls of Thebes by the sound of his lyre, with Zethus, who lugged the blocks of stone. The contrast between Amphion and Zethus is emblematic of the two vectors of architectural skill. Amphion is the magician/musician, a *mêtis*-man who, like Prometheus or Odysseus, can foresee the end product and enchant the several stones into a single solid structure, a weaver of the many into one. Zethus is the crude manual laborer, a sort of Polyphemus, who exhausts his brute force hauling the elements of a Cyclopean wall. In the case of Trophonius and Agamedes, the doubling explicitly involves political and economic power and thereby points to the status of the architect in the ancient Greek *polis*.

After having built many monuments, including the temple of Apollo at Delphi, Trophonius and his brother Agamedes build the treasury of a king. The king, like Zeus, requires the services of *mêtis* to control his political 'property'.[48] But like a woman who transgresses the boundaries of her *oikos* or misappropriates the product of her womb, the pair of architects try to steal the king's gold little by little through a secret passage they construct in the treasure house. The architects thus invert the 'regular' architectural function, building exposure instead of protection and dispossessing their client of his economic property, the talisman of political sovereignty. (It should be remembered that the *polis* is the sole commissioner of major architectural projects in Greece before the Hellenistic period.)[49]

The king – a *mêtis*-man, too, like his exemplar Zeus – retaliates by setting a trap of his own in which Agamedes is caught. Agamedes then asks his brother Trophonius to cut off his head to prevent his being recognized. After obliging his brother, Trophonius flees to a place where he is swallowed up by the earth and becomes an oracular hero.[50] After decapitating his alter-ego so that his identity cannot be determined – a feminization by castration – the architect becomes, like the Muses, a voice of transcendent truth.

In both phases of their activity – as illegitimate competitor for political power and as a split figure 'femininized' by emasculation and oracularization – these mythological architects allude to the status of their historical counterpart. The architect in ancient Greece is one of the general category of artisan termed *dêmiourgos* 'he who does the people's work'.[51] The moral and social status of the *dêmiourgos* is of the same marked, ambiguous structure as that of the female: despised for their manual and material labor, while magnified for their intellectual ingenuity. And although biologically male, the *dêmiourgos* shares the woman's specific attributes of *mêtis*, mobility (as an itinerant worker),[52] and graphic art. In terms of gender, the *dêmiourgos* is a virtual female.[53]

Among artisans, the architect rates relatively high by virtue of a particular closeness to the political function. The *dêmiourgos* is, to begin with, an ambiguous term in relation to political power. At Athens the word denotes a worker of low, non-land owning status, whether slave or citizen,[54] while elsewhere in Greece, the term *dêmiourgos* is used for a political office, of high status and great antiquity.[55] But the architect in Athens combines both vectors of meaning, receiving the low pay of a carpenter, but being paid by the year like a magistrate and, unlike other artisans, building not private, but public works that symbolize the power of the *polis*.[56] The orders of the architect are obligatory, like those of the magistrate.[57] These orders refer to the 'plans' as well as to the project itself. They are (like the woman's weaving) understood as a graphic entity and denoted by the term *sungraphê* 'a writing down, a contract'.[58]

This homology between the female and the architect in early Greek thought is inherited by Platonic philosophy.

Female and Architect: Platonic Philosophy

As with the texts of Freud, what Plato says explicitly about women offers only a partial account of the place and function of the female gender in his philosophy. The overt strategy of his text is to expel the female through silence (a philosophizing of Tereus' tactic) and to minimize the marked valence of any women it finds necessary to retain. The holding of wives and children in common and the engineering of eugenic reproduction (under the guise of random coupling) advocated for the ideal state in the *Republic*[59] attempts to eliminate marriage exchange and the father-ruled family, the very agents of the female's uncontrollable mobility and transcendent knowledge. Such practice would collapse gender difference into gender singularity and leaving women (guardian women, at least) as unmarkedly male as possible,[60] a social homogenization radically in keeping with a system of thought in which the relation of truth is that of the *homoion*, the 'like', 'same' or 'equal to itself'.[61] Both the force and the failure of this repression of the female mark are evident in the obscure but crucial *point de capiton*[62] where the Muses are invoked to utter the origin of the inevitable degeneration of the ideal state.[63] For it is these females with their transcendent knowledge in the sphere of reproduction who know the *archê* 'cause' and 'origin' of why the ideal state will fall, and of why, therefore, the entire edifice of the *Republic* can never be maintained in the real world. Outside of such lapses, however, it is not in overt reference to the female, but in the figure of the *dêmiourgos* that Platonic philosophy appropriates the traditional structure and function of the female gender.

Just as the term can designate both artisan and magistrate in the social sphere, so in Plato the *dêmiourgos* presents a 'study' in female-like ambiguity[64] – the statesman as weaver in the *Politicus*, the cosmic Demiurge of the *Timaeus*, and the status of the artisans in the *Laws*. The treatment of the *dêmiourgos* in Plato repeats the rhetoric of the female and the architect in pre-philosophical texts. Philosophy marks the 'other' as locus of transcendental knowledge, uncontrollable mobility, and graphic, material creativity and attempts to repossess these marked qualities, while either expelling or demoting the marked member. Weaving is marked as female, and while women are barred from politics, their characteristic art-form is displaced 'upwards' in the *Politicus* to become the paradigm of the statesman's *technê*, as it was of poetry and prophecy before.[65] We find a complex instance of the same process in the case of the *dêmiourgos*. In the *Timaeus* the figure is elevated and appropriated as the cosmic architect.

In the dialogue that bears his name, Timaeus, a politically and philosophically distinguished citizen of Locrus in Sicily (20a1-5, 27a), describes the construction of the universe. His can only be, he explains, a 'likely story' (*ton eikota mûthon* 29d, 59c6, 69c) or 'likely account' (*kata logon ton eikota* 30b7). Because the universe is a sensibly perceptible, material *eikôn* 'likeness, image, copy' of an unchanging, intelligible *paradeigma* 'model', it is describable only in 'likely' terms.[66] This verbal likeness is itself a three-part construction (Εἰς, δύο, τρεῖς):

> **part-one** (29d7-47e2) 'the things built by the artisanship of reason' (*ta dia nou dedêmiourgêmena*)
> **part-two** (47e3-68d7) 'the things coming into being through necessity' (47e2-4)
> **part-three** (69a6-92c9) the 'weaving together' of reason and necessity together.[67]

In *part-one*, the cosmos is created by a *dêmiourgos*, himself founded upon the repressed figures of the Muses and Metis (as swallowed by Zeus).[68] In his knowledge of the totality of the intelligible (30c2-31a1), this *dêmiourgos* is a philosopher.[69] He knows, that is, what the Muses know, and by virtue of that knowledge he is able to be a poet (*poiêtês* 'maker' 28c3) and to imitate the truth.[70] For he uses the eternal Forms as model (*paradeigma*)[71] in building (*tektainomenos* 28c6)[72] the cosmos as visible, material likeness (*eikôn*) of the intelligible[73] – and thereby as beautiful and good (*kalon*).[74] Here is the architect as figurative philosopher and the philosopher as figurative architect, building 'what he knows.' Like Zeus, this *dêmiourgos* is a god (*theos* 30a2). He, too, has 'swallowed' Metis. For he is a con-structor (*sunistas*: *sun* – 'together, with' + *istas* < *histêmi* 'make stand, set up' 29e1).[75] His construction is a harmony and a weaving.[76] And he is a father (*patêr* cf. 42e6-7),[77] who 'marvels at the marvel he engendered' without female consort (37c7).

His procreation is auto- and hom(m)o-erotic. Motivated by lack of envy, he creates an image of his own goodness,[78] a sphere of complete autarky (*autarkes*)[79] – auto-tropic (it 'turns on itself' 34a1-5),[80] auto-philic (*philon hikanôs auton* 'a sufficient friend to itself' 34b7-8), a 'blessed god himself' (34b8-9). His mortal creations are unmarked *anthrôpoi*, human and male only, of whom the wicked will be reincarnated as women, and if still unregenerate, then as animals (42b5-c4, 90e6-91a1). The absence of divine females and the repression of mortal women would seem complete.

The mark of the female is born in the *Timaeus* by the male *dêmiourgos*, elevated to a figurehead for the philosophic god. And what of mortal artisans? Like goddesses, the *Timaeus* makes no mention of them. For the place of the human architect in the Platonic economy, it is necessary to look away from the *Timaeus* briefly to the *Laws* – before returning to the *Timaeus* for *part-two* of its creation myth.

In the *Laws*, male artisans are marked as 'female' in politico-economic status and in spatial placement. In the projected city of Magnesia all citizens are male land-owners and no citizen is permitted to be a *dêmiourgos* (846d1). As in the myth of the architect Trophonius, therefore, the artisan is barred from acquiring the economic and political power of the male. The stationing of the artisans within the urban plan reflects their feminized role (848c7-849a2).

The *polis* is a circle divided into twelve sections, one for each tribe, with the center forming a thirteenth part, an Acropolis occupied by the gods (figure 1). Each citizen owns a portion of the two concentric zones that form the city and the surrounding country. The citizens live in the city, while the remaining territory is occupied by the artisans, segregated and divided into thirteen groups – one in a sub-urban periphery of the city, shaded in the plan, and the other twelve in villages located at the midpoint of each country district.[81] By this division and localization of the artisans, the plan attempts to control a spatial ambiguity parallel to that of the female in marriage exchange.[82] Like the woman, the *dêmiourgos* must be mobile, in the sense of being unlinked to any piece of land by ownership that would constitute citizenship.[83] But to be of regular and reliable use, he must also be put in a place and must stay put.

Read together with the *Timaeus*, this subordination of the 'real' *dêmiourgos* of the *Laws* indicates that in the economy of Platonic thought, the making of philosophy architectural in the figure of the cosmic Demiurge results in the feminization of the artisan himself in the economic and political sphere. In the context of intellectual or political creativity, the unmarked male assumes the ambiguous 'plus-interpretation' of signalling the female mark itself – thus requiring, in order to retain some diacritical difference, a re-marking of the female and of the male who creates not in mind or in law, but in matter. Each is re-marked with and as a female lack. In this negative incision, however, there re-appears in both the artisan of the *Laws* and the female principle of the *Timaeus* the imprint of the positive 'female' mark.

Looking again at the urban plan of the *Laws*, the very fragmentation and spatial restriction of the artisans is a symptom of their transcendent knowledge and creativity. For like the gods and like the land itself – and unlike the male citizen – the artisans are divided into thirteen groups, with the 'demiurgic suburb' echoing the divine Acropolis at the center of the city.[84] And of course it is as *dêmiourgos* – both architect and law-giver – that the text itself constructs this spatial arrangement and the political structure it supports.[85]

The case of the female in the *Timaeus* is similar, but more complicated. In the *Timaeus*

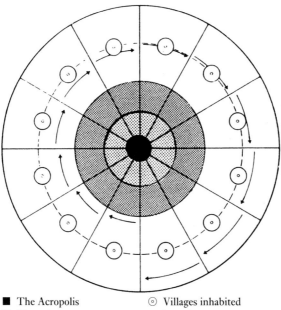

■ The Acropolis
▨ The urban center
▨ Artisan suburb
  Inner and outer rings
  of cultivated area
  (– – the border between
  the two)

⊙ Villages inhabited
  by artisans
→ Shows the monthly
  movement of the twelve
  troops of young men
  around the territory in
  an annual cycle (with
  the circuit switching
  direction year by year).

Figure 1 Plan of the city in Plato's
Laws, from P. Vidal-Naquet.

she returns as *anankê* 'necessity' and *chôra* 'place, space' – each principles of movement that must be controlled. These ontologically problematical powers are first described in *part-two* of the 'likely story' of creation, when hetero-erotic rivalry supplements the hom(m)o-/auto-erotic procreation of the same. *Part-one* of this creation myth, in which the demiurgic *nous* fathered alone phenomenal replicas of intelligible forms (*ta dia nou dedêmiourgêmena*), concealed a concomitant family drama founded upon an uneasy intercourse. The architecture of pure paternity sheltered what was always already going on inside the cosmic *oikos*, an unstable erotic hierarchy with *nous* on top.

Contrary to the impression created at the start of *part-one*, the world was not created with the Demiurgic *nous* as its sole *aitia* 'beginning, cause, principle' (28a4-9). Just as Zeus 'mixed' in sexual intercourse with Metis in order to 'incorporate' the power necessary to maintain his rule, so the cosmos was 'born' as a 'constructed mixture' of two causes – both *nous* 'intelligence' and *anankê* 'necessity' (47e5-48a2):

> For the becoming (*genesis*) of this cosmos was engendered (*egennêthê*) by having been mixed (*memeigmenê*) from the construction (*ex sustaseôs: sun* – 'together, with' + *stasis* 'standing, placing, erection') of both necessity (*anankês*) and intelligence (*nou*).

21

Embodied in this edifying intercourse is a political hierarchy, itself supported by romance, as *nous* is said to 'rule' (*archontos*) necessity by 'persuasion' (*tôi peithein*) (48a2) – the mark of the successful rhetoric not only in political, but also in erotic contests.[86] To govern Necessity, the Demiurgic mind must possess the rhetorical mastery of the Muses, able to speak '*pseudea* 'falsehoods' *homoia* 'like, equal' to real things'.

This structure of conjugal subordination is the architectural principle and the principal architecture of the universe (48a2-5).[87]

> Through necessity (*anankês*) subordinated (*hêttômenês* 'made inferior')[88] by intelligent persuasion (*peithoûs emphronos*) the universe was constructed (*sunistato*) in the beginning.

At stake in this containment of *anankê* within an *oikos* of persuaded submission is the regulation of her movement. For *anankê* 'necessity' is the *planômenê aitia* 'wandering cause' – both the cause of wandering and the cause that wanders (48a7),[89] just as the body 'wanders' in the six directions (43b4),[90] as symptoms 'wander' in the body (47c3, 86e7, 88e2), as the woman's womb 'wanders' (*planômenon*) all over her body when left 'fruitless' (*akarpon*) for a long time (91b7-c4), and as the sophists 'wander' (*planêton* 19e4-5) from city to city, without any home of their own. In their constructive intercourse, intelligence governs this necessary movement, for he persuades her

> to move (*agein*) most things (*ta pleista*) that come into being to what is best (*epi to beltiston*) (48a2-3).

To be 'truly' true, any account of cosmic architecture must be an icon of this intermingling of causes, a narrative mixture of the cosmic mixture (48a5-7):

> If anyone, therefore, is going to say truly (*ontôs*) how the world was born by these principles, it is necessary to mix (*meikteon*) also the category (*eidos*) of the wandering cause – in what way it is its nature (*pephuken*) to cause movement (*pherein*).

As the cosmic 'mixture' (*memeigmenê*) results from the 'con-struction' (*ex sustaseôs*) of the two causes, so its icon results from textual juxtaposition of 'the things built by the artisanship of reason set beside for oneself in the story' (*tôi logôi parathesthai*) with 'the things that come into being through necessity' (47e4-5). And as it is the nature of *anankê* to 'cause movement,' so its narrative necessity entails a narratological displacement (48a7-b3):

> So therefore it is necessary to go back again (*anachôrêteon*), and by taking again in turn (*authis au*) another befitting origin (*archê* 'first place, principle, sovereignty, authority') of these same things (*autôn toutôn*) – just as we did concerning things then, so now concerning these – we must begin (*arkteon*) back (*palin*) from the beginning (*ap' archês*).

In this other *archê* is the 'necessity' of the 'other' – the *anankê* that is *chôra*. For the ontological dyad of intelligible Forms and sensible images cannot stand alone. It requires a 'threesome' (Εἰς, δύο, τρεῖς). The *logos*, both logic and account, of the construction of the cosmos as a building of the 'same' entails the 'necessity of trying to show forth in words a difficult and obscure form.'[91] This is the *triton genos* 'third kind, kindred, gender' – *chôra*. The initial difficulty of this 'difficult form' lies in the repeated necessity of putting her in words:

> What power (*dunamin*) and nature (*phusin*) must we suppose it to possess? Such as this especially: to be the receptacle (*hupodochên*) of all becoming (*geneseôs*) like a nurse (*hoion tithênên*). This statement is true, but it is necessary to speak more clearly about it (49a4-7)… It is necessary to be eager to speak again still more clearly about this.(50a4-5)[92]

Chôra

'To speak more clearly about it,' the text continues its earlier verisimilitudes: the language of human psychology and reproduction informed by and informing the language of building and plastic production.[93] 'To speak again still more clearly about' the power and nature of *chôra* as 'receptacle of all becoming like a nurse,' Timaeus configures the moulding of figures and the begetting of children, each – like weaving and speech, and like architecture and philosophy – the 'original' of the other. In this reciprocal information of semantic fields there appears: not only the return of the pre-Platonic homology between 'graphic' art and reproductive (il)legitimacy, but also an attempt to regulate it. The iconological 'buildup' here manifests a single drive – to present the power and nature of *chôra* as absolute impassivity. The threat of Rhea is past. This mother will not be able to 'move' her offspring herself and present her husband with a supposititious de-Formation.

First deployed is the *eikôn* of sculpture.[94] As gold is moulded into various *schêmata* 'figures', but should always be called 'gold', so the 'nature (*phuseos*) that receives all bodies' never 'stands apart (*ex-istatai*) at all from its own power (*dunameôs*)' and must therefore always be 'called the same'.[95] Her *dynamis* 'power' as 'receptacle of all becoming' consists in continuously 'receiving' everything without ever 'taking' any *morphê* 'shape' of her own, a passive movement (*kinoumenon*) of impermanent figuration (*diaschêmatizomenon*) by entering and exiting agents.[96] The active members of this ontological intercourse are *mimêmata* 'copies' that have been 'formed by impress' (*tupôthenta*) from the eternal Forms.[97] Then, in a trope on the word *phuetai* 'is born' (50d2),[98] the three parties to this cosmic sculpture 'become' a family (50d2-4):

> And what is more (*kai de kai*) it is fitting to liken (*proseikasai prepei*) the one receiving (*dechomenon*) to a mother, the one from which [supply from 50d1-2: 'by being made like it, the one that becomes is born (*phuetai*)'] to a father, and the nature between these to an offspring (*ekgonôi*).

The *eikôn* is 'appropriate' because – *in this family* – the relation between father and child is the same as that between a good copy and its paradigm. It is the relation that proves both the legitimacy of the son (it is, for example, his uncanny resemblance to Odysseus that makes Helen recognize Telemachus before she knows his name) and the 'truth' of the copy: the reproduction of the same (*homoion*).[99] For the exactness of the replication is assured *in this family* by the function of *chôra*.

The *ekgonos* 'offspring' in this ontological family is a perfect replica of the paternal Form because of the mother's absolute morphological neutrality.[100] If *chôra* presented any *morphê* of its own, the copy would be vitiated.[101] The copy would be *kakos* 'bad, ugly, low-class, worthy of blame', the epithet of aesthetic, social, and 'natural' inferiority. Hence *chôra* must be without all fragrance, so that the copies may 'become' perfume.[102] To receive the impression of the Formal *schêmata*, she must be a tabula rasa, without any visible figure.[103] If the copies are to be *kalos* 'good, beautiful, aristocratic, worthy of praise' (as they must be),[104] the 'mother and receptacle' of material Becoming must be *by her nature* separate from all of its forms, and thus must not be called by the name of any of the four elements.[105]

> Rather, if we say that she is some form (*eidos*), invisible, without shape (*a-morphon*), and all-receiving (*pan-deches*), and that participates (*metalambanon*) in a most insoluble way (*aporôtata*, cf. *aporia* 'no way out')[106] in the intelligible (*noetou*) and is most hard to capture (*dusalôtaton*),[107] we will not speak falsehood (*pseudesometha*). (51a7-b2)

This Platonic model of material (re)production makes architecture a fixed image and the architect the fixer. And what does it make *chôra*? The sine qua non of the entire tradition of Platonized architecture, the *genos* 'kind, kindred, gender' that is a 'necessity' for the mutual construction of classical architecture and philosophy – not the program of its 'dislocation'. Back before the making of a cosmos out of the disordered universe, the *chôra* used to shake, in the manner of a winnowing basket, displacing the precursors of the four elements each to a different region of herself (52e5-53a7). But that movement was emphatically pre-architectural. Since the coming of the cosmic Demiurge, all material construction is Typical Becoming. But *chôra* cannot write or draw or imprint or build these Types (on) herself. The *chôra* is not auto-graphic. She is like Philomela with her hands (as well as her tongue) cut off,[108] a *pornê* without the means of *graphê*, a 'pornography of power-less-ness'. The copies entering *chôra* are themselves fixed by the immutability of the Forms they imitate, until they die away. By virtue of their Formal paternity, these images can do nothing more than 'symbolize their use'. To become works of 'dislocating' architecture, they would have to have something of their mother active within them.

But an active *chôra* – an active, non-metaphysical, material event – is precluded even as it is revealed by the institution of Platonic philosophy as architectural. It would be the work of architecture outside of participation in the Forms, architecture outside of transcendental metaphysics – before the feminization of practical building in compensation for philosophical construction. It would be pre-architectural architecture, a building before building. As the city-plan of the *Laws* marks the artisan's power and its suppression in the same configuration, so the architect of the Platonic *chôra* builds architectural dislocation as the erection of its impossibility.

Chôra 'after as before' the Demiurge

'Persuaded to move most things to what is best,' Necessity moves to question the founda-

23

tion of this impossibility.

The ambiguous movement of female and artisan in pre-Platonic thought makes it necessary to question the 'passification' of *chôra*. If the Platonic architecture of philosophy is constructed upon a previously shaking and now impassive *chôra*, how firm can its foundation be? In this now Classic instance of a now classic move by which a constitutionally mobile female is *maintenant* supposed to stay put, can the Platonic text escape the *pharmakon*-logic of female placement?

It is not only the pre-Platonic perspective that presses this question.

The text of the *Timaeus* calls itself an architecture. It is, in fact, a meta-architecture, pointing to its principles of construction at its constructed points. Its principles are those of classical architecture and philosophy: spatial and temporal displacement of material (re)ordered and (re)joined in a 'completion' (*teleutê*, cf. *telos* 'end, completion') with the organic harmony of the human body.[109] At the juncture via recapitulation of *part-three* to *part-two*, Timaeus describes himself in terms that recall the pre-Platonic nexus of architecture and gender under the sign of *mêtis*. He calls himself a builder and a weaver and a fitter of textual joints (69a6-b1)[110]:

> Since then indeed now (*ta nun*) as material (*hulê*) for us builders (*tektosin*), the kinds (*genê*) of causes lie beside (*parakeitai*) thoroughly separated, from which it is necessary to weave together (*sunuphanthênai*)[111] the remaining account (*logon*), let us go back (*epanelthômen*) again (*palin*) to the beginning (*archên*) briefly and quickly proceed to the same place from which we have arrived here,[112] and then try to put a completion (*teleutên*) and head (*kephalên*) upon the story (*muthôi*) that fits with (*harmottousan*, cf. *harmonia* 'means of joining, fitting') the things before.

Then from this point in the present, Timaeus goes back to the time of disorder, and recapitulates the creation of the cosmos by the Demiurge in similarly tectonic terms (69b2-d6).[113] This recapitulation itself repeats the principle that regulates the composition of the *Timaeus* – including the placement of *chôra*.

The structure by which the architecture of the *Timaeus* places and displaces *chôra* is itself classic in the Greek (re)construction of meaning. It was known in antiquity as *hysteron proteron Homêrikôs* or the 'later thing placed before the earlier thing the way Homer does.'[114] It may be understood in the terms of contemporary narratology, which distinguishes three 'levels' of a text[115]:

the HISTORY narrated (the return of Odysseus)
the NARRATIVE (the text of the *Odyssey*)
the NARRATING (a poet reciting the *Odyssey*)

In *hysteron proteron*, what is 'later' (*hysteron*) in the HISTORY is 'earlier' (*proteron*) in the NARRATIVE. By chiastic reversal, the historically later event is moved – as it were – and put in an earlier place in the narrative, there to be followed by what happened before it:

HISTORY	earlier event	later event
NARRATIVE	*later event (hysteron)*	earlier event (*proteron*)

A sort of narrative *mêtis*, the aim of this reversal is a circle, as the narration of the earlier event proceeds to the point of the later event again, thus producing an A-B-A circum-structure in which the 'past' is framed within the 'present' account[116]:

	A	B	A
NARRATIVE	*later event*	earlier event	*later event*
	(hysteron)	*(proteron)*	
e.g.	present	past	present

Anachronistic and metastatic, this *hysteron proteron* order defies as it defines a logic of identity, making the last first and the first last. It is a narrative instance of the fundamental tectonic power to displace an element from a temporal sequence and spatial location that might be called real, historical, or natural and to join it to another place. In the case of *hysteron proteron*, the (re)placement erects an icon of truth as the (re)presentation of the same. When the 'present' is stated before the 'past' and then (re)occurs as previously described, the text acquires the veridical authority of accurate pre-dication. It becomes an *eikôn* 'likeness' of the Muses' transcendental memory and an *eikôs logos* 'likely account' of truth as that which (re)occurs as *homoion* 'same, like, equal' to itself.[117] But truth so constructed depends upon construction for its truthfulness. The architecturalization of philosophy is its deconstruction.

For Timaeus' 'likely account' of *chôra* is built upon just such a *hysteron proteron* order. *Part-two* of his creation myth is arranged in an A (*hysteron*: later event) B (*proteron*: earlier event) A (later event again) sequence. The creation of the cosmos by the Demiurge in the impassive *chôra* is moved out of chronological order and placed *before* the description of the pre-cosmic *chôra*,[118] which then continues with the creation of the cosmos by the Demiurge:

A	B	A
later event (hysteron)	earlier event (*proteron*)	*later event*
Demiurge creates in *chôra*	**pre-cosmic *chôra***	**Demiurge creates in *chôra***
48e2–52d1	52d1–53a7	53b1–69a5

The text stresses the opposition between the two times – 'at that time' (*tote* 53a2), 'even before' (*prin kai* 53a7), 'indeed, on one hand, to be sure, in the time before that' (*kai to men de pro toutou* 53a7-8), 'these indeed being then' (*tote* 53b4), 'for the first time' (*proton* 53b4) – the more securely to exclude the movement of the pre-cosmic *chôra* from (the return of) Platonic architectural order.[119]

The Demiurgic creation encases the pre-architectural *chôra* in the constitutive vocabulary of classical architectural excellence.[120] Describing the condition of the elements 'before the birth of heaven' are alpha-privative adjectives – *a-logôs* 'without rational account, reason' and *a-metrôs* 'without measure' – that present the absence of rationality (*ratio*) and proportion (*summetria*, *proportio*) as a temporary spatial precondition.[121] Thus mathematics and measurement (*exactio commensus, mensura*) become instruments of the Demiurgic 'order' *kosmos* (*kosmeisthai* 53b1, cf. *kosmos* 24c1, 27a6, 28b3, 29a2, 29b2, 29e4, 30b7, 30d1, 32c1, 6, 42e9, 48a1).[122] For a *kosmos* is no mere aggregation of *morphai* 'material appearances', but a *schêma* 'shape, figure' (*diaschêmatisato* 53b4, cf. *diaschêmatizomenon* 50c3 of *chôra* as *ekmageion* 'plastic medium' shaped by the entering *mimêmata* 'copies') made by means of *eidesi* 'forms, shapes' and *arithmois* 'numbers' (53b5).[123] By this configuration, the Demiurge 'constructs' (*sun-istanai* 53b6) the four elements, before only the *ichnê* 'footprints' of themselves, as representations of the divine beauty and virtue (*kallista kai arista* 53b5-6) they previously lacked.[124] For these material *mimêmata* of Being to be born and die true to Type, they must enter and exit *chôra* without any threat of maternal (dis)placement to distort the resemblance. The pre-architectural condition of *chôra* must be absolutely past.

For 'before the birth of heaven,' *chôra* moved actively in a reciprocal mobilization of herself and the four pre-cosmic 'kinds' (*genos* 'kind, kindred, gender'). Likened to a work of weaving and weaving herself with the diathetic ambiguity of the female (she displaces in being displaced), pre-architectural *chôra* figures a *mêtis*-like movement. Because the four 'kinds' she contains are heterogeneous 'powers' (*dunameôn*) of unequal weight, *chôra* lacks all equilibrium.[125] Her condition is one of complete and continuous *anômalia* 'lack of the same level, anomaly': she is 'shaken' (*seiesthai*) and thereby 'shakes' (*seiein*) the elements.[126] Hers is the movement of elements ever differing and deferring. For the shaking of *chôra* (dis)locates the four 'kinds' according to their weight and texture. Continuing the iconology of mother and nurse, Timaeus illustrates this process with a simile drawn from the sphere of Demeter, goddess of motherhood and agriculture: *chôra* is likened to a *plokanon* 'woven basket' that winnows by shaking the corn from the chaff 'so that the thick and heavy go in one direction, and the thin and light are carried into another place and settle there.'[127] But 'once (dis)placed' the elements do not 'stay put'. Quantitative differentiation (re)produces disequilibrium (re)produces quantitative differentiation. The 'circular reciprocity' between what is shaken and what shakes is a perpetual weaving as unweaving, unweaving as weaving the four elemental 'kinds'.[128] All gen(d)eric resemblance – the condition of truth within the Platonic cosmos – is at once constructed and reversed without possibility of arrest. Here the working of gender not constructed as a marked versus unmarked opposition. Time and identity contradict without self-contradiction: the elements remain *ichnê* 'footprints' of themselves, past results of future causes.[129] The pre-cosmic *chôra* programs a universe in the condition of the trace.

This is the 'choral work' that must be 'passified' within the circumstructure of the Demiurgic order. 'Swallowing' this *mêtis* within itself, the *hysteron proteron* Form binds her architectural power of displacement within its (re)presentation of the passive *chôra*. Once the 'latter' and the 'earlier' conditions of *chôra* are reversed, however, and once the 'earlier' joins up with the 'latter' again, the circle must stay closed. The truth of Timaeus' ontology rests upon an architecture that excludes return to difference from the return of the same.

But once active and passive can be reversed, how irreversible can any 'passification' be? Once there is displacement in and of time and space, no construction can escape its architecturality. There is no architectural law – and no law of an architectural ontology – to prevent B from coming *again* after A, to prevent *chôra* from shaking herself again. No ontology erected architecturally can be transcendental. This Platonic architecture (of A-B-A, with no return of B) cannot elude its foundation in 'the circular reciprocity between what is binding and what is bound.' It cannot certainly (re)occur as real and binding always. By its own criterion, it cannot be true.

The Platonic text does not fail to intimate this potential for dislocation within its ontological architecture. Over against the Demiurgic *taxis* 'order' produced by causes that are 'architects with the intelligence of the beautiful and the good' (*dêmiourgoi meta noû kalôn kai agathôn*)[130] work causes 'devoid of reason that produce each time a happening without order' (*to tuchon a-takton*) (46e3-6)[131] – causes that (re)produce the pre-architectural *ataxia* 'lack of order'.[132] Indeed, it is only 'most' things that Necessity – whose 'nature it is to cause movement' – can be 'persuaded' to 'move toward what is best' (48a2-3). Why only 'most' things? Is it that to rule by rhetoric the Demiurgic *nous* must speak like the Muses? Must the architectural mind be, like the Muses, able to construct *pseudea homoia etumoisin* 'falsehoods like (*homoia* 'like, same') to real things' – an *homoion* 'sameness' that does not distinguish between truth and falsehood?[133]

In any case, it is in the supplementary relation between architectural truth and the necessity of movement[134] – in the imperfectly arrested capacity of *chôra* to shake again – that the program of a dislocating architecture may be read. The impassive, post-architectural *chôra* is not a 'solicitation' of Platonism, but its illusion and its ideology of support. It can program only the repeated gesture of the Demiurge.

It is almost exclusively the post-architectural *chôra* that figures in the texts of the *Choral Works*.

Chôra 'after as before' Choral Works.

In the *Transcript* of their collaboration (as edited by Jeffrey Kipnis), both Eisenman and Derrida express the desire to dislocate the classical institutions of architecture and philosophy by which each has been formed. Eisenman describes how his past work has attempted to 'mount a critique of the systematic privileging of anthropocentric origins' in architectural classicism, the tradition of 'man' as the 'measure of all things.'[135] When Derrida apologizes for his 'foreignness to architecture,' Eisenman replies:

> Yes, but Jacques, you have to understand how unable I am vis-à-vis your work. My training, in its classical[136] extreme, probably means that I am less able to do the architecture of which we speak than you. My tendencies are all towards the anthropocentrism, aestheticism, and functionality which I am trying to critique. I gravitate towards them; they are in my bones. I must constantly work against this sensibility in order to do the architecture I am interested in. What is exciting in this circumstance is that you are going to provide the crutch for me to overcome certain resistant values that I constantly face. On the other hand, I could provide a corresponding crutch, in that I am familiar with operating in the realm of the sensible.[137]

As his initial contribution toward creating 'the architecture of which we speak,' Derrida offers the essay '*Chôra*' in which he criticizes the traditional attempt within western philosophy to fit *chôra* into the framework of classical oppositions.[138]

Despite the desire and the effort of each, Derrida and Eisenman emerge in *Choral Works* as names of institutions that remain undisturbed. As architectural program, the philosopher's '*Chôra*' became the 'crutch' of a return in *Choral Works* of the 'anthropocentrism' the architect desired to 'overcome.'

Why?

Among the forces determining the relative lack of architectural or philosophical dislocation in *Choral Works* is the treatment of gender in '*Chôra*.' By dismissing the gender of *chôra* as neither Being nor Becoming and so outside all anthropomorphism, Derrida turns from the direction of analysis that might have led toward what there is in the Platonic rendition of *chôra* – the power of gender with all it implies of the ambiguities of movement and fixity in the construction of truth – that might program architectural dislocation. By confining his analysis within the problematics of classical ontology, by maintaining, in effect, the truth of that ontology and accepting its foundation as an irreversible given,[139] he misses the potential for its deconstruction in the pre-architectural *chôra* and her 'passification'. In '*Chôra*' Derrida reconstructs the gender of *chôra* as a perpetual, non-anthropomorphic virginity. As such, gender lies between Eisenman and Derrida in *Choral Works*, supporting each in his reproduction of classical philosophy and architecture.

Derrida's essay '*Chôra*' deconstructs the traditional readings of *chôra* in western philosophy. This tradition centers upon the problem of whether *chôra* belongs to the category of *mythos* or serious *logos*, to the metaphorical or the philosophical proper. Derrida argues that *chôra* as the third ontological *genos* 'kind, kindred, gender' cannot belong to either member of any opposition (including that of gender, 'female' versus 'male'), since oppositions belong to the other two ontological kinds, Being and Becoming. For *chôra* as 'place' of inscription 'gives place' to intelligible and sensible oppositions, but is herself always outside of them.[140] She bears no property of Being or Becoming. Nothing can be predicated of *chôra*. Thus anything said of *chôra* should be put under some form of erasure, enclosing it in quotation marks or over-marking it with a slash-sign (/), for example. No pronouns or definite articles, whether feminine or neuter, are appropriate to 'her/it.'[141]

For Derrida, this function of *chôra* as the third ontological kind has implications for her temporality and for her gender. These two categories are connected: because she is outside all the temporal distinctions of the realms of Being and Becoming, *chôra* lacks all intelligible or sensible properties, including those of 'anthropomorphic' gender. To make this argument Derrida must suspend it in each category once. Apropos time, to be outside all spatio-temporal positions, *chôra* must occupy the one irreversible moment of her 'passification'. Apropos gender, while denying *chôra* all properties, those of receptivity and plastic impression are admitted as explanatory of her temporality and its 'structural law'.

Temporality
Chôra 'is' the space of all temporal and spatial divisions, while remaining outside their horizon. Hence, the temporality of *chôra* is anachronism.

All interpretations of *chôra* (including that of the Platonic text itself) share her anachronistic structure, one that makes them what Derrida calls 'retrospective projections.' All these interpretations (like everything else in the sensible realm) come into being in a *chôra* that 'receives' all their 'forms' without ever being permanently 'informed' by them. Because they all share this condition, every interpretation of *chôra* 'casts forth ahead of time' (pro-jection) all the interpretations to come, which themselves 'look back' (retrospective) on all that have come before. Such anachrony is an inevitable result of what Derrida calls 'the structural law of *chôra*.' The *chôra* 'is' the structural law by which all 'being' is anachronized, that is, comes 'after as before' itself.[142]

But this law of *chôra* can be valid, only if and after it is invalid once. For *chôra* may be said to 'be' outside the horizon of temporal oppositions only *after* the institution of the Demiurgic cosmos and only *if chôra* herself never moves again 'after as before' Platonic architecture. *Chôra* 'is' outside all attribution – temporal and otherwise – only *if* 'she' or 'it' bears the attribute of this single, original, unanachronizable moment.[143]

Gender
'She' or 'it'? Neither 'is' ontologically true. But each is a 'necessity' of Platonic architecture and (as) philosophy in language.

Attempting 'to speak still more clearly' about *chôra*, Plato configures the language of gender with the language of building, sculpture, and inscription to describe an ontological family whose members reflect the unmarked versus marked construction of gender in Greek culture: father Being and his child Becoming share the unmarked attribute of real existence over against mother *chôra*'s marked lack of any property of her own. In his treatment of the gender of *chôra*, Derrida constructs, in effect, a similar unmarked versus marked opposition between the two iconologies used to describe her.

Derrida is not uninterested in the function of *genos* 'kind, kindred, gender' in the *Timaeus*. He analyses masterfully Socrates' ambiguous status inside and outside the *genera* of politicians and sophists.[144] Of the gender of *chôra*, however, Derrida confines his analysis to its 'radical rebellion against anthropomorphism.'[145] He is aware that this limitation may elicit objection. Apropos using the term *chôra* without a definite article and thus creating (in French, that is) a proper noun, he says:

> Does that not aggravate the risks of anthropomorphism against which we would like to guard? Are these risks not run by Plato himself when he seems 'compare', as one says, *chôra* to a mother or a nurse? Is the value of a receptacle not also associated, like passive and *virgin* matter, with the feminine element, and precisely in Greek culture? These objections are not without value. [Emphasis added.]

But in answer to these objections he only reiterates *chôra*'s non–existence:

> But if *chôra* indeed presents certain characters of the word as proper noun, would it not be only by its apparent reference to something of the unique [*à de l'unique*] (and there is in the *Timaeus*, more rigorously in a certain passage of the *Timaeus*, which we will approach later, *only one chôra*), the referent of that reference does not exist.[146]

Dismissing the gender of *chôra* as ontologically non–existent (besides resting on the truth of the ontology) fails to account for why her gender is in the text at all, why it is emphasized as part of a family whose other, male members are not non–existent. It leaves unanalyzed, as if its politics had no philosophical import, Plato's 'risk' in systematically gendering the whole cosmic drama, not only *chôra*, but the *dêmiourgos* as father, the gods as obedient children, Being as father, Becoming as son. But it is not just for what it omits that Derrida's treatment of the gender of *chôra* is open to criticism.

Derrida's overriding concern is to establish that the structural law of *chôra* removes her from all existential properties and attributes, making this 'third *genre*...only the moment of a detour in order to signal a *genre* beyond *genre*.'[147] But Derrida deduces this very structural law from language no less anthropomorphic, no less iconic, no less improper to to her than that of gender.[148] *Chôra* lacks the properties of gender by the same ontological law and to the same degree that she or it lacks the properties of the receptacle, the amorphous gold that receives *schêmata*, the plastic medium of typographic information, or any other of the attributes that 'she' does not *really* possess, all the improper properties from which Derrida deduces 'her' function. Derrida's analysis effectively marks the language of gender as solely a lack, leaving the language of plastic modelling alone as unmarked indication of how *chôra* works. Ostrasized as anthropomorphic from the field of relevance, gender returns under the alias of this marked versus unmarked division of choral iconology. Stipulating its ontological illegitimacy cannot exclude gender from the *genos* of *chôra*.

Indeed Derrida himself, while priviledging the language of impression, cannot – or at least, does not – exclude the language of gender completely. For he does admit into his analysis one presumably female term[149]:

> The hermeneutical *types* are not able to inform, are not able to give form to *chôra* except to the degree to which, inaccessible, impassive, 'amorphous' (*amorphon*, 51a) and always virginal, with a virginity radically rebellious against anthropomorphism, she/it *appears to receive* these types and *to give place* to them.[150]

This version of the gender of *chôra* as a 'virginity radically rebellious against anthropomorphism' stages a revolt of its own against the Platonic text. Where Derrida assumes exclusive separation of the ontological genres, Plato poses a more enigmatic relation. For according to Plato, *chôra* is not simply divorced from Being and Becoming *tout court*, but rather 'participates in a most insoluble way in the intelligible.'[151] And as for the gender term itself, Derrida chooses a sexual and social category of the female, perpetual virginity, not only absent from the Greek text, but indeed radically divergent from its emphasis on the roles of mother and nurse within a full family constellation. As it divided the plasticity from the gender of *chôra*, so here the marked versus unmarked structure divides the gender of *chôra* itself, between the exclusively female functions of the *Timaeus* and Derrida's more ambiguous, almost androgynous (for a virgin need not, of course, be female) creature, as devoid of marked female powers as are the guardian women of the *Republic*. This reconstruction of the gender of *chôra* raises the question of why Derrida, after such careful effort to eliminate anthropomorphism, would choose a term he must qualify as non-anthropomorphic, why does he – must he – have recourse to the language of gender at all? Why must he reconstruct (female) gender to say what he means?

By what philosophical and architectural *anankê* 'necessity' must the mark of the female return? Perhaps it is because all discourse on *chôra* is a construction *maintenant*, a 'now' that 'maintains,'[152] a 'projective retrospection' that must reinscribe the classical philosophy and architecture of gender. All Platonic 'choral work' maintains the mark of *thinking*: of the ontological category as a *genos*, a *genre*, a *naturally* reproducing kind (contrast the term 'class', for example, which does not entail the model of generation and sexual difference) and of *constructing* gen(d)eric difference as unmarked versus marked opposition. If the ontological category is a *genos*, (its) gender must return.

Eisenman's ultimate response to Derrida's *'Chôra'* is a project – a version of his trademark 'scaling' schemes – whose anthropocentrism and classical totalizations were recognized acutely by the participants, who tried 'after as before' to 'overcome' them.

It was nearly otherwise.

By the necessity of Platonic architecture and (as) philosophy in language, in his essay *'Chôra'* Derrida makes use of the metaphorical representation of *chôra*, even as he condemns its ontological illegitimacy. But in the collaboration of the *Choral Works*, Derrida refuses architecture the comparable license of material embodiment. While admitting the 'metaphor of impression or printing' in the philosophy of *'Chôra,'* in the *Transcript* Derrida avers of architecture:

> Of course, *chôra* cannot cannot be *represented in any form, in any architecture*. That is why it should not give place to an architecture – that is why it is interesting. What is interesting is that *the non-representable space* could give the receiver, the visitor, the possibility of *thinking about architecture*.[153]

Here philosophy recreates the Platonic text's treatment of the 'real' female and artisan: while appropriating the architectural mark of constructing *chôra* in metaphorical form, philosophy relegates architecture to architectural lack. Reconstructing its classical subordination of formal representation to thought, philosophy requires architecture to do what it does, 'thinking about architecture', but denies her 'representation in *any* form, in *any* architecture' by which to do so. As the Freudian female is condemned to hopeless envy of the logo-phallus, architecture here must emulate philosophy with her tongue cut out.

Despite this stricture – later in the collaboration, but before the formulation of his own 'scaling' scheme – Eisenman ventures a materialization of *chôra*, almost a cognate of the pre-architectural *anômalia* in its 'circular reciprocity' of formant and trace :

> I am describing an analogy of the receptacle and the object. The object is formed by the receptacle and the traces of the receptacle are left on the object. At the same time, the object forms the receptacle and leaves traces on it. It is a reverberating, displacing activity.[154]

But Derrida refuses this 'physical analogue' of a receptacle as being an 'inadequate metaphor' along with 'figure/ground', even as he admits the unavoidability of both metaphors and buildings:

> JD: This is more difficult. The receptacle does not receive anything. Everything is inscribed in it, but, at the same time, the receptacle remains *virgin*... The problem is that there is no physical analogue. Plato uses many metaphors to describe something for which metaphors are essentially inadequate. Receptacle is a metaphor...
> PE: But why, then, isn't a receptacle a ground?
> JD: Because it [i.e., *chôra*] is nothing... It is not a being.
> PE: ... We are constrained to make being in architecture.
> JD: Of course. That is the trouble. We have to make being out of something which is not being... What is being? The paradigm, the intelligible paradigm, the sensible emanation, these are beings. The intelligible is more being than the sensible, but they are both beings, the mother[155] and the copy. But *chôra* is nothing... So we have the use only of bad metaphors; indeed the concept of metaphor itself is 'bad', it has no pertinence. So, for instance, to get rid of figure/ground is very good...
> PE: And metaphor/metonymy also?
> JD: Also. But we cannot avoid metaphors. We know they are inadequate but we cannot simply avoid them, just as we cannot avoid buildings.[156]

At this point, Eisenman does not resist the impasse or pursue his intimation of choral anomaly.

Later, instead, architecture reverses its classical feminization by philosophy. Eisenman re-appropriates the unavoidable license of building to produce a model of what Derrida in '*Chôra*' terms the 'absent support' or 'absence as support' – the 'binary or dialectical determination' – into which *chôra*, while 'provoking and resisting' it, cannot be 'translated'.[157]

What Eisenman makes of Derrida's '*Chôra*' is a version of the 'scaling' method of design that he has practiced in previous projects. This design process is devoted to avoiding the anthropocentrism of architectural classicism, in which 'man' functions – as in the meta-architecture of the *Timaeus* – as the original measure or scale of all things.[158] Instead, the parts of the project are measured or 'scaled' to non-anthropomorphic elements of the site – such as topographic features (the bend of a river, the grid of the streets) or previous buildings (the course of a wall, the foundations of a slaughterhouse, the plan of an unbuilt hospital) or narratives, whether historical or fictional (the traditions of Romeo and Juliet), for example.[159]

In *Choral Works* the 'scaling' method is devoted to figuring the permutations of the complex relationship between Eisenman and Bernard Tschumi. As supervising architect of the whole Parc La Villette, it was Tschumi who invited Eisenman and Derrida to collaborate on a portion of the project. Tschumi is thus Eisenman's client. He is also a fellow architect, having designed a portion of the park himself, a design Eisenman saw as recalling an earlier one of his own. Eisenman explains to Derrida at their first meeting:

> This situation is very strange for me, because Bernard Tschumi's La Villette project is, I believe, related to an earlier one of mine. The grid in particular is reminiscent of a project that I did some years ago for Canareggio in Venice; many of my colleagues have also made this association. Bernard's invitation to work with you on a small project for La Villette therefore creates an opportunity for a misreading of a misreading – a displacement of a certain irony.[160]

This 'misreading' takes the form of a 'scaling' that involves the two sites, Parc La Villette in Paris and Canareggio in Venice, and the two projects, Tschumi's at La Villette and Eisenman's earlier one at Canareggio. These two sites and projects are correlated by: time (present, past, future), space (present, absent), scale (full scale, half scale), materiality (solid, void), and what might be called the ontological status of these factors (real, fictional).

Eisenman's 'scaling' scheme for *Choral Works* derives from manipulating these parameters of relationship. The scheme is described by Eisenman's associate, Thomas Lessor, at the fifth meeting of the team:

> What I did was to set up a scheme with four elements – the site of La Villette, Tschumi's project [there], the site of Canareggio in Venice, and Peter's project there. I then arranged these four elements vertically, one on top of the other, and elaborated them through their four possible permutations. By letting each horizontal level represent a different time as well as a different condition of solid and void, form and receptacle, a system was created in which each element is related to the others in various conditions of past, present, and future, absence and presence, and materiality: solid and void.[161]

Referring to a diagram like this one:

1 Tschumi's project at La Villette
2 Site of La Villette in Paris
3 Site of Canareggio in Venice
4 Eisenman's project at Canareggio in Venice

			Real	Fictional			
			I	**II**	**III**	**IV**	
Solid	**present**	half scale	*1*	**4**	**3**	**2**	**Future**
		full scale	*2*	**I**	**4**	**3**	
Ground							**Present**
Void	**absent**	full scale	*3*	**2**	**I**	**4**	
		half scale	*4*	**3**	**2**	**I**	**Past**

Lessor continues:

> As you can see, the first column of the diagram, which shows Tschumi's scheme and La Villette as presences and Peter's scheme and Venice as absences, represents facts as they exist relative to

the site. So, we will not build that column, but the other three, 'fictional' columns. For example, in the next condition Venice [4] as a future for Bernard's project [1] and La Villette [2] as the present for Peter's Canareggio scheme [3]. So in this permutation, Bernard's scheme is the influence on Peter's scheme. Each column contains a different fiction, created by different ordering of the four elements in the horizontal conditions of presence and absence, solid and void.[162]

In the model of the scheme (figure 3), in which fictional version II is worked out, 'present solids' appear as vertical extrusions of the ground, those of the 'future' reaching higher than those of the 'present'. 'Absent voids' appear as negative depressions, those of the 'past' dug deepest into the ground. In the three 'fictional' transformations of the 'real' condition, elements are scaled up or down from their original dimensions, whichever is necessary, in order for the 'future' and 'past' to be superimposed at 'half-scale' upon the 'present' rendered at 'full scale'. Lessor explains:

> Which way to scale, up or down, comes from the relations of the schemes. So, in the fourth column [the third fictional scheme] in which Peter's project [4] and Venice [3] are at real scale, Paris [2] is scaled to, that is, superimposed with Peter's project [4] and Bernard's project [1] is superimposed with Venice [2]. So, Paris [2] must be scaled down and Bernard's [1] scaled up.[163]

33

While producing a 'reversal of reality and meaning,'[164] the scheme is not satisfying either to Eisenman or Derrida.

Both architect and philosopher recognize in the proposal classical limitations. While neither points overtly to the obvious 'anthropocentrism' of making Eisenman's and Tschumi's rivalry the 'original measure' of the scheme, the features each does choose to criticize and the measures he takes to correct them are not arbitrary. In them, the materials, matters, and forces co-constructing classical architecture, gender, and philosophy reconverge. The final movement of *Choral Works* replays the architecture of the *Timaeus* as the Demiurge again 'passifies' the pre-architecture *chôra*.

For Eisenman, the problem with the project concerns the hierarchy of 'whole' over 'hole'. His scheme does not, he believes, sufficiently reverse its subordination to Tschumi's larger design. Speaking of the 'three [fictional] sites' he proposes to build in relation to the 'entire park', he explains:

> PE: I see the whole project as a continuous fabric, with the three sites as holes within it. So, what I would like to see is a notation of a larger scale which erases these other scales at each site. That's what I think is missing from this project at the moment... Let's say the three sites are like holes in a fabric and that the entire park is also a hole in the same fabric. Therefore, what we do on these three sites makes Bernard's project as a whole an aspect of the same fabric and the three sites part of a scheme underlying the whole thing. Thus the elements in each of the three sites would not only relate to each other at various scales and times, but also to the scale of the fabric... As it stands now, everything is in the same scale relative to a human being. What we need somewhere is a notation of one of the schematic elements, say one of the Tschumi/Eisenman squares, that would be larger, at real scale relative to the actual park. This would break the boundary of the scheme and relate it and the park to a larger fabric.[165]

In Eisenman's own terms, the 'whole project' of the Parc La Villette is a 'continuous fabric' with his three sites as smaller-scale 'holes within it'. Because they are scaled in relation to Tschumi's larger design, these three smaller 'holes' become 'part of a scheme underlying the whole thing' and 'make Bernard's project as a whole an aspect of the same fabric'. But

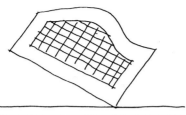

Figure 2 Derrida's drawing
Figure 3 Choral Works, a project for Parc La
Villette, by Peter Eisenman, Jacques Derrida,
and Renato Rizzi.

currently every element in the three smaller sites is 'in the same scale relative to a human being.' The 'hole' is still subordinate to Tschumi's 'whole'. To reverse the relegation, Eisenman wishes to scale up an element of his smaller sites to 'real scale relative to the actual park,' thus extending the 'boundary of his scheme' to that of a 'larger fabric' that would encompass both 'it and the park'. In this vision, the Parc La Villette becomes a woven allomorph of *chôra*, one that rival Platonic architects, *mêtis*-endowed masters of the weaving art, compete to contain as and by a (w)hole.

For Derrida, the problem is a version of (w)holeness that he terms 'totalization'. By including all the possible permutations that retain the original relations of project and site (Peter at Venice and Bernard at Paris), the three 'fictional' sites theoretically offer visitors all the data needed to reconstruct the 'real' situation. So the project needs, says Derrida, 'something which prevents them from closing the circle' (as Platonic architecture encloses the pre-cosmic *chôra*) 'something temporal perhaps…something which should not only prevent you from totalizing but also motivate an infinite desire to start again.'[166] 'What is needed here is some heterogeneity. Something impossible to integrate into the scheme… We might call this a 'lateral focus' because, since it is totally heterogeneous, it could become *the* focus.'[167] Derrida's call for 'total heterogeneity' initiates the final turn in the gen(d)eric contest of *Choral Works*.

As he could not complete his description of *chôra* without reconstructing her gender, so Derrida cannot leave *Choral Works* 'without gender'. Derrida asks for radical difference, a totally 'other (*heteron*) gender (*genos*)' within Eisenman's male-only scheme. Eisenman concurs, ominously reciting what he expels. He proposes that Derrida himself provide what will prevent 'closing the circle' and 'totalizing'. so that it will be 'totally heterogeneous' and will bring 'closure' to the project:

> PE: I'll tell you what we could do – we could have Jacques put what feels right to him. Then it would be *totally* heterogenous. It will bring the final *closure* to the project, in the sense that we started with your program, *chôra*. We took it and developed it, and now you add the heterogenous element. It will be terrific… That finally *closes* the thing from the *totally* heterogeneous to the *totally* rational. If you think of the text that we are making together as some sort of narrative, then we began with the program, then we drew and had discussions and various attempts at this, and the last thing is M. Le Philosophe draws the piece. I think it is perfect. It gives us no responsibility.[168]

Apparently ready to share, if not concede, its 'responsibility,' architecture asks philosophy to 'draw' its 'other gender.'

Derrida's drawing almost returns the pre-architectural *chôra* to *Choral Works*. Enjoined to play architect, the philosopher gamely supplements his programmatic *'Chôra'* (figure 2). Now availing himself lavishly of philosophic iconology, the representation in material form that he refused architecture and the anthropomorphism he refused himself before, Derrida not only draws Plato's metaphor of the pre-architectural *chôra*, the *plokanon* 'winnowing basket', but assimilates it to a lyre, thereby configuring a graphic title for the entire collaboration:

> JD: I drew a lyre, which is also a sieve. In Plato's text, *chôra* is compared to a sieve which separates things into the world of the sensible and intelligible. So this is both sieve and lyre, for what we did together was like a musical event. We call it choral work – music.[169]

The 'difference' between architecture and philosophy blurs, as the philosopher has drawn his 'other gender'. Confronted with this program of classical dislocation, this *graphê* of the 'universe in the condition of the trace', what does the architect do?

A true avatar of the Demiurge, Eisenman at once locates and stabilizes this 'other' *chôra*, indeed as the very centerpiece of the *Choral Works*. As Zeus would swallow *mêtis*, as the *oikos* would contain female mobility, as Platonic architecture would enclose the pre-cosmic *chôra*, and as Derrida refused Eisenman's 'physical analogue' of choral *anômalia*, so Eisenman makes Derrida's 'other gender' into a radically non-anthropomorphic, perpetually virgin 'hole' in middle of his 'ground'.

This paper was originally written for the Conference on Architectural Theory at the Chicago Institute for Architecture and Urbanism (CIAU), Skidmore, Owings, and Merrill Foundation, Chicago, Illinois, September 9-11, 1988. It is a pleasure to thank Mark Wigley and Jeffrey Kipnis for inviting me to be a part of this event, John Whiteman for making the conference possible, and John Rajchman for commenting upon my paper and for talking with me about philosophy over the past twenty years.

An expanded version of the paper was presented to the departments of Classics and Architecture at the University of California, Berkeley and the Peter Eisenman office in New York. I have profited from the questions and comments of those audiences.

The essay was completed with the support of a Fellowship from the CIAU, helpful reading by Andrew Dyck and Sarah Morris, valuable discussion of the *Timaeus* with David Blank, the constructive criticism of Peter Eisenman, the inspiration of Daniel Selden, and the abiding solicitation of Jeffrey Kipnis. The reading of John Whiteman saw it through.

Copies of the transcripts, drawings, and models of the *Choral Works* project were kindly provided by Judy Geib of the Peter Eisenman office.

1 *Perspecta* 23 (1986), pp. 78-91.
2 Derrida's essay was first published in a volume honoring the classicist Jean-Pierre Vernant, 'Chôra.' *Poikilia. Études offertes à Jean-Pierre Vernant* (Paris, 1987), pp. 265-295 (cited below as Derrida, '*Chôra*'). Its epigraph is a quote from Vernant's 'Raisons du mythe' in *Mythe et société en grèce ancienne* (Paris, 1974), pp. 195-244 = 'The Reason of Myth' in *Myth and Society in Ancient Greece*, tr. J. Lloyd (Atlantic Highlands, 1980), pp. 186-242 in which Vernant distinguishes the logic of *mythos*, of ambiguity, equivocality, and polarity, from that of the *logos*, the philosophical logic of non-contradiction. Derrida presents to Vernant, as scholar of the opposition *mythos/logos* and of the 'incessant inversion of poles,' the 'homage of a question' with regard to the Platonic *chôra*: 'how are we to think that which, while exceeding the regularity of *logos*, its law, its natural or legitimate genealogy, does not, however, belong, *stricto sensu*, to *mythos*?' (*Chôra*, p. 266). For the thought of Vernant on the *mythos/logos* opposition, Derrida refers also to Vernant's essay, 'Ambiguity and Reversal: The Enigmatic Structure of the Oedipus Rex,' *New Literary History*, 9.3 (1978), pp. 475-501.

English translations of Derrida's essay here are mine. An English translation by Geoff Bennington will appear in a volume documenting the collaboration, *Choral Works: A Collaboration between Peter Eisenman and Jacques Derrida*. Ed. J. Kipnis (New York, forthcoming). This text contains a transcript of the tape-recorded meetings between Derrida, Eisenman, and other members of the design team edited by Jeffrey Kipnis (cited below as *Transcript*) as well as an extensive commentary on both Derrida's essay and the design process of *Choral Works* by Kipnis, 'Twisting the Separatrix' (cited below from the typescript as Kipnis, *Separatrix*). Jacques Derrida writes of the collaboration in 'Pourquoi Peter Eisenman écrit de si bons livres,' *Psyche. Inventions de l'autre* (Paris,1987), pp. 495-508 = 'Why Peter Eisenman Writes Such Good Books,' tr. S. Whiting, *Threshold* 4 (1988), Journal of the School of Architecture, The University of Illinois at Chicago, eds. M. Diani and C. Ingraham, pp. 99-105 (cited below as Derrida, *Why Peter Eisenman*).
3 For the mutual construction of philosophy and architecture, see M. Wigley, 'The Translation of Architecture, the Production of Babel,' published in this volume and *Assemblage* 8 (February 1989), pp. 7-21, esp. pp. 11-12:

> Metaphysics produces the architectural object as the paradigm of ground-as-support in order to ground its own ungrounded condition. Philosophy represents itself as architecture, it translates itself as architecture producing itself in translation. The limits of architecture are established by the metaphorical status of architecture... Philosophy describes itself in terms of that thing which it subordinates... It produces an architecture of grounded structure which it then uses for support, leaning on it, resting within it. The edifice is constructed to make theory possible, then subordinated as a metaphor in order to defer to some higher, non-material truth. Architecture is constructed as a material reality in order to liberate some higher domain. As material, it is but a metaphor. The most material condition is used to establish the most ideal order, which is then bound to reject it as merely metaphorical.

4 For the 'archeology,' see, e.g., R. Wittkower, *Architectural Principles in the Age of Humanism* (New York, 1988), esp. pp. 32, 38-39, 104-137. Wittkower notes that the Renaissance knew the principles of Greek classicism from texts such as the *Timaeus* rather than from temples (p. 41).
5 The following quotations are excerpted from my tape recordings of the sessions.
6 Compare the remarks of Eisenman (PE) and Derrida (JD) *Transcript*, 17 September 1985:

> PE: What I would suggest is that we try to find a mechanism which, in a sense, initially destabilizes the work we produce from a traditional architectural reading. It is also possible to destabilize its traditional functionality. We could, for example, make part of it inaccessible.
> JD: In La Villette you cannot make it inaccessible.
> PE: But you can make part of it inaccessible.
> JD: The concept of the garden is something that contains access, the product of the garden is the pleasure of walking.

and *Transcript*, 3 April 1986:

> PE: Ordinary Parisians... should feel dislocated. This is the important thing – the dislocation from the ordinary expectation of what is a garden. It should be like reading *Finnegan's Wake* for the first time.

Derrida argues for the *maintenant* of architecture – the 'now' that 'maintains' – in 'Point de Folie – Maintenant l'Architecture.' *AA Files-Folio VIII, La Case Vide,* with English translation by K. Linker, 1986, pp. 4-19. = *Psyche. Inventions de l'autre* (Paris, 1987), pp. 477-494.

7 For consideration of gender at the Conference on Architectural Theory, see the comments by Mark Wigley following his paper and the papers of Beatriz Colomina and her respondent Silvia Kolbowski, Jennifer Bloomer, and her respondent Durham Crout, Robert Segrest, and Robert McAnulty. (The full transcripts of the conference are available at the CIAU.)

8 See, for example, D. Favro, 'In a Different Voice,' lecture, Julia Morgan Conference, University of California, Los Angeles, April 11, 1987 and 'Ad-Architects: Women Professionals in Magazine Ads,' in *Architecture: A Place of Women,* eds. E. P. Berkeley, M. McQuaid (Washington, 1989), a collection of articles grouped under the categories of I. 'Researching the Past,' II. 'Recounting Personal Involvement,' III. 'Suggesting Various Possibilities,' and IV.'Envisioning Future Roles'; D. Hayden, *Redesigning the American Dream: The Future of Housing, Work, and Family Life* (New York and London, 1984); and *The Grand Domestic Revolution: A History of Feminist Designs for American Homes, Neighborhoods, and Cities* (Cambridge, Mass., 1981), ed. S. Torre, *Women in American Architecture: A Historic and Contemporary Perspective* (New York, 1977). *Making Room: Women and Architecture, Heresies* 11 (1981).

9 See, for example, C. Erlemann,'What is Feminist Architecture?' in *Feminist Aesthetics.*, ed. G. Ecker, tr. H. Anderson (London, 1985), pp. 125-134.

10 For the relation between gender and what is understood as biological sex, as articulated by psychoanalysis and anthropology, see e.g., J. Mitchell and J. Rose, eds. *Feminine Sexuality: Jacques Lacan and the école freudienne* (New York, 1982), and C. MacCormack and M. Strathern, eds., *Nature, Culture and Gender* (Cambridge, U.K., 1980). For a recent review of the research on gender, see T. Laqueur, *Making Sex: Body and Gender from the Greeks to Freud* (Cambridge, Mass., 1990), pp. 1-24.

11 A pervasive example is the classification of nouns by gender (the chief referent of the English noun 'gender' until the development of the concept of 'gender identity' by the social and psychological sciences). The phenomenon of classifying nouns by gender is ambiguous in what linguists term 'motivation': in some languages, the total of feminine nouns contains nearly all feminine living beings and correspondingly for the masculine, while in other languages the genders have 'no discernable semantic core'. J. Greenberg, *Language Universals* (The Hague and Paris, 1966), p. 39. Ambiguity of motivation is one of the characteristics of semiotic 'marking' – as it is defined below – and thus makes gender itself a 'marked' category. This marking of gender implies the existence of an unmarked, gender-neutral condition – a condition repressed by the universality of differentiation by gender.

12 This phenomenon occurs at both the phonological, the grammatical, and the semantic levels of language. L. Waugh, 'Marked and Unmarked: A Choice between Unequals in Semiotic Structure,' *Semiotica* 38.3-4 (1982), pp. 299-318, esp. p. 299 stresses the need for semiotic analysis of conceptual categories to be based upon the model of markedness in the semantic system, where the oppositions obtain in the *signatum* and are correlated with differences in form, rather than the phonological system, where differences obtain in the

signans and are correlated 'only with 'differentiatedness' (= otherness) in the *signatum*… [P]honology is that area based primarily on the 'differentiatedness' of the *signatum*, while semantics is that area based primarily on the 'significativeness' of the *signatum*, its association with a given conceptual category. Since most work in semiotic systems deals with significative domains, it would seem then to be a phonological (and perforce linguistic) contraband to apply notions such as 'differentiatedness' to domains that are properly 'significative'.' The point is that at the semiotic level, it is the significance of a term, its differential meaning, rather than its difference or otherness per se – its 'gender' rather than its 'sex' – that marks it.

13 See J. Greenberg, p. 25 and L. Waugh, pp. 302-303. Waugh (p. 300) quotes Jakobson in a letter to Trubetskoy: 'It seems to me that it [the marked/unmarked opposition] has a significance not only for linguistics but also for ethnology and the history of culture, and that such historico-cultural correlations as life ~ death, liberty ~ non-liberty, sin ~ virtue, holidays ~ working days, etc., are always confined to relations a ~ non-a, and that it is important to find out for any epoch, group, nation, etc., what the marked element is. For instance, Majakovskij viewed life as a marked element realizable only when motivated; for him not death but life required a motivation' and notes that Majakovskij committed suicide.

14 'Male human being' or as Gregory Nagy used to say, 'male man'.

15 Man = human bears the 'zero-interpretation' (zero degree of x), man = not-female bears the 'minus-interpretation' (minus x). It is the context alone that determines the 'plus-interpretation,' thus imposing special effort upon the interpreter (cf. J. Greenberg, pp. 28, 51,who designates this usage 'facultative'). Waugh (p. 305) gives an example of the plus-interpretation of 'man': 'everyone in New York State is entitled to an abortion if he wants it.' We shall see a plus-interpretation of 'man' below in the figure of the Greek male appropriating powers his language has marked as 'female'.

16 See J. Greenberg, p. 26, and pp. 52-53 for other such pairs of adjectives. Cf. L. Waugh, pp. 308-309 on 'speech' versus 'writing' as an illustration that markedness is hierarchical rather than derivational, since writing is marked in relation to speech, despite possessing its own properties and structure.

17 See J. Greenberg, p. 26.

18 Waugh (p. 309) notes the marked versus unmarked pairs: barrenness/fertility, homosexuality/heterosexuality, black person/white person. As in the example of 'barrenness', the 'something different' possessed by the marked member may be conceived as a 'lack'. In the Aristotelian construction of gender, for example, females are marked as members of the same *genos* (defined by Aristotle in *Metaphysics*, 1024a as 'the continuous *genesis* 'generation' of those having the same *eidos* 'visible or intelligible form'') as males, but lacking sperm (defined by Aristotle as the sole principle of movement, form, and soul in human reproduction, cf. *Generation of Animals,* Book II, Chapter 3). Aristotle maintains this marking, despite the difference in the *eidos* 'visible form' of male and female genitals and despite the regular Greek usage, followed by Aristotle himself in *Rhetoric,* 1407b, of *genos* to designate the masculine, feminine, and inanimate grammatical 'genders.' Giulia Sissa unfolds this 'sexual politics' in Aristotle's philosophy of gender in 'Philosophes du genre: Platon, Aristote et la différence des sexes,' *Histoire des femmes*, eds. M. Perrot and G. Duby (Paris and Bari, 1990), pp. 58-100.

Another example from ancient Greek is the term *barbaroi* from which European languages inherit the notion of the 'barbarian'. So greatly do the ancient Greeks privilege their language that ethnic, local, national, and cultural differences are subsumed under the linguistic. As females lack sperm, so non-Greeks lack all of the Greek language, for *barbaroi* are those who cannot speak Greek, but only 'bar-bar-bar'. In this 'lingui-centric' reduction, 'race' is constructed as language. The unmarked versus marked division between Greeks and barbarians is criticized in Plato, *Politicus*, 261e1-264b2, where it is claimed that the correct division of racial *genera* should take the 'separate but equal' form of an odd versus even or female versus male split, see below, n. 65.

19 Compare Jakobson to Trubetzkoy (L. Waugh, pp. 300-301): 'I'm convinced that many ethnographic phenomena, ideologies, etc., which at first glance seem to be identical, often differ only in the fact that what for one system is a marked term may be evaluated by the other precisely as the absence of the mark.'

20 See J. Greenberg, p. 66.

21 See J. Greenberg, pp. 39, 79-80. See also Waugh, pp. 309-310, on some instances of the reversal of the markedness relation over time.

22 For the details of the material sketched below, see A. Bergren, 'Language and the Female in Early Greek Thought,' *Arethusa*, 'Semiotics and Classical Studies' 16.1-2 (1983), pp. 69-95.

23 All translations of Greek texts are mine.

24 Compare the dilemma of the male as represented by Jacques Lacan in relation to the knowledge and the desire of the female in 'God and the *Jouissance* of The Woman,' in J. Mitchell and J. Rose (above n. 10), pp. 137-149.

25 For the work and the intelligence of the artisan as *mêtis*, see P. Vidal-Naquet, 'A Study in Ambiguity: Artisans in the Platonic City,' *The Black Hunter: Forms of Thought and Forms of Society in the Greek World*, tr. A. Szegedy-Maszac (Baltimore and London, 1986), pp. 224-245 = 'Étude d'une ambiguité: les artisans dans la cité platonicienne,' *Le chasseur noir: Formes de pensée et formes de société dans le monde grec* (Paris, 1981), pp. 289-316, esp. pp. 227-228.

26 The essential work on *mêtis* is by M. Detienne and J.-P. Vernant, *Cunning Intelligence in Greek Culture and Society*, tr. J. Lloyd (Atlantic Highlands, 1978). = *Les ruses d'intelligence: la Mêtis des grecs* (Paris, 1974).

27 Classic examples: the hunter fox reverses itself, plays dead, and turns into a trap for the hunter. The fox-fish on the hook turns its body inside out, so that its interior becomes its exterior, and the hook falls out. See J.-P. Vernant and M. Detienne, pp. 34, 37.

28 See J.-P. Vernant and M. Detienne, p. 46: 'The ultimate expression of these qualities is the circle, the bond that is perfect because it completely turns back on itself, is closed in on itself, with neither beginning nor end, front nor rear, and which in rotation becomes both mobile and immobile, moving in both directions at once…the circle unites within it several opposites each one giving birth to its opposite, it appears as the strangest, most baffling thing in the world, *thaumasiotaton*, possessing a power which is beyond ordinary logic.'

29 See J.-P. Vernant and M. Detienne, p. 305.

30 For the construction of war machines as a part of the ancient architectural repertoire, see Vitruvius, *De architectura*, Book 10, Chapters 10-16, the climax of his treatise.

31 For the connection between weaving and architecture, Daniel Selden adduces Callimachus, *Hymn to Apollo*, lines 55-57: 'Men follow Phoebus when they measure out cities.

For Phoebus always delights in founding cities, and he himself weaves (*hyphaineî*) their foundations (*themeilia*).'

32 The trick of the stone is termed a *mêtis* at Hesiod, *Theogony*, 471 when Rhea begs Gaia and Ouranus to 'devise together with her (*sumphrassasthai*) a *mêtis* by which she could make him forget that she bore her dear child.' It is Gaia who takes the newborn Zeus to be raised secretly in the Cretan cave (479-484) and she could be the subject of 'having swaddled a great stone, she handed it to the son of Ouranus' (485), unless a change of subject back to Rhea is to be understood. M. West, *Hesiod: Works and Days* (Oxford, 1978) on 485 adduces the Arcadian parallel in which it is Rhea who gives Cronus a foul to swallow instead of Poseidon. For the architectural significance of such swaddling, compare the *Bekleidung* 'dressing, cladding' of a building in the theory of nineteenth-century comparative architectural historian and theoretician, Gottfried Semper in *The Four Elements of Architecture and Other Writings*, tr. H. Mallgrave and W. Herrmann (Cambridge, U.K., 1989), pp. 24, 34, 36-40, 103-110, 240-243.

33 *Theogony*, line 500.

34 As Detienne and Vernant observe (pp. 57-130, esp. 67-68, 109), Zeus 'attacks Metis with her own weapons' and the text of the *Theogony* calls him *mêtieta Zeus* 'Zeus endowed with *mêtis*' even *before* his defeat of the goddess. The anachronism is central to the goal of the text, the validation of Zeus' rule: Zeus is able to acquire *mêtis* and the 'right to rule' it brings, because he has already always possessed it. The ruler takes what has always been inherently his own.

35 Compare the architectural 'battle of the sexes' between the sperm as dynamic carpenter endowed with informing soul and the menstrual fluid as passive material in the embryology of Aristotle's *Generation of Animals*: 'The sperm of the male differs, because it possesses a principle (*archê*) in itself of such a kind as to cause movement (*kineín*) and to concoct thoroughly the ultimate nourishment, but the [sperm] of the female contains matter (*hulên*) only. If [the male sperm] gains mastery (*kratésein*), it brings [the matter] into itself, but if it is mastered (*kratêthen*), it changes into its opposite or is destroyed' (766b). See also 730b, 736a, 737a, 765b, 767b.

36 Apollodorus, Book I, Chapter 3, paragraph 6.

37 For the *main-tenant* of architecture, see J. Derrida, above, n. 6.

38 See C. Lévi-Strauss, *The Elementary Structures of Kinship*, tr. J. Bell, J. von Sturmer, R. Needham (Boston, 1969), pp. 478-497.= *Les structures élementaires de la parenté* (The Hague and Paris, 1967).

39 For Helen as the figure of such female placement, see A. Bergren, 1983 (above n. 22 and 'Helen's 'Good Drug,' *Odyssey*, IV 1-305' in *Contemporary Literary Hermeneutics and the Interpretation of Classical Texts*, ed. S. Kresic (Ottawa, 1981), pp. 200-214.

40 Weaving is taught to women by the daughter of Metis, Athena.

41 'Femininity,' *Standard Edition* 22.132:

> It seems that women have made few contributions to the discoveries and inventions in the history of civilization; there is, however, one technique which they may have invented – that of plaiting and weaving. If that is so, we should be tempted to guess the unconscious motive for the achievement. Nature herself would seem to have given the model which this achievement imitates by causing the growth at maturity of the public hair that conceals the genitals. The step that remained to be taken lay in making the threads adhere to one another, while on the body they stick into the skin and are only matted together. If you reject this idea as fantastic and regard my belief

in the influence of a lack of a penis on the configuration of femininity as an *idée fixe*, I am of course defenceless.

In a nice stroke of irony, Freud hits upon a certain truth in the aetiology of architecture, namely the lack – lack of shelter, protection, beauty, meaning, value – that it attempts to supplement. And in naming that lack, the female lack of a penis, Freud repeats, against the will of his text (which would downplay the woman's construction) the Greek attribution of a female gender to *mêtis* and thus to architecture.

Compare G. Semper's theory of weaving as the origin of architecture as vertical space enclosure. See, for example, 'Structural Elements of Assyrian-Chaldean Architecture' = Chapter 10 of 'Comparative Building Theory' (*Vergleichende Baulehre*, 1950), tr. W. Herrmann, in *Gottfried Semper: In Search of Architecture* (Cambridge, Mass., 1984), pp. 204-218, especially:

> It is well known that any wild tribe is familiar with the fence or a primitive hurdle as a means of enclosing space. Weaving the fence led to weaving movable walls… Using wickerwork for setting apart one's property and for floor mats and protection against heat and cold far preceded making even the roughest masonry. Wickerwork was the original motif of the wall. It retained this primary significance, actually or ideally, when the light hurdles and mattings were later transformed into brick or stone walls. The essence of the wall was wickerwork. Hanging carpets remained the true walls; they were the visible boundaries of a room. The often solid walls behind them were necessary for reasons that had nothing to do with the creation of space; they were needed for protection, for supporting a load, for their permanence, etc. (p. 205). Even where solid walls became necessary, they were only the invisible structure hidden behind the true representatives of the wall, the colorful carpets that the walls served to hold and support' (p. 206).

42 See A. Bergren, above n. 22 and M. Durante, 'Ricerche sulla prehistoria della lingua poetica greca, La terminologia relativa alla creazione poetica,' *Atti della Academia Nazionale dei Lincei* (Classi de scienze morali, storiche, critiche e filologiche), 15, pp. 231-249.

43 This ambiguity is obscured in languages that attempt a clean break between the graphic and the linguistic, between building as 'dumb object' and language: for example, English 'draw' versus 'write' (though 'draw' means 'write' in 'draw a contract'), French *dessiner* versus *écrire*, German *schriben* versus *zeichen*, Italian *scrivere* versus *disegnare*. On the glossary of drawing, see J. Derrida, 'Cartouches,' *The Truth in Painting*, tr. G. Bennington and I. McLeod (Chicago and London, 1987), pp. 185-247, esp., 191-193 = *La vérité en peinture* (Paris, 1978), pp. 213-289. For painting (*zôgraphia* 'writing/drawing living things') in Greek as a special case of writing (*graphê* 'writing'), since in both cases, the graphic object remains silent when questioned, see Plato, *Phaedrus*, 275d4-7.

44 The root of *gramma* is *graph* (as in *graphê*): *graph* + *ma* > *gramma*.

45 Apollodorus, Book 3, Chapter 14, paragraph 8.

46 For the details of the summary below, see Z. Petrie, 'Trophonius ou l'architecte. A propos du statut des techniciens dans la cité grecque,' *Studii Clasice* 18 (1979), pp. 23-37. For the ancient sources of the 'myth' of Trophonius and its many variants in other cultures, see the note of J. G. Frazer on Pausanius, Book 9, Chapter 37 in *Pausanias's Description of Greece: Translated with a Commentary* (London, 1913), pp. 176-179. Together these stories reveal a complex and pervasive account within traditional thought of the relationship between architectural and politico-economic power.

47 On the problematic status of the architect in *polis*, its local and historical variations, and the lack of scholarly consensus on the evidence, see J. Coulton, *Ancient Greek Architects at Work, Problems of Structure and Design* (Ithaca, 1977), pp. 23-29.

48 Political power in archaic Greek thought is dependent upon the products of *mêtis*. In addition to Metis herself, Zeus' sovereignty depends upon acquiring his characteristic weapon, the thunderbolt (flashing phallic power of the sky), a work of *mêtis* by the Cyclopes. See Vernant and Detienne, pp. 57-105.

49 See Z. Petrie, p. 24.

50 Like Oedipus, Trophonius illustrates the mark of the ancient hero, excess both above and below the human norm. See J. P. Vernant, 'Ambiguity and Reversal,' above n. 2.

51 See M. M. Austin and P. Vidal-Naquet, *Economic and Social History of Ancient Greece: An Introduction*, tr. and revised by M. M. Austin (Berkeley and Los Angeles, 1977), p. 12. = *Économies et sociétés en Grèce ancienne* (Paris, 1973 [1972]).

52 In the Homeric world, *dêmiourgoi* were 'travelling specialists who offered their services to the community [*dêmos*]' (M. M. Austin and P. Vidal-Naquet, pp. 45-46; cf. p. 201). Compare *Odyssey*, Book 17, lines 384-386: '…those who are *dêmiourgoi* -.the prophet, the healer of sicknesses, the builder with beams (*tektona dourôn*), or the inspired bard, who delights by his singing – for these are the mortals invited from place to place upon the limitless earth…' The analogy with the sophists is obvious and suggestive.

53 Compare Vidal-Naquet, p. 240: 'In likening artisans to women I am not indulging in a simplistic comparison.'

54 Aristotle records that in some city-states, before the institution of radical democracy, the *dêmiourgos* was excluded from political office (*Politics*, 3.1277b1-7). Compare also the ancient practice of admiring the work without mentioning the artist and of denigrating those who attain a professional level of skill in any performing art (M. M. Austin and P. Vidal-Naquet, pp. 177-178).

55 M. M. Austin and P. Vidal-Naquet, 12, pp. 190-193, 246-248, and L. Brisson, *Le même et l'autre dans la structure ontologique du Timée de Platon* (Paris, 1974), p. 92.

56 The salary of Archilochus, architect of the Erectheum, was 1 drachma/day, comparable to that of a carpenter (Z. Petrie, p. 24). Greek legendary history preserves accounts of architects vying with the political power of the client for the 'paternity' of the building. For example, the architect of the lighthouse of Alexandria builds his authority into the structure's future, its deterioration through time: he covers his construction with a coating of plaster bearing the king's name – which falls away after a few years to reveal his own (Z. Petrie, p. 29).

57 Inscriptions record the name of the architect just after that of the magistrate and a repeated phrase indicating the architect's authority: 'however, the architect orders…' (Z. Petrie, pp. 26-27).

58 The *sungraphê* was not a pre-figuration of the project, but rather a detailed description of the phases of execution and of their cost – the ancient architect was a writer and a contractor – and it was as such that his orders carried obligatory force (Z. Petrie, p. 27). Compare the *diagrammata* 'diagrams' by 'Daedalus or some other *dêmiourgos* or painter,' Plato, *Republic,* 529e1-3.

59 For eugenic marriage and communal child-rearing, see *Republic*, Book 5. For an alternate vision in Platonic thought of how to regulate marriage, see *Laws,* 771d5-772a4 and for another eugenic scheme, *Politicus,* 310b.

39

60 Compare the resumé of an argument like that of the *Republic* at the start of the *Timaeus*, where the assimilation of female to male is described as an architectural construction – a 'harmonization' (18c 1-2):

> And indeed we also made mention of women, how it would be necessary to fit together (*sunarmosteon* < *harmozo* 'fit, join' of carpentry, cf. *harmonia* 'fitting together, harmony') their natures so that they are nearly beside (*paraplesias: para* 'beside, nearly' + *plesias* 'beside, near') men.'

Compare the desire of the Demiurge that the cosmos be 'as nearly like (*paraplêsia*) himself as possible' (29e2-3), and see below, n. 78. For the verb *sunarmozo* 'fit together' of the Demiurgic architecture, see, e.g., 32b3, 35a8, 53e7-8, 56c7, 74c7, 81d5.

Contrast this universalization of unmarkedness in the zero-interpretation, whereby all human beings become male, with the gender-neutral unmarkedness entailed by the marking of gender per se (see above, n. 11) in which neither gender would differentiate.

61 In Platonic idiom to be 'true to yourself' is to be 'like' or 'same'; see, e.g., *Symposium*, 173d4, *Republic*, 549e2. For the collocation of 'like' and 'true' as synonymous, see *Sophist*, 252d1 and *Philebus*, 65d2-3, as reciprocal, *Phaedrus*, 273d1-6. The basis of this relation is the 'likeness' or 'sameness' of the sensible particular and the intelligible form or paradigm; besides the description in the *Timaeus*, see, e.g., *Republic*, 472c9-d1, *Parmenides*, 132d1-4 (where the participation of the particular in the paradigm is precisely the relation of likeness), and *Sophist*, 264c-268d. The vulnerability of this mimetic conception of truth is registered in the Muses' speech, when they claim they can 'say many falsehoods (*pseudea*) like (*homoia* 'like, equal') to real things' (see pages 14 and 27)– such is the revenge of ambiguous 'female' alterity.

62 For the *points de capiton* 'upholstery buttons' as the anchoring or nodal points that bind together associative material of the unconscious in the 'knotted' structure of the symptom, see J. Lacan, 'The Agency of the Letter in the Unconscious,' *Écrits: A Selection*, tr. A. Sheridan (New York, 1977), p. 154 = *Écrits* (Paris, 1966), p. 503 and J. Muller and W. Richardson, *Lacan and Language: A Reader's Guide to Écrits* (New York, 1982), p. 113.

63 The text (*Republic*, Book 8.546b-c) is a tissue of anxiety imperfectly disguised as irony. The Muses 'express themselves to us, as to children, in tragic language, playfully and in banter, though their language is lofty, as if in earnest,' articulating a perfect number for the divine creature and for the human creature, in ignorance of which the guardians will mate couples at the wrong time and thus cause the birth of unworthy offspring – who will display their degeneracy above all in the neglect of the Muses, 'thinking the arts less important than they ought!' The sober translator Grube expresses the ambiguity with which this pivotal passage is viewed: 'The mock heroic invocation to the Muses and their talking in tragic language should warn us not to take the mathematical myth which follows too seriously or too literally. It is perhaps the most obscure and controversial passage in the whole of Plato's works.' The description of the numbers is grotesque:

> For a divine creature which is born there is a cycle contained in a perfect number; for man it is the first number in which are found root and square increases, taking three dimensions and four limits, of the numbers that make things like and unlike, cause them to increase and decrease and which make all things correspond and rational in relation to one another. Of these the

lowest numbers in the ratio of four to three, married to five, give two harmonies when multiplied three times, the one a square, so many times a hundred, the other of equal length one way, but oblong, the one side a hundred numbers obtained from the rational diameters of five, each reduced by one, or from the irrational diameters reduced by two, the other side being a hundred cubes of three.

But the numbers themselves are calculable and significant, the human one being apparently the sum of the cubes of the numbers of the 'right triangle' (3, 4, 5) – 216, the shortest period of human gestation in days, plus the Pythagorean marriage number, 6. Cf. *Plato's Republic*, tr. G. M. A. Grube (Indianapolis, 1974), p. 197.

64 See P. Vidal-Naquet (p. 240) who concludes his essay by citing Plato, *Republic*, 10.620, where the soul of Epeius, architect of the Trojan Horse, 'enters the nature of a female skilled in *technê*.'

65 See *Politicus*, 278e4-279c3. Although posing a 'separate but equal' division of the genders at 261e1-264b2 (see above, n. 18), the text returns the unmarked versus marked hierarchy: the female mark of weaving is appropriated as the paradigm of the Statesman's *epistêmê* 'knowledge' (while the weaving *technê* itself is degraded as a small, material, visible *eidolon* 'image' of one of 'the most honorable, bodiless, most beautiful, and greatest things,' 285d4-286b1) and in the dialogue's creation myth the male *dêmiourgos* governs cosmic cycles that move back and forth like the woven thread (268d8-274e4). See also P. Vidal-Naquet, p. 227. On the figure of weaving in Platonic thought, see J. Frère, 'La liaison et le tissue,' *Revue internationale de philosophie* (1986), pp. 157-181.

66 See 28b-29d, especially 29b3-c2:

> So therefore concerning an *eikôn* and its *paradeigma* it is necessary to draw a distinction (*dioristeon*): that accounts (*logous*) are cognate (*suggeneis*) with those things of which they are the interpreters (*exêgêtai*). So of what is abiding and stable and clearly seen with the intelligence (*meta nou*), the accounts are abiding, and unchanging – to the degree it is possible and appropriate for accounts to be irrefutable and invincible, these must lack nothing. But of what is likened (*apeikasthentos*) to that [the intelligible] as a likeness (*eikonos*), the accounts are likenesses (*eikonas*) and in analogical relation with the former accounts: as being (*ousia*) is to becoming (*genesin*), so truth (*alêtheia*) is to belief (*pistin*). If then, Socrates, in many respects concerning many things – the gods and the becoming (*geneseos*) of the universe – we are not able to render accounts that are everywhere entirely consistent and accurate, do not be amazed. But if we present accounts no less likely than any other, we must greet them with affection, remembering how I who speak and you who are the judges possess human nature, so that it is fitting for us to receive a likely tale (*eikota muthon*) concerning these things and to seek nothing beyond this.'

Timaeus frequently reiterates the iconological status of his narrative (34c2-4, 44c7-d1, 48c1, d2, 49b6, 53d5-6, 55d5, 56a1, d1, 57d6, 72d5-8, 90e8) and at 59c5-d1 defends it (on which passage, see J. Derrida, '*Chôra*,' p. 282). See also 49a6-50a4 where Timaeus insists that terminology should match ontological status, so that no perpetually changing element should be called a 'this', as if it possessed permanent being, but rather a thing 'of such a quality always recurring as the same': for example, not 'fire', but 'something with the quality of fire that always recurs with the same quality'. On the metonymic relation between the kinds of being and the kinds of discourse in the *Timaeus*, see J. Derrida, '*Chôra*,' pp. 266ff.

67 For these divisions, see the complete translation and

40

commentary on the dialogue by F. M. Cornford, *Plato's Cosmology: The Timaeus of Plato Translated with Running Commentary* (New York, 1937).

68 The *dêmiourgos* is the appropriate term for the creator of the cosmos insofar as it covers the whole world of construction and production, both concrete (e.g., shoes, *Gorgias,* 447d3, *Theatetus,* 146d1, beds, *Republic,* 597d9, 11, buildings, 401b1-7, women's *kosmos* 'adornment', 373b8-c1, musical instruments, 399d1, Silenus-statues, *Symposium,* 215b2, brass-ware, clay pots, cooked meat, *Euthydemus,* 301c3,6, Phidias' Parthenon sculptures, *Hippias Major,* 290a5,9, refined gold, *Politicus,* 303d10) and figurative (e.g., justice, *Protagoras,* 327c7, moderation, justice, and virtue, *Republic,* 500d4-8, crimes, 552d6, freedom, 395c1, love between gods and men, *Symposium,* 188d1, painted images in the soul, *Philebus,* 39b3, names, *Cratylus,* 431e1, noble deeds, *Laws,* 829d2, *eikones* 'likenesses' in speech, 898b3). The particular craft of architecture is indicated here in the *Timaeus* by the use with the *dêmiourgos* of verbs of building: *tektaino* (cf. *tektôn* 'builder' and *architektôn* 'architect') and construction: *sun* – 'together, with' + *histêmi* 'make stand, set up'. The *Timaeus* is not the only dialogue in which a *dêmiourgos* figures as architect of the cosmos: see also *Republic,* 507c, 530a4-b4, *Politicus,* 270a5, 273b1.

69 For the *dêmiourgos* as characterized by special knowledge, see also Plato, *Republic,* 360e7, *Sophist,* 232d6.

70 For the linking of *dêmiourgos* and *poiêtês* 'maker, poet', see also *Republic,* 599d3, *Symposium,* 205b5-c2, 209a5.

71 See also 31a4, 37c8 (for the cosmos as *homoion* 'like' its paradigm), 38b8-c1 (for time as *homoiotatos* 'most like' its paradigm of eternal nature), 39e7 (for the cosmos as wrought *eis homoiotêta* 'in the likeness of' and *apotupoumenos* 'typed from' its paradigm), 48e5, 49a1.

72 For the verbs *tektaino* 'build' and *suntektaino* 'build together' of the Demiurge and the gods as his deputies, see 33b1, 36e1, 68e5, 70e3, 91a2, and 30b5, 45b3.

73 See 29b1-2, 37d5,7, 52c2, 92c7 (for the cosmos as *eikôn tou noêtou* 'likeness of the intelligible').

74 See 28a6-b1:

> Whenever the *dêmiourgos*, by looking toward what is always the same and using something of this sort as model (*paradeigmati*), produces the visible form (*idean*) and power of his work, by necessity everything he accomplishes will be beautiful and good (*kalon*).

75 See also 29e1, 30b4-5:

> Having constructed (*sunistas*) intelligence (*nous*) in the soul and the soul in the body, he built together (*sunetektaineto*) the totality (*to pan*).

See also 30b5, c3, 32c7. The verb *sun* – 'together, with' + *histêmi* 'make stand, set up' is used of the *dêmiourgos* of the heavens at *Republic,* 530a5.

76 See 36d8-e3:

> And when the whole construction (*sustasis*) of the soul had come into being according to the intelligence (*kata noûn*) of the constructor (*sunistanti*), then he built (*etektaineto*) within it the whole of the corporeal and bringing them together, middle to middle, he fit them together (*prosêrmotten,* cf. *harmonia* 'fitting together'). And the whole soul was woven (*diaplakeisa*) throughout heaven everywhere from the middle to the extremity.

77 See 28c3, 37c7, 41a7, 42e6-7.

78 As the plot of the *Iliad* represents the *boulê* 'wish, design' of Zeus (Book I, line 5), so the *archê* 'origin, cause' (29d4) of the cosmos is located in the psychological condition – the goodness (*agathos*), the lack of envy (*phthonos*), the wish

(*eboulêthê, boulêtheis*), the considered judgement (*hêgêsamenos*) – of its anthropomorphic creator (29e1-6).

79 See 33d2, 68e3 and compare 28a6-7, 29a1.

80 See also *Laws,* 898a8-b3.

81 Compare the segregation of the artisans and the farmers from the elite guardian class in the *Republic,* 415a7, 466b2, 468a6.

82 Vidal-Naquet (p. 238) notes the closest thing in all of Greek history to 'a collective action with political goals' mounted by artisans: the plan of Cinadon in the 4th century B.C. to overthrow the Spartan constitution, leading a group whose weapons were the tools of the artisans (Xenophon, *Hellenica,* 3.3.7). Lacking any independent political identity, the artisans are regulated by the city, rather than participating as a group in its governance.

83 Note also the linkage between the artisans and *xeinoi* 'foreigners', *Laws,* 848a3, 849d5.

84 In addition, it is the two tutelary deities of the artisans, Athena and Hephaestus, who preside over the city in the *Timaeus* and the *Critias*. And like the gods, the artisans have a right to be paid and to collect interest if it is late, a practice usually forbidden in the *Laws* (921a-b). See P. Vidal-Naquet, pp. 231, 233.

85 See G. Morrow, 'The Demiurge in Politics: The *Timaeus* and the *Laws.*' *Proceedings and Addresses of the American Philosophical Association* 27 (1954), pp. 5-23.

86 For *peithô* 'persuasion' (and *apatê* 'deception') as the powers of Aphrodite, see the *Homeric Hymn to Aphrodite*, especially lines 7, 33. With the Sophists' ability to 'make the worse argument seem the better' compare the Muses' ability to speak 'many falsehoods (*pseudea*) like (*homoia* 'like, equal') to real things' (see above, p. 14). For the linkage of rhetorical and erotic persuasion in the rhetorician Gorgias' 'Defense of Helen' see A. Bergren, above n. 22, pp. 82-86. The argument of G. Morrow, 'Necessity and Persuasion in Plato's *Timaeus*,' *Studies in Plato's Metaphysics,* ed. R. E. Allen (London and New York, 1965) is compromised by reducing 'persuasion' to its putative result, 'cooperation.' For rhetoric as the *dêmiourgos* of persuasion, see Plato, *Gorgias,* 453a2, 454a3,5, 455a1.

87 Compare 68e4-5, where the *dêmiourgos* is said to use necessary (as opposed to divine) causes as *hupêretousais* 'subordinate' in his 'building (*tektainomenos*) of the good in all things that come into being.'

88 Compare the use of this verb in Aristotle's embryological contest between the sexes: 'whenever the [male] principle (*archê*) does not gain mastery (*kratêi*) and through lack of heat is unable to concoct and lead [the material] into its own proper form (*eidos*), but in this it is subordinated (*hêttêthêi* 'made inferior'), it must change into its opposite. The female is opposite of the male, and [it is so] in that by which one is male, and the other female.' *Generation of Animals,* 766a. See also above, n. 35.

89 On *Anankê* as a divine power and principle of irregular and unpredictable movement, see F. M. Cornford, above n. 67, pp. 163-177. On the homelessness of the sophists, see J. Derrida, '*Chôra,*' pp. 278-279.

90 To endow the circular cosmos with the motions proper to *nous* 'intelligence' and *phronesis* 'mind', the Demiurge removes these six-directional movements and makes the cosmic 'body' *aplanes* 'free from wandering' (34a5).

91 See *Timaeus,* 48e1-49a3:

> So let the new *archê* of the universe be divided more than the one before: for then we distinguished two forms (*eidê*), but now we must disclose another, third kind (*genos*). For the two

were sufficient for what was said before: one form supposed (*hupotethen*) as that of the model (*paradeigmatos*), intelligible and always being the same; and the second, as the copy (*mimêma*) of the model, possessing becoming (*genesin*) and visible. Then we did not distinguish a third, considering that the two would be sufficient. But now the account (*logos*) seems to introduce the necessity (*eisanakazein*) of trying to show forth in words (*emphanisai logois*) a difficult and obscure form (*eidos*).

92 Between the two assertions, Timaeus links the problem of speaking about *chôra* with that of how to speak of the four elements: terms like 'this' or 'that' denoting perdurable being should be used not of the four elements (fire, earth, air, and water), since these are ever-changing qualities, but only of 'that in which (*ekeino en hôi*) these things always come into being, appearing and then vanishing from there again' (49e7-50a1).

93 The *nous* as father, demiurge (*dêmiourgos patêr te ergôn* 41a7), and poet, the gods as his children (42e6-8), Being as a model, Becoming as a copy.

94 The prejudicial assimilation of architecture to sculpture in western philosophy is founded here (the stone *sêma* of Zeus – above, p. 15 – being lost under the rubric of 'mythology' to the tradition of philosophy and architectural theory). See J. Kipnis, *Separatrix* for the Hegelian hierarchy of architecture as unsublimated sculpture and its influence on Derrida's contributions to *Choral Works*.

95 See 50a5-b8:

> For if someone should mould figures (*schêmata*) out of gold and not cease moulding each of them into all the rest, and if someone should point to one of them and ask what it is then, it is by far most secure in relation to truth to say that it is gold, and – of the triangle and as many other figures as have come into being – never to speak of these as *being*, which indeed are changing even while someone asserts their *being*. Instead we should be content if ever they are willing to receive even a qualitative description with security. Indeed the same account (*logos*) applies also to the nature (*phuseôs*) that receives (*dechomenês*) all bodies (*sômata*). It must always be called the same (*tauton prosrêteon*). For it never stands apart (*ex-istatai*: *histêmi* 'stand') at all from its own power (*dunameôs*).

96 See 50b8-c3:

> For it both always receives (*dechetai*) all things and never in any way whatsoever has it taken on (*eilêphen*) any shape (*morphên*) like (*homoian*) to any of those going in. For by nature (*phusei*) it is there for everything as a plastic medium (*ekmageion* 'that which wipes off, that in or on which an impression is made'), moved (*kinoumenon*) and figured (*diaschêmatizomenon*) by those going in, and through those it appears (*phainetai*) to be of different qualities at different times.

97 See 50c4-6:

> The things going in (*eisionta*) and going out (*exionta*) are copies (*mimêmata*) of the eternal things, impressions (*tupôthenta* 'things formed by impress, moulded, typed') from them in a certain way that is marvelous and hard to explain, which we will pursue again.

98 See F. M. Cornford, p. 185, on the pivotal function of 'is born' (*phuetai*) in 50c7-d1.

99 See *Odyssey*, Book 4, lines 140-146. Compare Hesiod, *Works and Days*, line 182, where the evils of the Iron Age of humankind include a father who is not *homoiios* (like) his children and line 235, where justice in the city is manifested by women giving birth to children who are *eoikota* (like) their parents (on both usages, see C. West, *Hesiod: Theogony*, above n. 32) and Aristotle, *Generation of Animals*, 767b, where any child who is not *eoikôs* (like) its parents is a *teras* 'monstrosity'.

100 See 50d4-e1:

> And it is necessary to understand that if the impression (*ektupômatos* 'that which is modelled out') is going to be visually varied with every diversity, the thing itself in which (*tout' auto en hôi*) it stands modelled out (*ektupoumenon*) would in no way be well prepared except by being without the shape (*a-morphon*) of all the forms it is going to receive (*dechesthai*) from elsewhere (*pothen*).

101 See 50e1-4:

> For if it were like (*homoion*) any of those going in, whenever those of an opposite or wholly other nature came, in receiving them it would copy (*aphomoioi* 'make like', cf. *aphomoioumenon* 50d1) them badly (*kakôs* 'bad, ugly, low-class, worthy of blame') by making its own aspect appear besides (*paremphainon*).

102 See 50e4-8:

> Therefore it is necessary that what is going to receive all the kinds (*genê*) in itself must be free from (*ektos* 'outside') all the forms (*eidôn*), just as in the case of unguents – as many as they contrive by skill to make sweet-smelling – they create this condition first: that the waters about to receive the scents are especially without smell.

103 See 50e8-10:

> And any who try to take impressions (*apomattein* 'wipe off', cf. *ekmageion* 50c2) of figures (*schêmata*) in any of the soft substances, allow absolutely no figure (*schêma*) to exist visible, but by levelling it first they make it as smooth as possible.

104 The copies that constitute *genesis* 'becoming' must be *kalos*, for the Demiurge who created the universe of becoming is himself *aristos* 'most good, well-born, brave', and it is not *themis* 'what is put or placed as law' – it is not 'architectural' – for anyone who is *aristos* to do anything except the *kalliston* 'what is most *kalos*' (30a6-7). For the Demiurgic construction as *kallista*, see also *Republic*, 530a5.

105 See 51a1-6:

> So, in the same way, to that which is going to receive beautifully (*kalôs*) many times over the entirety of itself the copies (*ap-homoiômata* 'that which is made like') of all the eternal things it belongs also to be by nature (*pephukenai*) free from all the forms (*eidôn*). For this reason, then, the mother (*mêtera*) and receptacle (*hupodochên*) of what has become visible and in every way perceptible we must not call earth or air or fire or water nor any of their compounds or components.

106 On this passage, see L. Brisson, above n. 55, pp. 197-208. In his analysis of the 'connaissance du milieu spatial' Brisson argues that *chôra* 'participates in the intelligible' insofar as she, like Being, is forever imperishable and thus knowledge of her can be certain, but 'most insolubly' because she is without an intelligible Form (*a-morphon*). The description of *chôra* as 'third kind' specifies her condition as eternal and indestructible (52a8-b1):

> And then there is the third kind, being that of the eternal *chôra* (*on to tês chôras aei*), not admitting destruction (*phthoran ou prosdechomenon*) but providing a seat for all things as many as have becoming (*genesin*).

The description continues with a critical account of how this 'third kind' is known (52b1-3):

> And it [is] graspable (*hapton*) without sense-perception (*met' anaisthêsias*) by a certain bastard logic (*logisthmôi tini nothôi*), hardly an object of belief (*mogis piston*), toward which indeed looking we also dream (*pros ho dê kai oneiropoloûmen blepontes*)

Brisson understands *logisthmôi tini nothôi* (by a certain bastard logic) as employing the image of a numerical calculation (*logismos*) made illegitimate (*nothos*) by the fact that it ends up in a number that does not exist, so as to indicate a logical calculation leading to the impossible fact that the *chora* 'participates in the intelligible' although there is no Form in which as a 'father' she may participate. Apropos this interpretation it should be noted that Greek term *nothos* 'bastard' describes not a child without a known father, but one whose parents are not married and who is thus deprived of citizenship and possibly of inheritance. The Greek 'bastard' is a child deprived of the 'father function' as a social construction. The logic leading to *chora* ends in a form (*eidos*, 51a7) that is not a Form. The text goes on to explain this 'bastard logic'. Reinforcing *met' anaisthēsias* 'without sense-perception,' *mogis piston* 'hardly an object of belief' reiterates that *chora* does not belong to the realm of Becoming of which knowledge can be only variable 'belief'. Rather, our illegitimate reasoning about *chora* takes the form of a dream. The phrase *pros ho dê kai oneiropoloûmen bleptones* 'toward which indeed looking we also dream' does not mean, as the phrase is understood by Brisson ('the representation that we make for ourselves of it is related to a dream,' pp. 201-202) and Derrida ('here is how one catches a glimpse of *chora*... as in a dream,' '*Chôra*,' p. 272), that we see *chora* as in a dream, i.e., that the dream is the cognitive mode proper to *chora*. Rather, the dream is here, as elsewhere in Plato, a mode of cognitive error, specifically, a failure to distinguish copy from model, semblance from true Form (see, e.g., *Republic*, 414d5, 476c2-d3, 533b1-c5, 534c6, *Theatetus*, 158b1-d4). The image of the dream continues, as the mistaken understanding of *chôra* is specified (52b3-c):

> toward which indeed looking we also dream (*pros ho dê kai oneiropoloûmen bleptones*) and say that everything that exists (*to on hapan*) must somehow be in some place (*topôi*) and possess a certain *chôra*, and that what is neither in the earth nor somewhere in heaven does not exist. Because of this dreaming we are not able, even when awakened, to speak the truth by making all the following distinctions indeed and others cognate with them even concerning the sleepless and truly existing nature: namely that, for a *eikôn*, since the thing itself on the basis of which it has come into being is not its own and it is moved always as the semblance (*phantasma*) of something else, for these reasons it is proper to come into being in something else, by clinging in some way to existence, or be itself in no way at all; but for what is really existing, the accurately true account is an ally: how so long as the two [the *eikôn* and its model] are distinct, neither ever will come into being in the other and become at once one and the same thing and two.

The point is that we apprehend *chôra* by supposing that every Being must be somewhere, but it is in fact only the *eikôn* 'copy' of Being that requires *chôra* in which to be born. We dream in mistaking the copy's need for that of its model.
107 The term intimates a link between *chôra* and *mêtis* via hunting, in which nets, traps, and reversals, both material and mental, enact the 'circular reciprocity' between the hunter and the hunted. See J. P. Vernant and M. Detienne, pp. 27-54 and L. Brisson, p. 199. For the 'hunting' of the sophist as master of rhetorical feints and shape-shifting, see Plato, *Sophist*.
108 Thus precluding the *main-tenant* of architecture. See above, n. 37.
109 Compare the Aristotelian teleology in the Vitruvian ideal of the temple as reproducing the proportions of the body of a *hominis bene figurati* 'well shaped man,' *De Architectura*, Book III, Chapter 1, especially paragraph 5, where the body parts providing the crucial dimensions are said to have been grouped by the Greeks into the 'perfect number which the Greeks call *teleon*.'

110 Derrida closes '*Chôra*' by quoting this passage from the *Timaeus*, having observed:

> Homology or analogy at least formal, one more time: in order to think *chôra*, it is necessary to return to a beginning more ancient than the beginning, namely, the birth of the cosmos, just as the origin of the Athenians must be recalled to them from beyond their own memory. In that which it has of the formal, precisely, the analogy is declared: a concern for composition that is architectural, textual (histological) and even organic is presented as such a little further on.

This observation of the textual architecture of the *Timaeus* is not mentioned in the *Transcripts* or discussed by Kipnis in *Separatrix*. Nor does Derrida return to it in *Why Peter Eisenman*.
111 Compare the gods' creation of mortals 'weaving together (*proshuphainontes*) mortal with immortal' (41d1-2) and the Demiurge as weaver, see above, n. 76.
112 To gloss 'the same place from which we have arrived here' F. M. Cornford (p. 280, n. 2) writes: 'The 'same position' is sensation and sense-perception, which we reached at the end of the first part (45b-47e), and have now reached again in the concluding paragraphs of the second part.' The resumé, in other words, is meant to cover only *part-one* of the account. It does include, however, elements from *part-two*: the disorder of the pre-cosmic chaos and the terminology of the cosmic order. See the translation below.
113 The passage is replete with architectural language:

> For just as was said also at the beginning (*kat' archas*), because these things were in disorder (*ataktôs*), in each itself in relation both to itself and to the others the god created (*enepoiêsen*) symmetries (*summetrias*), both as many and in whatever way it was possible for them to be analogous (*analoga*) and symmetrical (*summetra*). For then (*tote*) they had no share of these, except insofar as it happened by chance, and there was nothing at all of those things named now worthy to name – like fire and water and the rest. But all these he put in order (*diekosmēsen*) for the first time, then from them constructed (*sunestēsato*) this totality, one living thing having all in itself both mortal and immortal. And of the divine he himself was the artisan (*dēmiourgos*), while the generation of mortals he commanded his own offspring to fabricate (*dēmiourgein*). They, imitating him, took an immortal principle (*archēn*) of soul, next framed (*perietorneusan* 'turn as in a lathe') a mortal body around it and gave the whole body as a vehicle and in this built in addition (*prosôikodomoun*) another form (*eidos*) of soul, the mortal.

114 For the operation of this structure in the composition of the *Odyssey*, see A. Bergren, 'Odyssean Temporality: Many (Re)Turns,' *Approaches to Homer*, eds. C. Rubino and C. Shelmerdine (Austin, 1983), pp. 38-71.
115 For these categories of narratological analysis, see, e.g., G. Genette, *Narrative Discourse: An Essay in Method*, tr. J. Lewin (Ithaca, 1980), pp. 25-32, whose original French terms are: *histoire* 'story, history of events', *récit* 'narrative', and *narration* 'narration, narrating instance'.
116 This structure produces the 'abyss' of narrative 'encasings' (*enchâssement*) examined by Derrida to show how the multiple-layered, chronological containments in the prologue of the *Timaeus* prefigure *chôra* as 'receptacle of all becoming' ('*Chôra*,' pp. 282-290). Derrida enumerates: F1 (the whole dialogue entitled *Timaeus*) is a 'receptacle' containing F2 (a dialogue yesterday, 17a2), which contained F3 (the fictive model of an ideal city, 17c1-3) – 'a structure of inclusion makes of the *included* fiction the theme in some way of the prior fiction which is its *including* form, its capable container, let us say, its receptacle' (p. 286) – and F4 (the

young Critias mentioned an ancient story yesterday, 20d1) containing F5 (the story told to the young Critias by his grandfather Critias – who heard it from Dropides, 20e1-4, a layer not counted by Derrida) containing F6 (the story told to Dropides by Solon) containing F7 (the story told Solon by the Egyptian priest of the 'amazing achievements' of Athens as recorded in Egyptian writings, 20e5, 21d4-25d6). Derrida observes that 'the whole of the *Timaeus* is thus scanned by these returns backward' (p. 291), but does not observe the 'return backward' that contains the pre-cosmic *chôra*.

117 Compare the Muses' capacity to (re)present in its totality a past presence and sight in any present place, above, p. 14.

118 The description of the pre-cosmic *chôra* follows a mini-recapitulation of the three ontological kinds and the assertion of their existence as 'three in three ways' (*tria trichêi*) 'even before the birth of heaven' (52d2-4). The repetition of triadic form in the *Timaeus* is compulsive. Timaeus himself is called the 'third companion' (20d4). With the three sides of the Nile's 'Delta' (called *chôra*, 22e2) – the inverted 'delta' being a frequent symbol for the female genital in antiquity and later, compare Wittkower (pp. 104-107) on significance of the number 'three' in Renaissance architectural theory with its Christian as well as classical resonances.

119 Indeed, it is important to note that while the *logos* 'necessitates' introducing *chôra* into the cosmology, there is no 'logical' necessity for describing the prior condition of *chôra*. The necessity, rather, is architectural: to *establish* a temporal and qualitative difference between the two conditions.

120 See 53a7-c2:

> Indeed, on one hand, to be sure, in the time before that (*kai to men de pro toutou*), all these were irrational (*a-logôs* 'without speech, rational account, reason') and disproportionate (*a-metrôs* 'without measure'). But when he took it in hand to order (*kosmeisthai*) the whole, fire first and water and earth and air – having some traces (*ichnê* 'tracks') of themselves, but in every way disposed as it is likely (*eikos*) that anything is, whenever the god is absent – these indeed being then (*tote*) by nature in this condition he for the first time (*prôton*) shaped them (*diaschematisato*, cf. *schêma* 'shape, figure') by both forms (*eidesi*) and numbers (*arithmois*). That the god constructed (*sun-istanai*) them with the greatest possible beauty and excellence (*kallista kai arista*) out of what is not thus, beyond all else let this stand as asserted by us always.

121 For *symmetria* and *proportio*, see Vitruvius, *De Architectura*, Book I, Chapter 2, paragraphs 1, 3 and Book III, Chapter 1, paragraph 1. Compare also the description of the pre-cosmic condition by the alpha-privative *a-taktôs* 'without arrangement' (30a5) with Vitruvius' initial pronouncement that 'architecture consists of order (*ordinatio*) which the Greeks call *taxis*' (Book I, Chapter 2, paragraph 1). For the aesthetic and moral power of *taxis* 'arrangement' and *kosmos* 'order' and *ataxia* 'lack of arrangement' in the work of all *demiourgoi* including architects, see Plato, *Gorgias*, 503a4-504a8, especially:

> Socrates: Each places each thing he places in a certain arrangement (*taxin*) and compels the one to be fitting and to harmonize with the other, until he has constructed (*sustêsêtai* < *sun+histêmi* 'make stand together') a whole thing both arranged (*tetagmenon*, cf. *taxis*) and ordered (*kekosmêmenon*, cf. *kosmos*)...
> Socrates: If a house should achieve arrangement (*taxeôs*) and order (*kosmou*), it would be good (*chrêstê* 'useful, honest, beneficent'), but if lack of arrangement (*ataxias*), then bad (*mochthêra* 'wretched, unsafe, wicked'). Callias: Right.

For the pre-architectural *chôra* as an alpha-privative condition of *an+omalia* 'not levelness', see below.

122 For mathematics in the architectural training, see Vitruvius, *De Architectura*, Book I, Chapter 1, 4.

123 For example, the *eidos* 'form, shape' of a triangle has a certain *arithmon* 'number' of sides.

124 For such representation as the philosophical paradigm of architecture, compare M. Wigley (above, n. 3, p. 12):

> The eventual status of architecture as a discipline began to be negotiated by the first texts of architectural theory, which drew on the canons of the philosophical tradition to identify the proper concern of the newly constituted figure of the architect with drawing (*disegno*) that mediates between the idea and the building, the formal and the material, the soul and the body, the theoretical and the practical.

125 See 52d4-e3:

> Indeed the nurse of becoming, being made wet and fiery and receiving (*dechomenên*) the forms (*morphas*) of both earth and air, and experiencing all the other conditions that accompany these, appeared by sight to be of every sort. And because of being filled with powers (*dunameôn*) neither alike (*homoiôn*) nor of equal balance (*isorropôn*), in no part of herself was she equally balanced (*isorropein*).

Contrast the ideal of symmetrical balance in classical proportions.

126 See 52e3-5:

> But swaying unevenly everywhere (*anômalôs pantêi talantoumenên*) she herself was shaken (*seiesthai*) by these powers, and by being moved (*kinoumenên*) she shook them (*seiein*) again in turn (*au palin*).

Compare 57e1-58a1 for motion as requiring a lack of *homalotês* 'evenness' between mover and moved. By the term *anômalôs*, *chôra* is again described by an alpha-privative: *a(n)* 'not' + *homalos* 'even, level'. Both *homalos* and *homoios* 'same, equal' derive from the root *homo-* 'one and the same'. The *anômalia* of *chôra* precludes concomitant spatial and temporal 'sameness' and thus Platonic truth.

127 See 52e5-53a6:

> Because of being moved (*kinoumena*), they were continually separated and carried in different directions – just as when things are shaken (*seiomena*) and winnowed (*anikômena*) by baskets (*plokanôn* 'woven basket') and tools (*organôn*) for the cleaning of corn, the thick and heavy go in one direction, and the thin and light are carried into another place and settle there. At that time (*tote*) in the same way the four kinds (*genê*: pre-cosmic water, fire, earth, and air) were shaken (*seiomena*) by her who received them, producing (*parechontos*) a shaking (*seismon*) by being moved herself (*kinoumenês autês*) like a tool, so as to separate (*horizein*) the most unlike kinds farthest from one another and to thrust the most alike close together into the same place.

On the *plokanon* 'woven basket' and its relation to the cult of Demeter, see F. M. Cornford, pp. 199-202.

128 Compare G. Vlastos, 'The Disorderly Motion in the 'Timaeus,' *Studies in Plato's Metaphysics,* ed. R. E. Allen (London and New York, 1965), pp. 395-396.

129 The criticism by Vlastos (p. 390) of the usage of 'footprints' *ichnê* as 'self-contradictory' misses the (attempted) differentiation between a cosmos, in which the putative stability of opposites makes contradiction possible and the 'anomaly' of pre-cosmic 'choral work'.

130 For architecture as *taxis*, see Vitruvius, above n. 121.

131 Compare G. Vlastos, p. 395, n. 2.

132 See above n. 113.

133 For the entire speech of Timaeus as a rhetorical presentation before 'you who are judges,' see 29c8-d1.

134 Compare J. Derrida, '*Chôra*,' p. 292:

The strange (*insolite*) difficulty of this whole text derives from (*tient à*) the distinction between these two modalities: the true and the necessary.

135 *Transcript,* 17 September 1985:

> In my own work I have been mounting a critique of the systematic privileging of anthropocentric origins. As well as looking a questions of scale, I have regulated the concept of function as origin in the traditions of architectural aesthetics, which reinforce the status of anthropocentric origins such as scale and function... Traditional architectural aesthetics takes for granted hierarchy, closure, symmetry and regularity, thus foreclosing the possibility of dissonance, non-closure, non-hierarchy, and so on. For me, this is no longer tenable.

136 The editor prints 'classical' rather than 'Classical' in the proofs of *Transcript,* but the tradition in which Eisenman is trained and which he critiques is that of western classicism and thus the capitalized form would best render his meaning graphically.

137 *Transcript,* 17 September 1985.

138 *Transcript,* 17 September 1985:

> So, let me go very quickly to the single idea I have. When Tschumi asked me to participate in this project, I was excited, but at the same time, I was totally, totally empty. I mean, I had no ideas at all. I was in the midst of writing a text in homage to the philosopher Jean-Pierre Vernant, which had to do with something I taught twelve years ago concerning a very enigmatic passage in the *Timaeus*, a passage which has amazed generations of philosophers. In it, Plato discusses a certain place. The name for this singularly unique place is *chôra.*

139 Compare Kipnis' aim in analyzing *chôra* (*Separatrix*, pp. 29-30):

> Deconstruction is not destruction, it does not pursue the separatrix to destroy it and the laws it enables; it does not seek the *chaos* which would result from the destruction of either the separatrix or *chôra*. It seeks, instead, to expose the hidden agenda behind an untenable reification of the order that the separatrix imposes. Deconstruction questions the repressions of the instability that the separatrix, like *chôra*, reflects into order, making order possible. Deconstruction, returning to Nietzsche's question, What if truth were a woman? respects the mark for what it/she is.

My deconstruction of the institution of *chôra* does not destroy her, but exposes the valorization of Platonic order made possible by the maintenance of choral stability and the repression of choral instability in 'respecting the mark for what it/she is.'

140 J. Derrida, '*Chôra*,' p. 268:

> While giving place to oppositions, she herself would never submit herself to any reversal. And that, another consequence, not because she would be inalterably *herself* but because in going beyond the polarity of meaning (metaphorical or proper), she would no longer belong to the horizon of meaning, nor of meaning as the meaning of being.'

141 J. Derrida, '*Chôra*,' pp .270-271.

142 Compare J. Derrida, '*Chôra*,' pp. 268-269, especially:

> It would be a question of a structure and not of some essence of the *chôra*, the question of essence no longer having any meaning on the subject of her. The *chôra*, we will say, is *anachronic*, she 'is' the anachrony in being – better – the anachrony of being. She anachronizes being.

143 J. Kipnis, *Separatrix,* p. 28, notes the 'absolute anteriority' of *chôra*, but does not deconstruct the institution of a moment when 'all true movement begins':

> ...*chôra* is neither word nor concept, neither proper noun nor

common noun, and it is a condition of absolute anteriority. Moreover, though Derrida treats of it only in passing, *chôra* shakes, shakes the whole, separating before the separation; it is movement before movement begins, since in the *Timaeus* all true movement begins with the world-soul and comes after the Demiurge does his work. Yet *chôra* shakes and orders even the chaos.

Similarly, Kipnis' account of the relation between *chôra* and the Demiurgic inscription (p. 28):

> *Chôra* has no existence, no pure being anterior to and free from inscription, outside of rhetoric and trope: it *is*, though it *is* only and always in the text as before it.

144 J. Derrida, '*Chôra*,' pp. 278-279.

145 J. Derrida, '*Chôra*,' p. 269.

146 J. Derrida, '*Chôra*,' p. 271.

147 J. Derrida, '*Chôra*,' p. 266.

148 Derrida reiterates the metaphorical status of *both* categories of language, but privileges that of 'impression or printing'. See, e.g., *Transcript,* 17 September 1985:

> To discuss this, he has to use what generations of philosophers have called 'metaphors.' These are the mother, the matrix or the nurse. You can compare, he says, the paradigm with the father, the sensible world with the child or the infant, and *chôra*, this place of inscription, with the mother or nurse. But these are only metaphors, because they are borrowed from the sensible world. So *chôra* is not the mother, nor the nurse who nurtures infants.

continuing a moment later with,

> *Chôra* is the spacing which is the condition for everything to take place, for everything to be inscribed. The metaphor of impression or printing is very strong and recognizable in this text. It is the place where everything is received as an imprint.

149 The quality of 'virginity' can, of course, be male: compare the Greek term *parthenos* indicating either a male or female virgin, depending upon the gender of the article used with it. But in apposition with 'inaccessible' and 'impassive', as in the passage cited above, 'Is the value of a receptacle not also associated, like passive and virgin matter, with the feminine element, and precisely in Greek culture,' 'virginity' appears to be intended as female here.

150 See J. Derrida, '*Chôra*,' p. 269. See also *Transcript,* 17 September 1985:

> What interests me is that since *chôra* is irreducible to the two positions, the sensible and the intelligible, which have dominated the entire tradition of Western thought, it is irreducible to all the values to which we are accustomed – values of origin, anthropomorphism, and so on. I insist on the fact of this non-anthropomorphism of *chôra*. Because *chôra* looks as though it were were giving something, 'giving' place... yet Plato insists that in fact it has to be a virgin place, and that it has to be totally foreign, totally exterior to anything that it receives. Since it is absolutely blank, everything that is printed on it is automatically effaced.

It should also be noted that the 'effacement' of what is 'printed' on *chôra* may be 'automatic' but not in the sense of 'immediate,' or else there would be no sensible objects at all.

151 See above, p. 23.

152 For *maintenant* as a virtual 'technical term' in Derrida's philosophy of architecture, see above, n. 6.

153 Emphasis added. *Transcript,* 8 November 1985. See also *Transcript,* 3 April 1986:

> PE: As Thomas will tell you, La Villette is a killer project. The theoretical paradigms which you set up are so difficult to make.
> JD: Do not worry; it is an impossible program for architecture.

It is the challenge in itself that is important.

154 *Transcript,* 3 April 1986.
155 Derrida's 'feminine slip' here is corrected by the editor to 'paradigm' in the proofs of the *Transcript*.
156 Emphasis added. *Transcript,* 3 April 1986.
157 J. Derrida, *'Chôra,'* p. 273:

> Simply that excess is nothing, nothing which may be or be said onto-logically. That absence of support, that one cannot translate into absent support or absence as support, provokes and resists every binary or dialectic determination, any examination [*arraisonnement*] of a philosophical *type*, let us say more rigorously, of an *ontological* type.

158 For the *locus classicus* in Vitruvius, see above, n. 109.
159 For *Choral Works* as an instance of Eisenman's 'scaling' method, as practiced in the 'Romeo and Juliet' and 'Long Beach Museum' projects, and for a defense of this design process as 'avoid[ing] the trap of architectural totalization (not literary totalization) by replacing the universalizing discourse which drives traditional design with a local fiction,' see J. Kipnis, *Separatrix*, pp. 7-8 and 13-14.
160 *Transcript,* 17 September 1985.
161 *Transcript,* 21 April 1986.
162 *Transcript,* 21 April 1986.
163 *Transcript,* 21 April 1986. Lessor also explains site one/column two:

> Let's look at site one (column 2). Venice, which appears at the top, is scaled up, is solid, and is the highest. It is the future plan. The only part of Venice which you will see is the canal of Venice as a wall, three or four meters high. Bernard's scheme, the second element in the column, is at full scale, since it is in the present, and solid, but it only comes a little bit out of the ground... La Villette, the third element in the column, is also in the present, but as a small void. It is a receptacle, as in its superposition it is both the wall of Paris and the canal. Peter's scheme, the bottom element in the column, is the past, and is a deeper void.

164 Lessor and Eisenman observe (*Transcript,* 21 April 1986):

> TL: For [fictional] site two (column 3)... If you look at this diagram in which La Villette [2] is scaled down to make the squares in Bernard's project [1] the same size as those in Peter's [4], the Parisian abattoirs seem to be at the right scale, but they aren't. The Parisian abattoirs are so much bigger than the ones in Venice, that when you scale Paris down, the abbatoirs appear to be at the same scale.
> PE: Which is nice.
> TL: Yes, it is a reversal of reality and meaning.
> PE: You get this terribly strange play of scale and reality, as if half is always at the same scale and half not, as if something terrible has happened.

165 *Transcript,* 21 April 1986.
166 *Transcript,* 21 April 1986. Derrida explains:

> JD: To put it in an abstract way, I would be interested in a way of opening the dimension of either the future or the past in such a way that they could never be integrated into the totality as present-future or present-past. In that way, the relationship to the future could be totally open; this could motivate the visitor to stop and read, and even gain a virtual perception of the whole.

Eisenman describes 'virtual perception of the whole' as a feature of classical architecture:

> PE: Traditional architecture provides a virtual perception of the whole. When you walk through a Palladian plan, you schematize it in your mind – you don't have to walk through the whole building to understand its symmetries. The somatic memory puts these things together. Classical architecture always provided parts in different places to allow the whole scheme to be put together. What Jacques is saying is that maybe there could be something in each piece that would provide an aperture, a kind of opening to nowhere.
> TL: That breaks the circle.

167 *Transcript,* 21 April 1986.
168 Emphasis added. *Transcript,* 21 April 1986.
169 See *Transcript,* 1 October 1986.

Jennifer Bloomer is the Director of Graduate
Programs in Design at Iowa State University.
She was a fellow of the CIAU in 1989-90, and
is the author of *Desiring Architecture*
(New Haven, forthcoming) and *Tabbles of
Bower* (Bloomfield Hills, forthcoming).

A lay a stone a patch a post a pen the ruddyrun
Minor Architectural Possibilities[1]

Jennifer Bloomer

'Nature is therefore purely poetic, and so it is a magician's den, a physicist's laboratory, a children's nursery, an attic and a lumber-room.' It must not be assumed that there is anything accidental about the fact that the allegorical is related in this way to the fragmentary, untidy, and disordered character of magicians' dens or alchemists' laboratories familiar above all to the baroque. Are not the works of Jean Paul, the greatest allegorist in German literature, just such children's nurseries and haunted rooms?[2]

It is well known that the potato is a root vegetable that grows in stony soil and has Irish affiliations. The potato, which grows in the dark, sports grotesque protuberances known as eyes. When digging for these tubers, one must sift through many stones before finding all the potatoes contained within the volume of soil at hand. There are seven potatoes in the children's rhyme and there are seven potatoes in this stony text. It may take some digging to find them.

One potato

Humpty Dumpty sat on a wall
Humpty Dumpty had a great fall
All the king's horses and all the king's men
Couldn't put Humpty Dumpty and his bleeding, seeping, exuding, leaking, dribbling, trickling, oozing, streaming, flowing, discharging, runny, riveting, emissive self together again.

P.S. Had he not fallen among stones, this story might have been different.

Before we come into the world, we are beings in motion, blind projects in the dark, bodies tossed and rolled, rocked, on the move. This is the way we are. Once we come in, assaulted by the light, rocking makes us feel at home. We are nomads born, haptic creatures, and we spend our lives forgetting it. Architecture is the evidence of this denial.

It stands between the unrepresentable and us. Architecture is the petrified droppings of an authoritative, insensible God. Our existential projects are the denial of death by the denial of bodies. Immortalizing by the veiling of the mortal. We pile up stones feverishly in an attempt to reproduce the container, the vessel, the thing, producing the image at the expense of the voluptuous. We, like Sisyphus, never reach the goal because the impossibility of so doing is programmed into the rules of the game.

Two potato

I have a bone to pick – or chomp on – with the recent 'alliance' of architecture with the discourses of deterritorialization and dissemination that all comes out as style. 'What does it look like?' is not the same question as 'How does it work?' or 'What is the itinerary?' or 'What constitutes the assemblage?' But perhaps the bone I think I am biting is my own tail.[3] Perhaps Mark Wigley has played a vague and duplicitous game, operating on a razor's edge, making of deconstruction so ridiculous a proposition that, now happily and easily consumed as having something to do with an architectural 'look' (as in I don't know how to define it, but I know it when I see it), the margins have been cleared. In the realm of possibility of this 'perhaps', even the *grosse pierre* has been rolled aside, leaving a gaping dark hole. The work can now begin. Again.

David pitched a well-aimed pebble and hit Goliath right where it hurts (in the eye). Folks who live in glass houses should beware of inviting in boys who talk softly but carry big slingshots.

Three potato

Sometimes pebbles seem simply to be underfoot, as in the following from Roger Kimball, writing in *The New Criterion* in June 1988. The piece is called 'The Death and Resurrection of Postmodern Architecture,' and it is about rolling away that same big rock:

> Immersed in Mr. [Peter] Eisenman's chatter, one easily forgets that architecture is essentially about building habitable buildings, buildings that we live in and work in, play and worship in, not buildings that we struggle to decode.[4]

Let us crack open a few of these stones. 'Immersed': we are under water, perhaps in hot water, perhaps we are drowning, in chatter. (To chatter is to verbalize whatever comes to mind, without restraint or order.) Heterosexual, white adult males DO NOT CHATTER. Who chatters? Magpies, women, children, black mammies, and jovial Uncle Toms in the movies, flamboyant gay males. Eisenman has been hit where it hurts – with a word, his position in the power structure has been challenged. Architecture is here a simple, unified discipline with its own pure essence: building habitable buildings. The Being (essence) of architecture is building buildings in which we dwell. A familiar model. But Kimball fails to mention the thinking part of architectural *Dasein*, putting it by implication over in an other category, that of 'struggling to decode.' To decode presumes a prior encoding, which is implied here as an additional facet of NOT ESSENTIALLY ARCHITECTURE. And it is this 'not' that draws the line and ties it at both ends. With this 'not', Kimball has laid the cards of positivism on the table. The duality architecture/not architecture can be mapped as follows:

Eisenman	architecture
chatter	essence
drowning	building and dwelling
struggling	living working playing
decoding	worshipping

Clearly, Eisenman is not on the side of architecture.

Four

Architecture stands. *Stat.* '*Fidem meam obligo vexillo civitatium Americae Federatarum, et rei publicae pro qua stat. Uni natione, deo ducendi, non dividendae, cum libertate iustitiaque omnibus.*'⁵ Architecture stands and stands for. Like a flag or symbol, a sign. *Pro qua stat? Pro statu quo.* Architecture is the supplement of – it both stands in for and is in excess to – the State, the *civitas, pro qua stat*. The power of architecture rests in its potential to stand up and in for the powerful, the potentate, which stands under and in for the Omnipotent. When the nation under God bleeds out of its boundaries and finds itself in a state of global multinational capitalism, the questions 'Who are all?' and 'What are liberty and justice?' become difficult – slippery. When that for which architecture stands becomes slippery and difficult, it stands to reason that architecture becomes slippery and difficult.

The sorceress – hysterics of Helene Cixous appear as – repressed other makers in Monique Wittig's *Les Guerillères*. In this fictional world, the women use the tools of patriarchal material culture to make assemblages that work against it. They make a Deleuzian minor architecture⁶: they collect the tools of capitalist culture – mass production machinery of all sorts, washing machines, vacuum cleaners, and stoves – and make of them a great allegorical dumping ground, a petrified landscape, which they set on fire. 'Then, starting to dance around it, they clap their hands, they shout obscene phrases, they cut their hair or let it down. When the fire has burnt down, when they are sated with setting off explosions, they collect the debris, the objects that are not consumed, those that have not melted down, those that have not disintegrated. They cover them with blue green red paint to reassemble them in grotesque grandiose abracadabrant compositions to which they give names.'⁷

These are Towers of Babble, chatterers' architecture, the hatchery,⁸ an architecture of the carnivalesque that has exited the sanctioned and bounded midway.⁹ The amusement park or funhouse is the reification and *topos* of – still – authoritatively controlled desire. Desire here is filtered through an assemblage of safety valves. Power and ideology are as present here as in the Pentagon, or perhaps more to the point, as in the Penthouse, where desire is reconstituted as will to power and served up as sexuality. (In this sense, the pet is better clothed than the emperor.) What is pent up in the Penthouse or the fun house is the desire of the other, which apparently is not satisfied (as the barkers in the midway or the caption writers in the tit mags would have us believe) by being petrified, objectified. The ejaculations of the other, when they come, are not easily wiped away. They can be messy and ugly, 'hysterical constructions,' 'grotesque grandiose abracadabrant compositions,' circulating partial objects. Dark, polysemous, and out of control, like the dreamy fall.

For the other, the penthouse, the fun house, and the prison house bear a remarkable similarity: they are orderly stacks of 'mill and stumpling stones.' And, as Nietzsche reminds us, we will more easily break a leg in our stumblings than one of these stones. It is a losing battle to attempt to tear down or replace these solid constructions. What is to be done is the building of 'unsafe buildings' in their shadows. 'Inasmuch as [history] is a criticism of signifying practices, it will have to 'shift the stones' by shifting around its own stones. Criticism speaks only if the doubt with which it attacks the real turns back on itself as well. Operating on its own constructions, history makes an incision with a scalpel in a body whose scars do not disappear; but at the same time, unhealed scars already mar the compactness of historical constructions, rendering them problematic and preventing them from presenting themselves as 'truth'… The certainties that history presents should…be

51

read as expressions of repressions. They are nothing but defenses or barriers that hide the reality of historical writing. They incorporate uncertainty: 'true history' is not that which cloaks itself in indisputable 'philological proofs,' but that which recognizes its own arbitrariness, which recognizes itself as an 'unsafe building'.[10]

An unsafe construction, then, not only questions its object of criticism, but always throws itself into crisis as well. The work is always in progress. It is generative. It is never complete. It is never completely clear. 'She had been working on it for fifteen years, carrying about with her a shapeless bag of dingy, threadbare brocade containing odds and ends of colored fabric in all possible shapes. She could never bring herself to trim them to any pattern; so she shifted them like pieces of a patient puzzle-picture, trying to fit them to a pattern or create a pattern out of them without using her scissors, smoothing her colored scraps with flaccid, putty-colored fingers.'[11]

Architecture is the material expression that stands for (*stat*) ideology. It also stands in the metaphor of hierarchical and structural thinking (gravity, Cartesian logic). It is tautological (Joyce's 'tootoological') – it is incised – and in this sense Eisenman is right: 'Architecture will always look like architecture.' But, the 'looks like' must be called into question.

An architecture of desire – a minor architecture – will operate in the interstices of this architecture. Not opposed to, not separate from, but upon/within/among – barnacles, bastard constructions – *une batarde architecture* – tattoos (ornament, embellishment). An other writing upon the body of architecture. Architecture becomes the ground, or stone, on which its mapping is inscribed – on which its processes bleed. KAFKA.

Five potato

Allos agoreuein. The other speaks in public, in the agora. For the other, as for Walter Benjamin – reject, outcast, melancholic, who met his end among pure, finely cut, white, proper stones – the line between the political and the personal is utterly imaginary. The contest between the libidinal and the political – desire and ideology – is no contest.

As Craig Owens[12] has pointed out, the theory of allegory of Benjamin 'defies summary.' Benjamin's text is a patchwork of fragments and seams, stitched both horizontally across each layer of pieces and vertically through the layers to hold the thing together. Because Benjamin's treatise on allegory and *Trauerspiel* is itself allegorical, it is not approachable by summation (which would merely be a recitation of the text at best). It is, however, appropriate to plot an itinerary through this text, and by so doing, to map it (misread it).

Benjamin's treatise is an 'exasperated articulation of a theme [allegory] originally taken as absolute,' a critical experimentalism of Tafuri's type 'E', the classification of 'Piranesi's *Iconographia Campi Martii,* of many 'critical restorations' by Albini and Scarpa, of Kahn's last work.'[13] And, one might add, of James Joyce's *Finnegan's Wake* (an 'exasperated articulation' of the 'nightmare from which I am trying to awake').

Let us begin with the word 'emblem'. 'In the baroque, especially, the allegorical personification can be seen to give way in favour of the emblems, which mostly offer themselves to view in desolate, sorrowful dispersal.'[14] An emblem (in German, *Sinnbild*, which, with its perverse homophonous similarity to 'symbol,' and its more appropriately perverse homophonous similarity to 'sin-build', suggesting a connection to illicit building) is an image that serves as a decoding apparatus of an allegory. Emblems, which 'mostly offer themselves to view in desolate, sorrowful dispersal,'[15] are themselves kinds of maps of the complex, fragmented, hieroglyphic mode of allegory that Benjamin finds in baroque tragic drama (and also well-seeded in sections of early modernism – in Baudelaire, for example). In their dispersal, the emblems that serve as switching mechanisms of Benjaminian allegory differ radically from the personifications of conventional allegory, which are simple and possess simple, causal relationships between figure and meaning. Benjamin cites Johann Joachim Winckelmann's *Versuch einer Allegorie besonders fur die Kunst*[16]: 'The best and most perfect allegory of one or of several concepts is comprised of one single figure, or should be thought of as such.' And Friedrich Creuzer[17]: 'The German emblem…is quite lacking in that dignity and substance. It ought therefore…to remain confined to the lower sphere, and be completely excluded from symbolic tests.'

Here, an opposition between emblem and symbol (or the allegorical and the symbolic) is being set up, to which we will return shortly. What Benjamin accomplishes here is a decisive cleavage between types of allegory. Both involve 'convention and expression'[18], but that to which I shall refer as 'conventional allegory' (as opposed to Benjaminian allegory) 'is not convention of expression [which points in the direction of allegory's connection to writing], but expression of convention…[and] expression of authority, which is secret in accordance with the dignity of its origin, but public in accordance with the extent of its validity.'[19]

A return to 'emblem' will allow us access to this cleavage, this place between, this perhaps abysmal split. The Latin word *emblema* means inlaid work, like mosaic, made of bits of stone, or like certain ('primitive') forms of jewelry. ('Metalworking was the 'barbarian', or nomad, art par excellence…'[20])

The Latin word emerged from the Greek *emballein*, which means 'to throw' in. The making of a pot or jug or vessel is called 'throwing'. The twisting of fibers into thread, which is then wound about the *rochetto*, a shuttling projectile (a rocket) used to make textiles, is called 'throwing'. Throwing is casting, as in casting a fishing line (which describes a trajectory) or in casting a shadow (which describes a projection). To 'throw up' is to evacuate the stomach of contents. When accomplished hurriedly, this is called projectile vomiting. To 'throw up' is also to erect a construction hurriedly. If we trace a trajectory back through 'throw' to the Latin, we encounter the verb *iaceo*, 'I throw,' whose past participle is embedded in the object, the project, and the trajectory, as well as in rejection, abjection, and injection. And ejaculate.

A 'throw' is also a radius described by a crank or cam in a machine. And this will return us to Benjamin, and the distinction between symbol and allegory. For Benjamin, the 'genuine' concept of the symbol is that which comes from theology, a paradoxical concept of 'the unity of the material and the transcendental object.'[21] He castigates the nineteenth-century romantic aestheticians for distorting the concept into a simplistic one that is dependent on an 'indivisible unity of form and content.'[22] In such a construct, 'the beautiful is supposed to merge with the divine in an unbroken whole,'[23] making a perfect, circular relationship between what something looks like and what something is (between appearance and essence). Benjamin insists that the cornerstone of this nineteenth-century idea was laid in classicism. His lengthy description of the 'harmonious inwardness' of the classical subject and the classical conception of the symbol is worth quoting verbatim:

> In classicism the tendency to the apotheosis of existence in the individual who is perfect, in
> more than an ethical sense, is clear enough. What is typically romantic is the placing of this per-

53

fect individual within a progression of events which is, it is true, infinite but is nevertheless redemptive, even sacred. But once the ethical subject has become absorbed in the individual, then no rigorism – not even Kantian rigorism – can save it and preserve its masculine profile. Its heart is lost in the beautiful soul. And the radius of action – no, only the radius of the culture – of the thus perfected beautiful individual is what describes the circle of the 'symbolic.' In contrast the baroque apotheosis is a dialectical one. It is accomplished in the movement between extremes. In this eccentric and dialectic process the harmonious inwardness of classicism plays no role, for the reason that the immediate problems of the baroque, being politico-religious problems, did not so much affect the individual and his ethics as his religious community... Simultaneously with its profane concept of the symbol, classicism develops its speculative counterpart, that of the allegorical. A genuine theory of allegory did not, it is true, arise at that time, nor had there been one previously. It is nevertheless legitimate to describe the new concept of the allegorical as speculative because it was in fact adapted so as to provide the dark background against which the bright world of the symbol might stand out.[24]

The opposition of symbol and allegory involves the centered, bright unity of the one and the eccentric, dark assemblage of the other in a figure-ground relationship. Allegory *is* the other. It exists outside, but somehow lies underneath, both classical and romantic discourses.

In a series of twists, Benjamin demonstrates the identity of the modern (he names Yeats) attitude and the nineteenth-century (he quotes Goethe and Schopenhauer) attitude toward the allegory/symbol relationship, an identity whose template is the alignment of symbol with the expression of Idea and allegory with the expression of content; and retrieves from the pejorative remarks of Schopenhauer on allegory one of the dominant structural elements of his own argument. Schopenhauer (in *The World as Will and Representation*) equates the expression of concept with 'the trifling amusement of carving a picture to serve at the same time as an inscription, as a hieroglyphic.'[25] Benjamin takes Schopenhauer's dismissal of allegory as being merely a form of writing (picture writing) and says 'Yes!' This is an important aspect of allegory, this muddying of the distinction between word and image, between the verbal and the visual. And here he suggests what Stephen Melville will later state, 'that the allegorical impulse is one which would acknowledge explicitly the futility of trying to sort the 'mere' from the 'pure,' [*la mère* from *le père*, *la mer* from *la pierre*] an impulse to embrace the [heteronomous and heterological].'[26]

Manfredo Tafuri suggests (although he does not write it) that, because architecture is such a complex structure, it is always already of an allegorical impulse; for when 'symbolic signs' are introduced into architecture, they acquire an '*ambiguous* character.'[27] 'In reality every work of architecture can be referred to several symbolic systems. The fact that in Borromini's S. Ivo the myth of Babel's Tower, the ascent to Truth and Knowledge, the divine anti-Babel, the Pentecostal space, the superimposed [conventional] allegories of Modesty and Knowledge (the emblematic bee and the *Domus Sapientae* as the seven-pillared house) are fused with the passage from a space uncertain of its hierarchy (that of the lower level) to the unitary space of the dome, is not irrelevant to the formation of meanings specific to the spatial in-fill.'[28] Tafuri's architectural symbol (and particularly in the example of Borromini), resembles closely Benjamin's allegorical sign: 'The symbol is, in fact, something that because of its nature rejects a univocal reading. Its meanings tend to escape and its characteristic is that of *revealing and hiding at the same time*. Otherwise, instead of a symbol we should speak of an 'emblem'... It follows, therefore, that the qualities of the [architectural] symbol are the same as those of the artistic 'sign': ambiguous, disposed to accept different meanings, transparent and fixed within a pre-established code, and, at the same time, able to transgress the laws of that code.'[29]

In another essay,[30] Tafuri reports that, with the rise of allegory and symbolism in the seventeenth and eighteenth centuries, 'architecture realizes the impossibility of finding its own reasons exclusively in itself.'[31] The presence of an 'interlocutor' who 'does not simply receive the messages, but…is asked to complete them, even to change their meaning while they are being deciphered,' is necessary to what Sedlmayer called '*an architecture that describes itself*' (the work of Brown, Kent, Chambers, Soane, Lequeu, et al). In the assemblages of the so-called 'picturesque' landscape gardens (or of Soane's museum), architecture's status as absolute object approaches that of the ambiguous and relative, moving from the autonomous to the didactic (in the vague direction of what Eisenman terms a 'dislocating text of architecture'[32]: 'As didactical instruments they are turned towards man, awakening his senses and injecting into them, immediately afterwards, a critical stimulus: Nature, by now not a reflection of the divine Idea but a structure shared by man, can merge with the history of the entire human species, showing that the rational course of civilization is *natural*, because it moves (Gian Battista Vico) from the realm of the senses to that of the intellect... The Gothic, Chinese, Classical and eclectic pavilions inserted [*emballein*] in the texture of a 'nature trained to be natural,' are ambiguous objects. They allude to something other than themselves, losing their semantic autonomy. It is the same phenomenon that will move into *major* architecture…'[33]

There are several points of intensity here. One lies in the term '*major* architecture.' 'Major' is not only used; it is italicized. Major architecture implies the presence of an other architecture, which would be, by the logic of the implication, 'minor architecture'. And into this category of minor architecture, it follows, the 'ambiguous objects' fall. Thus, through Tafuri, the construction 'minor architecture', which may contain within it 'ambiguous object', 'dislocating text of architecture', allegory, and decipherability, may be tracked to the constellation of architectural constructions as they exist in oscillating difference to their context at Kew. Kew, here, becomes the ghost of the expanded field with which Rosalind Krauss tracks the allegorical impulse in contemporary art.[34] This vaguely minor architecture is an assemblage of partial objects, a tesseraic text, a patchwork. (The picture of the picturesque – what it looks like – is overshadowed by the complex of joints.) And it stands in difference to *major* architecture, instruments of reflection of the 'divine cosmos', Tablets of Stone with the WORD OF GOD writ large.

A second generative collision is located in Tafuri's merging of interlocution and decipherment. At the point where the messages of '*l'architecture parlante*' are intercepted by an 'interlocutor', speech shifts to writing: the role of the participatory, critical subject ('(s)he among the speakers') involves a deciphering. This deciphering interlocutor is tantamount to a decoding chatterer. The switching mechanism of the spoken shifts grindingly to the switching mechanism of the written. Benjamin: 'In the baroque the tension between the spoken and the written word is immeasurable.'[35] The writing of the baroque *Trauerspiel* 'does not achieve transcendence by being voiced; rather does the world of written language remain self-sufficient and intent on the display of its own substance. Written language and sound confront each other in tense polarity.'[36] The philosophical basis of the allegorical lies in 'those comprehensive relationships between the spoken language and script.'[37]

In the Benjaminian allegorical, writing is a Derridean *supplément* – a substitute for and in excess of spoken language. It is the excessive act that points to a lack in that in for which it stands. Writing is other. It is the glyphing of writing – the black marks on the page, the script – in which otherness may reside. Sounded only, writing pretends to be the transparent medium that the rational order requires it to be. Marked, inscribed, encrypted, it is something other; there is something hidden and secret beneath its *maquillage* and manners.

'There is nothing subordinate about written script; it is not cast away in reading, like dross. It is absorbed along with what is read, as its 'pattern'. The printers, and indeed the writers of the baroque, paid the closest possible attention to the pattern of the words on the page.'[38] In allegory, words are tattoos: ornamental patterns on the body, ink in crypts.

Allegory is the nightmare of Adolf Loos. It is primitive, barbaric; the urge to tattoo is in all of us, he warns, but 'we must overcome the Indian in us.'[39] Gazing upon the pristine boxes of Loos, we might succumb to a sense of match between his spoken (into the void) and his written (onto the landscape). Until we venture over the threshold. 'Every bit as characteristic of [the verse of the baroque *Trauerspiel*] is the contrast between the logical – if one will, the classicistic – structure of the façade, and the phonetic violence within.'[40] The white box of Loos is a geode: inside there is unbounded sensuality, its 'primitivism' shaded by the most transparent of Ruskinian veils. Loos' box and the allegorical box are relatives of Pandora's box, which was not a box at all, but a jug. A sin-build. It is, according to Benjamin, by keeping the lid on the box, that allegorical language comes into being. It is the church's authoritative repression of the pagan, the barbaric, its 'banish[ment of] the gods from the memory of the faithful' that gave rise to the allegorical impulse.[41] Allegory is the possibility of a return of a repressed, a writing of that which has been imprisoned, in the dark, in the hollow vessel, the void, the jug.

The third, and most intense intersection is that of Nature and History: 'Nature, by now not a reflection of the divine Idea but a structure shared by man, can merge with the history of the entire human species…'[42] At this point, we will return to Benjamin's discussion of allegory and symbol. It is to Friedrich Creuzer's 1819 work on symbol and myth[43] that Benjamin turns to give us insight into the allegorical. And here the concept of time enters the picture. Because of the brevity, or momentariness, of the symbol, it cannot embrace myth as does allegory, which involves progression and series. Benjamin quotes Creuzer quoting Gorres: 'We can be perfectly satisfied with the explanation that takes the one [the symbol] as a sign for ideas, which is self-contained, concentrated, and which steadfastly remains itself, while recognizing the other [allegory] as a successively progressing, dramatically mobile, dynamic representation of ideas which has acquired the very fluidity of time. They stand in relation to each other as does the silent, great, and mighty natural world of mountains and plants to the living progression of human history.'[44] 'Man's' subjection to nature and the tangential and 'enigmatic' question of the nature of existence and of the individual being's biographical historicity coincide here. And it is death – the ultimate subjection to nature – that inscribes the boundary between nature, which is always subject to death and always allegorical, and signifying. Allegory in the baroque *Trauerspiel* is a history of signifying nature analogous to myth in the epic poem of classicism. So, baroque allegory represents a shift of perspective upon signifying nature, that is, a shift from myth to history.

But, at this point, Benjamin confronts us with a challenge to negotiate the clashing rocks of history and nature: 'It is by virtue of a strange combination of nature and history that the allegorical mode of expression is born.'[45] And we track this treacherous itinerary aboard the hieroglyph. For the hieroglyph itself in Benjamin is the emblem of *his* allegorical journey through knowledge.

It will be important to recall at this point that the maps of Giambattista Piranesi – the drawings of *Il Campo Marzio* – are represented as pictures carved into ancient broken tablets of stone and are thus coded as hieroglyphic maps. Hieroglyphs, those 'images of desire that are the non-stuff of which dreams are made,'[46] are ubiquitous in the *Vedute* as well, appearing properly – tattooed – on the shafts of obelisks.

In *Finnegan's Wake* there are two proper rebuses, or hieroglyphs, both of which appear in the margins at the close of section II.2 (two point two, which opens with a tattoo: 'As we are there are where are we are we there from tomtittot to teetootomtotalitarian. Tea tea too oo.'[47] And in the margin here: 'Menly about peebles', the peoples who are pebbles: the progeny of Deucalion and Pyrrha, the victims of Medusa, caryatids and atlantids, orders, the dead, the petrified. This is, after all, the section in which the calculus goes skimming; and an impotent Nietzsche – gotten up in the main text as Giambattista Vico (via the recurring (Wagnerian) leitmotif of Edgar Quinet, Vico's French propagandist) – Nietzsche, the proponent of eternal returns and the breaking up of stony words, is invoked in another margin: 'Also Spuke Zerothruster.'[48] The two rebuses are[49]:

jake, jack and l
(the babes th:

[1] Kish is for anticheirst, a:

[2] And gags for skool and
our drawings on the line!

and each is located adjacent to a footnote which is targeted in the main text above, a countdown to the close of the section which is a cryptic letter, a 'cryptogam' (words on which we might stumble and break a leg, *una gamba*, a gam). The letter is called 'NIGHTLETTER' and is from children to parents. It extends 'youlldied greedings' and is thus readable as a Christmas card and as an (Oedipal) death wish.

Let us examine the second picture. It accompanies the footnote that is marked at the word 'geg' in the text. 'Geg' appears in the following series: 'Aun Do Tri Car Cush Shay Shockt Ockt Ni Geg. Their feed begins,' which precedes the NIGHTLETTER. 'Geg' is both 'gag' and the number ten in the countdown of this frozen projectile, this zerothruster, these 'autocratic writings of paraboles of famellicurbs'[50] that prefigure the landscape of

Thomas Pynchon's rockety heterotopia, *Gravity's Rainbow.*[51]

The rebus is the Roman numeral X, or ten, a chiasmus, a crossing, a place where something happens. It is the letter X, of crossing out, of authoritative censorship and of crossing – transgression, of darkness. It is the night letter. X is a *chi*, which stands in for Christ, as in 'Xmas'. This invokes Joyce's 'crossmess parzle,'[52] which is *Finnegan's Wake* itself: both Christmas parcel and crossword puzzle, it is the near relative of Tafuri's (borrowed) jigsaw puzzle (*giocho di pazienza*) of historical research. X maps an intersection, as in the (rotated) intersection of the *cardo* and *decumanus*, or as in the intersection of the two lives of Oedipus, the point where he took Jocasta's stickpin of glittering stones and jabbed out his eyes. X is an Oedipus map, an Oedipa Maas. X marks the (blind) spots of history. X is four V's, or is it two, converging; a T prior to decapitation. X is the mark of Cain, the wanderer, the outcast with blood on his hands. It is the illogical incision made on the bite of the serpent. X is the letter of the repressed, rated X. X is the monogram of Xanthippe, who poured a pot of piss on the head of her husband, Socrates.

The footnote that accompanies this picture says 'And gags for skool and crossbuns and whopes he'll enjoyimsolff over our drawings on the line!'[53] The rebus depicts spanking instruments and the symbol of poison, the skull and crossbones (with death's head *in absentia*). Thus, it is the X of the *pharmakon*, both poison and cure. Derrida: 'If the *pharmakon* is 'ambivalent', it is because it constitutes the medium in which opposites are opposed, the movement and the play that links them among themselves, reverses them or makes one side cross over into the other (soul/body, good/evil, inside/outside, memory/forgetfulness, speech/writing, *etc.*)... We will watch it infinitely promise itself and endlessly vanish through concealed doorways that shine like mirrors and open onto a labyrinth. It is also this store of deep background that we are calling the *pharmacy*.'[54] This is the promise of Benjaminian allegory, and is as well the promise of *Finnegan's Wake*. This *pharmakon* is that which is represented by the image from which Joyce's rebus is appropriated: the alchemical symbol of the hermaphrodite – the crossing of female and male, of the feminine and masculine, of the excremental (the dirty, the bloody) and the precious (the divine): the Philosopher's Stone. The point of X change.

But this rebus is more than a purloined letter. It is as well *une lettre volée* – please note, it bears vestigial wing tips opposite its club feet.[55] These winglets fly with difficulty, like a rocket with no thrust, or like Icarus or Lucifer, whose parents reversed the direction of flow of the NIGHTLETTER's wishes. They bear a remarkable resemblance to the pathetic five-feathered wings of Paul Klee's *Angelus Novus*, a watercolor owned by Benjamin and of which he wrote: 'His face is turned toward the past. Where we perceive a chain of events, he sees one single catastrophe which keeps piling wreckage upon wreckage and hurls it in front of his feet. The angel would like to stay, awaken the dead, and make whole what has been smashed. But a storm is blowing from Paradise; it has got caught in his wings with such violence that the angel can no longer close them. This storm irresistibly propels him into the future to which his back is turned, while the pile of debris before him grows skyward. This storm is what we call progress.'[56]

The pile of debris, the ruin upon ruin, is what the melancholic Benjamin called history, and it is here that the petrified landscape of allegory and pile of ruins that is history intersect. This intersection, or point of exchange between nature and history encoded in the hieroglyph, is articulated a decade after the *Ursprung* by Benjamin's prodigal son, Theodor

W. Adorno. For Adorno, Benjamin's 'strange combination of history and nature,' entities traditionally held in opposition to each other, must be one in which the opposition is 'transcended'. Richard Wolin writes: 'According to Adorno, this act of transcendence can be accomplished, given the present constellation of socio-historic forces, *only if each side of the antithesis can be perceived as passing over into its opposite*.'[57] So, the relation between history and nature must work across a *chiasmus*, where 'historical being, in its most extreme historical determinacy, where it is most historical, is grasped as a natural 'being' and 'nature', where it apparently hardens itself most thoroughly into nature, is grasped as an historical being.'[58]

It is the *Trauerspiel* itself that figures this chiasmus in Benjamin's text. 'The writer must not conceal the fact that his activity is one of arranging, since it was not so much the mere whole as its obviously constructed quality that was the principal impression which was aimed at. Hence, the display of the craftsmanship…shows through like the masonry in a building whose rendering has broken away. [Here Benjamin marks the intersection of allegory and section, the conceptual apparatus of the generative work, with its embedded map, a 'concept' that is also about achronological structure: space.] Thus, one might say, nature remained the great teacher for the writers of this period. However, nature was not seen by them in bud and bloom, but in the over-ripeness and decay of her creations. In nature they saw eternal transience, and here alone did the saturnine vision of this generation recognize… In the process of decay, and in it alone, the events of history shrivel up and become absorbed in the setting.'[59]

History meets nature on its back side, the side not that of 'an eternal life so much as that of irresistible decay.'[60] This nature, nature as a stony setting, meets history coming around and collides in the emblem: 'For where nature bears the imprint of history, that is to say where it is a setting, does it not have a numismatic quality?'[61] This quality of having been engraved (of space having been inserted, or thrown in) is that of the emblem, the hieroglyph, and the ruin. Nature as setting (nature approaching history) and History as decay (history approaching nature) – itself a kind of setting or stage prop against which *human* nature plays – coincide in the ruin. It will be important to bear in mind that the ruin is a construction where temporality is a sluggish or slothful operator, and becomes, for all intents and purposes, anachronized, petrified, and thereby is legible as spatiality. In the ruin, the dialectical movements of the Great Dichotomy of space and time are frozen. The ruin calls the Great Dichotomy into question. (We will pick up this thread again, but for the moment leave it dangling.)

In the ruin – the catacombs, the crypts – those things which we are desirous of preserving or keeping secret may be buried, or encrypted. 'The enigmatically mysterious character of the effect of the grotesque seems to have been associated with its subterraneously mysterious origin in buried ruins and catacombs. The word is not derived from *grotta* in the literal sense, but from the 'burial' – in the sense of concealment – which the cave or grotto expresses…'[62] Here Benjamin is doubling: the quotation refers to the concept of the grotesque in antiquity, the 'secret storehouse of invention'[63] of baroque allegory. So, the grotesque is the burial place of secret things that drive allegory and in this way is related to hieroglyphic script, which performs similarly. At this point, script and crypt enjoy a confluence, which we shall call *(s)crypt*, a signifier for this hole, this writing of something which is empty space, where something secret or sacred – something unspeakable or unrepresentable – is kept, a holey space.[64]

The intersection of allegory and the grotesque in Benjamin marks a beginning of a significant itinerary. Writing out of and upon the grotesque body of Georges Bataille, Mark Taylor indicates that 'this chiasmic body [Bataille's 'tube with two orifices' with ramificatory complications, which calls interiority/exteriority distinctions into question] cannot be articulated in terms of the binary opposites that structure thought and language. Never 'proper, clean, neat, or tidy', the body is inescapably transgressive... In examining (sperm, menstrual blood, urine, fecal matter, vomit, tears, sobs, screams, cries and laughter), Bataille develops a scatology through which he attempts to subvert the eschatology of speculative philosophy and traditional theology. [At this point, Taylor reminds us in a note of 'the use of the word 'altar' to refer to a toilet.'] While Hegel is preoccupied with securing the System 'proper' by wiping or flushing away *Kote*, Bataille struggles to expose the gap through which the repressed eternally returns.'[65] The grotesque body is the body of crypts, invaginations, and folds – of secret voids, burial chambers where secrets and sacreds may be preserved. In this body, Nature, History, Theology, and Psychoanalysis slide around and in and out of each other in utter indistinguishability.

The chiasmic body is a hieroglyphic text. It represents the unrepresentable (the unspeakable): the hissing holes 'through which the repressed eternally returns.' An illegible text. Benjamin likens baroque allegory to texts written in intertwined Egyptian, Greek, and Christian pictorial languages – a place where theology could preserve the power of sacred things (by embedding them in the profane). This kind of writing is also capable of providing 'a refuge for many ideas which people were reluctant to voice openly before princes.'[66]

Fredric Jameson has noted this capability of allegory in the literature of what he generalizes as 'the third world': 'All third-world texts are necessarily, I want to argue, allegorical, and in a very specific way: they are to be read as what I will call *national allegories...*'[67] Jameson argues that in these allegorical texts the gap between the libidinal (personal, private, unconscious) and the political (collective, world of classes), which is a major determining characteristic of capitalist culture, is erased; that in 'third-world' texts (he cites primarily African and Chinese texts) '*the story of the private individual destiny is always an allegory of the embattled situation of the public third-world culture and society.*'[68] Jameson here locates allegory as that place where ideas under repression by the dominant might be hidden, as well as the place where the personal and political may coincide. The reading of such allegories requires a 'new mapping process' in which 'we must rethink our conventional conception of the symbolic levels of narrative (where sexuality and politics might be in homology to each other, for instance) as a set of loops or circuits which intersect and overdetermine each other...'[69] These allegories, in distinction to what Jameson labels 'the unconscious allegories of our own ['first-world'] cultural texts,' are 'conscious and overt.'[70] What Jameson's text suggests (albeit obliquely) for present purposes is the potential of allegory as a vehicle for the return of any repressed. Jameson's concept of 'mapping', of which 'national allegory' is a form, is 'structurally available to the dominated rather than the dominating classes.'[71]

MAPPING: The midden heap – the emblematic dumping ground in *Finnegan's Wake* – is a mapping of the hen's letter: *une lettre volée*, both obvious and hidden, and not legible to all in the same way. The little biddies can scratch up the most wee ('tea tea too oo') bits.[72]

60

Benjamin quotes Opitz: 'Because the earliest rude world was too crude and uncivilized and people could not therefore correctly grasp and understand the teachings of wisdom and heavenly things, wise men had to conceal and bury what they had discovered for the cultivation of the fear of God, morality, and good conduct, in rhymes and fables, to which the common people are disposed to listen.'[73] That which is hidden in the allegorical is theological, the sacred buried in the profane. This is what is hidden in the *Trauerspiel*: 'TRAGEDY, like a festival given in honor of horror-spreading TIME, depicted for gathered men the signs of delirium and death whereby they might recognize their true nature.'[74] But this aspect has been carved away – properly – from religion, now a cagey structure of domination. Taylor: 'Bataille maintains that art now provides a more effective access to the uncanny time-space of the sacred… In *Lascaux, or the Birth of Art*, he argues that art 'begins' in the bowels of mother earth… From the beginning (if indeed there is a beginning), there is something *grotto-esque* and *dirty* about art. Bataille is convinced that the dirt of art's grotesque, subterranean 'origin' can never be wiped away. Art, like religion, emerges from the filth of the sacred.'[75] We might add architecture, 'the mother of the arts.'

This emerging mirrors the merging (albeit a collisive one) in the *Trauerspiel*, as Bataille's effective erasure of the dialectic mirrors Benjamin's invocation of it. (The dialectic prepares the way for its own dissolution, after all. The introduction of mediation makes it possible to throw the whole business into question.) Allegory in Benjamin, like the Dionysian orgy in Bataille, is a 'harsh disturbance of the peace and a disruption of law and order'[76] that occurs at the place where the sacred and the profane are indistinguishable. And this place is allegorizable (or emblematizable) by allegory itself. Because in allegory, 'any person, any object, any relationship can mean absolutely anything else,'[77] the profane world, the material world is rendered a world in which each person, object, or relationship is of no particular significance (importance). At the same time, these 'things' that are used to signify acquire a power that makes them then different, locates them on a 'higher plane', that is, renders them of the sacred. 'Considered in allegorical terms, the profane world is both elevated and devalued.'[78] This dialectic is echoed in the dialectic of convention and expression. Allegory is, again, both. 'Here too the solution is a dialectical one. It lies in the essence of writing itself.'[79] Here allegory connects to criticism, both convention of expression ('like every kind of writing'[80]) and expression of convention. 'The strategy of criticism is located in the object of criticism'[81] as 'the allegorical work tends to prescribe the direction of its own commentary.'[82]

The *Trauerspiel* is an object with no outer form (like that of the symbol). 'Its outer form has died away.'[83] An intricately constructed ruin of 'extraordinary detail', petrified, mortified. 'Criticism means the mortification of works.'[84] This returns allegory (complex, timeless, hieroglyph script) to its position of opposition to the symbol (simple, fleeting, transparent image), where 'in it the baroque reveals itself to be the sovereign opposite of classicism.'[85] Allegory, which 'at one stroke…transforms things and works into stirring writing,'[86] thereby resting on an unstable ground 'between sacred standing and profane comprehensibility,'[87] is a stormy 'synthesis' reached 'as a result of the conflict between theological and artistic intentions, a synthesis not so much in the sense of a peace as a *treuga dei* between the conflicting opinions.'[88]

Allegory is associated with the melancholic. 'For the only pleasure the melancholic permits himself, and it is a powerful one, is allegory.'[89] It is the gaze of melancholy which caus-

61

es life (time) to flow out of objects – petrifies them – so that they remain, dead, but pre-served. Melancholy is the attribute of Saturn, or Cronos (who castrated his father and brother Uranus, birthing Aphrodite from the blood), the dualistic god of extremes. One of the forgotten symbols of melancholy, Benjamin points out, is the stone, which is also (for reasons we have seen) an allegorical emblem par excellence. 'He was by nature pensive and of a melancholy complexion, which dispositions ponder a matter more constantly and pro-ceed more cautiously in all their actions. Neither the serpent-headed Medusa, nor the African monster, nor the weeping crocodile of this world could mislead his gaze, still less transform his limbs into an unfeeling stone.'[90] 'Melancholy betrays the world for the sake of knowledge.'[91] The melancholic, the allegorist, gazes into a 'bottomless pit of contempla-tion.'[92] Craig Owens' citation of Robert Smithson bears appropriation here:

> The names of minerals and the minerals themselves do not differ from each other, because at the bottom of both the material and the print is the beginning of an abysmal number of fissures. Words and rocks contain a language that follows a syntax of splits and ruptures. Look at any word long enough and you will see it open up into a series of faults, into a terrain of particles each containing its own void...[93]

At the stopping of his text, Benjamin leaves us with a final dialectic of allegory, so that it does not, 'as those who lose their footing through somersaults in their fall,...fall from emblem to emblem down into the dizziness of its bottomless depths... Ultimately in the death-signs of the baroque the direction of allegorical reflection is reversed; on the second part of its wide arc it returns, to redeem... These allegories fill out and deny the void in which they are represented, just as, ultimately, the intention does not faithfully rest in the contemplation of bones, but faithlessly leaps forward to the idea of resurrection.'[94]

Six potato

The geography of *Finnegan's Wake* is a petrified corpse, the body of the Dead Father. Joyce's friend and publisher Sylvia Beach affectionately called him 'Melancholy Jesus' and his wife Nora Barnacle called him 'good-for-nothing' (sloth and dullness are characteristics of the melancholic). The melancholic's passion is knowledge, which Benjamin associates with evil. ('One demon knows more than you.') Recall that it is knowledge that is associat-ed with evil in the Bible. Benjamin notes that the attribute of Adam is melancholy and the attribute of Eve is joyfulness.[95] He also points out the problem with this duality: it is mad-ness that is associated with melancholy, but it is Eve who is instigator of the Fall. The only way out of this conundrum is to call the division into question. It was Eve, after all, who first consumed the evil knowledge, the secret knowledge of the sacred/profane. Eve, born of Medusa, with her melancholic's stony gaze and her intimacy with serpents. Eve, who bore two sons Cain and Abel, the passionate, murderous, wanderer (Cain was his mother's son) and the gentle, obedient favorite of God. Cain and Abel, who in *Finnegan's Wake* appear as Shem and Shaun, the sons of the petrified landscape, Humphrey Chimpden Earwicker, and the flowing, disseminative river, Anna Livia Plurabelle. Shem, the Penman, is his mother's son: a sinister writer, he is always blaspheming, with 'an artificial tongue with a natural curl' (p. 169). Shem lives in the House O'Shame (the 'Haunted Inkbottle') where he is 'an ineleuctable phantom...writing the mystery of himself in furni-ture' (184.08-10). Shaun, the Postman, is a man's man: rational, right, orderly, 'dogmestic' (411), 'decent' (419), 'gracious' (424), and, notably, 'able' (427).

Shem is perhaps nowhere more present than in the 1,500-word sentence occupying pages 119 to 123 that confuses the act of writing and the 'vaulting feminine libido,' which is, in the end, 'sternly controlled and easily repersuaded by the uniform matteroffactness of a meandering male fist' (123.08-10).

Mapping: When we are geographically distant, my lover constructs my body with imagery, aestheticizes – lips, breasts, eyes, curves, colors. Medusa is a masculine projection. The voyeur petrifies the body. (What does it look like?) I, eyeless and with no *aegis*, map the deep surfaces of his body with the memory of the tongue, or of the skin. I write his body with dark, olfactory ink, from scalp to armpit to groin to behind the knee to between the toes. I trace the complex of nuances among these points of intensity. I write the feminine. An un-visible tattoo. When it (*jouissance*) comes to (bleeds into) architecture, what it looks like hardly matters. The distant pleasures of the *voyeur* are pale as ice in the presence of the *scrypteuse*. The *ombre elle*.[96]

Question: What has eyes but cannot see?

The Penman is a chatterer. (Remove the 'ise' from P. Eisenman and see what you get.)[97] Also the possessor of peculiar tattoos: 'the first till last alshemist wrote over every square inch of the only foolscap available, his own body, till by its corrosive sublimation one continuous present tense integument slowly unfolded all marryvoisubg moodmoulded cyclewheeling history' (185-186).

Shem is 'middayevil.' Benjamin: 'In their supreme, western, form the mosaic and the treatise are products of the Middle Ages; it is their very real affinity which makes comparison possible.'[98]

Shem writes, Shaun delivers. Shaun and Shem appear in *Finnegan's Wake* as Same and Th'other: both the twins of Plato and Thamous – regal representative of Amon Ra, the sun god who creates by speaking – and Thoth – the inventor of writing, a 'cure' for memory loss, which is rejected (as a poison) by Thamous.[99] Helene Cixous: 'Shaun boasts of being the possessor of all words as he is the master of all men, and thus establishes his allegiance to capitalism and patriarchy.'[100] At this point, Fredric Jameson's happy typo in 'Postmodernism, or the Cultural Logic of Late Capitalism' is telling. ('Who has known how to metamorphose a 'typo' proper to protect the one with a slip into which the other can fall?'[101]) After noting the commercial failure due to the inability of shoppers to find the boutiques in John Portman's Westin Bonaventure Hotel in Los Angeles, Jameson writes: 'When you recall that Postman is a businessman as well as an architect, and a millionaire developer, an artist who is at one and the same time a capitalist in his own right, one cannot but feel that here too something of a 'return of the repressed' is involved.'[102]

The Postman gazes into the depths of a glassy surface and sees reflection, like Narcissus, who spurned Echo, the ceaseless chatterer. The Penman sees into the abysmal liquid, the void, the Pandora's jug. Th'other speaks with stylish instrument.

In *Finnegan's Wake*, Shem and Shaun are unstable as individuals. They flow in and out of each other; they are always becoming. There is always difference, but it will not hold still. It is mercurial. 'The *pharmakon* always penetrates like a liquid; it is absorbed, drunk, introduced into the inside, which it first marks with the hardness of the type, soon to invade it and inundate it with its medicine, its brew, its drink, its potion, its poison. In liquid, opposites are more easily mixed. Liquid is the element of the *pharmakon*.'[103] Liquid is the matrix of the mosaic: it bleeds among the stones; it separates them and holds them together. 'Just as mosaics preserve their majesty despite their fragmentation into capricious particles, so philosophical contemplation is not lacking in momentum. Both are made up of the distinct and the disparate; and nothing could bear more powerful testimony to the transcendent force of the sacred image and the truth itself. The value of fragments of thought is all the greater the less direct their relationship to the underlying idea, and the brilliance of the representation depends as much on this value as the brilliance of the mosaic does on the quality of the glass paste.'[104]

Seven potato

My daughter Sarah, who is eight and wants to be a writer when she grows up, has brought me her latest production, a 'book for little kids' called *The Pattern Book and Other*. This book contains information which Sarah, the Diderot of the third grade,[105] deems it necessary for little kids like her four-year old cousin Kate to know. The book consists of four chapters:

> Chapter I: 'Patterns' – a mosaic (with obscene glue globs displaying themselves shamelessly) of colored paper patterns in circles, squares, triangles, and ellipses.
> Chapter II: 'Math' – an illustrated 2+2=4, 4+4=8.
> Chapter III: 'Knock Knock Jokes' – ('Knock Knock. Who's there? Banana, etc.')
> Chapter IV: 'Meshering' – which includes the fact that there are 'four quarks in a galleon.'

It astounds me that that which I labor so hard to understand is mere, and pure, child's play. Children perhaps know the untruth of the mantra that we teach them. Children (those little nomadic androgynes that we carve away at from the moment they come into the world) know, like Nietzsche knew, that words – the wall material of the symbolic order – are as likely to break our bones (our matrix)[106] as are sticks and stones. And the constructions – historical, philosophical, etc. – they embody are as present, as familiar, as beloved, as oppressive, as cold and pale, as the architectural constructions that stand for them.

In Wim Wenders' film, *Wings of Desire*, it is only Peter Falk, playing a simulacrum of himself – an actor known for playing a bumbling, babbling, one-eyed detective in another role, who occupies his spare time making drawings – but also the ghost of what the protagonist angel is to become (an *Angelus Novus*), and the children, the little chattering magpies, who understand. The chiasmus of the film, the place where the angel's blood flows red (the image shifts from black and white to Technicolor), occurs at the Berlin wall, a wall made of pure – or is it mere – ideology.[107]

OR[108]

1 This paper is an early version of an introductory chapter to *Desiring Architecture: The Scrypts of Joyce and Piranesi*, forthcoming from the Yale University Press. The chapter alludes to other parts of the book (which is itself an allegorical 'mapping', the subject of the work) at many points. Whenever it has seemed potentially helpful, I have directed the reader to other parts of the book that have been published and are therefore available. This is by no means required or even necessarily recommended reading.
2 W. Benjamin (1928), quoting Novalis' *Schriften* to illuminate his concept of the allegorical in *The Origin of German Tragic Drama*, tr. J. Osborne (London, 1985), p. 188.

3 The reader has just encountered the first indication that this project is an historical one. See footnote 10.
4 R. Kimball, 'The Death and Resurrection of Postmodern Architecture,' *The New Criterion* (June 1988), p. 26.
5 A mystorical element: growing up in East Tennessee, I recited this every school day of my adolescent life.
6 I am here suggesting a transfer (with modifications) of the concept of 'minor literature' of Gilles Deleuze and Felix Guattari to architecture. For elucidation, see J. Bloomer, 'D'or,' in *Sexuality and Space*, ed. B. Colomina (Princeton, 1991).
7 M. Wittig, *Les Guerrillères*, tr. David Levay (London,

1979), p. 93.

8 The hatchery is expounded upon in 'In the Museyroom,' *Assemblage* 5 and in 'Towards an Architecture of Desire: Architecture, Writing, the Body,' in *Proceedings of the ACSA National Conference* (Miami, 1988).

9 The following paragraphs represent an oblique commentary upon Robert Segrest's 'Frank Lloyd Wright at the Midway,' included in this volume.

10 M. Tafuri, 'The Historical Project,' *The Sphere and the Labyrinth*, tr. P. d'Acierno and R. Connolly (Cambridge, Mass., 1987), p. 12.

11 W. Faulkner, *Sartoris* (New York, 1956), p. 151, cited in G. Deleuze and F. Guattari, *A Thousand Plateaus: Capitalism and Schizophrenia*, tr. B. Massumi (Minneapolis, 1987), p. 476.

12 C. Owens, 'The Allegorical Impulse: Toward a Theory of Postmodernism,' *October* 9 (Summer 1979), pp. 67-86.

13 M. Tafuri, *Theories and History of Architecture*, tr. G. Verrecchia (New York, 1980), p. 111.

14 W. Benjamin, *The Origin of German Tragic Drama*, p. 186.

15 Ibid.

16 Ibid.

17 Ibid.

18 Ibid.

19 Ibid.

20 G. Deleuze and F. Guattari, *A Thousand Plateaus*, p. 401.

21 W. Benjamin, *The Origin of German Tragic Drama*, p. 160.

22 Ibid.

23 Ibid.

24 Ibid., pp. 160-161.

25 Ibid., p. 162.

26 S. Melville, 'The Forgetting of Modernism, the Necessity of Rhetoric, and the Conditions of Publicity in Art and Criticism,' *October* 19 (Winter 1981), p. 80.

27 M. Tafuri, *Theories and History of Architecture*, p. 196.

28 Ibid., p. 198.

29 Ibid., emphasis mine.

30 M. Tafuri, 'Architecture as Indifferent Object and the Crisis of Critical Attention,' *Theories and History of Architecture*, pp. 79-102.

31 Ibid., pp. 80-82.

32 P. Eisenman, 'Architecture as a Second Language: The Texts of Between,' in *Threshold* IV, eds. M. Diani and C. Ingraham (New York, 1988), pp. 71-75.

33 M. Tafuri, 'Architecture as Indifferent Object,' p. 82.

34 R. E. Krauss, 'Sculpture in the Expanded Field,' *The Originality of the Avant-Garde and Other Modernist Myths* (Cambridge, Mass., 1985), pp. 276-290.

35 W. Benjamin, *The Origin of German Tragic Drama*, p. 201.

36 Ibid.

37 Ibid., p. 215.

38 Ibid.

39 A. Loos, 'The Luxury Vehicle' (1898), *Spoken Into the Void*, tr. J. O. Newman and J. H. Smith (Cambridge, Mass., 1982), p. 40.

40 W. Benjamin, *The Origin of German Tragic Drama*, p. 206.

41 Ibid., p. 223.

42 M. Tafuri, *Theories and History of Architecture*, p. 82.

43 F. Creuzer, *Symbolik und Mythologie der alten Volker, besonders der Griechen* (Leipzig, 1819).

44 W. Benjamin, op. cit., p. 165.

45 Ibid., p. 167.

46 M. Taylor, *Altarity* (Chicago, 1988), p. 240.

47 J. Joyce, *Finnegan's Wake* (New York, 1965), p. 260.

48 Ibid., p. 281.

49 Ibid., p. 308.

50 Ibid., p. 303.19.

51 M. Foucault: '[Heterotopias are] the disorder in which fragments of a large number of possible orders glitter separately… *Heterotopias* are disturbing, probably because they secretly undermine language, because they make it impossible to name this and that, because they destroy 'syntax' in advance, and not only the syntax with which we construct sentences but also that less apparent syntax which causes words and things (next to and also opposite to one another) to 'hold together'.' M. Foucault, *The Order of Things: An Archaeology of the Human Sciences* (New York, 1973), p. xviii.

52 The phrase comes to me from Anthony Burgess… See his *Joysprick: An Introduction to the Language of James Joyce* (New York, 1973).

53 J. Joyce, *Finnegan's Wake*, p. 308.

54 J. Derrida, *Dissemination*, tr. B. Johnson (Chicago, 1981), pp. 127-128.

55 I build here upon Derrida's pun on 'The Purloined Letter' from *The Post Card: From Socrates to Freud and Beyond*, tr. A. Bass (Chicago, 1987), p. 423. Poe's story is there the subject of Derrida because it was the subject of Jacques Lacan's '*Seminar*.' The fact that it was translated into French by Charles Baudelaire, the poet of spleen (melancholy) and flowers of evil, and the subject of Walter Benjamin, may or may not be important here.

56 W. Benjamin, 'Theses on the Philosophy of History,' in *Illuminations*, ed. H. Arendt, tr. H. Zohn (New York, 1969), pp. 257-258.

57 R. Wolin, *Walter Benjamin: An Aesthetic of Redemption* (New York, 1982), p. 166. Emphasis mine.

58 T.W. Adorno, *Gesammelte Schriften I: Philosophische Fruhschriften* (Frankfurt, 1973), cited by R. Wolin, *Walter Benjamin*, p. 167. Emphasis is Adorno's.

59 W. Benjamin, *The Origin of German Tragic Drama*, p. 179.

60 Ibid., p. 178.

61 Ibid., p. 173.

62 Ibid., p. 171. Benjamin is quoting Borinski, *Die Antike*.

63 Ibid.

64 The itinerary through Owens ('The Allegorical Impulse') to Robert Smithson ('A Sedimentation of Mind: Earth Projects') to Edgar Poe (*The Narrative of Arthur Gordon Pym*) (and, one might add, to the holey space of Deleuze and Guattari in *A Thousand Plateaus* - see note 11) is important to bear in mind because it is a kind of underground passage to so many others here.

65 M. Taylor, *Altarity*, p. 126.

66 W. Benjamin, *The Origin of German Tragic Drama*, p. 172.

67 F. Jameson, 'Third-World Literature in the Era of Multinational Capitalism,' *Social Text* 15 (Fall 1986), p. 69. Jameson's blind spots (the construing of the 'third world' as an entity, the construing of the 'first world' as white, heterosexual male) have been well-illuminated by Aijaz Ahmad, so I will not dwell on them here. See A. Ahmad, 'Jameson's Rhetoric of Otherness and the 'National Allegory',' *Social Text* 17, vol. 6, no. 2 (1987), pp. 3-25.

68 Ibid., emphasis Jameson's.

69 Ibid., p. 73.

70 Ibid., pp. 79-80

71 F. Jameson, 'Third-World Literature,' p. 88, note 26.

72 This bit of mapping tracks a conduit via Heraclitus' Fragment LXXX ('The hidden attunement is better than the obvious one'), here marking a paradoxical chiasmus at the site of the purloined letter, to Bloomer, 'Vertex and Vortex:

A Tectonics of Section,' in *Perspecta* 23 (New York, 1987), pp. 40-53.

73 W. Benjamin, *The Origin of German Tragic Drama*, p. 172.

74 G. Bataille, *Visions of Excess*, quoted by M. Taylor, *Altarity*, p. 141.

75 M. Taylor, *Altarity*, pp. 141-142.

76 W. Benjamin, *The Origin of German Tragic Drama*, p. 177. Benjamin is quoting Carl Horst.

77 Ibid., p. 175.

78 Ibid.

79 Ibid.

80 Ibid.

81 M. Serres, *Hermes: Literature, Science, Philosophy,* eds. J. Harari and D. F. Bell (Baltimore, 1983), p. 38.

82 C. Owens, 'The Allegorical Impulse,' p. 69.

83 W. Benjamin, *The Origin of German Tragic Drama*, p. 182.

84 Ibid.

85 Ibid., p. 176.

86 Ibid.

87 Ibid., p. 175.

88 Ibid., p. 177.

89 Ibid., p. 185.

90 Ibid., p. 154.

91 Ibid., p. 157.

92 Ibid., p. 231.

93 C. Owens, 'The Allegorical Impulse,' p. 85.

94 W. Benjamin, *The Origin of German Tragic Drama*, pp. 232-233.

95 Ibid., p. 147.

96 It should be abundantly clear, on the evidence of the gender of the producers of the work in question, that my use of 'the feminine' does not have a simple relationship to gender. On this I will line up with Kristeva. However, it is my belief that the propensity (the pent-up rage, pent-up desires) to 'write the feminine' exists perhaps closer to release in those human beings whose existences have been dominated by forms of oppression, i.e., those who benefit least from the status quo. Women, persons of color, lesbians and gay men, the poor, and nomadic people (a category which will include the 'homeless') fall into this category. Clearly, the majority of human beings on this planet fall into this category, pointing to the subtlety and power of phallogocentric culture, the culture of 'Catch 22'. Catch 22 is a wall or cage. Writing the feminine is mole work. Writing on the wall.

97 A voyeur without eyes is ex-orbitant.

98 W. Benjamin, *The Origin of German Tragic Drama*, p. 29.

99 H. Cixous, *The Exile of James Joyce* (London, 1976), tr. S. A. J. Purcell, pp. 741-742.

100 Ibid., p. 743.

101 J. Derrida, *The Post Card*, p. 515.

102 F. Jameson, 'Postmodernism, or the Cultural Logic of Late Capitalism,' *New Left Review* 146 (July/August 1984), p. 83. An additional error here, interesting because of the chains of textual relationships it generates, is Jameson's misnaming of the Westin Bonaventure, which he repeatedly calls the 'Bonaventura'. Many have jumped to correct Jameson's error, including N. Katherine Hayles, who gets it wrong by reversing the names in *Chaos Bound: Orderly*

Disorder in Contemporary Literature and Science (Ithaca, 1990), and Edward W. Soja, who corrects correctly in *Postmodern Geographies: The Reassertion of Space in Critical Social Theory* (London, 1989).

103 J. Derrida, 'Plato's Pharmacy,' *Dissemination*, p. 152.

104 W. Benjamin, *The Origin of German Tragic Drama*, pp. 28-29.

105 As this chapter goes to publication, Sarah is ten and has recently completed a play about Mutant Ninjas.

106 M. Taylor: 'As the irreducible interval in which time and space interweave, *différance* is the '*matrix*' of all presence and absence.' *Altarity*, p. 276.

107 A statement which has been in some ways strengthened and in some ways challenged by the recent erasure of the wall, an event that was virtually unthinkable when this paper was written in 1988.

108 I would like to address the difficult problematic of the presence of Peter Eisenman in this work. When I presented this construction to the Chicago working session group, the most incisive response was Silvia Kolbowski's. She questioned my 'need to defend Peter Eisenman.' (At least, that is the question as I remember it.) At the time, caught of-guard and feeling caught at something illicit, I babbled some inanity denying such a project and postulating Eisenman's presence in this paper as being due to the fact that I was simultaneously gestating an essay for the Ohio State Eisenman monograph. But of course this answer is inadequate. The need is not so much to defend as to come to terms with a father. (This, to be sure, may include defenses of all sorts…) Eisenman's production over the past two decades has in large part constituted the nourishment which has sustained the growth of my thinking about architecture. And certainly not only mine: I have many siblings; some are represented in this collection. Perhaps my brothers have killed *Pater* to their satisfaction and no longer suffer angstuous influenzas.

The problem of the daughter may be different. For me, it is the problem of locating the excluded middle – not to kill Dad and not to live invisibly in his shadow. It is perhaps the problem of living tangibly in the shadow, making of the shadow something else which is my own, a something else which abandons the linearity of comparison and which embraces its own other-ness. While Eisenman is much named here, the construction itself contains an implicit critique of his work, a critique which recognizes a reflexivity among its objects and its genealogy (which includes Tafuri and Benjamin, as well). My project is neither to revere nor to murder, but to recognize the perhaps more complex entanglement of the father–daughter relationship. Wrestling and copulation have their similarities, after all. (Of course, I learned this from my (m)other father, James Joyce…)

The figure on page 57 is from *Finnegan's Wake* by James Joyce. Copyright 1939 by James Joyce. Copyright renewed © 1967 by George Joyce and Lucia Joyce. Used by permission of Viking Penguin, a division of Penguin Books USA, Inc.

Beatriz Colomina is an architect who teaches
history and theory at Princeton University.
She has written extensively on questions of
architecture and the modern institutions of
representation, particularly the printed media,
photography, advertising, film and television.
She is the editor of *Architectureproduction
(Revisions 2)* and *Sexuality and Space*. Her
forthcoming book is entitled *The publicity of
Modernism: Loos and Le Corbusier.*

Intimacy and Spectacle
The Interior of Loos

Beatriz Colomina

'To live is to leave traces,' writes Walter Benjamin, in discussing the recent birth of the interior. 'The interior emphasizes them. An abundance of covers and protectors, liners and cases is devised, on which the traces of objects and everyday use are imprinted. The traces of the occupants also leave their impression on the interior. The detective story that follows these traces comes into being… The criminals of the first detective novels are neither gentlemen nor apaches, but private members of the bourgeoisie.'[1]

There is an interior in the detective novel. But can there be a detective story of the interior itself, of the hidden mechanisms by which space is constructed as interior? Where would the traces be imprinted? What clues do we have to go on?

A little-known fragment of Le Corbusier's *Urbanisme* (1925) reads as follows: 'Loos told me one day: 'A cultivated man does not look out of the window; his window is made of ground glass; it is there only to let the light in, not to let the gaze pass through.''[2] This quotation points to a conspicuous, yet conspicuously ignored feature of Loos' houses: not only are all the windows either opaque or covered with sheer curtains, but the organization of the spaces and the disposition of the built-in furniture (the *immeuble*) seems to hinder access to them. A sofa is often placed at the foot of a window so that the occupants sit with their backs to it, facing the room (figure 1). This even happens with those windows which look into other interior spaces – as in the sitting area of the ladies' lounge of the Müller house in Prague, of 1930 (figure 2). Moreover, upon entering a Loos interior one is continually turning around to face the space one has just moved through, rather than the space ahead or the space outside. With each turn, each look backward, our progress is halted. Looking at the photographs, it is easy to imagine oneself in these precise, static positions, usually indicated by the unoccupied furniture, and further to imagine that it is intended that these spaces be comprehended by occupation, by using the furniture, by 'entering' the photograph, by inhabiting it.[3]

In the Moller house (Vienna, 1928) there is a raised sitting area off the living room, with a sofa set against the window. Although one cannot see out of the window, its presence is strongly felt. The book shelves surrounding the sofa and the light coming from behind it suggest a comfortable nook for reading (figure 3). But comfort in this space is more than just sensual, for there is also a psychological dimension. The position of the sofa, and its occupant against the light, produces a sense of security. Any intruder ascending the stairs

Figure 1 Flat for Hans Brummel, Pilsen, 1929. Bedroom with a sofa set against the window.

Figure 2 Müller house, Prague, 1930. The raised sitting area in the *Zimmer der Dame*, with the window looking on to the living room.

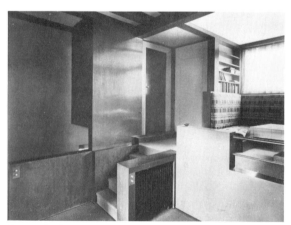

Figure 3 Moller house, Vienna, 1928. The raised sitting area off the living room.

from the entrance (itself a rather dark passage) and entering the living room would take a few moments to recognize anyone sitting on the sofa. Conversely, any intrusion would soon be detected by a person occupying this area, just as an actor entering the stage is immediately seen by a spectator in a theater box (figures 4, 5).

Loos observed that 'the smallness of a theater box would be unbearable if one could not look out into the large space beyond.'[4] Both Kulka and Münz interpret this as a reference to the economy of space provided by the *Raumplan*, but they have overlooked its psychological dimension. For Loos, the theater box exists at the intersection between claustrophobia and agoraphobia.[5] This spatial-psychological device could also be read in terms of power, regimes of control inside the house. The raised sitting area of the Moller house provides the occupant with a vantage point overlooking the interior. Comfort in this space is related to both intimacy and the control of the scene.

This area is the most intimate of the sequence of living spaces, yet, paradoxically, it occupies a volume that projects from the street façade, just above the front entrance and, moreover, it corresponds with the largest window on this elevation (figure 6). A person inside the space can easily see anyone crossing the threshold of the house (while screened by the curtain) and monitor any movement in the interior (while 'screened' by the backlighting).

In this space, the eye is turned towards the interior. The window does not frame a view but is merely a source of light. The only exterior view that would be possible from this position requires that the gaze travel the whole depth of the house, from the alcove to the living room to the music room, which opens on to the back garden (figure 7). Thus, the exterior view depends upon a view of the interior.

The look folded inward upon itself can be traced in other Loos interiors. In the Müller house (Prague, 1930), for instance, there is an increasing sense of privacy in the sequence of spaces articulated around the staircase, from the drawing room, to the dining room and study, to the 'ladies' room' (*Zimmer der Dame*) with its raised sitting area, which occupies the center, or 'heart', of the house (figures 2 and 8). But this space has a window that looks on to the living space (figure 9). Here, too, the most intimate room resembles a theater box, and overlooks the entrance to the communal area of the house, so that any intruder could easily be seen. Likewise, the view of the exterior, towards the city, from this 'theater box', is contained within a view of the interior. There is also a more direct and more private route to the sitting area, a staircase rising from the entrance of the drawing room. Suspended thus in the middle of the house, this space assumes a dual character: it has a 'sacred' quality, but it is also a point of control. Paradoxically a sense of comfort is produced by two seemingly opposing conditions, intimacy and control.

This is hardly the idea of comfort that is associated with the nineteenth-century interior as described by Walter Benjamin in his essay 'Louis-Philippe, or the Interior.'[6] In Loos' interiors the sense of security is not achieved by simply turning one's back on the exterior and becoming immersed in a private world – 'a box in the world theater,' to use Benjamin's metaphor. It is no longer the house that is a theater box; there is a theater box inside the house, overlooking the internal social spaces, so that the inhabitants become both actors in and spectators of family life – involved in, yet detached from their own space.[7] The classical distinctions between inside and outside, private and public, object and subject, are no longer valid.

Figure 4 Moller house. Plan of elevated ground floor, with the alcove drawn narrower than it was built.
Figure 5 Moller house. Staircase leading from the entrance hall into the living room.

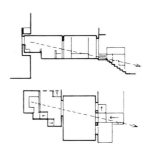

Figure 6 Moller house. View from the street.
Figure 7 Moller house. Section and plan tracing the path of the gaze from the raised sitting area to the back garden.

74

Figure 8 Müller house. Main floor.
Figure 9 Müller house. The living room,
view toward the dining room. The window
on the right.

Figure 10 Müller house. Library.

Traditionally, the theater box provided for the privileged a private space within the dangerous public realm, by re-establishing the boundaries between inside and outside. When Loos designed a theater in 1898 (an unrealized project), he omitted the boxes, arguing that they 'didn't suit a modern auditorium.'[8] Thus he removed the box from the public theater, only to insert it into the 'private theater' of the house. The public realm had entered the private house by way of the social spaces,[9] and the domestic theater box represented a last stand of resistance to this intrusion.

The theater boxes in the Moller and Müller houses are spaces marked as female, the domestic character of the furniture contrasting with that of the adjacent 'male' space, the library (figure 10). In these, the leather sofas, the desks, the chimney, the mirrors represent a 'public space' within the house – the office and the club invading the interior. But it is an invasion which is confined to an enclosed room – a space which belongs to the sequence of social spaces within the house, yet does not engage with them. As Münz notes, the library is a 'reservoir of quietness' 'set apart from the household traffic,' whereas the raised alcove of the Moller house and the *Zimmer der Dame* of the Müller house not only overlook the social spaces but are positioned at the end of the sequence, on the threshold of the private, the secret, the upper rooms, where sexuality is sequestered. At the intersection of the visible and the invisible, women act as the guardians of the unspeakable.[10]

But the theater box is a device that both protects its occupants and draws attention to them. Münz describes entry into the Moller house thus: 'Within, entering from one side, one's gaze travels in the opposite direction till it rests on the light, pleasant alcove, raised above the living room floor. Now we are really inside the house.'[11] That is, the intruder has penetrated the house only when his/her gaze strikes this most intimate space, turning the occupant into a silhouette against the light.[12] The 'voyeur' in the 'theater box' has become the object of another's gaze; she is caught in the act of seeing, entrapped in the very moment of control.[13] In framing a view, the theater box also frames the viewer. It is impossible to abandon the space, let alone leave the house, without being seen by those over whom control is being exerted. Object and subject exchange places. Whether there is actually a person behind either gaze is irrelevant:

> I can feel myself under the gaze of someone whose eyes I do not even see, not even discern. All that is necessary is for something to signify to me that there may be others there. This window, if it gets a bit dark, and if I have reasons for thinking that there is someone behind it, is straight-away a gaze. From the moment this gaze exists, I am already something other, in that I feel myself becoming an object for the gaze of others. But in this position, which is a reciprocal one, others also know that I am an object who knows himself to be seen.[14]

Architecture is not simply a platform that accommodates the viewing subject. It is a viewing mechanism that produces the subject. It precedes and frames its occupant.

The theatricality that we sense in interiors by Loos does not depend on the buildings alone. Many of the photographs, for instance, tend to give the impression that someone is just about to enter the room, that a piece of domestic drama is about to be enacted. The characters absent from the stage, from the scenery, and from its props – the conspicuously placed pieces of furniture (figure 11) – are conjured up.[15] One of the few published photographs of a Loos interior that includes a human figure is a view of the entrance to the drawing room of the Rufer house (figure 12). The photograph shows a barely visible male figure who is about to cross the threshold through a peculiar opening in the wall and play

Figure 11 Adolf Loos flat, Vienna, 1903. View
from the living room into the fireplace nook.
Figure 12 Rufer house, Vienna, 1922. Entrance
to the living room.

his part.[16] But it is precisely at this threshold, slightly off stage, that the actor/intruder is most vulnerable, for the window of a reading space looks down on to the back of his neck. Traditionally considered to be the prototype of the *Raumplan*, the Rufer house also contains the prototype of the theater box.

In his writings on the question of the house, Loos describes a number of domestic melodramas. In *Das Andere*, for example, he wrote:

> Try to describe how birth and death, the screams of pain for an aborted son, the death rattle of a dying mother, the last thoughts of a young woman who wishes to die…unfold and unravel in a room by Olbrich! Just an image: the young woman who has put herself to death. She is lying on the wooden floor. One of her hands still holds the smoking revolver. On the table a letter, the farewell letter. Is the room in which this is happening of good taste? Who will ask that? It is just a room![17]

One could well ask why it is only the women who die and cry and commit suicide. But, leaving aside the question for the moment, Loos is saying that the house must not be conceived of as a work of art, that there is a difference between a house and a 'series of decorated rooms.' The house should be a stage for the theatre of the family, a place where people are born and live and die. It is an environment, or stage, whereas a work of art presents itself as an object to a detached viewer.

In order to break down the condition of the house as an object, Loos radically convolutes the relation between inside and outside. One of the strategies he employs is to use mirrors which, as Kenneth Frampton has pointed out, appear to be openings, and openings that can be mistaken for mirrors.[18] Even more enigmatic is the placement, in the dining room of the Steiner house (figure 13), of a mirror just beneath the window to the exterior.[19] Here, again, the opaque window is only a source of light. The mirror, placed at eye level, returns the gaze to the interior, to the lamp above the dining table and the objects on the sideboard, recalling Freud's studio in Berggasse 19, where a small framed mirror hanging against the window reflects the lamp on Freud's work-table. In Freudian theory the mirror represents the psyche, thus the reflection in the mirror is also a self-portrait projected on to the outside world. The placement of Freud's mirror on the boundary between interior and exterior undermines the status of the boundary as a fixed limit. Similarly, Loos' mirrors promote the interplay between reality and illusion, between the actual and the virtual, undermining the status of the boundary between inside and outside.

This ambiguity between inside and outside is intensified by the separation of sight from the other senses. Physical and visual connections between the spaces in Loos' houses are often separated. In the Rufer house, a wide opening establishes a visual relation between the raised dining room and the music room, which does not correspond to the physical connection. At the rear of the dining room is a mirror that returns the eye to the interior. Similarly, in the Moller house there appears to be no way of entering the dining room from the music room, which is seventy centimetres below; the only means of direct access is to unfold steps hidden in the timber base of the dining room (figure 14).[20] This strategy of 'framing' is repeated in many other of Loos' houses. Openings are often screened by curtains, enhancing the stage-like effect. It should also be noted that it is usually the dining room that acts as the stage, and the music room as the space for spectators. What is being framed is the traditional scene of everyday domestic life.

But the breakdown of the distinction between inside and outside, and the split between

Figure 13 Steiner house, Vienna, 1910. View of
the dining room, showing the mirror beneath
the window.
Figure 14 Moller house. View from music
room into the the dining room. In the center
of the threshold are steps that can be let down.

sight and touch, is not located exclusively in the domestic scene. It also occurs in Loos' project of 1928 for a house in Paris for Josephine Baker (figures 15, 16) – a house that excludes family life. However, in this instance the 'split' acquires a different meaning. The house contains a large top-lit, double-height swimming pool entered at the second-floor level. Kurt Ungers, who collaborated with Loos on this project, wrote:

> The reception rooms on the first floor arranged round the pool – a large salon with an extensive top-lit vestibule, a small lounge and the circular café – indicate that this was intended not solely for private use but as a *miniature entertainment centre*. On the first floor, low passages surround the pool. They are lit by the wide windows visible on the outside, and from them, thick, transparent windows are let into the side of the pool, so that it was possible to watch swimming and diving in its crystal-clear water, flooded with light from above: an *underwater revue*, so to speak.[21]

As in Loos' previous houses, the eye is directed towards the interior, which turns its back on the outside world; but the subject and object of the gaze have been reversed. The inhabitant of the house – Josephine Baker – is now the primary object, and the visitor – the guest – is the looking subject. The most intimate space – the swimming pool, paradigm of a sensual space – occupies the centre of the house, and is also the focus of the visitor's gaze. As Ungers writes, 'entertainment in this house consists of looking.'[22] But between this gaze and its object – the body – is a screen of glass and water, which renders the body inaccessible. The swimming pool is lit from above, by a skylight, so that inside it the windows would appear as reflective surfaces, impeding the swimmer's view of the visitors standing in the passages. This view is the opposite of the panoptic view of a theater box, corresponding, instead, to that of a peep-hole, where subject and object cannot simply exchange places.'[23]

The *mise-en-scène* in the Josephine Baker house recalls Christian Metz's description of the mechanism of voyeurism in cinema:

> It is even essential…that the actor should behave as though he were not seen (and therefore as though he did not see his voyeur), that he should go about his ordinary business and pursue his existence as foreseen by the fiction of the film, that he should carry on with his antics in a closed room, taking the utmost care not to notice that a glass rectangle has been set into one of the walls, and that he lives in a kind of aquarium.[24]

But the architecture of this house is more complicated. For example, the swimmer might also see the reflection, framed by the window, of her own slippery body superimposed on the eyes of the shadowy figure of the spectator, whose lower body is obscured by the frame. Thus she sees herself being looked at by another: a narcissistic gaze superimposed on a voyeuristic gaze. This erotic complex of looks in which she is suspended is inscribed in each of the four windows opening on to the swimming pool. Each, even if there is no one looking through it, constitutes, from both sides, a gaze.

The split between sight and the other physical senses that can be detected in Loos' interiors is explicit in his definition of architecture. In his essay 'The Principle of Cladding' he writes: 'the artist, the *architect*, first senses the *effect* that he intends to realize and sees the rooms he wants to create in his mind's eye. He senses the effect that he wishes to exert upon the *spectator*:…homeyness if a residence.'[25] For Loos, the interior is space before the analytical distancing that language entails – pre-Oedipal space, space as felt. We sense it as we might a fabric, with our eyes averted, as if the sight of it would constitute an obstacle to the sensation.

79

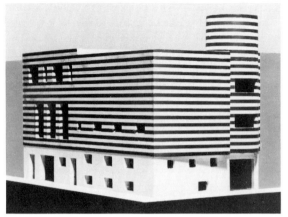

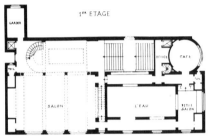

Figure 15 Baker house (project), Paris, 1928.
Model.
Figure 16a and 16b Baker house. Plans of first
and second floors.

Figure 17 Adolf Loos flat. Lina Loos'
bedroom.

Loos seems to have reversed the Cartesian schism between the perceptual and the conceptual. Where Descartes deprived the body of its status as the seat of valid and transmissible knowledge ('In sensation, in the experience that derives from it, harbours error.'[26]), Loos privileges the bodily experience of space over its mental construction: the architect first senses the space, then he visualizes it.

For Loos, architecture is a form of covering, but it is not the walls that are covered. Structure plays a secondary role, and its primary function is to hold the covering in place:

> The architect's general task is to provide a warm and livable space. Carpets are warm and livable. He decides for this reason to spread out one carpet on the floor and to hang up four to form the four walls. But you cannot build a house out of carpets. Both the carpet on the floor and the tapestry on the wall require a structural frame to hold them in the correct place. To invent this frame is the architect's second task.[27]

The spaces in Loos' interiors cover the occupant as clothes cover the body (each occasion has its appropriate 'fit'). José Quetglas has written: 'Would the same pressure on the body be acceptable in a raincoat as in a gown, in jodhpurs or in pyjama pants?... All the architecture of Loos can be explained as the envelope of a body.' From Lina Loos' bedroom – 'this bag of fur and cloth' – to Josephine Baker's swimming pool – 'this transparent bowl of water' – the houses of Loos always contain a 'warm bag in which to wrap oneself'(figure 17). It is an 'architecture of pleasure,' an 'architecture of the womb.'[28]

But space in Loos' architecture is not just felt. It is significant in the quotation above that Loos refers to the inhabitant as a spectator, for his definition of architecture is really a definition of theatrical architecture. The 'clothes' have become so detached from the body that they require structural support independent of it. They become a 'stage set'. The inhabitant is both 'covered' by the space and 'detached' from it. The tension between the sensation of comfort and comfort as control disrupts the role of the house as a traditional form of representation. More precisely, the traditional system of representation, within which the building is but one of many overlapping mechanisms, is dislocated.

The status of the architectural drawing, for example, is radically transformed. Loos writes in his essay 'Architecture' that 'the mark of a building which is truly established is that it remains ineffective in two dimensions.'[29] By 'ineffective' he means that the drawing cannot convey the 'sensation' of space as this involves not only sight but also the other physical senses.[30] Loos invented the *Raumplan* as a means of conceptualizing space as it is felt, but, revealingly, he left no theoretical definition of it. As Kulka noted, he 'will make many changes during construction. He will walk through the space and say: 'I do not like the height of this ceiling, change it!' The idea of the *Raumplan* made it difficult to finish a scheme before construction allowed the visualization of the space as it was.' But Loos was not simply setting sensual experience against abstraction; he was dealing with the untranslatability of languages. In 'Architecture' he writes:

> Every work of art possesses such strong internal laws that it can only appear in its own form... If I could erase the most powerful architectural phenomenon, the Palazzo Pitti, from the memory of my contemporaries and then have it drawn by the best draughtsman to enter in a competition scheme, the jury will throw me into a mad house.[31]

Because a drawing cannot convey the tension between sight and the other senses, it cannot adequately 'translate' a building. For Loos the architect's drawing was a regrettable consequence of the division of labour, and it could never be more than a mere technical state-

81

ment, 'the attempt [by the architect] to make himself understood by the craftsman carrying out the work.'[32]

Loos' critique of the photography of architecture and its dissemination through architectural journals was based on the same principle, that it is impossible to represent a spatial effect or a sensation:

> It is my greatest pride that the interiors which I have created are totally *ineffective* in photographs. I am proud of the fact that the inhabitants of my spaces do not recognize their own apartments in the photographs, just as the owner of a Monet painting would not recognize it at Kastan's. I have to forego the honor of being published in the various architectural magazines. I have been denied the satisfaction of my vanity.[33]

The inhabitants of a house perceive it as an environment, not as an object, whereas a photograph of a house published in an architectural journal requires a different kind of attention, which presupposes a certain distance and is therefore closer to the contemplation of a work of art in a museum. Loos interiors are experienced as a frame for action rather than as an object in a frame.

There is, nevertheless, a certain consistency in photographs of Loos interiors, which seems to suggest that he had some involvement in their production. The presence of certain objects, such as the Egyptian stool, in nearly every interior view has been noted by Kenneth Frampton. Loos also seems to have adjusted the photographs so as to better represent his own idea of the house. The photographic archives of the images in Kulka's book reveal a few tricks: the view through the 'horizontal window' in a photograph of the Khuner villa (near Payerbach, 1930) is a photomontage,[34] as is the violin in the cupboard of the music room of the Moller house. A storey was added to the photograph of the street façade of the Tristan Tzara house (Paris, 1926-27), in order to make it more like the original project, and numerous 'distracting' domestic objects (lamps, rugs, plants) were erased throughout. These interventions suggest that the images were carefully controlled and that the photographs of Loos' buildings cannot simply be considered as a form of representation that is subordinate to the building itself.

For example, Loos often frames a spatial volume, as in the bedroom of the Khuner villa or the fireplace nook of his own apartment. This strategy has the effect of flattening the space seen through the frame, making it seem more like a photograph. As with the device of obscuring the difference between openings and mirrors, this optical effect is enhanced, if not produced, by the photographs themselves, which are taken only from the precise point where the effect occurs.[35] Loos' critique of the photographic representation of architecture should not be mistaken for a nostalgia for the 'complete' object. What he achieves in this play with reflective surfaces and framing devices is a critique of classical representation. Such framing devices undermine the referential status of the photographic image and its claim of transparently representing reality. The photographs draw the viewer's attention to the artifice involved in the photographic process. Photographs (like drawings) are not representations in a traditional sense; they literally construct their object.

Loos' critique of traditional notions of architectural representation is bound up with the phenomenon of an emergent metropolitan culture. He recognized social institutions as systems of representation, and his attacks on the family, Viennese society, professional organizations, and the state, launched in *Das Andere*, were implicit in his architecture. Architecture, in all its possible manifestations – drawing, photograph, text, or building – is, after all, only a practice of representation.

The subject of Loos' architecture is the citizen of the metropolis, immersed in its abstract relationships and striving to assert his independence and individuality in the face of the levelling power of society. This battle, according to Georg Simmel, is the modern equivalent of primitive man's struggle with nature, clothing is one of the battlefields, and fashion is one of its strategies.[36] He writes: 'The commonplace is good form in society… It is bad taste to make one's self conspicuous through some individual, singular expression… Obedience to the standards of the general public in all externals [is] the conscious and desired means of reserving their personal feelings and their taste.'[37] In other words, fashion is a mask that protects the intimacy of the metropolitan individual.

Loos writes about fashion in precisely such terms: 'We have become more refined, more subtle. Primitive men had to differentiate themselves by various colours, modern man needs his clothes as a mask. His individuality is so strong that it can no longer be expressed in terms of items of clothing… His own inventions are concentrated on other things.'[38] Fashion and etiquette, in Western culture, constitute the language of behavior, a language that does not convey feelings but acts as a form of protection – a mask. As Loos writes, 'How should one dress? Modern. One is modernly dressed when one stands out the least.'

Significantly, Loos writes about the exterior of the house in the same terms that he writes about fashion:

> When I was finally given the task of building a house, I said to myself: in its external appearance, a house can only have changed as much as a dinner jacket. Not a lot therefore… I had to become significantly simpler. I had to substitute the golden buttons with black ones. The house has to look inconspicuous.[39]
>
> The house does not have to tell anything to the exterior; instead, all its richness must be manifest in the interior.[40]

Loos seems to establish a radical difference between interior and exterior, which reflects the split between the private life and the social life of the metropolitan being: outside, the realm of exchange, money, and masks; inside, the realm of the inalienable, the non-exchangeable, and the unspeakable. Moreover, this split between inside and outside, between senses and sight, is gender-loaded. The exterior of the house, Loos writes, should resemble a dinner jacket, a male mask, as the unified self, protected by a seamless façade, is masculine. The interior is the scene of sexuality and reproduction (childbirth, sickness, death), all the things that would divide the subject in the outside world. However, this dogmatic division in Loos' writings between inside and outside is undermined by his architecture.

The suggestion that the exterior is merely a mask that clads some pre-existing interior is misleading, for the interior and exterior are constructed simultaneously. When he was designing the Rufer house, for example, Loos used a dismountable model that would allow the internal and external distributions to be worked out simultaneously. The interior is not simply the space enclosed by the façades. A multiplicity of boundaries is established, and the tension between inside and outside resides in the walls that divide them, its status is disturbed by Loos' displacement of traditional forms of representation. To address the interior is to address the splitting of the wall.

Take, for instance, the displacement of drawing conventions in Loos' four pencil drawings of the elevation of the Rufer house (figure 18). Each one shows not only the outlines of

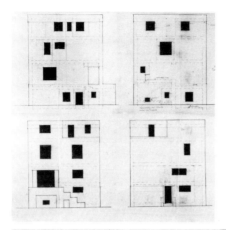

Figure 18 Rufer house. Elevations.
Figure 19 Showroom, Goldman & Salatsch
menswear shop, Vienna, 1898.

the façade but also, in dotted lines, the horizontal and vertical divisions of the interior, the position of the rooms, the thickness of the floors and the walls, while the windows are represented as black squares with no frame. These are drawings that depict neither the inside nor the outside, but the membrane between them: between the representation of habitation and the mask is the wall. Loos' subject inhabits this wall, creating a sense of tension at the limit.

This is not simply a metaphor. In every Loos house there is a point of maximum tension, and it always coincides with a threshold or boundary. In the Moller house it is the raised alcove protruding from the street façade, where the occupant is ensconced in the security of the interior yet detached from it. The subject of Loos' houses is a stranger, an intruder in his own space. In Josephine Baker's house, the wall of the swimming pool is punctuated by windows. It has been pulled apart, leaving a narrow passage surrounding the pool, and splitting each of the windows into an internal window and an external window. The visitor literally inhabits this wall, which enables him to look both inside, at the pool, and outside, at the city, but he is neither inside nor outside the house. In the dining room of the Steiner house, the gaze directed toward the window is folded back by the mirror beneath it, transforming the interior into an exterior view or scene. The subject has been dislocated; unable to occupy the inside of the house securely, it can only occupy the insecure margin between window and mirror.

This tampering with limits is intensified in Loos' Goldman & Salatsch menswear store in Vienna of 1898. Occupying the intersection between body and language, between the space of domesticity and that of social exchange, of economy, the interior of the shop exists halfway between the private universe of the interior and the outside world. Goldman & Salatsch provided its clients with underwear and external accessories such as ties, hats, and walking sticks – that is, with the most intimate garments, as well as the objects that support (literally and symbolically) the body as a figure (the body's props, its prostheses). In this store the most intimate garments are being exhibited and sold; they have abandoned the sphere of domesticity for the sphere of exchange. Conversely, the objects that most obviously represent the site of exchange, the mask that safeguards the coherence of the human figure in the public realm, have entered the interior.

A photograph published in *Das Interieur* in 1901 shows a space clad with tall rectangular mirrors set in dark frames (figure 19). Some of the mirrors are fixed, others are cupboard-doors, and yet others coincide with openings into other spaces. There are two male figures, one a client emerging from the intimate atmosphere of the fitting-room, the other an accountant who has entered from the exterior world of finance. They both occupy the same wall, but the nature of that occupation is unclear. One of them seems to be standing at the threshold of an opening, his image reflected on the mirror-door and perhaps again in the cupboard door to the right. Even more enigmatic is the other figure, for only the upper part of the body is visible, behind bars, as if confined within a cage. Even now that the plan of the shop has been reconstructed, it is impossible to establish the actual position of these figures within the space. One of them stands beside the image of his back – or is it the other way around? The depth of his body, its material presence, has been erased. Other reflections appear throughout the space, without any body to ground them. This dissolution of the figures into the wall surfaces questions not only their position but also that of the person viewing the photograph.

Furthermore, the illusion of Loos as a man in control of his own work, an undivided subject – an illusion I myself have fostered in this article – is also rendered suspect. In fact, he is constructed, controlled, and fractured by his own work. Take the idea of the *Raumplan*, for example: Loos constructs a space (without having completed the working drawings) and then allows himself to be manipulated by this construction. Like the occupants of his houses, he is both inside and outside the object. He is not simply an author, the object has as much authority over him as he has over the object.[41]

The critic is no exception to this phenomenon. Incapable of detachment from the object, the critic simultaneously produces a new object and is produced by it. Criticism that presents itself as a new interpretation of an existing object is in fact constructing a completely new object. The Loos of the 1960s, the austere pioneer of the modern movement, was replaced in the 1970s by another Loos, all sensuality, and in the 1980s by Loos the classicist. Each era creates a new Loos. On the other hand, there are the readings that claim to be purely objective inventories, the standard monographs on Loos – Münz and Künstler in the 1960s and Gravagnuolo in the 1980s, but they are thrown off balance by the very object of their control. Nowhere is this alienation more evident than in their interpretations of the house for Josephine Baker.

Münz, otherwise a wholly circumspect writer, begins his appraisal of this house with the exclamation 'Africa: that is the image conjured up more or less firmly by a contemplation of the model,' but he then confesses not to know why he invoked this image.[42] In his attempt to analyze the formal characteristics of the project, all he can manage is the opinion that 'they look strange and exotic.'[43] What is most striking in this passage is the uncertainty as to whether Münz is referring to the model of the house or to Josephine Baker herself. He seems unable either to detach himself from this project or to enter it.

Like Münz, Gravagnuolo finds himself writing things without knowing why, reprimands himself, and then attempts to regain control:

> First there is the charm of this gay architecture. It is not just the dichromatism of the façades but – as we shall see – the spectacular nature of the internal articulation that determines its refined and seductive character. Rather than abandon oneself to the pleasure of suggestions, it is necessary to take this 'toy' to pieces with *analytic detachment* if one wishes to understand the mechanism of composition.[44]

He then institutes a regime of analytical categories ('the architectural introversion,' 'the revival of dichromatism,' 'the plastic arrangement'), which he uses nowhere else in his book. And he concludes:

> The water flooded with light, the refreshing swim, the voyeuristic pleasure of underwater exploration – these are the carefully balanced ingredients of this gay architecture. But what matters more is that the invitation to the spectacular suggested by the theme of the house for a cabaret star is handled by Loos with discretion and intellectual detachment, more as a poetic game, involving the mnemonic pursuit of quotations and allusions to the Roman spirit, than as a vulgar surrender to the taste of Hollywood.[45]

The insistence on detachment, on re-establishing the distance between critic and object of criticism, architect and building, subject and object, is of course indicative of the obvious fact that Münz and Gravagnuolo have failed to separate themselves from the object. The image of Josephine Baker offers pleasure, but it also represents the threat of castration posed by the 'other': the image of woman in water – liquid, elusive, unable to be controlled or pinned down. One way of dealing with this threat is fetishization.

The Baker house represents a shift in the status of the female body. The theater box of the domestic interiors places the woman's body against the light. She appears as a silhouette, mysterious and desirable, but the backlighting also draws attention to her as a physical volume, a bodily presence within the house, with its own interior. She is both in control of the interior and trapped within it. In the Baker house, the female body is produced as spectacle, the object of an erotic gaze, an erotic system of looks. The exterior of the house cannot be read as a mask designed to conceal its interior; it is a tattooed surface which neither conceals nor reveals. This fetishization of the surface is repeated in the 'interior'. In the passages, the visitors consume Baker's body as a surface adhering to the windows. Like the body, the house is all surface; it does not simply have an interior.

1 W. Benjamin,'Paris Capital of the Nineteenth Century,' *Reflections*, tr. E. Jephcott (New York, 1986), pp. 155-156.
2 'Loos m'affirmait un jour: 'Un homme cultivé ne regarde pas par la fenêtre; sa fenêtre est en verre dépoli; elle n'est la que pour donner de la lumière, non pour laisser passer le regard.' Le Corbusier, *Urbanisme* (Paris, 1925), p. 174. In F. Etchells's translation of 1929, published under the title *The City of To-morrow and its Planning* (London), the sentence reads thus: 'A friend once said to me: 'No intelligent man ever looks out of his window; his window is made of ground glass; its only function is to let in light, not to look out of.' (pp. 185-186). Was Loos a nobody for Etchells, or is this just another example of the kind of misunderstanding that led to the mistranslation of the title of the book? Perhaps it was Le Corbusier himself who decided to erase Loos' name. Of a different order, but no less symptomatic, is the mistranslation of 'laisser passer le regard' (to let the gaze pass through) as 'to look out of', as if to resist the idea that the gaze might take on a life of its own.
3 The perception of space is produced by its representations; in this sense, built space has no more authority than do drawings, photographs, or descriptions.
4 L. Münz and G. Künstler, *Der Architekt Adolf Loos* (Vienna and Munich, 1964), pp. 130-131. English translation, *Adolph Loos: Pioneer of Modern Architecture*, tr. H. Meek (London, 1966), p. 148: 'We may call to mind an observation by Adolf Loos, handed down to us by Heinrich Kulka, that the smallness of a theatre box would be unbearable if one could not look out into the large space beyond; hence it was possible to save space, even in the design of small houses, by linking a high main room with a low annexe.'
5 Georges Teyssot has noted that 'the Bergsonian ideas of the room as a refuge from the world are meant to be conceived as the 'juxtaposition' between claustrophobia and agoraphobia,' a dialectic already found in Rilke. G. Teyssot, 'The Disease of the Domicile,' *Assemblage* 6 (1988), p. 95.
6 'Under Louis-Philippe the private citizen enters the stage of history... For the private person, living space becomes, for the first time, antithetical to the place of work. The former is constituted by the interior; the office is its complement. The private person who squares his account with reality in his office demands that the interior be maintained in his illusions. This need is all the more pressing since he has no intention of extending his commercial considerations into social ones. In shaping his private environment he represses both. From this spring the phantasmagorias of the the interior. For the private individual the private environment represents the universe. In it he gathers remote places and the past. His

drawing room is a box in the World theater.' W. Benjamin, 'Paris, Capital of the Nineteenth Century,' pp. 154-156.
7 This calls to mind Freud's paper 'A Child is Being Beaten' (1919), where, as Victor Burgin has written, 'the subject is positioned in the audience and on stage – where it is both aggressor and aggressed.' Victor Burgin, 'Geometry and Abjection,' *AA Files* 15 (summer 1987), p. 38. The *mise-en-scène* of Loos' interiors appears to coincide with that of Freud's unconscious. S. Freud, 'A Child is Being Beaten: A Contribution to the Study of the Origin of Sexual Perversions,' *The Standard Edition of the Complete Works of Sigmund Freud*, vol. XVII, pp. 175-204. In relation to Freud's paper, see also: Jacqueline Rose, *Sexuality in the Field of Vision* (London, 1986), pp. 209-210.
8 L. Münz and G. Künstler, *Adolf Loos*, p. 36.
9 See my note 6. There are no social spaces in the Benjaminian interior. He writes: 'In shaping his private environment he [the private person] represses both [commercial and social considerations].' Benjamin's interior is established in opposition to the office. But, as Laura Mulvey has noted, 'the workplace is no threat to the home. The two maintain each other in a safe, mutually dependent polarisation. The threat comes from elsewhere,... the city.' L. Mulvey, 'Melodrama Inside and Outside the Home,' *Visual and Other Pleasures* (London, 1989), p. 70.
10 In a criticism of Benjamin's account of the bourgeois interior, Mulvey writes: 'Benjamin does not mention the fact that the private sphere, the domestic, is an essential adjunct to the bourgeois marriage and is thus associated with woman, not simply as female, but as wife and mother. It is the mother who guarantees the privacy of the home by maintaining its respectability, as essential a defence against incursion or curiosity as the encompassing walls of the home itself.' L. Mulvey, 'Melodrama Inside and Outside the Home,' in *Visual and Other Pleasures*, op. cit.
11 L. Münz and G. Künstler, *Adolf Loos*, p. 149.
12 Upon reading an earlier version of this manuscript Jane Weinstock pointed out that this silhouette can be understood as a screened woman, a veiled woman, and therefore as the traditional object of desire.
13 In her response to this paper during the conference Silvia Kolbowski pointed out that the woman in the raised sitting-area of the Moller house could also be seen from behind, through the window to the street, and therefore she is also vulnerable in her moment of control.
14 J. Lacan, *The Seminar of Jacques Lacan: Book I, Freud's Papers on Technique 1953-1954*, ed. J. Miller, tr. J. Forrester (Cambridge, 1988), p. 215. In this passage Lacan is referring

to Jean-Paul Sartre's *Being and Nothingness*.

15 There is an instance of such personification of furniture in one of Loos' most autobiographical texts, 'Interiors in the Rotonda' (1898) where he writes: 'Every piece of furniture, every thing, every object had a story to tell, a family history.' A. Loos, *Spoken Into the Void: Collected Essays 1897-1900*, tr. J. O. Newman and J. H. Smith (Cambridge, Mass. and London, 1982), p. 24.

16 This photograph was published only recently. Kulka's monograph (a work in which Loos was involved) presents exactly the same view, the same photograph, but without a human figure. The strange opening in the wall pulls the viewer towards the void, towards the missing actor (a tension that the photographer no doubt felt the need to conceal). This tension constructs a subject, as it does in the built-in couch of the raised area of Moller house, or the window of the *Zimmer der Dame* overlooking the drawing room of the Müller house.

17 A. Loos, *Das Andere* 1 (1903), p. 9.

18 K. Frampton, unpublished lecture, Columbia University, New York, autumn 1986.

19 It should also be noted that this window is an exterior window, as opposed to the other window, which opens on to a threshold space.

20 The reflective surface in the rear of the dining room of the Moller house (halfway between an opaque window and a mirror) and the window in the rear of the music room 'mirror' each other, not only in their locations and their proportions, but even in the way the plants are disposed in two tiers. All of this produces the illusion, in the photograph, that the threshold between these two spaces is virtual - impassable, impenetrable.

21 Letter from Kurt Ungers to Ludwig Münz, quoted in L. Münz and G. Künstler, *Adolf Loos*, p. 195. Author's emphasis.

22 Ibid.

23 In relation to the model of the peep show and the structure of voyeurism, see Victor Burgin's Project *Zoo*. L. Tickner, 'Sexuality and/in Representation: Five British Artists,' in *Difference: On Representation and Sexuality*, ed. K. Linker (New York, 1984).

24 C. Metz, 'A Note on Two Kinds of Voyeurism,' in *The imaginary Signifier* (Bloomington, 1977), p. 96.

25 A. Loos, 'The Principle of Cladding' (1898), in A. Loos, *Spoken into the Void*, p. 66. Author's emphasis.

26 F. Rella, *Miti e figure del moderno* (Parma, 1981), p. 13 and note 1. René Descartes, letter to Hyperaspistes, August 1641. *Correspondance avec Arnould et Morus*, ed. by G. Lewis (Paris, 1933).

27 A. Loos, 'The Principle of Cladding,' in A. Loos, *Spoken into the Void*, p. 66.

28 J. Quetglas, 'Lo Placentero,' *Carrer de la Ciutat* no. 9-10 (special issue on Loos), January 1980, p. 2.

29 A. Loos, 'Architecture' (1910), in *The Architecture of Adolf Loos*, eds. Y. Safran and W. Wang, tr. W. Wang (London, 1985), p. 106.

30 See, in this connection, Loos' use of the word 'effect' in other passages, for example in the fragment of 'The Principle of Cladding,' in *Spoken into the Void*, quoted in my note: '[the] *effect* is the *sensation* that the space produces in the spectator...the feeling of warmth, when in his own house.'

31 A. Loos, 'Architecture,' in *The Architecture of Adolf Loos*, pp. 105, 106

32 A. Loos, 'Ornament und Erziehung' (1924), *Trotzdem* (Innsbruck, 1931].

33 A. Loos, 'Architecture,' op. cit. Author's emphasis.

34 This window, the only 'picture' window to appear in a Loos building, points to the difference in his work between architecture in the context of the city and that of the countryside (the Khuner villa is a country house). This difference is significant, not only in terms of architectural language, as it is often discussed (Benedetto Gravagnuolo, for example, talks of the differences between the 'whitewashed masterpieces' – the Moller and Müller houses – and the Khuner villa, 'so vernacular, so anachronistically alpine, so rustic.' See B. Gravagnuolo, *Adolf Loos* [New York, 1982].), but in terms of the way the house relates to the exterior world, the construction of its inside and outside.

35 Looking again at the photograph of the dining room of the Moller house (figure 14), the illusion that the scene is virtual, that the actual view of the dining room is a mirror image of the space from which the view is taken – the music room (thus collapsing both spaces into each other) – is produced not only by the way the space is framed by the opening, but also by the frame of the photograph itself, where the threshold is made to coincide exactly with the sides of the back wall, making the dining room into a picture inside a picture.

36 'The deepest conflict of modern man is not any longer in the ancient battle with nature, but in the one that the individual must fight to affirm the independence and peculiarity of his existence against the immense power of society, in his resistance to being levelled, swallowed up in the social-technological mechanism.' G. Simmel, 'Die Grosstadt und das Geistleben' (1903). English translation: 'The Metropolis and Mental Life,' in *George Simmel: On Individuality and Social Forms*, ed. D. N. Levine (Chicago, 1971), pp. 324-329.

37 G. Simmel, 'Fashion' (1904), ibid.

38 A. Loos, 'Ornament and Crime' (1908), tr. W. Wang, in *The Architecture of Adolf Loos*, p. 103.

39 A. Loos, 'Architecture' (1910) in *The Architecture of Adolf Loos*, p. 107.

40 A. Loos, 'Heimat Kunst' (1914) in *Trotzdem* (Innsbruck, 1931).

41 One of the ways in which the myth of Loos as an author has been sustained is the privileging of his writings over other forms of representation. These are used to legitimize observations made about his buildings. In demonstrating the way in which these systems of representations have been displaced, I have also treated Loos' words as a stable authority. This practice is problematic at many levels. Critics use words. By privileging words, they privilege themselves. They maintain themselves as authors (authorities). As this convention is dependent on the classical system of representation, this paper remains in complicity with the system that it claims to criticize. It is therefore necessary to reinterpret all of this material.

42 L. Münz and G. Künstler, *Adolf Loos*, p. 195.

43 Ibid.

44 B. Gravagnuolo, *Adolf Loos*, p. 191. Author's emphasis.

45 Ibid.

Douglas Graf is an Associate Professor of
Architecture at The Ohio State University,
a recurrent visitor to the program at the
University of Washington, and a practicing
architect with projects primarily in
Massachusetts and Texas.

Strange Siblings –
Being and No-Thinness
An Inadvertent Homage to
Ray and Charles Eames

Douglas Graf

Architecture and the written word are a strange couple. Sometimes they pass themselves off as siblings, as in two of the language twins, sometimes they're involved in a revival of 'The Servant,' one becoming the hand-maiden to the other, both being able to play each role. Sometimes they, along with others, are forced to masquerade as the class structure of the Prussian state, a strange brew that architecture finds particularly annoying.

When Victor Hugo said (and I hardly need to say it) 'This will kill that,' perhaps he envisioned the possibility of successive generations of media indulging in repeating patterns of patricide, print succumbing to cinema, and cinema to video. It would be curious to know what he envisioned as a future for print in light of his prediction for architecture, whether he might have seen it also as an embalmed present to the present from the past, kept in the main in a state of life in death in vast mausoleums maintained by the state at an increasingly painful economic price, ironically synthesizing the first great libraries and the mausoleums of Hellenistic society, itself a mummification of the Periclean state. The library itself, as edifice, might be regarded as an earlier attack on architecture by text, to edify evolving from *aedificare*, to build a house. The Hellenistic libraries to a large extent reflected the critical inclinations of late Greek culture and the explosion of scholarly rather than creative writing, for erudition rather than imagination. It seems only fitting that Pergamon's ambassador to Rome, the herald of the state's cultural achievements, was the librarian, possibly explaining the degree to which Greek culture actually impacted Roman civilization.

At any rate, it is interesting to note that the potent image of 'The Hunchback of Notre Dame' was created not by Hugo, but by Lon Chaney, Jr., and that what's killing what at the moment might be circumscribed by the hysterically funny idea of a writers' strike in Hollywood. But although one might argue that the twentieth century has been the great age of the image, language is still in there kicking, allied now with late capitalism rather than late Hellenism, with mergers and outright buy-outs, absorbing its weakened former competitors like philosophy into its empire.

Language has been trying to buy into architecture for quite some time now, and its advance men, like Hugo, have been trying to knock the price down by knocking the product, an operation that was wonderfully lampooned by Hegel in his much misunderstood spoof on criticism, *The Philosophy of Fine Art*. Among the great lines that the language boys don't think are the least bit funny must be included:

> The Chinese, Hindoos, and Egyptians, for example, in their artistic images, sculptured deities and idols, never passed beyond a formless condition, or a definition of shape that was vicious and false, and were unable to master true beauty.[1]

But seriously, what if there were a system that established some sort of hegemony among various disciplines? Or what if there were some sort of basic structure that operated among all forms of communication?

Ten years ago, a conference such as this would certainly have been an opportunity for the discussion of semiology, and the dreaded Ogden/Richards semantic triangle would have been much in evidence. Today, this will almost certainly not be the case. It might be interesting to ruminate on the possible reasons for this. Fashion is always a possibility. Perhaps it is the result of a resurgent historicism and its tendency to demote the value of function. However, since to a large extent, 'semantic meaning' in architecture has tended to focus on function, its current de-emphasis has left the linguistic argument somewhat high and dry. And yet here it is, architecture as 'text'. I would like to use Umberto Eco and Peter Eisenman to represent two peaks in this linguistic landscape.

In a recent publication, *Mies Reconsidered*, Eisenman presents a brilliant formal analysis of some of Mies' early work.[2] His intention, however, is to use the discussion to showcase the manifestation of 'textuality' in architecture. Furthermore, he argues that this textuality will only be evidenced by the application of textual analysis, that is, as opposed to formal or symbolic analysis. Eisenman argues that while formal analysis is concerned with aesthetics and symbolic analysis with traditional meaning as derived through metaphor,

> ...the 'meaning' revealed through textual analysis is, however, a structural meaning, not a metaphoric one. A structural meaning is one in which there is a differentiation and not a representation.

He goes on to argue that:

> ...a sign of difference and a trace of presence are textual notations. It is the operation of these kinds of notations which is usually ignored by the traditional analysis of meaning; the textual level is left unconsidered because of a fixation on symbol as metaphor that suppresses sign as difference.[3]

Here, the triumvirate of formal, symbolic, and textual analysis has been replaced by the opposition of symbol and text, which now assumes synonymity with 'sign'. The insistence that what seems to be perceptually based formal arguments must be considered textual seems to underscore a desire to invoke the authority of a linguistic approach even in the absence of its clear applicability or relevance. It is especially not clear how textuality manifests its presence within forms, since Eisenman argues that 'not all objects are necessarily texts.'[4]

Eisenman says in reference to Mies' Brick Country House Project:

> ...the walls speak to the fact that there is no space in the house. The walls do not define space; rather they define their own condition of being – that is, their capacity to support and their capacity to divide.
>
> Traditionally, walls are read as the perimeter of space: they either contain, enclose, or exclude space. But the walls in the Brick Country House are merely object presences, divisions where there is no space to divide or where the space has been removed and only surfaces exist.'[5]

The 'traditional' here seems to mean 'non-textual,' that is, that it lacks those qualities necessary to permit unmistakable communicated meaning of mono-thematic simplicity. By assuming this to be obvious he appears to strengthen the connection between architecture and 'formal analysis', which, as defined by Eisenman,

> ...looks for formal order, such as sequences, closures, or proportions: the interval between columns, the relationship of wall lengths, the ratios of solids to voids or parts to the whole.[6]

The assumption seems to be that formal analysis doesn't entail any decisions or interpretation, but rather that it is arrived at through the mere recording of largely quantifiable data from organizations within the object that somehow manifest themselves quite conspicuously. Symbols are subject to symbolic analysis, signs are subject to textual analysis, and thus presumably formal analysis is left to focus on these unidentified organizational systems that are somehow neither symbols nor signs. This raises questions not only about where and how this category might be manifested but also whether it can even exist at all, whether its assumed evidence can vanquish interpretation, ambiguity, undecidedness and a multiplicity of readings. Within Eisenman's argument, however, these unnamed formal systems seem to share the qualities that require textual readings. According to this position the introduction of a single simple element into a larger context creates a crisis for the elemental and 'obvious' reading and necessitates new strategies for interpretation.

One such reading of Mies' Brick Country House is the distinction made between the wall as divider and the wall as container. In the first instance the wall is seen as neutral and elemental; in the second instance, it achieves valence and is configurational. If two walls are compared, one existing in isolation and the other sited in juxtaposition with another object, the first can be seen exercising its capacity to establish a position and divide. The second wall, however, while it too divides and establishes a position it does so more ambiguously because it begins to exercise another capacity, that of making closure or an edge. This capacity is less ambiguous configurationally because it accounts for the presence of the object. It brings the object and wall together in a relationship in which the presence of one element becomes subsumed within the configuration. The reduction to and search for configurational unity from an alternative and simultaneous state of elemental multiplicity is embodied in the word 'configuration' itself, both in the sense of recalling a compound origin and in the sense of conceptually calculating or figuring with the material present.

Whatever capacities an element has, the introduction of configuration stresses some and represses others. The notion of configuration can be very simple. But it can also be ambivalent. Specifically with regard to the wall and the object. For example, we can imagine two types of configurations, one of similarity, and one of difference. In the former, the two elements become equivalent, wall as object and object as wall, bracketing space like unequal bookends (figure 1). In the second case, they are contrasted, each adopts capacities that reinforce a configuration of difference, such as the relationship between the center and the edge (figure 2). In both cases, however, it is the context that galvanizes and focuses the interpretive opportunities.

For Mies' Brick Country House Project, it seems clear that the walls maintain their elemental-ness, but it is impossible for them to avoid addressing their context simultaneously. It is the nature of their contextual relationships which reinforce their qualities as static elements while at the same time suggesting a dynamic ('where the space has been removed') as they are read as fragments of configuration. If it is seen that 'the walls do not define

93

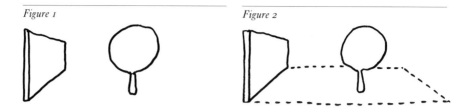

Figure 1   *Figure 2*

space: rather they define their own condition of being,' this would seem to support the distinction between the elementary notion of isolation and the configurational notion of context, walls as perimeter and 'the traditional distinction of inside and out.' As demonstrated by the wall and the object, inside and outside are configurational, not elemental, notions.

In 1973, Umberto Eco published an article in *VIA* entitled 'Function and Sign: The Semiotics of Architecture,' in which he argued that 'architecture [is] a particular challenge to semiotics…because apparently most architectural objects do not *communicate* (and are not designed to communicate), but *function*.'[7] He then proceeds to argue that function is sort of a form of communication and that symbolism is a form of function, but he insists that the primary form of architectural communication is the denotation of function. Furthermore he argues that:

> Architectural discourse is experienced inattentively, in the same way in which we experience the discourse of films and television, the comics, or advertising – not, that is, in the way in which one is meant to experience works of art and other more demanding messages, which call for concentration, absorption, wholehearted interest in interpreting the message, interest in the intentions of the 'addressor'.[8]

One can see time and again in Eco's argument that his conception of architectural purposiveness continuously intrudes into his attempt to subject architecture to semiotic principles. When the focus is on the possibilities of language, the perspective enlarges:

> Much of the discussion of architecture as communication has centered on *typological* codes, especially semantic typological codes, those concerning functional and sociological types… We will return to typological codes…but it is clear that they constitute only one, if perhaps the most conspicuous, of the levels of codification in architecture.[9]
>
> But what stands out about these codes is that on the whole they would appear to be, as communicative systems go, rather limited in operational possibilities. They are, that is, codifications of already worked-out solutions, codifications yielding standardized messages – this instead of constituting, as would codes truly on the model of those verbal languages, a system of possible relationships from which countless significantly different messages could be generated.[10]

Eco thus discards a very provocative trail of his own argument:

> …one might be tempted to hypothesize for architecture something like the 'double articulation' found in verbal languages, and assume that the most basic level of articulation (that is, the units constituting the 'second' articulation) would be a matter of geometry. [11]

If architecture is the art of the articulation of spaces, then perhaps we already have, in Euclid's geometry, a good definition of the rudimentary code of architecture.

This approach he jettisons because 'this geometric code would not pertain specifically to architecture,' but would constitute a meta-language.[12] Thus, the lack of exclusivity demands that architecture look for meaning entirely within itself.

However, in an interview in *Precis* 6 he apparently reverses his position. In reacting to Rossi's Modena Cemetery, Eco says:

> Quite frankly, I must tell you that Rossi's work frightens me. It really is cemeterial. We must question whether architecture can or should autonomously provide meaning.[13]

Evidently, the very success with which Modena triggers the denotation of function is itself now found suspect. The implication is that Eco now seems ready to explore the meta-language of geometry as it relates to architecture. It could be said that here the notion that any discussion of what is 'purely' architecture is contaminated by the introduction of geometry has collided with the idea that architecture is a criticism of geometry rather than an embodiment of it. Perhaps architecture is concerned with the implications of geometry rather than mere descriptions of it. The sheer physicality of architecture, even its conceptual physicality, requires that architecture be a 'simulation' of geometry. Or perhaps one could say that the material presence of architecture constitutes a meta-geometry that absorbs and fuses the external dissonance between existence and essence. When taken separately both the vacuousness of geometry and the density of materiality can be seen as potentially pejorative. But when they are combined the result is both something and nothing, something that is there and not there, thin and not thin, the embodiment of 'being and no-thinness.'

Given this critical relationship, in which inherent to the object is a simultaneous commentary on configuration, perhaps a micro-meta-language could be proposed. Within the semiotic universe, certain basic building blocks have been proposed: phonemes, lexemes, sememes, classemes, choremes, myththemes, morpho-semes, metasemes, morphemes, and just plain old phemes and semes. From a brief survey of the literature, it seems that these classifications reflect nothing more than personal attempts to understand the nature of language. This should encourage others to make the same effort. In this spirit, a morpheme sounds like the perfect building block for architecture, but modesty of scope requires that we pursue first the sub-morphemic units, the eames, of which there are two: rayeames, or elements, and charleseames, or configurations. The eames, thus, constitute a framework for a minimal structure in architecture.

If architecture is the criticism of geometry, perhaps a framework for minimal structure would be located in the implications of the Pythagorean series as explored in its materiality. Rayeames might be so named, at least in part, because a ray is a co-generational organization that directly relates a point to a line. Obviously, there would be a similar relationship between a line and a plane and a plane and a volume. In a more general way the first is denoted as edge, and, in a more architectural manner, the second is denoted as façade. Something along these lines might generate a series of basic elements. A charleseames, then, would constitute the relational structure between these elements.

The connection between the basic elements is perhaps further underscored etymologically. For example, the Latin word for stake, aligned here with the idea of 'line', is *vallus*. A rampart, or a series of stakes, becomes singular again as 'plane', *valli* to *vallum*, from which

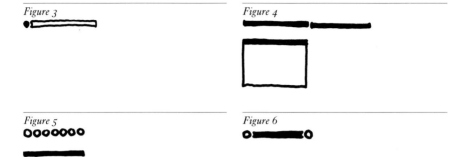

Figure 3

Figure 4

Figure 5

Figure 6

the word 'wall' is derived. *Vallus* has a common ancestry with *volvere*, to roll, and thus itself constitutes 'a roll,' which is a line wrapped with, or extruded into a plane, therefore confounding linearity with a conflicting lateral dimension, an operation which suggests that the roots of 'volume' are spiral (e.g., toilet paper; a 'volute', of course, is a planar section of volumetric generation). It's interesting that this origin unites the usages of the word in various degrees of stability, reflecting the underlying indeterminacy of their construction.

The interrelationships, transformations, and instabilities manifested by the words that constitute the etymological 'volume family' are mirrored by, or perhaps even the resultants of, a coextensive system described within the configuration of objects. With regard to an object, any presumed unity of the whole is abnegated by the difficulty (perhaps impossibility) of determining the system by which the various constituent elements are demarcated, related, stabilized, and interpreted. The elusiveness of decidability with relation to formal constituency is related at least in part to the ability of the rudimentary elements of geometry to constitute re-presentations of each other.

The elements of the Pythagorean series constitute extensions of one another, based first on the notion of extrusion from the non-dimensional to the dimensional, or once again from nothingness to somethingness. The extrusion of a point inevitably becomes a line (figure 3), but a line can be extruded into just more line unless the extrusion is along an axis of no dimension, i.e., across the axis on length (figure 4). Secondly, there is present the notion of replication, that 'point' by becoming 'points' becomes 'line', etc. (figure 5); and thirdly, of juxtaposition, 'two points make a line, two lines make a plane' (figure 6), and so on (and thus through a strange lineage 'linen'). Extension and replication result in the production of a new element, but juxtaposition defines a new element without producing it. What it produces is more ambiguous: it concerns the limits of the new element, including the limitations of its boundary.

Thus, juxtaposition simultaneously results in something less and something more than another element. It creates a situation that manifests the existence of multiple pieces and therefore constitutes the most fundamental form of configuration. It also makes evident the connection between elements, as that element defined by configuration elides into the elements established by a paired presence. The relationship between singular and multiple

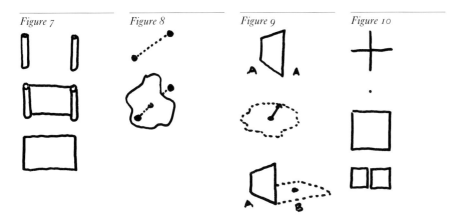

Figure 7   Figure 8   Figure 9   Figure 10

manifestations across the elision is made clear, as is a sense, of limitation and boundary in the singular element (figure 7). But more is established as well. The separation of the juxtaposed elements, the stark evidence of their multiplicity and exchangeability, establishes the notion of equality. The existence of multiples and the idea of equality allow for the definition of more than one figure. For example two points establish a line, but they also establish a plane, that sum of points that lie equidistant from each other (figure 8). Thus the two points, each of which still manifest their own separate existence, establish a line, a plane, and the inter-relationships between all four elements. Taken together these constitute a configuration of the sort which could be called 'intersection'.

Replicative juxtaposition (i.e., two points, two lines, etc.) thus raises the possibility of simultaneously composing multiple and different elements. This resultant could be defined as composite juxtaposition, involving adjacency of non-similar elements, such as point and line. This latter combination creates a configuration in which the inequalities work to propel certain latent qualities of the elements to the forefront, such as the point as a 'center' and the line as an 'edge' (figure 9). In each case, it is the presence of difference, which each element provides for the other, that allows the qualities or roles to be actively manifested. Thus, the configuration as a whole and the particular roles exhibited by the elements are only present to the degree that the relationship between the elements is manifested. Otherwise the qualities remain latent.

Four candidates for the categories of configuration are therefore intersection, center, perimeter, and module (figure 10). The last being simply the configuration of juxtaposition itself. Except for center, which stresses a singularity of position, any one of these categories can be made by any combination of elements. Thus, they maintain that same quality of elisiveness that make any ultimate sense of configurational fixity elusive. Furthermore, any one configuration tends to generate the other three, extending the same sense of latent familial familiarity from element to element and element to configuration, to configuration, to configuration (figure 11).

Some of these familial relationships are worth scrutinizing. For example the intersection of two lines particularizes a point that is activated by its presence in a configuration to become a center. A bend in a line, a special form of intersection, becomes a perimeter. It does something very similar to an intersection except not only does the bend articulate

Figure 11

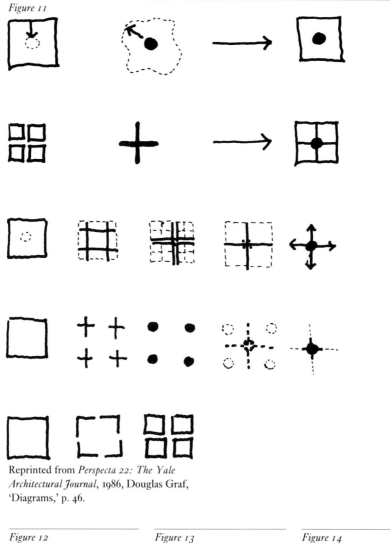

Reprinted from *Perspecta 22: The Yale
Architectural Journal*, 1986, Douglas Graf,
'Diagrams,' p. 46.

Figure 12   Figure 13   Figure 14

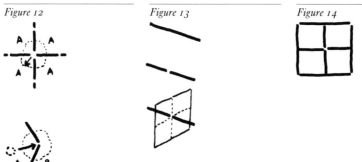

difference along the line, the point, it also articulates difference across the line, the sidedness of 'perimeter', implying the presence of an absent 'center' (figure 12). The particularization of any point on a line articulates difference along the line implying the presence of multiple lines and a connecting 'center'. The multiple lines create a 'module', articulating a plane whose points are equidistant from each, and thus begetting 'intersection' (figure 13).

Thus, a basic organization of formal, and by extension architectural, language seems poised between two omnipresent structures, elements and configurations, each of which simultaneously exhibit two very strong tendencies, fecund expansion and enfeebling contraction. This calls into question the strategies of both Eco and Eisenman: on the one hand, the accuracy of semiological analysis and, on the other hand, the dichotomy of text versus object. The first proposes a stability of archetype, and the second supposes a specificity of configurational meaning, both of which seem unattainable given the expanding, contracting, elisive, elusive organizations of the eames.

The 'paradise garden' (figure 14), is able to manifest all four basic configurations. It is therefore a useful paradigm for architectural composition, or perhaps a meta-eames, to extend the liberties being taken, or more specifically in this case, a 'Ray-Charles'. The structure of this simple figure is thus yet highly composite and redundant given the fact that each of the configurations within it seem to carry with it a 'code' by which the others can be generated. Given the assumed ubiquity of the proposed list of elements and configurations, the paradise garden, as befits a meta-eames, looms as an implication or potential presence in virtually any given situation. In this sense, Eisenman's argument about texts strikes a resonant cord:

> Texts always contain something else. That something else is the approximation or simulation of another object.[14]

By this reading, a text might be seen to be the assertion onto a locus by a configuration, or perhaps more simply, no text, no context.

The difficulties of interpretation, of developing strategies, or even merely of trying to establish the inventory of the constituent pieces of a building underscore the impossibilities of fully 'knowing' a building. We can only understand it as a simultaneously manifested set of abstract patterns, parts, and series, any one of which achieves support only by ignoring a large quantity of available data. Their properties and the boundaries between them tend to drift apart and back together as the areas of their operation expand and contract. The history of ideas and certainly the recent history of literary criticism have been marked by the relentless revision and supplanting of old orthodoxies with new heresies, heterodoxies, and ultimately new orthodoxies regarding the critical interpretation and the decidability of meaning.

What seems especially peculiar with regard to the world of architectural criticism is the rather belated impact of the idea of undecidability upon a discipline that has been so impoverished of developed interpretive strategies in the first place. The current revelation provides the promise of interminable debate and raucous uncertainty when for years there has been no debate and rampant disinterest in the possibilities of architectural purport. Certainly one of the reasons we are all drawn to literary criticism in the first place is the fact that it is just more, well, critical. Something seems to be at stake. At least to an outsider, scrutiny seems directed on areas of tight focus. Much architectural discourse, however,

99

seems impaled on either the mythologies of history, or 'typological' analyses that parody architectural precedent. The proclivity displayed by postmodernism toward each of these tendencies helps to explain their resurgence while at the same time exposing their weaknesses. It also exposes the critical weaknesses within the theories of modernism, which largely focussed on a techno-functional cant at the expense of more specifically interpretive material to deal with an architectural polemic that should have felt itself forced to confront the compositional problems of abstraction. That so substantial a twentieth-century figure as Le Corbusier can be said to be such a relatively indifferent critic of his own work is perhaps a reflection of this critical weakness. And his conspicuous aversion to or repression of the hermeneutic discussion seems especially bizarre given the configurational significance associated with his projects.

A brief digression might further illuminate the weakness of our position. In an article published in *Architectural Review* soon after the completion of Ronchamp, James Stirling contrasted the 'trends toward the arbitrary'[15] as displayed by the chapel to those that manifest 'the rationale of the modern movement'[16] manifested by such buildings as Lever House. In the present context, Stirling's argument has an eerie resonance of Eco's. Except that now the assurance of certainty has been transferred from function to technology.

> In the U.S.A., functionalism now means the adaptation to building of industrial processes and products, but in Europe it remains the essentially humanist method of designing to a specific use. The post-war architecture of America may appear brittle to Europeans and, by obviating the hierarchical disposition of elements, anonymous; however, this academic method of criticism may no longer be adequate in considering technological products of the 20th century. Yet this method would still appear valid in criticizing recent European architecture where the elaboration of space and form has continued without abatement; and the chapel by Le Corbusier may possibly be the most plastic building ever erected in the name of modern architecture.[17]

Although the dichotomy he establishes might lead one to believe that Ronchamp would thus be scrutinized by the 'academic method of criticism' and be prepared for an inspection of 'the hierarchical disposition of elements,' instead his approach is reduced to this, 'As a building it functions extremely well and appears to be completely accepted.'[18] This out of the way, the focus of the critique begins to emerge, it is not just the inappropriateness of modernist rationale to Ronchamp, but more importantly the inappropriateness of Ronchamp to modernism.

> It may be considered that the Ronchamp chapel being a 'pure expression of poetry' and the symbol of an ancient ritual, should not therefore be criticized by the rationale of the modern movement. Remembering, however, that this is a product of Europe's greatest architect, it is important to consider whether this building should influence the course of modern architecture. The sensational impact of the chapel on the visitor is significantly not sustained for any great length of time and when the emotions subside there is little to appeal to the intellect, and nothing to analyze or stimulate curiosity. This entirely visual appeal and the lack of intellectual participation demanded from the public may partly account for its easy acceptance by the local population.[19]

There is a treasure trove of material in this passage, much of which helps to place in perspective the critical fulcrum of the 1950s. Although it might be extremely difficult for the contemporary eye to contemplate the privileged positions being awarded to the 'opponents' of Ronchamp such as Lever House, perhaps the strangest declaration is that 'there is little to appeal to the intellect, and nothing to analyze or stimulate curiosity.'[20] Not only is the certainty of this declaration stupefying, especially when applied to what 'may possibly be the most plastic building ever erected in the name of modern architecture,'[21] but it raises the question of what precisely there is in a building that is open to interpretation particularly if Ronchamp doesn't have it and yet still lends itself to 'easy acceptance' by the local population. The answer still doesn't seem to be 'hierarchical disposition of elements.' After reviewing Ronchamp's 'incorrect' technology, Stirling noted:

> This freedom from the correct use and expression of materials, apparent in other post-war European architecture, has little parallel in the New World where the exploitation of materials and the development of new techniques continues to expand the architectural vocabulary.[22]

Thus, surprisingly, the relatively unreadable nature of Ronchamp is at least partially due to its inability to expand modern architectural vocabulary. This argument is then developed with the observation that European architecture has looked to 'popular art and folk architecture, mainly of an indigenous character, from which to extend their vocabulary,'[23] and further, that 'there seems to be no doubt that Le Corbusier's incredible powers of observation are lessening the necessity for invention.'[24] The argument goes thus. New forms will emerge from modern technologies and will necessitate invention, and therefore stimulate analysis, whereas old forms are so obvious as to become opaque and must be regarded primarily, and quickly, as '*objets trouvés* of considerable picturesqueness.'[25]

It is ironic that the observation 'an appreciation of regional building…has appeared frequently in Le Corbusier's books'[26] could be applied equally to Stirling's work. Presumably, Mediterranean *Gemeinschaft* is less appropriate to modernism than nineteenth-century *Gesellschaft*. Further, Stirling noted in his discussion that 'Far from being monumental, the building has a considerable ethereal quality, principally as a result of the equivocal nature of the walls.'[27] Alternatively, it was the inability of the walls to be equivocal, with their transparent origins in traditional regional architecture that prevented their 'appeal to the intellect' and 'provid[ed] nothing to analyze.' Thus, interpretation seems both to demand and reject clarity simultaneously and requires the use of a 'vocabulary' that is invented rather than absorbed. Finally, Stirling concludes:

> The desire to deride the schematic basis of modern architecture and the ability to turn a design upside down and make it architecture are symptomatic of a state when the vocabulary is not being extended, and a parallel can be drawn with the Mannerist period of the Renaissance. Certainly, the forms which have developed from the rationale and the initial ideology of the modern movement are being mannerized and changed into a conscious imperfectionism.
>
> Le Corbusier, proceeding from the general to the particular, has produced a masterpiece of a unique but most personal order.[28]

It is interesting that vocabulary is not being extended when its being 'mannerized', which I take to mean broadly being made to do something that it wasn't 'meant' to do, but evidently can do anyway. This would seem closer to some notion of extension, exploring the meanings, which a form might support, than Stirling's argument, which seems to be less about extension than accumulation. Stirling seeks to locate certainty of meaning within the ideologies, which somehow legitimize the production of form, rather than open form to the possibilities of independent, if uncertain interpretations, free from the intentional ideologies of the zeitgeist.

There is again the echo of Eco, however, in the fact that Stirling credits the walls with the ability to effectuate a reading by which the building is given a 'considerable ethereal quality,' without extending this investigation as to how or why this reading is effectuated, but rather, merely using the observation as an opportunity to enumerate various technological and typological 'abnormalities'. Perhaps using the eames, one might explore 'the equivocal nature of the walls' in any number of buildings to glean some of the uncertainties proposed by configuration itself and extend the operating range of vocabulary, independent of intentional ideologies.

It is interesting that Stirling contemplates the decline of invention signaled by the lateness of Le Corbusier's 'indigenous Mediterranean' period, but seems to find little parallel with Ronchamp in the rubble wall of the 'heroic' Swiss Pavilion (figure 15). To some degree, they operate within the same system of implication.

In the latter, the rough-textured rubble wall and the dormitory block can be seen to bracket the history of the artifact, from the origins of manipulation and the first scene of space-making. The rough stones, gathered to produce a wall, the slight bend in which creates difference across it; the suggestion of the first enclosure and implication of a primal center, the recognition of which removes the focus of 'volume' from the stones to the space itself; the stones themselves, reconceived as 'plane,' transformed to weightless thinness by the aggressive web of mortar that binds them into a singularity (figure 16). The first focus is left behind as the building develops away from it. The wall, by repetition, turns edge into bar, which finds further elaboration into modular segments, mirroring the wall's segmentation into a columnar series (figure 17). This ensemble creates its own version of focus in its *cortile*, the distant edge of which evidences separation of the wall plane from the columnar structure and the birth of the *plan libre* (figure 18). Space and structure are re-synthesized in the dormitory block (itself a reconstitution of the missing third leg of the palazzo), and pushed towards a permanent future as it heroically expands into the void, 'picked up' (*aufhebungated?*) and no longer earth-bound by the 'anti-wall' of the pylons, the stones (assembled volumes) making their reappearance as dormitory rooms (figure 19). Presumably, Swiss students may contemplate the prospect of the end of time from the comfort of the porch, as architecture abdicates its attempt to make place as it reunites with space itself. Thus, the inevitable tendency of the eames to call forth or defer to each other results in a very intricate system of cross-referencing, in which even those that are absent are maintained to some degree.

Perhaps Ronchamp argues for a more complex version of this scenario, in which the King James version of history intersects with Hegel's. As Stirling has noted, '...the building has a considerable ethereal quality, principally as a result of the equivocal nature of the walls.' One might mull over the sense of equivocation proffered, 'having two or more significations,' 'undecidable,' or 'of doubtful advantage, genuineness, or moral rectitude.' Surprisingly, given Stirling's argument it would seem to be the last, that is, moral rectitude, which produces the 'equivocal nature of the walls.' The eames, however, conspire to embrace the first two and put to rout suspicions of doubtful advantage. They move toward a rectitude that is terminal, if not moral.

There are seemingly an infinite number of situations in which the walls at Ronchamp configure to produce dichotomous pairs. In the first example, the east and south walls combine to produce a conspicuous emergent corner to the building. In some ways, the view from the southeast recapitulates the argument of the Swiss Pavilion, in which the genesis of a palazzo is suggested by the juxtaposition of a primary wall and an accommodating vol-

Figure 15

Figure 16

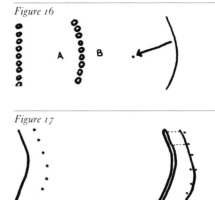

Figure 17

103

Figure 18

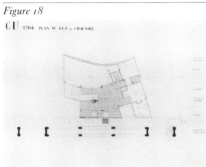

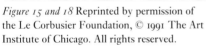

Figure 19

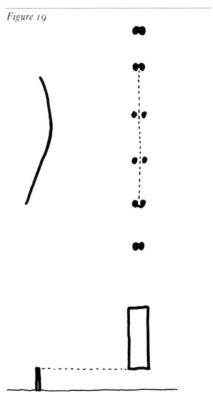

Douglas Graf

Figure 20

Figure 21

Figure 22

Figure 23

Figure 20 © Le Corbusier
Foundation

ume beyond it (figure 20). The sense of similarity across the corner, virtually absent at the dormitory, is very strong here, given the symmetries that are established. This sense of equivalence extends to equate the elements that bracket the scene, the two towers to the west and north, although between the two dominance is given to the former, as it 'towers' over the smaller one, incomplete by comparison (short and *sans* 'hood') and still within the protection of the roof. Similarly, between the corner walls, dominance is given to the south wall by virtue of its tailing edge, the end of which soars upward to provide a synonymous frame with the roof structure. Perhaps this corner also recalls Chaumont, in which part of the perimeter of the château, exposed by a missing wall, must compete with the opposing towers in an attempt to situate the organization of the palazzo form. Ronchamp critiques the château by supplying the absent wall in the role of initiator, thereby establishing a clearer relationship between this corner and its opposite, in a way which indicates the influence of the former on the latter, a relationship that is not reciprocated nor even acknowledged (figure 21).

As the 'initiating' wall unravels the perimeter to the west, a continuous series of reciprocities present themselves. The concavity of its exterior surface is opposed by the convex wall of the first chapel tower. As at the Swiss Pavilion, the wall is presented at the moment at which it suggests the enclosing of space rather than merely existing as a presence within it; as defining an object rather than being the object itself. Unlike the Swiss Pavilion, however, the wall is transformed along its length, from a soaring razor's edge of a plane at the outside corner, to a massive earth-bound volume as it extends toward the southwest. On the exterior, as a space encloser, the concavity of the exterior wall is countered by the increasingly volumetric reading of the wall itself. On the inside, space-making is again the suggested province of the wall, in this instance by its accommodation of the windows, which are carved from its mass to produce a discrete series of volumes. Within this scenario, the large chapel might be seen as the latest and greatest in this series of glyptic voids.

The conditions at the south portal, however, argue for a different interpretation. The westernmost window arrayed in the wall might be said to carve only along its eastern perimeter, as it is flanked on the west by a wall segment of continuous depth, not easily read as a residual solid (figure 22). Rather, it is as though the surface of the void has begun to transform the gathering volume of the wall into an enclosing plane, a transfiguration of object from solid to void, and volume-definer from mass to edge. The south portal thus marks that point at which wall-as-mass, and thus as auto-defined object, becomes reconceptualized to wall-as-plane and as the definer of volume adjacent to itself; the transformation is evidenced uniformly across the entire length of the rubble wall of the Swiss Pavilion and occurs sequentially along the perimeter of Ronchamp (figure 23). *Vallus* is thus resurrected to re-perform the act of archegenesis from stake to wall to volume as the south façade of Ronchamp unrolls toward the first chapel. The metamorphosis establishes both the continuity of the perimeter and the break within that continuity: similarity of surface and dissimilarity of implication, and dissimilarity of surface and similarity of implication.

These two opposing/cooperating configurations, wall as volume and plane as volume-definer, join together as particularity turns to generality and concept replaces percept. It is noteworthy that the south doorway occurs at that point on the perimeter at which the power of the wall to make perimeter is first manifested, thus making entry 'into' conceivable. One enters, then, at that point of entelechy where rationality reclassifies the immediate materiality of the object into a larger category, that of a general principle, the abstraction of surface and the immateriality of object as space. The first chapel can therefore be seen as a configuration in opposition to the wall even as it is, in a sense, a continuation of it.

The discontinuation of the overhanging, bounding roof to the west reinforces the moment of change at the same time as it demarcates by its absence the volume-defining role of the chapel walls, a role that the roof itself performed as it sheltered the configurations beneath it. The roof structure disappears from among the perimeter elements until it re-emerges at the northeast corner, where its circumscription of the northeast 'tower' reinforces its connection to the first chapel, while at the same time raising questions as to the implications of these repeated gestures of equivalence bracketed within partially countermanding gestures of difference.

The nature of this connection is offered as further evidence for inspection at that part of the perimeter not subject to restraint and incorporation by the roof canopy, the west and north walls. If the theme established by the development of the south façade of Ronchamp is as perimeter, its destiny is closure, a condition, which if met, however, would terminate any possibility of future development. After definition of the first chapel, the exterior plane continues in a manner that eventually forms the second chapel, an effort at completion that both succeeds and fails. It succeeds in that the surrounding plane maintains a unifying concavity, the edges of which establish the notion of closure (figure 24). It fails in that this promise of unity is broken as the configuration creates two distinct areas within the overall area, the first and second chapels. These areas are thus as distinctly separate from each other as they are singularly united. The perimeter offers additional examples of this sort of 'difficult' closure. The third chapel brackets symmetrically with the second in compensatory opposition to the configurational relationship that exists between the first two (figure 25). The inversion of this bonding, however, is situated necessarily by convexity, rather than the previously deployed concavity. This device both maintains the continuity and development of the perimeter at the same time as it closes and reopens it. In either case, the third chapel and the subsequent areas along the north wall reinforce a further reading of identity with the second chapel in separating the first chapel from the rest of the ensemble as a void rather than as a 'solid', or an absence rather than a presence (figure 26).

In this case, the development of the north wall can be seen as uncannily mirroring that of the south. 'Volume as mass' is thus subtly and surreptitiously reintroduced as a theme almost immediately after its banishment at the south portal, but in a symmetry that forces an ironic equivalence between the heroic and the banal (figure 27). The axis established by the configuration of the interior space – the axis of symmetry for the building at least in respect to the interior plan configuration – creates a notion of similarity between these two rather disparate aggregates, that is, the opposing interior elevations. This notion reinforces the idea that 'the Wall' and the first chapel are to be read with reference to each other and that the array of spaces along the north wall may betray similar relationships, especially those supporting notions of progressive development. Thus the vestry can be seen as an extension of the third chapel, as well as an opposition to it: first as its continuation, or second, as its reconstitution, replicated and abstracted to become a potentially infinitely repeatable module, undramatically symmetrical to any and all of its progeny. The relative neutrality of this space and the relative disinterest of the walls to the center, as opposed to

Figure 24

Figure 25

Figure 26

Figure 27

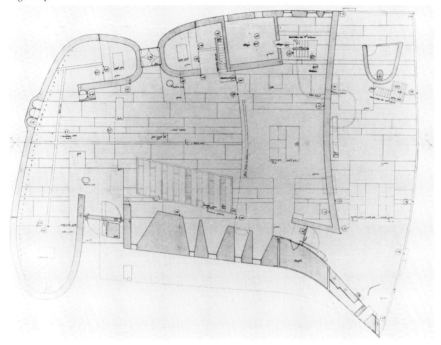

Figure 27 Le Corbusier Foundation, © 1991
The Art Institute of Chicago. All rights
reserved.

Figure 28   *Figure 29*

the situation with regard to the three chapels, are qualities that are extended even further in the next space in the sequence (figure 28), in which only the suggestion of enclosure is certain, while each of the 'enclosing' walls averts its interest in this space by establishing a primary responsibility elsewhere.

Within this scenario, another symmetry superimposes its organization around the center axis, a symmetry in which the north and south walls are paired in directional opposition to each other but in developmental equivalence (figure 29). Each configuration proposes a progression in which a 'new' space is the resultant, a space in which definition is achieved by an advance in the relative isolation of the void from the elements that define it. Whereas the 'wall' and the eroded pylons of the Swiss Pavilion bracket the development of the composition as end conditions of opposition and equivalence, the two spaces at Ronchamp additionally mirror each other in symmetry, as they maintain similar positions in similar sequences, while at the same time (and/or similar times, and or opposing times) mirroring/contrasting the focus and dissolution of space. Here, Ronchamp '*aufhebt das Aufhebung selbst.*'

Perhaps this reading of a beginning and an ending, which is itself a beginning again, a re-incorporation of the particular with the Other, does have strong associations with an Hegelian historicism. The perimeter of Ronchamp might be read as a sort of history of architecture, from the genesis along the 'Wall' of sculptural mass from pure position: the reconceptualization of edge as plane and the creation of volume through perimetrical enclosure at the first chapel; completion of the first precinct and its replication at the north portal: the extraction of precinct from an object of singular significance to the interchangeability of cell, as displayed by the relationship of the third chapel to the vestry; and the reintegration of inside to outside and the reduction of precinct to nuance at the 'last space'. It is interesting to note that the client for Ronchamp never seems to have programmed any request for the small chapels' existence, nor made any request for their number. Perhaps Le Corbusier might be regarded as having invented them for the purposes of setting up this architectural paradigm, a sort of 'stations of the cross' to document an evolution, as the perimeter of the building itself evolves. From the initial isolation of closure, to the re-incorporation of inside with outside, and the reduction of precinct to vicinity and enclosure to fragmented object, the review extends from Ramses to Riegl.

Figure 30

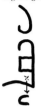

Returning to an earlier argument, however, requires that another element be read within this series, the outdoor 'sacristy' (the 'fourth chapel'). Its mirroring of the first chapel from the perspective of the southeast corner, its bracketing the symmetry of the north portal, and its recollection of the configuration of the three chapels all conspire to reinforce this connection. Moreover, its qualities of fragmentation and displacement match it in sympathy to some extent with the 'last space,' which might now be read additionally as a record of the absence of the 'sacristy' (figure 30). As part of the architectural paradigm, this relationship might be viewed as a longing for, or the promise of, a simple closure to the more complex second series of northern perimeter configurations, the eventuation of which is prevented by the dividing/connecting 'separatrix' quality of the east wall. Perhaps this might be interpreted as the permanent positioning of a sort of utopian primitivism perpetually beyond the grasp of the present, but always within its promise, a sort of special case of the 'future present' with a perpetual 'can't' attached to it, an antimillenial twist very much absent from the promise of the Swiss Pavilion.

Speaking of cant, however, the outdoor 'sacristy' provides it in excess, since it first configures a rather shockingly abrupt corner to the building, second, as its rotation introduces an abrupt thrust to the perimeter back towards the initiating corner, and third, as its form re-presents the expression or repetition of a conventional, 'trite', stock phrase. This return to the initial corner, moreover, within a vocabulary that has seemingly evolved successfully from it, constitutes a bit of a revelation, although it continues the metaphor of return established between the two sets of concave shapes. In this regard, it is worth remembering that the initiating corner was seen as being 'predictive' of the division into two sets, or perhaps even the instrument of the division itself via the extension of the diagonal axis across the composition. Thus, rather than remain content with the role of mere 'beginner', the initiating corner can be read as maintaining control over significant aspects of the perimeter's development, including its ultimate recall, in a somewhat complex version of 'cat and mouse'.

In this case, there is yet another version of beginning and end, a more theological one, one scenario of which might have the initiating wall becoming a metaphor for Genesis, and the abrupt return constituting an equivalent Revelations. Perhaps the chapels reenact the evolution of the Godhead, from Jehovah to Jesus the son and the break at the north portal,

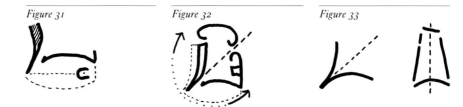

Figure 31   Figure 32   Figure 33

and from the Holy Spirit to the Second Coming, fracturing the enclosure into an Old and New Testament, both of which continue the theme of a promised return (figure 31). Perhaps in this reading the 'last space' should be read as 'loss of focus/loss of faith', as the 'separatrix' wall might be read as the moving armature of history. It is interesting that the phenomenal overhanging roof at Ronchamp never occurs along the conscious/conceptualized/historical perimeter, but only beyond it, and always with a drama that is completely hidden in its absence. In its presence, its configuration supports the supremacy of the southeast corner and a certain equivalence along the diagonal axis of intervention (figure 32). In the areas in which its presence is absent from the exterior, however, it conforms to a different organizational notation, one which finds axiality along the longitudinal axis of the interior space.

This particular division of allegiance is not unique to the roof. As has already been noted, the north and south perimeters find enough equivalence to support the longitudinal axis as easily as enough difference to deny it. The 'separatrix' wall is in much the same situation as the roof. It supports the diagonal axis by its capacity to mirror the 'initiating wall', yet it supports simultaneously the longitudinal axis. Its ability to mirror is compromised by the strong relationship between the outdoor 'sacristy' and the southeast corner, a relationship that tends to configure the outside space in a way that allows the 'separatrix' wall to be seen as an internal membrane and therefore relatively unstable given the usual severity of the perimeter (figure 33). In this regard, it further reinforces the longitudinal axis as it seems to achieve some degree of fixity by the axis' control. Thus the 'separatrix' wall is to one axis what the north portal is to the other: the somewhat surprising incursion of one authority into the domain of another, a condition that at Ronchamp presents the interrelational conflict of two different systems.

Among the other elements that might belong to the longitudinal system could be included the cistern beyond the western perimeter of the building, an ellipsoidal concrete pool containing several 'pure' solids to function as splash blocks for the water collected from the roof. The trapezium plan of the interior seems to pay homage to this element from which it seems to grow. Conversely, the trapezium associates itself with the space beyond the membrane wall, which it gestures to incorporate (figure 34). The longitudinal axis further evidences this dual relationship between an absent, idealized center to the west (the cistern

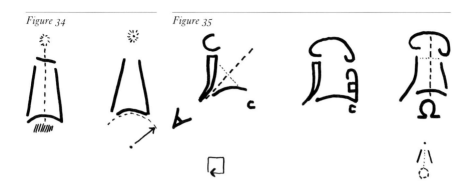

Figure 34   Figure 35

and its forms) and an absent, unrealized perimeter to the east (the porch and its environs). Thus yet another model positions Ronchamp: the axis between an ideal, inaccessible, timeless 'beginning', which can reference, but never actually 'begin,' and its proposed eventual 'realization,' equally problematic to achieve, but sufficient to position its contemplation. Here, then, is a sort of timeless version of positioning history inside 'time' in opposition to the generative, manipulative, bounded versions of a history, a sort of classicist's Revenge on both Hegel and theology.

The two axes might thus be seen as a particular version of Plato versus the Pentateuch, a version that by finding numerous parallels achieves as uneasy a synthesis as Plutarch. In both cases, however, the east wall proposes a dilemma of anticipation, whether the future evolves from the past or returns to it. This dilemma is also central to the production and interpretation of architecture and to the role of the eames in its recognition, to the degree that the making of architecture is reduced to repeating, the search for text isolated from its manipulation is a quest for reduction rather than for inspection. Invention is the struggle with tradition; in fact, it is the tradition.

It is interesting to note that Le Corbusier made a note to consult the Apocalypse in his notebooks during the design of Ronchamp. In addition to numerous presumed similarities between text and building (such as the backwards flowing rivers = the water collection system), 'I am the Alpha and the Omega' has particular resonance, not only as a recapitulation of the continuous theme of beginning/end and similarity/difference, but also because of the letters themselves. The diagonal axis thus assumes the role of Alpha while the longitudinal axis adopts that of Omega, an event that permits various re-synthesizing strategies of configuration to be proposed (figure 35). Given Ronchamp's promise of and progress towards completion, one may further understand that at the end of time, when history ceases and the necessity for interpretation and its dependence on similarity and difference vanishes, when tradition is reunited with origin, Ronchamp's plan will become one with its perimeter and the building will become its own Jerusalem, the paradise garden (figure 36).

Ronchamp is evidence simultaneously of the uniqueness of all buildings and the eternal, internal dialogue among all buildings, which allows each one to become a critique of all others. It should console Eco, as it underscores the continuity of argument within configuration, and therefore design, and to the potential consistencies of architectural 'lan-

III

Douglas Graf

Figure 36

Le Corbusier, Le Poème de L'Angle Droit, 1984 edition. © 1991 ARS, N.Y./Spadem

112

guages'. That the latter seem to always have the qualities of 'textuality', thanks to the eames, perhaps is consolation to Eisenman, although the infinitude within which they operate might argue that a specificity of interpretation will inevitably be elusive. On the other hand, perhaps it merely underscores the common non-verbal ancestry of 'figuring', both as thinking and shaping, a worthy bond for limitless acts of edification.

1 G. H. Hegel, 'The Philosophy of Fine Art,' in *Philosophies of Art and Beauty,* ed. A. Hofsteder (New York, 1964), p. 429.
2 P. Eisenman, 'miMises READING: does not mean A THING,' *Mies Reconsidered: His Career, Legacy, and Disciples* (New York and Chicago, 1986).
3 Ibid., p. 87.
4 Ibid.
5 Ibid., p. 88.
6 Ibid., p. 86.
7 U. Eco, 'Function and Sign: Semiotics of Architecture,' VIA 2 (New York and Philadelphia, 1973), p. 131.
8 Ibid., p. 143.
9 Ibid., p. 141.
10 Ibid., p. 142.
11 Ibid., p. 141.
12 Ibid.
13 U. Eco, 'Adjustment and Conjecture in Architecture,'

Precis 6 (1987), p. 79.
14 P. Eisenman, 'miMises READING,' p. 86.
15 J. Stirling, 'Ronchamp: Le Corbusier's Chapel and the Crisis of Rationalism,' *The Architectural Review* (February 1956), p. 160.
16 Ibid., p. 161.
17 Ibid., p. 155.
18 Ibid., p. 156.
19 Ibid., p. 161.
20 Ibid.
21 Ibid., p. 55.
22 Ibid., p. 161.
23 Ibid., p. 161.
24 Ibid.
25 Ibid.
26 Ibid., p. 161.
27 Ibid., p. 156.
28 Ibid., p. 161.

K. Michael Hays is Associate Professor
of Architecture in the Graduate School of
Design at Harvard University and editor of
*Assemblage: A Critical Journal of Architecture
and Design Culture.*

**Inscribing the Subject
of Modernism**
The Posthumanist Theory
of Ludwig Hilberseimer

K. Michael Hays

**Strategies in
Architectural Thinking**

Within the discourse of modernism was developed a critical practice, associated with an ongoing bourgeois humanism, which confines a 'correct' reading of an architectural object to an acceptance of the position from which the immanent characteristics of the object have precedence over its external historical and ideological determinants: the position of a transcendental subject. Recent critical theory has taken an explicitly anti-humanist turn, which has come to be thought of as definitively postmodern. It is my thesis that a rigorous anti-humanist trajectory can be found historically within modernism, but that its consequences prove at times to be less desirable than current anti-humanists (and I count myself among them) might hope.[1]

What I propose to offer in this essay is a partial account of Ludwig Hilberseimer's so-called *sachlich* architecture in terms of the theory of the subject. What is important here is the link between the category of the subject and any ideological critique of modernism or of the present. Louis Althusser went so far as to *define* ideology in terms of the subject: ideology places the individual in an imaginary relationship to society as a social subject. 'The existence of ideology and the hailing [interpellation] of individuals as subjects are one and the same thing.'[2] It is this sense of the category of the subject that I believe is helpful in a study of modernism.

A contemporary of Hilberseimer's, the architect turned sociologist, Sigfried Kracauer, writing about the culture of Weimar, put his own perception of the problematic of modernism this way:

> The world is split into the diversity of what exists and the diversity of the human subject confronting it. This human subject, who was previously incorporated into the dance of forms filled by the world, is now left solitarily confronting the chaos as the sole agent of the mind, confronting the immeasurable realm of reality. [The subject is] thrown out into the cold infinity of empty space and empty time.[3]

What I take such statements to be – and they can be found throughout the literature of Weimar – is a crisis of humanist thought.

The crisis of humanism and its objects

The rather startling image of Mies van der Rohe's 1922 skyscraper project reveals two basic architectural strategies that diverge from conventional compositional methods. One is a

Figure 1 Georg Grosz, Friedrichstrasse,
from *Ecce Homo*, 1923. Malik-Verlag Berlin,
Ausgabe C. The Department of Rare Books
and Special Collections, The University of
Michigan Library.

building surface qualified no longer by patterns of shadow on an opaque material, but by the reflections and refractions of light by glass. The other is a building form conceived not in terms of separate, articulated masses related to one another by a geometrically derived core, but as a complex unitary volume that does not permit itself to be read as emanating from an internal formal logic. With these two related propositions Mies puts into crisis the cognitive status of the humanist object and the corresponding conception of the viewing or creating subject as an ideal, unified, centered self, unencumbered in its contemplation of the abstract unity of the object that was to be both an inducement to and a metaphor for a position of transcendence.

Against the autonomous formal object of humanism – in which the viewer can grasp in purely mental space an antecedent logic, deciphering the relationships between its parts and connecting every part to a coherent formal theme – the alternative posited by Mies is an object intractable to decoding by an analysis of what is only immanent and apparent. The glass curtain wall – alternately transparent, reflective, or refractive depending on light conditions and viewing positions – absorbs, mirrors, or distorts the immediate, constantly changing images of city life and foregrounds the context as a physical and conceptual frame for the building. (Compare the drawing of the Friedrichstrasse by Georg Grosz [figure 1].) The convex, faceted surfaces are perceptually contorted by the invasion of circumstantial images, while the reflection each concavity receives on its surface is that of its own shadow, creating gaps, which exacerbate the disarray.

These surface distortions accompany and accentuate the formal inscrutability of the volumetric configuration. It is impossible, for example, to reduce the whole to a number of constituent parts related by some internal armature or transformed through some formal operation; indeed, no such compositional relationships exist. Neither is it possible to explicate the object as a deflection from some formal type; Mies has rejected the meanings that such classical design methods tend to promote. The very body of the building contorts to assume the form demanded by the contingent configuration of the site and to register the circumstantial images of the context. Mies thus invests meaning in a sense of surface and volume that the building assumes in a particular time and place, in a contextually qualified moment, continuous with and dependent upon the world in which the viewer actually moves. This sense of surface, severed from the prior knowledge of an internal order or a unifying logic that is characteristic of humanist architecture, is enough to wrench the building from the atemporal, idealized realm of autonomous form and install it in a specific situation in the real world of experienced time, open to all the chance and uncertainty of life in the metropolis.

Mies here exemplifies a central strategy of anti-humanist thought: against the a priori categories of rational understanding, in which the mind is supposed to have a preformed and permanent structure that parcels out the objects of experience, it is now the temporal, historically developed, and irrational structure of society that is determinant. Adorno – rewriting Marx's dictum that philosophy is not a 'matter of logic' (*Sache der Logik*), but the 'logic of the matter' (*Logik der Sache*) – puts the point succinctly: 'The fetish character of commodities [the reality of the metropolis] is not a fact of consciousness, but dialectic in the eminent sense that it produces consciousness.'[4] And if our reading of Mies' project is thus far largely phenomenological, it is that very phenomenological reality of the metropolis that throws humanist conceptions of the subject into question, even as it is the vestiges

117

K. Michael Hays

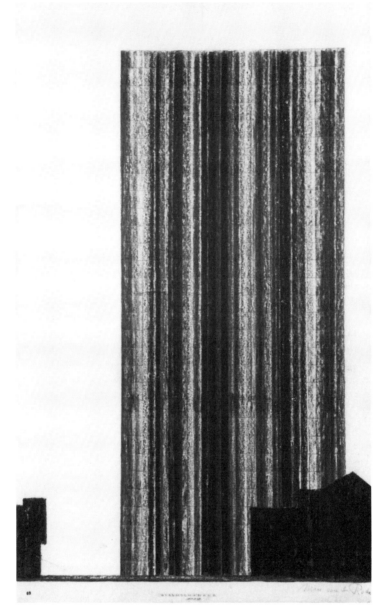

Figure 2 Ludwig Mies van der Rohe, *Glass
Skyscraper Project*, 1922. Elevation (schematic
view). Charcoal, brown chalk, crayon on brown
paper, 54½ × 32¾ in. Collection Mies Van der
Rohe Archive, The Museum of Modern Art,
New York. Gift of Ludwig Mies van der Rohe.

of humanist thought that allow the reality to be gauged as unsatisfactory. The avant-garde thus dramatizes in its very internal structures a crucial contradiction in the ideology of the subject, the force of which we can appreciate rather concisely in this example of Mies' project.

The project attests to the fact that the humanist conceptions of formal rationality, 'obvious' intelligibility, and self-creating subjectivity cannot cope with the irrationality of actual experience. In the modern city, such constructs fail to function, and the mind, the subject, is consequently unable to perceive a pattern in the chaos. At such a moment, the subject has its one opportunity to escape reification: by thinking through what it is that *causes* reality to appear to be only a collection of fragmented images, by looking for structures and processes operating in time behind what appears to be given and objectified. Crisis, in short, is converted into critical mediation between various levels of form and its social context.[5] And the other aspect of Mies' skyscraper – the black, silent elevational drawing (figure 2) – attempts to negate the status quo, asserting itself as a radically different, subversive object within an unsatisfactory social and physical fabric.[6]

The turn to the objective effects of capitalism, to its structures and processes understood as (over)determinants of form, and to the construction of some kind of causality among the levels of everyday social experience, new modes and materials of production, and architectural form: this is the similarity between Mies' 1922 skyscraper project (figure 3) and Hilberseimer's Chicago Tribune project of the same year (figure 4). The distinction between them is the different terms in which these mutual relationships are grasped – the difference between the *displacement* and criticism of the social subtext by form, as is the case with Mies, and the *absorption* or envelopment of this subtext into form, as is the case with Hilberseimer. A definite epistemological shift separates the two, and it is this shift and its consequences for the conceptualization of the subject that will concern us here. For I believe, and will try to argue, that the shift is nothing less than the beginning of an era of *post*-signification. By this term I mean not only the abolition of architecture as a communicative action or representational practice, not only the evacuation of significations and subjectifications, but also the negation of all dimensions of critique and conscious resistance available to architectural practice – a condition, I would assert incidentally and polemically, of which we are the heirs.

Mies' skyscraper is a sign still laden with meaning – projective, referential, intrusive – in a negative dialogue with the context of its production, one that is sustained at many levels. Hilberseimer's project, on the other hand, begins not with some notion of context or situation to which it is a critical response, but rather with a technical principle dissimulated as an architectural configuration. The technical principle is cellular reproduction. As hypothesized by Hilberseimer, modern building production requires that each building unit – each structural and spatial cell – be identical to all others, not in a linear series, but in a multi-dimensional matrix of repetitive cells. The reproducible elements at the molecular level translate and relay information received from the global structure of the city, even as these same elements are, in turn, the prime constitutive units of that structure. The abolition of the gap between the homeostatic urban order and the individual cell eliminates the possibility of attributing significance to the act of selecting or arranging forms.

Perhaps the collapse of this gap between the molecular and the molar reaches its ultimate form in Hilberseimer's *Hochhausstadt* project of 1924, in which there is an assimila-

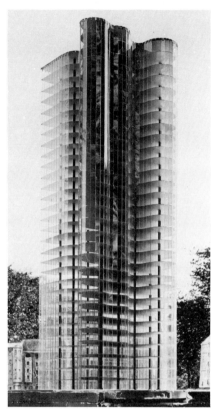

Figure 3 Ludwig Mies van der Rohe, *Glass Skyscraper Project*, 1922. Model no longer extant. Photograph courtesy Mies van der Rohe Archive, The Museum of Modern Art, New York.

Figure 4 Ludwig Hilberseimer, perspective rendering of entry for Chicago Tribune competition, 1922. Courtesy of The Art Institute of Chicago.

tion or absorption of all particularity in the raw material into the totalizing structure of the work itself, in which, in Hilberseimer's own words, 'the general case and the law are emphasized and made evident, while the exception is put aside, the nuance canceled.'[7] The auratic architectural object is systematically and utterly defeated by techniques of reproduction now radically rationalized and expanded. And the subject's conscious experience of interpretation (which used to correspond to its ability to contemplate, reason, and reflect) becomes little more than a process of witnessing the extension of a code, tracing the external network of socioeconomic and historical circumstances that determine and manipulate the subject.

But it must be insisted that this architecture does not really represent the technical, social, or economic conditions that produced it. On the contrary, Hilberseimer's architecture effectively truncates the complex network of colliding forces in which architecture originates to present us with a self-generating model that obeys only its own logic. It conceals the real origins and stories of a building's formation with an erased record, a kind of materiality that can communicate nothing detached from itself. And yet, *it can engender itself*. There are two towers, less a plastic manipulation of volume than a reduplication of the modular system, indefinitely repeated in ignorance of all circumstance. As Jean Baudrillard has written, 'For the sign to be pure, it has to duplicate itself: it is the duplication of the sign which destroys meaning.'[8] What is at issue here, then, is not the exchange of one image of reality for another, as is the case with Mies' project, but of substituting signs of the real for the real itself. 'So it is with simulation, insofar as it is opposed to representation,' writes Baudrillard. 'Simulation starts from the *utopia* of this principle of equivalence [of the sign and the real], *from the radical negation of the sign as value*, from the sign as reversion and death sentence of every reference.'[9]

Now this is all very close, as I have been trying to make it out, to what Baudrillard characterizes as the passage from representational objects to the 'hyperreality' of our present.[10] And perhaps a case could be made for reading Hilberseimer not as a paragon of modernism, but rather as an anticipation of that later and quite different thing we have come to call 'simulationism' or postmodernism. But I want to argue, to the contrary, for the historical specificity of Hilberseimer's transformation. Hilberseimer's architecture, I will try to show, can be conceived only as a production of, and a response to, the very particular conditions of the Weimar Republic. I want to argue that, having first recognized the determining conditions for a certain historically specific type of subjectivity, which I have broached here as a radical and potentially critical kind of anti-humanism, Hilberseimer's modernism itself increasingly hollowed out such subjectivity and rendered its articulation as a critical agency highly problematic.[11]

Analysis of the texts

I shall pursue my topic by turning now to an analysis of the writings of Hilberseimer, published for the most part before 1919 in *Der Einzige*, a journal edited by admirers of the nineteenth-century German anarcho-individualist Max Stirner and his follower (in their opinion) Friedrich Nietzsche,[12] and between 1920–24, for the *Sozialistiche Monatshefte*, a paper for which Hilberseimer was the art critic. Hilberseimer's articles elaborate Nietzsche's *The Birth of Tragedy* in terms of the epistemological status of art, the notion of the artist as a prophetic leader, and the concept of chaos as the constitutive condition of the

121

eternal return, and assimilate these ideas to Alois Reigl's assertion that the art of all cultures is measured by their *Kunstwollen*. The conjunction of Nietzsche and Riegl will
become key in Hilberseimer's 'total solution'.

There are several stresses found in Hilberseimer's theoretical and critical writings worth
distinguishing here. First, it should be noted that artistic creation is not conceived as a for-
mative power (as a development from craft and artisanry, or *techné*), or as a demiurgic production (an imposition of form by an individual force), but rather as prophetic intuition.
Art is ascribed not so much to a faculty – classically conceived and destined to a signifying
identification and function – as to compulsion, desire, and will. The point is the
Nietzschean one that both art and science are *together* illusory, that both are involved with
the production of images of the world, 'appearances' as Nietzsche called them, and that the
know-how *(Können)* characteristic of science leads us into the worst kind of self-blinded
illusion, an illusion that does not know itself to be one. This is important because it already
opens the way to a challenge both of a humanist conception of artistic creation and the
hubris of conventional bourgeois science into which much of the *neue sachlichkeit* fell.

The second point to be stressed is what is seemingly a contradictory formulation of the
structure of aesthetic totalization. According to Hilberseimer, at the present, when individual experience has been riven from the collective reality, artistic practice is left to straddle
the cleft; the modern artist must mediate between the objective world and its subjectively
comprehensible forms. Hilberseimer celebrates Nietzsche's Dionysian creative subject –
unschooled, unrestrained, naive, natural – as that which represents the original ground
(Urgrund) of reality, a primitive and non-contingent substratum of being. The artistic
subject reveals the contours of this reality, configures it in an art of invariant meaning,
spontaneously and subconsciously created, a 'magical banishment,' 'above time,' 'incapable
of development,' and antithetical to the art of the Apollonian self-consciousness.[13]
Hilberseimer's aesthetic and epistemological formulations thus set forth, on the one hand,
an ideal of relatively unrestrained contact with genuine experience or total content and its
passage through the creative subject into concrete form, presumably guaranteed by an
explicit bracketing of such encircling determinants as material, mode, technique, various
historical contexts, and the discursiveness of ordinary practice. 'The creator, then, is intuitive; free from law… And all science and knowledge, etc., cannot replace this naive security of creation.'[14]

On the other hand, Hilberseimer calls into question the individual freedom of artistic
creation and, more significantly, the very notion of the antithesis between reality and its
representation. He understands Riegl's concept of *Kunstwollen* as a complex and mediated
relationship between subject and object, a 'creative struggle' between artistic will and
material conditions, that allows itself to be understood historically as a special kind of
vision, dominant in a particular epoch. Hilberseimer summarized Riegl's analysis with an
often repeated aphorism: 'An artwork is a condition of tension brought to harmony.'[15] The
form and the material conditions of the artwork will not be in any easy balance; still less
will the material conditions have determined the form.[16] On the contrary, the autonomy of
the *Kunstwollen* assures that its formal demands will be fulfilled even in contradiction of
material conditions. Riegl's *Kunstwollen*, for Hilberseimer at least, is at once a reaction
against positivist science and a profound totalization and determinism. And as such, it is a
refusal of humanism's celebration of free consciousness, of artistic expression as an activity

Figure 5 Ludwig Hilberseimer, 1885-1967,
'Hochhausstadt' (high rise city), north/south
street, perspective view, 1924; ink
and watercolour on paper, 97 × 140cm.
The Hilberseimer Collection, gift of
George E. Danforth. Courtesy of The Art
Institute of Chicago.

controlled by an individuated, univocal subject.

But I must return to this later. For now it is enough to point to this second stress, and to a third: that for Hilberseimer, the condition for artistic practice endemic to modernism is a crisis of legitimation experienced primarily as a loss or breakdown of figurability. Artistic technique has been threatened from inside by virtuosity and detached academicism. Neoplasticism, suprematism, and cubism have guided abstract art to the point of total annihilation of the material and to extreme formal concentration. Hilberseimer called this the 'zero point of art.'[17] And art has been threatened from outside by industrialized technology and the specializations of science, with the results that the adequation of form to content – and both to their essential 'oneness' – is no longer possible. 'Our age is necessarily problematic. Perfection would appear now as hypocritical, just as comfortable methods neglect to admit of the abyss *(Abgrunde)*.'[18] The properties that distinguish artistic discourse as a primal compulsion no longer seem to inhere in that discourse itself. And the human subject is constrained by systems it may have produced, but in any case cannot seem to control. Meanwhile, 'chaos surrounds us, unformed, but certain to push into form,'[19] 'chaos, the attendant of civilization that brings all manner of frustration to formation *(Bildung)*.'[20] Again, what is important in this articulation of the inability of a culture to give form to its world is the recognition that the loss of signification, experienced as crisis, is the loss of the paternal fiction of humanist thought, of classical art's heritage and guarantee.

I should like now to try to situate Hilberseimer's essays more precisely in a discourse in which art's various moments are articulated according to the various possible relationships between subject and object, to pitch the logic of his argument toward some of the specific artistic practices with which he, in his writings between 1919-24, concerned himself, and ultimately to consider his conception of the synthesis of the primitive moment of completion against which all these practices are evaluated.

Expressionism and the agonistic subject

A preliminary indication of the shadings of Hilberseimer's conceptualization of what he called 'the primitive' and its relation to a utopian future is afforded by an consideration of his dissent from the romantic-expressionist pronouncements of the *Arbeitsrat für Kunst*. According to Hilberseimer, expressionist art is the attempt in modernity to recapture some of the quality of a lost primitive past – the reconciliation between matter and spirit, between daily life and life's essence. But its promise of a future of reconciliation and happiness, a utopian alternative to the perception of a degraded social existence, was bound up with its romantic retention of previous instances of joy and fulfillment, recoverable through some notion of *anamnesis*, 'a conscious inclination toward the past,' as Hilberseimer put it. The formal activities of the expressionists project their desire for a reconciled community of man into a psychic space that is not so different from that of the present save for the eruption of particular desired objects or effects presently lacking – curved lines, crafted details, and continuous metamorphoses of light and colors. The fantasies of the freed individual psyche maintain faith in a moralized and mythicized future where the most unhappy attribute of the present, alienation, has disappeared. But the nostalgia for past totalities, the welling up of subjective feeling and protest against the objective universe that threatens to crush the individual, along with the provincialism of the present, 'the unshakable belief in one's own face'[21] – all these expressionist tendencies effectively block the possibility of any genuine opening onto the future, of imagining a future that might be constitutionally *other* than the actual present. Expressionism's vision of the uncoerced self is generated by a thoroughly despairing understanding of the possibilities of historical life. Its hope is placed rather in the myth of absolute presence, the notion that being is a kind of plenum in which there exists a plenitude similar to past societies and that for this reason something like a substantial and meaningful present is ontologically possible even though actually unachievable. The expressionist anxiety before the future ends up, paradoxically, by glorifying both past and future and hypostatizing the present.

So it is that Hilberseimer here identifies expressionism's Platonic side (for the most tenacious version of the myth of an absolute presence is the Platonic doctrine of memory as a return to lost sources of plenitude before birth). 'Thus primitivism, exoticism, and infantilism arose within Expressionism... All these intentions that link themselves to the past are but attempts to substitute an intellectual rapport with the past for the *lost tradition*.'[22] But more important, it is here that Hilberseimer counters the Platonic doctrine of *memory as a return to significant objects* with the Nietzschean imperative of *chaos as the production of significant appearances*. Hilberseimer continues, 'But [this return to the primitive] is far from a return to nature. Expressed in all these aspirations is the search for the law that the art of the past manifests in almost all of its works. But every link to the past is destined to lead to eclecticism. The true [primitive] work of art will always be born *only from the chaos of time*. Only in this way can its image take on sense.'[23]

Dadaism and the dispersed subject

Hilberseimer's early contact with the disquietude of the radical art circles of Berlin gives specificity to his understanding of possible new sensibilities springing not from a false sense of the fullness of the past, but from the chaos of the present. Hilberseimer was associated with the Berlin Dadaists, such as Hans Richter, Hannah Höch, Raoul Hausmann throughout the teens and twenties. In his essay 'Dadaismus' of 1920, his characterization of that movement is put concisely in terms of subjectivity and Dadaism's adversarial relationship with bourgeois culture: '[In Dadaism] the ancient feelings of security are dissolved and replaced by an animated world, by restlessness, by excitement. *The I, now set free from meaningless bonds, flows freely into the cosmos.* Dada destroys the idols of culture and scorns the serious tedium of art.'[24] For Hilberseimer, Dada fulfilled the contestatory obligation of art to resist the security of habit and explode the nostalgias for a reconciliation between subject and object no longer possible, while maintaining a 'primitive' will to form.

Dada demonstrated that artistic production in society has an inescapable relationship with those mass-cultural formations that govern collective perception. For Dada the human subject (to put it in Althusserian language) is structured like a mode of production, and as such cannot be the centered subject of bourgeois epistemology and aesthetics, but is instead precisely decentered to the degree that it is the bearer of different and often contradictory structures.

Hilberseimer understood this, but it must be underscored here that the critical dissonance, shock, and '*Wahrheitsfanatismus*' of Dadaist activities, and the concomitant assault on the human center as the origin of sense, are interpreted by Hilberseimer as directed

125

toward a possible future. In speaking of Dadaism, Hilberseimer evokes Nietzsche's lesson of a world 'where we will be able to be original, something like parodists of the history of the world and God's clowns; to the point where, perhaps, our laughter possesses a future, out of the so many things belonging to the present time that are condemned to oblivion.'[25] If one cannot refute the experience of chaos, one can nevertheless mediate it, transforming it into that positive anticipation, which is its correlative. Indeed, artistic practice, for Hilberseimer, just *is* such mediation. Hilberseimer wishes to locate the positive within the negative itself: to grasp that the negative may serve as a means of access to the positive, and that chaos is the constitutive condition of a new order. The lacerating ambiguity of Hilberseimer's position follows from his wish to preserve the chaos-negating power of spiritual intuition at the level of the individual human agent without collapsing into either mysticism or individualism; and this crossed by his equally intense insistence that the content of that intuition is immanent in the very chaos of the world.

Hilberseimer's posthumanist subject

And so we can now say with some precision that the concept of the subject that emerges in Hilberseimer's account of expressionism, Dadaism, and other artistic practices by which he was surrounded is a subject that can be fitted into both a vision of effective human agency and some more radical notion of a subjectivity dispersed into the realms of industrialization, standardization, mass production, and consumption. That is, Hilberseimer understands the subject of modernism as *at once* the particular constitution of knowledge, history, and discourse in a historically specific and individual human agent, *and* the no less circumstantially dense plurality of forces that has passed from both an arrogant bourgeois humanism and the expressionist sentimentalization of individual distress to a new postindividualist framework. The subject as seen by Hilberseimer is continually called upon (interpellated) to take multiple and contradictory subject-positions, yet it is capable of binding these positions together into 'a new order springing from chaos.' 'The I, now set free from meaningless bonds, 'flows freely into the cosmos',' a dispersed subject, linked to reality but by only a thin thread, and destined to resolve itself in a superior if vaguely articulated consciousness, for which the signs are already given.

The psychic split perceived by Hilberseimer is, as we now know, the very condition of subjectivity under capitalism. The lived experience of individual consciousness as fragmented, compartmentalized, and reified, coupled with the hope of a more radical or utopian agency of mediation and colligation is not just some glitch in our conceptualization of subjectivity that can be resolved either by reasserting a notion of individuality as a monadic and autonomous center of activity and freedom or by voiding the category of the subject altogether. Rather the articulation of such an experience and such a hope conveys the precise and concrete historical situation in which the very emergence of the posthumanist subject can be understood. For if Hilberseimer's writings often attempt to sound timeless and universally valid, his theoretical position can be conceived only as a production of the very particular *Stimmung* of the Weimar Republic. Hilberseimer's ambivalence toward the metropolis – the sense of a disenchanted euphoria, the mood comprising almost equal parts of anxiety and elation, which finds its object in Berlin – is just the ambivalence of Weimar culture, where modernity and negativity, higher consciousness and alienation, sobriety and unhappiness, authenticity and depthlessness, become almost inseparable.[26]

It is at this point, then, that I wish to return to my earlier assertion that Hilberseimer's conceptualization of architectural practice turns on the deliberate confrontation with the objective conditions of the everyday metropolitan experience in an effort to find material for the construction of a new consciousness that might replace a dysfunctional and discredited humanism, and to make a few summary points that concern that turn.

First of all, Hilberseimer makes it clear in his publication of *Groszstadtarchitektur* that advanced capitalism is at once the structural precondition of modernism, whose force blasts subject from object and recolonizes the fragments of each in terms of purely instrumental and functional categories (thus promoting the overdevelopment of science, know-how, and technique), and the proleptic basis for, if not a direct experience, then at least the figural projection of a future restructuring into a rationalized totality. Capitalism is itself the only force capable of organizing and harmonizing the dissonance and random concatenation of objects and events. Banality, triviality, and everydayness are now seen as the proper material for a 'higher' theory of architectural production. A rarefied and autonomous aesthetic is no longer possible in the modern city whether for pleasurable aloofness or for resistance, but instead a practice enmeshed in the everyday.

Second, the subject itself, to the extent of its relation with the structure of the everyday, cannot be thought of as autonomous. Objectively structured like a mode of production, the subject is not so much an abstraction as what Heidegger called a '*Neutrum*'. The character of the subject is given from the outside, and contradictorily. And thus it is, precisely, distracted. Nevertheless, for Hilberseimer, the artistic subject must still be the principal agency of mediation between the realm of production and the realm of form. His solution to the dilemma, then, is to totalize: As the *Kunstwollen* becomes a kind of field phenomenon, it appears to operate as a virtual subject, accountable to no one while seeming to account for everything, thus resolving the tension between the objective reality and some future utopia to arise from it. But the form of that utopia is, of course, already presignified as a possibility, as a possible category, by the objective reality of the present. Hilberseimer's totality is an affirmational tautology – a surrender of the subject to the very force that assures its dissolution.

Now I would like to suggest that this particular inscription of the subject I have been trying to articulate – a subject that is at once subjected to material forces and systems of signification beyond its control, and at the same time, capable of mediating or totalizing those external forces and systems within the internal logic of architectural form – this doubled subject is not constructed for nothing: it is an attempt to compensate for the loss of figurability that I have already mentioned, the loss of signification, the loss of the paternal fiction of humanist thought to the inauthenticity of mass culture. Without ever leaving the terrain of the architectural, Hilberseimer's total solution projects a whole structure and image of subject/object relations, a vehicle for our understanding and experience of an actual, concrete historical situation of everyday social life that is intolerable but inescapable. The vocation of architectural theory is thereby revealed as the exigency to produce that very image, that very *Stimmung*, that very referent – the matter-of-factness, the new 'intensified rhythms of life,'[27] the new ascetic, desacralized, and disenchanted objects, as well as the marked and expectant absence at the heart of the actual, perceptible spaces in this city – in short, to produce that very life world of intolerable ambiguity and contradiction of which theory can then claim to be the resolution and displacement. What society gives us as an existential reality – a firmly ensconced structure of reification – already binds us to inauthenticity. And yet, a difference can be made, though the difference must needs look much the same as the condition it opposes.[28]

1 This essay was written in the summer of 1988 as a lecture for the conference at the Chicago Institute for Architecture and Urbanism. It is part of a larger study now nearing completion that investigates the anti-humanism of Ludwig Hilberseimer and Hannes Meyer, and the more reluctant constructions of the modern subject in the works of Adolf Loos and Heinrich Tessenow. In that study, I have developed and modified much of what is presented here as only preliminary and partial. For other preliminary statements see my 'Reproduction and Negation: The Cognitive Project of the Avant Garde,' in *Architecture, Production, Reproduction*, ed. Beatriz Colomina, Joan Ockman, et al (New York, 1988); 'Tessenow's Architecture as National Allegory: Critique of Capitalism or Protofascism?' *Assemblage* 8 (1989) and *9H* 8 (1989).

2 L. Althusser, 'Ideology and Ideological State Apparatuses,' *Lenin and Philosophy*, tr. B. Brewster (New York, 1971), p. 175.

3 S. Kracauer, *Schriften 1* (Frankfurt, 1971), p. 13. I have used the translation of the passage by D. Frisby, *Fragments of Modernity* (Cambridge, 1986), p. 120.

4 T. Adorno, in a letter to Walter Benjamin of 1935, in Adorno, *Über Walter Benjamin* (Frankfurt, 1970), p. 112.

5 Here I intend to invoke an Althusserian understanding that architecture is not simply a free-floating object in its own right, nor does it reflect some base, context, or ground and simply replicate the latter ideologically, but rather that the object possesses some 'semi-autonomous' force in which it can also be seen as negating that context. I must gloss over some problems with my use of the Althusserian term 'mediation'. For a discussion, see F. Jameson, *The Political Unconscious* (Ithaca, 1981), pp. 23 ff.

6 Mies' radical engagement with irrationality and chaos, his framing of circumstance, at once anguished and exhilarated, perhaps begins and ends here. His later work emphasizes again and again its ambition to salvage the purity of high art from the encroachment of urbanization, massification, technological modernization, in short, of modern mass culture.

7 L. Hilberseimer, *Grosstadtarchitektur* (Stuttgart, 1922), p. 2.

8 J. Baudrillard, *Simulations* (New York, 1983), p. 136.

9 Ibid., p. 11. Emphasis in original.

10 'The description of this whole intimate universe [of objects] – projective, imaginary and symbolic – still corresponded to the object's status as mirror of the subject, and that in turn to the imaginary depths of the mirror and 'scene': there is a domestic scene, a scene of interiority, a private space-time (correlative, moreover, to a public space). The oppositions subject/object and public/private were still meaningful. This was the era of the discovery and exploration of daily life, this other scene emerging in the shadow of the historic scene, with the former receiving more and more symbolic investment as the latter was politically disinvested... But today the scene and mirror no longer exist; instead, there is a screen and network. In place of the reflexive transcendence of mirror and scene, there is a nonreflecting surface, an immanent surface where operations unfold – the smooth operational surface of communication.' J. Baudrillard, 'The Ecstacy of Communication,' *The Anti-Aesthetic*, ed. H. Foster (Port Townsend, 1983), pp. 126-127.

11 The pertinence of this type of study will be apparent, I think, at a time when one of the central questions of critical practice is how to relinquish the armored subjectivity modelled on bourgeois individualism *without* abandoning whatever notion of critical agency is needed, first to perceive and then to militate against very real and institutionalized forms of coercion. By focusing an analysis on the status of the subject as determined and situated by architecture, I further intend to suggest that the disciplinary function of the centered subject is itself a kind of imposition of blindness or obstruction of inquiry into the hidden institutional frameworks and ideological factors that determine any work and the conditions under which it is apprehended. This is the case most obviously in the work of critics who look to architecture only to fulfill their desire for plenitude and affirmation.

12 On Stirner and the journal see H. G. Helms, *Die Ideologie der anonymen Gesellschaft, Max Stirners' 'Einziger'* (Cologne, 1966). Hilberseimer's articles, all published in volume 1 (1919), were: 'Schöpfung und Entwicklung,' Jan. 19, p. 46; 'Umwertung in der Kunst,' Jan. 26, pp. 24-25; 'Form und Individuum,' Feb. 2, pp. 30-31; 'Der Naturalismus und das Primitive in der Kunst,' March 9, pp. 88-89; 'Kunst und Wissen,' March 30, pp. 127-128. In the analysis here I shall refer, for the most part, to the longer manuscript, c. 1922, also entitled 'Schöpfung und Entwicklung,' (Ludwig Karl Hilberseimer Archives, Art Institute of Chicago, ser. 8/3, box 1/10), which is also the source for many later articles. Translations are mine unless otherwise noted.

13 L. Hilberseimer, 'Schöpfung und Entwicklung,' MS, p. 9.

14 Ibid., p. 11.

15 Ibid., passim.

16 Hilberseimer is explicit about this latter point: 'The problem of the 'material functionality' of architecture is finally, as in primitive architecture, a problem of limited relevance.' 'Kirchenbauten in Eisenbeton,' *Zentralblatt der Bauverwaltung* XLVII: 42 (1927), pp. 533-542, quotation on 533.

17 L. Hilberseimer, 'Schöpfung und Entwicklung,' MS, passim.

18 Ibid., p. 41.

19 Ibid., p. 39.

20 Ibid., p. 2.

21 L. Hilberseimer, 'Anmerkungen zur neuen Kunst,' *Sammlung Gabrielson Göteburg 1922-23*, tr. M. Tafuri in 'USSR-Berlin 1922: From Populism to the 'Constructivist International,' in *Architecture Criticism Ideology*, ed. J. Ockman, et al (Princeton, 1985), pp. 179-183; my emphasis. Hilberseimer's notion of chaos as a constitutive condition for meaning cannot be overemphasized, for it occurs again and again in his criticisms, and is the hinge on which his concepts of artistic mediation and subjectivity turn.

22 Ibid.

23 Ibid.

24 L. Hilberseimer, 'Dadaismus,' *Sozialistische Monatshefte* 26: 25/26 (1920), p. 1120.

25 Ibid., p. 1121.

26 Beatriz Colomina, in her essay in the present volume, has shown that Loos' interior architecture is a particularly vivid demonstration – over and against the *Gesamtkunstwerk* of

Jugenstil with its optical illusion of individual existence – of subject-positions still available to architectural representation in the early 1920s. What we must now observe, however, is that that demonstration traces its norms, however accommodating or liberating, on a background of an economy still not fully industrialized and rationalized. The characteristic, typal objects and motives of Loosian *sachlichkeit* – leather goods and umbrellas, wood and marble paneling, oriental carpets, Kokoschkas, and all – still show traces of production by artisanal labor and distribution by an organization of small shopkeepers over store counters; the individual human origins of the typal objects of this period have not yet been completely erased. Moreover, Loos' subject-positions as described by his architecture retain the ideal of individualism, and are based on a present in which the bourgeoisie was still a rising and progressive class, the nuclear family still a viable structure, and the monadic subject still in possession of some degree of resistance to the complete penetration of commodification into the innermost depths of the psyche.

27 L. Hilberseimer, 'Dadaismus,' p. 1122.

28 In the chapter 'Anyone, or: The Most Real Subject of Modern Diffuse Cynicism,' of his extraordinary study of Weimar culture, Peter Sloterdijk uses Heidegger's concept of 'Anyone' to characterize the *Stimmung* of Wiemar in terms of the condition of subjectivity.

This period senses that reality is dominated by spooks, imitators, remote-controlled ego machines. Each person could be a double (*Wiedergänger*) instead of itself. But how can one recognize this? In whom can one still see whether it is 'it-self' or only Anyone? This question stimulates in existentialists deep cares about the important but impossible distinction between the genuine and the nongenuine, the authentic and the inauthentic, the articulated and the inarticulated, the decided and the undecided (which is simply 'as it is'). [Heidegger put it this way:]

'Everything looks as though it is genuinely understood, comprehended and said, but basically it is not, or it does not look as though it is, but basically it is.'
…The Other can initially be asserted only by simultaneously averring that it looks precisely like the One; seen from the outside, the 'authentic' does not distinguish itself from the 'inauthentic' in any way.

P. Sloterdijk, *Critique of Cynical Reason* (Minneapolis, 1987 [orig. German, 2 vols. Frankfurt, 1983]), p. 199.

Hence, the vestigial dimension of resistance, hope, and redemption found within Hilberseimer's ambivalence can be understood. For as long as ambivalence is at least still asserted as a fundamental feature of existence, the possibility of an 'other' dimension remains formally salvageable within the domains of anticipation.

Catherine Ingraham teaches in the
architecture department at the University
of Illinois in Chicago. She was a fellow at
CIAU from 1988-1990 and has published
and lectured widely on architecture and
architectural theory. She is working on a
book entitled *The Burdens of Linearity:
Architectural Constructions.*

The Burdens
of Linearity

Catherine Ingraham

I will be referring in this essay to three overworked and, for me, strangely intertwined pieces of writing, the first Claude Lévi-Strauss' 'A Writing Lesson,'[1] the second Jacques Derrida's commentary on that essay in 'The Violence of the Letter,'[2] and the third the first chapter of *The City of Tomorrow* by Le Corbusier.[3]

Derrida's critique of Lévi-Strauss' writing lesson is an exemplary Derridean commentary on the problem of writing and the limitations of structuralist analysis; and Le Corbusier's writings are in some respects exemplary modernist polemics. However, neither Lévi-Strauss, Derrida, nor Le Corbusier are exemplary in any sense that would allow me to connect them to each other in the way I have in mind. It is their idiosyncratic rather than exemplary quality that sets up the magnetic field between them: between the anthropologist philosopher architect. The specific points of contact that interest me here lie in the odd but I think significant preoccupation of all these authors with two things: the first, Le Corbusier's and Derrida's (and implicitly Lévi-Strauss') obsession with lines and linearity; the second, Le Corbusier's and Lévi-Strauss' (and implicitly Derrida's) curious encounters with 'beasts of burden' – specifically mules, and donkeys.

My plan to use 'lines' (what lines?) and 'beasts of burden' as linkage elements between three very different texts requires some explanation. These things, or beings, occupy fundamentally different orders – the inanimate versus the animate is only the most obvious. And yet both Lévi-Strauss and Le Corbusier, and in a different way Derrida, use the inscription (or failed inscription) of lines on the one hand, and the antics of beasts on the other, to speak analogically of nature, culture, rationality, ethnology, and metaphysics. Just as the donkey in *The City of Tomorrow* is a recurrent figure of classical resistance to modernity, of ornamental fruh-fruhness and dilatory historicism, so the mule in 'A Writing Lesson' induces a certain confusion and humiliation – a waywardness – that opens into a meditation on the origins of writing. Derrida's critique of Lévi-Strauss' essay remarks, in turn, on the curious paraphernalia of Lévi-Strauss' ethnographic journey into the Brazilian jungle, the (im)possibility of a 'path' (made by oxen, mules, and men), ruined lines of communication (fallen telegraph lines), and inscriptionality and violence.

I am reminded here of at least two other taxonomies where things radically different become things alike (if only through the contamination of proximity): Emerson's obsession in his famous essay 'Nature' with the phenomena of 'language, sleep, madness, dreams,

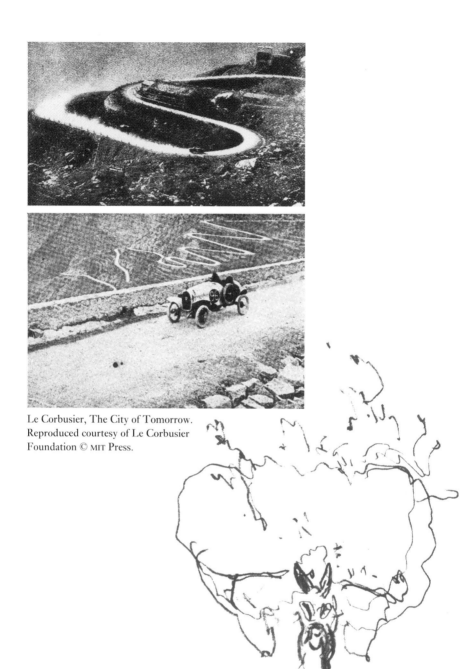

Le Corbusier, The City of Tomorrow.
Reproduced courtesy of Le Corbusier
Foundation © MIT Press.

Alvar Aalto, *Donkey*, Delphi, 1953.
Reproduced with permission of the Alvar
Aalto Foundation.

132

beasts [and] sex'[4] and Borges' 'Chinese Encyclopedia' cited by Foucault at the beginning of *The Order of Things* in which animals 'drawn with a very fine camel hair brush' are listed next to animals 'innumerable,' and animals 'belonging to the Emperor,' 'stray dogs,' 'et cetera.'[5] These lists (series) are provocative because they suggest, indeed remark exquisitely upon, the possibility/inevitability of everything being brought into relation with everything else – although this is, of course, both a wonderful and terrible dream. Taxonomies are neither endless or unfixed: an infinite number of relations are hypothetically possible, but only a few, very specific, connections are ever actually made. Taxonomies are only as persuasive as the institutional, cultural, linguistic, conventions that frame them – although here, especially in Borges, there is some kind of fragile interplay going on between taxonomic conventions themselves (alphabetic, numeric).

Thus when I propose to speak of lines and beasts in Derrida's, Lévi-Strauss', and Le Corbusier's texts, I should ideally clarify the framework from which I am speaking. I am not speaking out of a strict historical or scientific tradition – neither of which would put lines and beasts on the same list. Nor am I speaking from a strictly literary point of view, although both of the above examples (Borges, Emerson) are writers of literature. To be sure, the critical license granted by post-structural critical theory seems to permit one, in general, to conceive of homologous worlds where the lines made by certain beasts (in this case, mules and donkeys) on the landscape – the paths they make/follow, the direction they take, the marks/spoor they leave behind as they navigate the terrain, their willingness or stubbornness in all this – are intimately and significantly related to the lines (the marks) that one might draw or write or otherwise inscribe on paper and/or the lines and paths inscribed on a landscape by a building, more precisely, by architecture. But the authority/authorizing framework that governs my line/beast homology most pointedly is neither history nor science nor literary theory, but architecture, indeed, Le Corbusier himself.

In ways familiar to everyone, Le Corbusier disputes a certain genealogy of architecture by arguing that an orthogonal architecture (the 'orthogonal state of mind') best expresses the spirit of the modern age. Here the 'regulating line' (orthogonality, geometry, measurement) of humankind is opposed to what Le Corbusier calls the path of the pack-donkey.[6] This is interesting because it is the architect, in my triad of writers, who seems to mediate between the anthropologist and the philosopher of language by picking up one strand from each discipline – from philosophy a discourse about lines and rationality, from ethnology and anthropology a discourse about the paths of beasts and men – and intermingles them into a thesis about linearity, beastiality, and architecture. I am not subjecting Le Corbusier to a retrospective reading using texts that he would never (by historical reasoning) have read, much less appropriated. The only sense in which Le Corbusier might be said to mediate between Derrida and Lévi-Strauss is through the homologous relationship his text (and its mention of lines and beasts) bears to these other texts. I am interested in saying, on the one hand, that Le Corbusier, as an architect, was adept in the use of arguments from elsewhere,[7] and, on the other hand, that discussions about 'lines' and 'beasts' in Le Corbusier's texts are more ethnographic and philosophical than geometric or scientific, whatever he may claim. His bizarre connections between, for example, temples and cars, ocean liners and houses; his jerky assemblage of historical evidence and the infamous metaphor of the 'pack-donkey's way' versus 'man's way' in *The City of Tomorrow* argues for a style of architectural discourse and sensibility that treats the many parts of the world

Le Corbusier, The Contemporary City, detail.

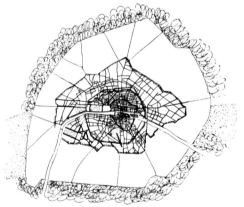

Le Corbusier, The City of Tomorrow.
The Six Successive Boundaries of Paris.
Reproduced courtesy of Le Corbusier
Foundation. © MIT Press.

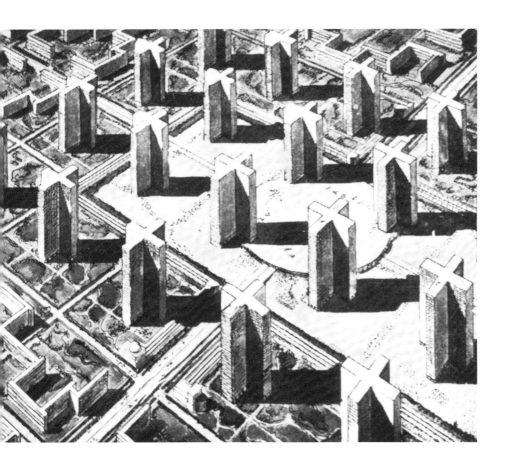

Catherine Ingraham

as structurally and morphologically related. This sensibility is aphoristic in its conclusions, witty in its appraisals, peripatetic in its assembly of source material (newspaper clippings, epigraphs, excerpts from poetry, philosophy, sociology, and so on) into a loose palimpsest of idiosyncratic polemics and typographical conceits. It is an oratorical discourse that is part of a long tradition in architectural thought (beginning perhaps with Vitruvius and ongoing with Aldo Rossi)[8] that takes the whole world as inhabitable by the architect. It is thus, most aptly, in architecture – inside an architectural discourse that is mediating between philosophy and ethnology – that lines and beasts can be said to have a shared life.

It is customary to compare, usually unfavorably, Le Corbusier's writing with his architecture. And, indeed, it is precisely this connection, among others, that I will be talking about, although not specifically with respect to Le Corbusier's projects. Certainly there is a difference between the writing and the architectural projects, but it is neither the simple difference between the themes of rectilinearity and curvilinearity nor the difference between the professions of writing and building. Le Corbusier was not the first or last architect to contradict his writing with his architecture (and vice versa), nor the first or last to oppose modernity to the 'barbarisms' (the beastialities) of the past. I use him, in a sense, because the line/beast connection he makes is so apparently connected to another line of inquiry of which he seems to have had no inkling – mainly the inquiry into the relation between writing and architecture. The writing and architecture connection, which are the general nodes of this essay, includes (but goes beyond) the problem of the book and the architectural project, the written text and the architectural text. Among other things, one might say that Le Corbusier's donkey gives a very specific, a very banal, shape and face to the outrages against the 'proper line' that architecture always seems to find and polemicize in its past.

Le Corbusier's remarks on the pack-donkey are easily recalled:

> Man walks in a straight line because he has a goal and knows where he is going; he has made up his mind to reach some particular place and he goes straight to it. The pack-donkey meanders along, meditates a little in his scatter-brained and distracted fashion, he zigzags in order to avoid the larger stones, or to ease the climb, or to gain a little shade; he takes the line of least resistance.[9]

Man thinks only of his goal. The pack-donkey thinks only of what will save him trouble. 'The Pack-Donkey's Way,' Le Corbusier goes on, 'is responsible for the plan of every continental city.'

According to Le Corbusier's mytho-poetical account of the history of architecture, covered wagons of an invading population 'lumbered along at the mercy of bumps and hollows, of rocks or mire [and] in this way were born roads and tracks.' These early tracks are made according to a donkey's idea of how to move from one point to another. Along these tracks houses are 'planted' and eventually these houses are enclosed by city walls and gates. 'Five centuries later another larger enclosure is built, and five centuries later still a third yet greater.'[10] The great cities, built according to this first track heedlessly traced out on an inhospitable landscape, have only capillaries, no arteries. In order to cure the problems of a city suffocated by these intersecting capillaries, Le Corbusier recommends surgery – cutting out central corridors in which the 'bodily fluids' of the cities can flow. The straight line that cuts through the congestion of the 'Pack-Donkey's Way' is, according to Le Corbusier, 'a positive deed, the result of self-mastery. It is sane and noble.'[11]

The pack-donkey recurs as a motif throughout *The City of Tomorrow* in an account of nature whose 'material' (beastly body) is chaotic but whose spirit (human rationality) is order; or again in an account of the human body as a 'fragmentary and arbitrary shape' but a pure and orderly idea; in an account of nations overcoming their 'animal existence'; in an account of the supremacy of orthogonality,[12] and so on. The pack-donkey is alternately the figure, in these architectural fables, of the chaotic and diseased body, the barbaric builder of antiquity, the maker of the 'ruinous, difficult and dangerous curve of animality,' the 'looseness and lack of concentration' of human beings in distraction, the disorderly material (debris) of nature and culture, the primitive. All of these things/forces threaten the triumph of geometry (and an architecture of geometry), of positive action, of overcoming (colonization), of sanity, nobility, and self-mastery.

The 'orthogonality' that Le Corbusier emphasizes in these parts of *The City of Tomorrow* does not refer simply to the rectilinearity that one finds in Le Corbusier's Unité d'Habitation, for example, although Le Corbusier remarks extensively on the 'rightness' of the right angle. The 'orthogonal state of mind,' which defines architecture for Le Corbusier,[13] governs *all* architectural thought and action that is devoted to self-mastery and the 'rational' line (which is not necessarily *straight* in a literal or graphic sense). Orthogonality is a theory about what it is proper for architecture to do,[14] and thus extends beyond the (merely) rectilinear to any form that is erected against the monstrous, speechless, wandering, pathless incoherence of the genealogical line itself, the history of architecture itself.[15] Orthogonality keeps culture hegemonically superior to nature and attempts to obliterate the trace of nature in culture. It is as operative in Le Corbusier's writing as in his architectural projects – indeed, one might say that it is operative in all architecture. The modulor – in its various contortionist positions but unfailing commitment to rectitude and measurement – is the Corbusian figure of this properness and it stands opposed to the misbehaving donkey.[16]

The resistance of the beast of burden to orthogonal thought (to the modulor) happens only when a proper path has already been laid out or imagined – as well as an economy and organization of labor, an (always already) human economy within which the beast is understood as a cultural, rather than a natural (or wild) entity. It is precisely the sense of the beast of burden as a measure of human work, transgression, and laziness that gives it currency in Le Corbusier's text. At the same time, the donkey possesses all the faults of an animal of 'nature' – indirection, slowness, enigmatic behavior, apparent mindlessness. The allegorical collapse of the donkey into the transgressive (human) body and, simultaneously, Le Corbusier's repeated surgeries, the *coup*, by which the animal body is separated from the mind and spirit in the modern city, reiterate an ancient nature/culture drama. Whether this drama is between two architectures – the orthogonal (proper) and the non-orthogonal (improper) – or between a 'natural' production (beast) and a 'cultural' production (line), its power is to forestall the collapse of the separatrix, the division between the proper and the improper, the cultural and the natural.[17] All the strategies by which we can separate a line (writing/drawing) on a piece of paper from a line (path, groove) made in the bush by a 'mindless' animal from a line (drawing/building) made by an act of architecture, are the strategies of Le Corbusier's polemic, and indeed, my own strategies of inquiry into the relation of writing and architecture. It might even be that the degree to which we can maintain/manipulate the separation between the categories of the line and the animal is the

Richard Fleischner, *Sudan Grass Maze – Maze
and Bluff* (executed in Rehoboth, Mass.), 1972.
500ft long × 7-8ft high. Sudan grass masked off
with masonite and plastic. From R. Lippard,
*Overlay Contemporary Art and the Art of
Prehistory* (New York, 1983).
Patricia Johanson, *Stephen Long*, 1968, acrylic
on plywood (red, yellow, and blue stripes)
2ft × 1,600ft × ½in.

degree to which architecture and writing remain apart from each other and different. And the degree to which that separation can be made problematic is the degree to which they are the same.

One might also say that all of Le Corbusier's (and my own) wanderings into fables, literary examples, word play, and so on is made possible through the bestiality (in Le Corbusier's sense) of writing itself – its writhings and wanderings, its refusal to remain tethered to the subject matter or to our intentions. The distinction between lines and beasts, writing and architecture, is always taken back, even as it is given, by the contaminating 'behaviors' of each side of the equation.

Le Corbusier's writing about architecture is itself a paragon of heedlessness, lack of self-mastery, lack of direction. There is, for example, a chapter in *Towards a New Architecture* that suggests to me a whole line of 'donkey readings' of Le Corbusier. It is entitled 'Eyes Which Do Not See,' with the subheading 'I Liners.'[18] Here, even as Le Corbusier is announcing the streamlined example of the ocean liner – its functional purity, its freedom from specious decoration and ornament – the language is slipping away from its taxonomic 'I: Liners' into 'Eye Liners', 'unhappy' eyes that cannot see because they have too much ornament, eyeliner, on them, or '*I* Liners,' a parody of the linings of the self and authorial identity.

But the modulor and the donkey of Le Corbusier's text is only half the story. The other half is the anthropologist and the mule. Genetically speaking, mules are the cross (point of intersection) of a horse mating with a donkey. The horse, through the discipline of dressage as well as lesser disciplines, is, at least mythologically, capable of being accurately directed by reins held in human hands. Mules, on the other hand, are bred for the strength and indirect guidance of the pack animal (who is frequently 'driven' rather than 'ridden'). Further, mules cannot reproduce their own kind and must be produced over and over again by the pairing between the two other species. The move from the donkey of Le Corbusier's text to the mule of Lévi-Strauss' text may seem slight (in genetic terms); indeed, it is very slight on one level. Both Le Corbusier and Lévi-Strauss use the movements of these animals as a counterpoint to another discourse about lines. As we have seen in Le Corbusier's text, this discourse on lines had to do with the 'straightness' (the properness) of modernity versus the 'crookedness' of architectural history. And yet, on another level, the move from the donkey to the mule is as drastic and as absolute as the move (left unstated in Le Corbusier) from the animal as a piece of nature to the animal as a piece of culture. Mules and donkeys, in this sense, are as different from each other as horses and cars. One reproduces. The other is produced. One of the differences between Le Corbusier's and Lévi-Strauss' texts – which I do not take up in any explicit detail here – might well be the character of the difference between things that reproduce (donkeys, humans) and things that are produced (mules, lines), although not in the way one thinks.[19]

I believe the writing/architecture connection – which, as we know, has been under discussion in one form or another since at least the Renaissance[20] – is so intimate, so isomorphic, that under normal circumstances we cannot see it and resist/argue it. The various historical instances where architecture has been connected to writing always seem to express a desire, on the one hand, for some sort of special interchange between these artistic kingdoms and, on the other hand, complete autonomy from each other. In a banal sense, architects traditionally 'write', but would rarely be considered 'writers'. Writers, on the

From R. Lippard, *Overlay Contemporary Art
and the Art of Prehistory* (New York, 1983).

other hand, certainly build narrative structures, but what they build would never be mistaken for architecture. However, the problem with a historical account of writing and architecture is that it stops at the level of inscriptional technique, whereas the sense of writing and architecture that I will be developing here goes beyond, without leaving behind, this narrow space of inscription where writing and architecture seem to share little. The importance of Derrida at this point is that he gives us a way of thinking about writing/language that exposes a certain inescapable relationship of writing to spatiality and structure.[21] Whereas the word 'structure' can refer to any number of different structures (cultural, political, ethnographic, anthropological, linguistic) part of my argument will be to suggest that all of these structures are underwritten initially by some gesture, some move, that is more architectural than anything else.[22]

What both Le Corbusier's and Lévi-Strauss' essays suggest is that writing and architecture are both about lines and a specific kind of bestiality/animality – and that this is a special, particularly fruitful, way of troping them. As inscriptional techniques, they are about the making of a line and a path (temporal/spatial) and, as sign systems, they are simultaneously about the transgression of or wandering away from the line and the path. Mules and donkeys are thus paradigmatic animals whose legendary reputation for resisting the so-called 'rational' human desire to progress makes them curious analogues for the way in which writing and architecture both resist and bear the burdens of linearity.

I should say at this point, however, that when I use the words 'writing' and 'architecture' I am speaking, as usual, very broadly. For the moment anyway, as I mentioned above, I am standing between the two senses of writing that Derrida articulates (writing-as-inscription and writing-as-originary violence), and I use this model to also suspend architecture between a narrow inscriptional sense and 'architectural thinking,' although I realize that the grammatological model is among the most problematic for architecture. The fact that I am using the Derridean formulation of this problem – of writing and architecture as having both an inscriptional sense and a 'more ancient' sense – raises serious problems in the application of a linguistic model to architecture and the architectural language. But this connection is also one of the connections being tested here. I am using the term 'linearity' to describe the temporal/spatial moment, common to both writing and architecture, in which something (a line, a path) unfolds according to a certain line of thought, a certain genealogy, a certain enclosure or corridor, a certain physical marking, psychic marking, and so on. The deviation from the linear into the network or rhizome, the meandering, drifting of the barely harnessed pack animal, upsets 'linear thinking' and subsequently the inscription of the line. For Le Corbusier, linearity is the way of the enlightened humanist/architect. For Lévi-Strauss, linearity is the path of the white (non-native) anthropologist through the forest. For Derrida, linearity is the end-project of western metaphysics.

Lévi-Strauss, like Le Corbusier and Derrida, is also concerned with reflecting on (and upsetting) a genealogy – in this case, the origin of writing. The line of descent that Lévi-Strauss claims for writing in 'A Writing Lesson' is, according to Derrida's subsequent critique, false in the sense that it fails to recognize its own ethnocentricity, its own love of ethnographic power. Derrida, in turn, disrupts this genealogy of writing, not in favor of a corrected point of origin (i.e., a linear beginning) for writing, but in favor of a genealogy whose path is bent around, a series of branching roots with no main root. Curiously Derrida seems to overlook the remarks that Lévi-Strauss makes on the relation of writing

d'après Contenau			D'après Morgan et Cooke		D
Carthage	Neo-punique	Grec archaïque	Nabatéen	Palmyrénien	

A. Kammerer, *Petra et la Nabatene*. Courtesy
of Librarie Orientaliste Paul Geuthner, Paris.

to architecture – remarks I will cite later. One should also bear in mind that all of Lévi-Strauss' remarks on writing are conditioned by (and what I mean by 'conditioned' is all important) adverse experiences he has with the mule that he rides into the Brazilian jungle. Derrida only notes this fact obliquely. Thus, in both Le Corbusier's and Lévi-Strauss'/Derrida's case, a certain genealogical line (of writing, of architecture) gets ruined, and the act of reflection on this ruined genealogy occurs in some kind of opposition to a recalcitrant beast of burden.

Now you may think I am speaking, like Le Corbusier, allegorically. But I am not merely telling an animal story in order to smuggle in a story about architecture and writing. What I would like to suggest is that it is not coincidental that Le Corbusier chooses to issue his accusations against classical and nineteenth-century architecture by refusing an architecture built according to the pack-donkey's way. Nor is it coincidental that Lévi-Strauss is forced to his musings about writing while riding a mule. It is not surprising that in the presence of animals (metaphorical, mythical or otherwise) we are forced to a consideration of our own animality – and thus to considerations of morality, rationality, order, civilization, and the primitive, which are, ostensibly, the larger philosophical concerns of Le Corbusier and Lévi-Strauss. At the same time, the banality of these particular animals (the donkey or mule), reduces these large concerns to the more pedestrian (perhaps more grotesque) status of local problems, such as how to find your way through the jungle, or how get an automobile up a hill. And these more local issues (for both Lévi-Strauss and Le Corbusier) become, primarily, issues of how to follow, draw, interpret, account for, *lines*. The donkey and the mule – and their various 'paths' and effects upon the humans that metaphorically or literally 'handle' them – come to bear the burden of the line and its local inscription in space (on paper, in the jungle, on the hillside). And these lines, isomorphic with the wanderings of the mythologized donkey and mule, start in the middle of things, aimlessly. Thus, these beasts act as fulcrums, or switching mechanisms, between the specific and the general, the point and the line, the beginning and the end. One might even say that the donkey and the mule lurk within all discourses that propose to analyze architecture and/or writing. They are the keepers and transgressors of inscriptionality.

But I should go back a bit and consider a few sections of 'A Writing Lesson.' At the beginning of Lévi-Strauss' essay, it appears that he and his fellow anthropologists cannot take the usual *picada* – the path in the forest – because the oxen carrying gifts for the natives cannot get through the heavy underbrush. The expedition is thus forced to take a route over the plateau, a route unfamiliar even to Lévi-Strauss' native guides, with the result that the whole expedition gets lost in the bush somewhere around the fifth paragraph of the account. After a crisis of authority having to do with the chief's inability to provide his people with direction and food, the Indians reorient themselves and the expedition pushes on to their rendezvous. Lévi-Strauss and his men effect their exchanges, count about seventy-five Indians gathered (since the purpose of his expedition in the first place was to take a census of the Indian population), and leave as quickly as possible. The situation directly after the exchange of goods is, as Lévi-Strauss remarks, always fraught with danger. However, it turns out that the danger for Lévi-Strauss does not lie in the latent violence of the natives but in the recalcitrance of his mule. Shortly after leaving the gathering Lévi-Strauss somehow finds himself and his mule alone and again lost in the jungle. He stops and gets off the mule in order to fire a shot for help, which in turn causes the mule to suddenly bolt. Lévi-Strauss spends the next several hours trying to catch him, but by the time he does, he has become more thoroughly lost. 'Demoralized by this episode,' Lévi-Strauss writes, he decides to rely on his mule to get him out of this predicament.

> Neither my mule nor I knew where they [the band] had gone… sometimes I would head him in a direction that he refused to take; sometimes I would let him lead, only to find that he was simply turning in a circle… I was not, admittedly, the first white man to penetrate that hostile zone. But none of my predecessors had come back alive and, quite apart from myself, my mule was a tempting prey for people who rarely have anything very much to get their teeth into.[23]

Fortunately, however, it seems that several of Lévi-Strauss' Indian guides had turned back as soon as they noticed his absence and had been following him all day (presumably because they found his wanderings amusing, or instructive). They now rescue him, lead him back to where he left his belongings at the foot of a tree, and together they rejoin the main party.

This episode is the central trauma of 'A Writing Lesson.' And it conditions Lévi-Strauss' reflections on something that happened earlier in the expedition. As the result of a sleepless night (caused by the 'torment' of getting lost), Lévi-Strauss thinks back on an episode with the chief of the tribe. During the transfer of gifts from whites to Indians, this chief pulled forth a piece of paper upon which he began to draw wavy lines (both paper and pencil were routinely given as gifts by the anthropologists). The chief pretends in front of his people to be the one who is authorizing the exchanges. He confers with Lévi-Strauss about each gift according to his 'false' list. Here, too, Lévi-Strauss in a sense gets lost in this 'false discourse' that does not correspond with anything that, for him, counts as writing, and has to be rescued by the chief's commentary, 'which was prompt in coming.' The wavy lines count as neither writing nor drawing for Lévi-Strauss.[24]

Reflecting on this episode the evening after his fiasco with the mule in the jungle, Lévi-Strauss concludes that the chief understood how writing works as a controlling mechanism without actually understanding how to write. He goes on to say:

> If we want to correlate the appearance of writing with certain other characteristics of civilization, we must look elsewhere. The one phenomenon which has invariably accompanied it is the formation of cities and empires: the integration into political systems, that is to say, of those individuals into a hierarchy of castes and classes. Such is, at any rate, the type of development which we find, from Egypt right across to China, at the moment when writing makes its debut; it seems to favour rather the exploitation than the enlightenment of mankind. This exploitation made it possible to assemble workpeople by the thousand and set them tasks that taxed them to the limits of their strength: to this, surely, we must attribute the beginnings of architecture as we know it.[25]

Now it is precisely the link between writing and architecture, tacked on to the end of this reflection about the origins of writing, which itself occurs as a kind of nightmare, or perturbation, as a result of Lévi-Strauss' episode with his mule, that interests me. For one thing, when Derrida radically 'corrects' Lévi-Strauss' perceptions of the relation between writing/violence/origins of culture, he apparently leaves the link with architecture untouched. If writing is pushed beyond its narrow inscriptional sense into 'arche-writing', one might well ask if architecture too gets pushed back from a narrow inscriptional sense into the 'more ancient' sense? One could also ask if this more ancient sense has something to do with the surreptitious (philological, homophonic) insinuation of architecture into the word 'arche' itself, or into the interstice, the hyphen that makes the arche-writing an always already divided place. For another thing, in some obvious way both writing and architecture rely on the making of lines and Lévi-Strauss' text is a continuous lament about how lines (paths, marks, inscriptions, writing, architecture, communication) are in the process of disintegration or loss. One might suggest that the surreptitious, productive, figure of connection between lines, architecture, and writing in Lévi-Strauss', and subsequently Derrida's text, is the recalcitrant mule.

I am not going to review Derrida's critique of Lévi-Strauss in detail, except to note a few points. Derrida does not refute Lévi-Strauss' claim that writing is connected to violence – he only resituates it. Lévi-Strauss' genealogy of writing is upset by Derrida's analysis, but this is not a classical upset that would relocate the origins of writing at some earlier historical period, at some different point in time. Instead Derrida's argument focuses on Lévi-Strauss' claim that there are cultures with writing and cultures without writing and that cultures without writing are somehow 'innocent', uncorrupted by the exploitation and violence that he (Lévi-Strauss) thinks writing inaugurates. Derrida's point is that all cultures, from their moment of inception, are violent in the sense that the inauguration of culture *per se* is an act of suppression (of the proper name). It is this 'originary violence' that Derrida calls the arche-writing.[26]

Derrida's critique centers primarily on how lost Lévi-Strauss is in his own ethnocentricity – too lost to see that his remarks on writing confirm his own uncrossable distance from the culture he is describing rather than the closeness (the 'fondness') he claims. 'Ethnocentricity,' in Derrida, is not only a cultural centricity, but also a blindness to how discourse structures observation in a certain direction. Lévi-Strauss is not unaware of this pitfall – indeed, he reminds us frequently in his writing about the mythology of his own investigation. And yet, in this story about Indians and writing, Lévi-Strauss does seem blind to the signs that his narrative – the many paths the story and the expedition takes – give him.

Derrida asks us to consider these paths in the following way:

> ...one should meditate on all of the following together: writing as the possibility of the road and of difference, the history of writing and the history of the road, of the rupture, of the *via rupta*, of the path that is broken, beaten, *fracta*, of the space of reversibility and of repetition traced by the opening, the divergence from, and the violent spacing, of nature, of the natural, savage forest. The *silva* is savage, the *via rupta* is written, discerned, and inscribed violently as difference, as form imposed on the *hyle*, in the forest, in wood as matter...[27]

I would add to this list of meditations a connection that seems implicit in them: the road, the way cut through (as either line or inscription in wood, or something even more faintly written) as the possibility of structure/architecture.

At the risk of reducing all of this to a graphic metaphor, I think one of the problems that Derrida articulates in this passage is our difficulty in reading or navigating the 'wavy' – the lines written by the donkey on the landscape, the mule in the forest, the chief in the village, or the twisted beginnings of language, self-identity, and culture. The failure to read wavy lines is not simply a technical failure but a metaphysical failure. Derrida remarks in a different section of *Of Grammatology* that the enigmatic model of the *line* is the very thing that philosophy could not see 'when it had its eyes open on the interior of its own history.' 'The end of linear writing,' Derrida continues, 'is indeed the end of the book, even if...it is

145

within the form of the book that new writings...allow themselves to be...encased.'[28] Writing 'without the line' and the death of the 'linear model' (delinearized temporality, pluri-dimensionality) describe, in effect, the post-structural universe.

'Writing as inscription' is not only the traditional sense of writing, but, until Derrida, it was the *only* sense of writing. By undoing (yet keeping) all the things associated with traditional writing (by undoing yet keeping the *line*, the inscription, the path) Derrida begins to 'unmask' the linear model and, in the process, unmasks the play of difference in language and culture. Architecture is, perhaps, unmasked at the same time, revealing in its innards the odd writings of donkeys and mules rather than modulors and anthropologists. Architecture approaches writing – writing approaches architecture – beyond their respective inscriptions (although their respective inscriptions are never fully transgressed), a landscape defined by the traces left by donkeys and mules, wayward and wavy lines, among other things/monsters. What is not so clear – and what is in the state of suspension and suggestion here – is how architecture builds itself in that beastial arche-space; and how the violence of spacing and architecture is thought before, or intimately related to, the violence of writing.

1 C. Lévi-Strauss, 'A Writing Lesson,' *Tristes Tropiques* (New York, 1972).
2 J. Derrida, 'The Violence of the Letter,' *Of Grammatology*, tr. G. C. Spivak (Baltimore, 1976).
3 Le Corbusier, *The City of Tomorrow*, tr. F. Etchells (Cambridge, 1982).
4 Cheyfitz, *The Transparent: Sexual Politics in the Language of Emerson* (Baltimore, 1981).
5 M. Foucault, *The Order of Things* (New York, 1973), p. xv.
6 Le Corbusier, *The City of Tomorrow*, p. 43.
7 This statement depends on another argument that I make in an article entitled 'The Faults of Architecture: Troping the Proper,' in *Assemblage* 7 (Fall 1988). Here I suggest that architecture historically depended on acts of metaphoric and metonymic (tropic) appropriation from other disciplinary languages. Architecture itself comes, then, from nowhere or elsewhere.
8 Aldo Rossi follows in this tradition because of his analogies between forms (coffee pots, buildings) and conceptual material. Unlike many of his predecessors, Rossi is alert to the failures of system in architecture. See especially *A Scientific Autobiography* (Cambridge, Mass., 1981).
9 Le Corbusier, *The City of Tomorrow*, p. 11.
10 Ibid., pp. 12-13.
11 Ibid., p. 18.
12 Ibid., pp. 41-43.
13 Ibid., p. 43.
14 'Orthogonality,' which means 'lying at right angles' or in a 'linear transformation,' is here broadened to include the related word 'orthographic,' which means the proper spelling of a word. This 'ortho-' state of the architectural mind is what interests Le Corbusier more than the right-angledness of architecture.
15 'Line' might be taken in a double sense here as both a line of descent from Greece and Rome, i.e., history, and a 'line' that Le Corbusier feels has been fed to the modern world by antiquated and irrational forces.
16 The modulor, as Hashim Sarkis pointed out to me, is a hybrid figure comprised of the module plus the 'or', i.e., the golden rule or the golden section. The golden state of measurement is won away from the bestiality of the donkey.

This brings to mind another donkey, mainly the gold-excreting donkey of Perrault's 'Peau d'An,' who is sacrificed for the sake of the princess. Here the donkey skin cloaks the princess, making her ugly, until her 'prince' comes along and sees the 'gold' beneath the skin. Louis Marin talks about this story as a fable of kingly power in L. Marin, *Portrait of the King* (Minneapolis).
17 See Jeffrey Kipnis' essay 'Twisting the Separatrix,' *AA Publications* (London, 1990). This remarkable essay, which discusses Peter Eisenman's and Jacques Derrida's collaboration on the La Villette park in Paris, articulates the power of the 'separatrix,' 'that divider whose ability to separate the inside from the outside establishes the solid ground upon which all the foundations of discourse rest.'
18 Le Corbusier, *Towards a New Architecture*, tr. F. Etchells (New York, 1986), p. 85.
19 This line of thought remains undeveloped in the subsequent pages, although it lurks beneath the different treatments of animals in each of these texts. Le Corbusier uses the pack-donkey as an allegorical figure (a figure of 'reproduction'), whereas Lévi-Strauss buys and sells pack animals for his expeditions (figures of 'production'). It would be too simplistic to align writing with reproducing and architecture with producing, or vice versa.
20 See especially M. Tafuri, *Theories and Histories of Architecture* (New York, 1980). In this seminal text, Tafuri situates the 'linguistic' in very early theories of architecture.
21 The arche-writing articulated in Derrida's essay 'The End of the Book and the Beginning of Writing,' in *Of Grammatology*, tr. G. C. Spivak (Baltimore, 1976) is a writing that is always already divided (deferring and differing), even if only by the 'time of a breath,' p. 180.
22 Here I am referring to what Derrida calls the 'force of the architectural metaphor in philosophy,' although I want to make larger claims for architecture than Derrida ever makes. I want to say that it is architecture that makes Derrida's so-called 'more ancient' sense of writing possible. Without architecture, and what Derrida calls 'architectural thinking' – which is either the possibility of diffusion through, inscription in, or closure of space – language and writing cannot inaugurate their violences. See E. Meyer,

'Interview with Derrida,' *Domus* 671 (1986), pp. 17-24.

23 C. Lévi-Strauss, *A Writing Lesson*, p. 290.

24 At another point in the narrative, Lévi-Strauss remarks that many of the Indians would draw wavy horizontal lines on the paper when given pencils and paper. This he claims is neither writing nor drawing (Ibid., p. 288). Lévi-Strauss goes on to say, 'The Nambikwara…do not know anything about design, if one excepts some geometric sketches on their *calabashes*…they imitated the only use that they had seen us make of our notebooks, namely writing, but without understanding its meaning or its end. They called the act of writing *iekariukedjutu*, namely 'drawing lines'.' Derrida notes this passage with surprise. 'It is,' he remarks, 'as if one said that such a language has no word designating writing – and that therefore those who practice it do not know how to write – just because they use a word meaning 'to scratch', 'to engrave', 'to scribble', 'to scrape', 'to incise', 'to trace', 'to imprint', etc. As if 'to write' in its metaphoric kernel, meant something else. Is not ethnocentrism always betrayed by the haste with which it is satisfied by certain translations…' J. Derrida, *Of Grammatology*, p. 123.

25 C. Lévi-Strauss, *Tristes Tropiques*, p. 292.

26 It is this point that compels Derrida to speak of writing in the narrow sense (inscriptional writing) and writing in the broad sense (arche-writing). Writing in the broad sense, however, depends for its force on writing in the narrow sense, since it is here that writing earns its reputation as something secondary to speech – a 'fallen secondary.'

27 J. Derrida, *Of Grammatology*, p. 108.

28 Ibid, p. 86.

Jeffrey Kipnis is an Assistant Professor
of Theory and Design in The Ohio State
University Department of Architecture and
a member of the Los Angeles design firm,
Shirdel and Kipnis. His publications include
*In the Manor of Nietzsche – aphorisms around
and about architecture* and *Choral Works:
The Eisenman/ Derrida collaboration.*

Forms of Irrationality [1]

Jeffrey Kipnis

I would like to begin with a mention of my design concerns, first, because I would be misrepresenting my work were I simply to discuss architectural theory as a scholarly endeavor that operated merely for its own sake. I do not believe that to be the case. In fact I believe that all architectural theories and histories always also operate, beneath their veil of objectivity and aside from their announced intent, in the service of a design agenda despite their frequent protestations to the contrary.

More importantly, though, I want to speak briefly about my design concerns because my work is from the outset motivated by the question of design, in particular, by design processes and by my attempt to move toward overcoming a sense of creeping intellectual and spiritual bankruptcy that I feel whenever I see and study much of the architecture of our times. In that sense, I am less interested in architectural discourse than I am in design.

Now, among those who more or less share this feeling of disappointment, there are many who believe that the situation is the result of external, economic, and political conditions that appropriate and trivialize architecture as it does art, literature and so forth. Perhaps that is the case, but if it is so, I believe it to be merely a proximate cause, as pneumonia is often the proximate cause of death in someone dying from lung cancer. These arguments neglect the question of the availability of architecture for appropriation, for trivialization through the mechanisms of fashion or commerce. I believe, rather, that the destitution of design is occurring from within, at what might be referred to as the level of design's metaphysic, if it is still possible today to employ that ancient term meaningfully. In other words, architecture is constitutionally unable to exceed the forces of appropriation and trivialization, which are therefore merely the symptoms, not the causes of the decline.

Let me make one point very clear. When I speak of disappointment in today's architecture, I do not by any means intend to suggest that I find it somehow incompetent or ugly. Quite to the contrary, much of it is beautiful and quite competent, occasionally even extraordinary. On its own terms it is therefore largely successful, whether from the hand of Charles Gwathmey, Hans Hollein, James Stirling or any of the other distinguished architects working today. This is a key issue, for from my point of view it is not because of architecture's failings that disappointment arises, but in spite of its successes.

The concept is easy enough to grasp. An example of an institution that is irrelevant and spiritually bankrupt, but which nevertheless is successful on its own terms, is to be found in today's British monarchy. Queen Elizabeth, Prince Charles, and their peers seem very human, very likeable, very attractive people who are genuinely concerned with acquitting themselves as responsibly and nobly as possible. Nevertheless, no amount of ingenuity, knowledge or skill exercised on their parts in presenting themselves to the world can eradicate the antiquated notion that royalty as such implies, the presumption of innate, genetic superiority, and right to power. Thus, though perhaps I can enjoy the appearance, the pomp, and circumstance of the British monarchy, I cannot quiet the uneasiness within me provoked by the untenable premises that found that institution.

Perhaps the situation with architecture is similar; one plausible speculation is that no matter how beautiful or skillful the architecture of today is, if it, like royalty, is founded on and disseminates archaic notions, then we can do nothing to stem the tide of its growing irrelevance. From this point of view, it may be no coincidence that Prince Charles is so deeply devoted to proselytizing a reactionary architecture, to keeping an irrelevant architecture in place.

Now, in this speculation, at least two possibilities exist. The first is that architecture is metaphysically complete and thus in its essence irretrievably irrelevant, a position argued, for example, by Hegel in his *Aesthetic*.[2] The concept of metaphysical completion is complex and beyond the scope of this talk. Suffice it so say that the implication of a metaphysically complete architecture would be that the process of discovery – particularly self-discovery – had gone as far as it could go in architecture. In other words, all individual and cultural themes that can be taken up in architecture have already been manifested. This would not mean the end of architecture, which would continue to creatively redeploy those themes, but it would mean that architecture could no longer be the primary scene of new themes, and thus relevant to the development of either culture or the individual.

On the other hand, it is possible that the waning significance of architectural design today is evidence of the operation of very powerful forces that nevertheless can be overcome, the position, for example, of Nietzsche as found explicitly in *Dawn*[3] and implicitly throughout his work.

Postulating and theorizing just such forces is the distinguishing characteristic of one of the major species of modern discourse whether by Marx, Nietzsche, Freud, Heidegger, Derrida or others. Irrespective of the significant differences among these, one theme in them remains constant: that disciplines can and do take for granted certain assumptions as self-evident postulates that ground all other work, and that these assumptions, which cannot sustain scrutiny, are the vector through which destituting forces operate.

Hence, one class of architectural speculation that seeks to confront the growing irrelevance of architecture – implicit in the work of Peter Eisenman, John Hejduk, and Daniel Libeskind – has argued over the last decade or two that despite the apparent diversity of styles, attitudes, and aesthetics that we see today, most architectural design continues to share a fundamental problem in the way it takes for granted what architecture 'is'. I would like to consider the thesis that there remain significant doctrines of architectural design that function as self-evident architectural truths but which are untenable and thus sources of intellectual and spiritual inadequacy.

If the vacuity of architectural design today is the result of such false groundings, then it becomes clear why criticism has been ineffective in the task of revitalizing the discipline. Were the problem to be, as is so often heard, a case of ignorance or insufficient skills or even a dearth of talent, criticism would be the appropriate medium for addressing the problem and stimulating its solutions. As I suggested, however, the evidence is that we live in a time when the intelligence, the knowledge, the skills, and the talents of architects are at a zenith. If, however, the problem lies in architecture's founding canons, then criticism is necessarily insufficient to the task inasmuch as it can only operate in respect of those canons. Therefore the probe into architecture's waning relevance must be conducted at a level deeper than criticism, that is, at the level of architectural design theory.

I often turn to what is termed 'popular culture' – television, movies, and so forth – but not as sources of images, say in the manner of Robert Venturi, but rather as material through which to analyze what might be called the metaphysics of everyday life. In other words, the truths, metaphysical assumptions, and self-evidencies that permeate popular culture are representative of those that operate in our culture as a whole. Thus, for example, in the television series 'Star Trek' the character Mr. Spock is the very incarnation of a traditional western view of man and his historical development. The Vulcan civilization of which Spock is a member is an advanced and highly evolved form of life that has conquered the emotions and become a population of pure reason. The antiquated and no longer accept-able notions of teleological perfection and the separation of mind and body nevertheless continue to operate uncritically in this television show and, by extension, throughout everyday life.

In this spirit, I would like to consider a moment from a wonderful science fiction movie from the late 1950s, *Forbidden Planet*. In the movie a scientific crew from earth ventures to another planet where they discover the still-functioning physical structures of an unimag-inably advanced civilization who, mysteriously, have completely disappeared. The first crew fails to maintain contact with earth, so, twenty years later, a second expedition is dis-patched to discover the fate of first. Upon arrival, they find that only two members of the original survive, a scientist and his daughter.

The leaders of the second expedition are naturally curious about the civilization and learn from the surviving scientist that the people were called the Krell, and they were the most intelligent and highly developed civilization ever to have existed. Now, when asked what the Krell looked like, the scientist responded that they never depicted themselves in their art nor did they write descriptions of themselves in their literature. 'Nevertheless,' he said, 'perhaps some clue can be derived from this characteristic arch' (figure 1). Obviously, the implication is of a somewhat midriff heavy creature.

As the movie proceeds we discover that, alas, the crowning achievement of the Krell was also the vehicle of their total destruction. Though possessed of virtually infinite intellectu-al power, the Krell nevertheless felt trapped by their bodies, which limited and inhibited their considerable possibilities of expression. So, they built the largest computer ever con-ceived, one which occupied a cube 50 miles on a side and consumed the power of a 1,000 stars. Abandoning their bodies, the Krell deposited their minds into this marvellous machine that could manifest any and every intention of each individual.

It turns out, unfortunately, that the Krell overlooked a fundamental flaw in their vision-ary enterprise. They forgot that when you deposit your mind into a machine, you deposit not only your intentional and intellectual ego, but also your id, a lapse, I am sure, that would have given Freud reason to pause. So, in what must have been one of the lustiest

Figure 1 'The characteristic arch' from
Forbidden Planet.

and most violent nights in the history of the universe, the Krells' individual ids, given unbridled power to express their aggressions and appetites, turned against one another, ultimately destroying the entire civilization in a single night.

Though there is much of interest here, let us consider only the scientist's theory of Krell architecture. Implicitly, he puts forward the following argument: because all human architecture, despite whatever other significations it may host, ultimately represents an idealized human body, therefore all architecture always represents an idealization of its occupant. I will take up this proposition in the general case in a moment, but let's first consider the validity of the scientist's analysis of Krell architecture in face of the empirical evidence at our disposal.

By the scientist's own testimony, the Krell never represented their body, idealized or otherwise, in their art or literature. Moreover, they were particularly obsessed with the limitations of their body; after all, they devoted all of their energy to constructing a fabulous machine expressly for the purpose of abandoning their corporal being. It therefore seems unlikely that this most advanced of all civilizations would unthinkingly produce an architecture that puts forward an attitude that is inconsistent with or even contradictory to the spirit evidenced in all of their other work. Rather, it seems more likely that they were keenly aware of the significations of architecture, which occurs beneath and beyond style, and no doubt took full advantage of those. Therefore no conclusion whatsoever about the body of the Krell can be drawn from the 'characteristic arch.' Moreover, it might even be speculated that the doorway was entirely unaccommodating to their body or for that matter possibly not a doorway at all. The scientist's 'theory' is plagued by anthropocentric projection.

Now, to consider the proposition that we found implicit in the erroneous interpretation of Krell architecture, let us recall and generalize its basic premise: all architecture, despite stylistic variation and aside from whatever other symbolic or signifying gestures it contains – all architecture ultimately represents an idealization of its occupant. As I am sure you recognize, this 'self-evident' principle not only permeates western culture in general, determining in large part its response to architecture, but is one of the fundamental assumptions implicit in architectural design theory from the Renaissance to the present. Not only is it evidenced in the Vitruvian Man and the Modulor for example, but it also underlies the assumptions of Marxist, empiricist, program-centered, social, behavioral, and perceptual/aesthetic theories.

Ultimately, one would want to consider whether or not this principle is necessarily true, whether this thought states an inevitable consequence of the unique relationship of architecture to habitation or merely an archaic assumption that retains its power in architecture uncritically. However, in this talk I merely want to consider those recent efforts in contemporary theory and design, which, in trying to come to grips with architecture's waning relevance, have turned their attention to this principle. In general, these efforts argue that the intellectual and spiritual insufficiency of design today grows out of this principle in the following way: since architecture always has and always will represent an idealization of its occupant, then contemporary design may be seen to be failing to respond to the fact that the idealized occupant of today is a very different being from the anthropocentric, egocentric, phallocentric idealization of 'man' that developed from the sixteenth through the mid-nineteenth century and that, this line of argument holds, continues to be represented

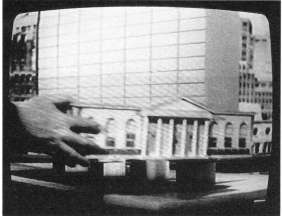

Figures 2, 3, 4 Old text, new veneer –
scenes from *The Fountainhead*.

in architecture today.

In this all-too-familiar view, the ideal occupant is an adult male. He will, at least teleo-logically, know himself univocally and comprehensively in terms of his rational and histor-ical representation of himself to himself – recall Mr. Spock. This idealization, which thrives on the criteria of the good, the true, and the beautiful, reached nearly perfect repre-sentation in modernist architecture. Is this why today's architecture is so disturbing, so dissatisfying? From this point of view, contemporary design is seen to persist in presenting to us an obsolete view of ourselves that we know and inescapably feel to be fundamentally inadequate. Yet postmodernist architecture, with its seductive appeal to fragments and a richer symbolic vocabulary, does nothing but provide a stylistic veneer to the same under-lying text (figures 2-4).

This, of course, is no great revelation. Theorists and architects have understood this for some time, and the thrust of their various projects has been to understand why this regres-sive condition prevails, despite the expressed intention to overcome it. As a consequence we have seen the development of a new respect for the emotional and cultural stakes that exist in architectural design and theory, which begin to consider why architectural design is one of those few realms where resistance to change is at its highest and therefore repres-sion in the Marxist, Freudian or Derridean sense is at its severest.

Much of the speculative work of the last two decades, though quite different in specifics, can be considered from this point of view as directed towards a more complete representa-tion in architecture of what we know today to be its occupant: a being/becoming who is at once infant, child, adolescent, and adult, who is at once male and female, who is at one and the same time rational and irrational, empirical and mystical. These theories and architec-tures hold ambivalence and multivocality to be not a weakness to overcome, but a strength to be valorized. They indulge in the unusual not for the sake of fashion, but in order to explore aspects of design and discourse that have always existed as a possibility but that we have never desired nor ever dared to face.

However, despite its argumentative power and its promise of new directions toward a meaningful and relevant architecture, certain problems arise in a theory of design founded on an effort to update the principle of the idealized occupant. I believe that it can be shown that all such efforts will contain internal, structural contradictions that cannot be eliminat-ed. Let us consider four of those problems.

First, such a theory remains a theory of the architectural object in the classical sense, from which definitions and analyses it derives the authority for its various design process-es. As such, it is a rational theory firmly within the traditional form of architectural theo-ries. In this form, a theory of architecture seeks to define the architectural object, to tell us what that object ideally 'is' (or 'really does'). Then, by implication, architectural design is the process by which an architect objectifies the ideal architectural object as defined, given the idiosyncratic constraints of any particular circumstance. In that way architectural theory always claims to precede and condition the design process. Perhaps modernist and postmodernist architectural theories are the cases par excellence in which an inadequate architecture was produced by the effort to reduce the design process to the production of a defined object.

The problem here is that categorical definitions of the architectural object are not mere-ly historically insufficient; they are necessarily and congenitally insufficient. Several issues are at work here; to point out but two, the incomprehensible numbers and qualities of relationships into which the architectural object enters makes impossible any definition of it. But more importantly, the architectural object is a metamorphic, though not historical, entity. One cannot define that object comprehensively, since internal to what it 'is' is its indeterminacy, its undecidability. This is not only true from object to object in time and space, but also of each object 'itself'.

The efforts of theory to take control of this undecidablilty, temporally under the name 'history,' inter-spatially under the name 'context' and intra-spatially under the name 'program,' fail, because history, context, and program flow from the object (both within an object and from object to object). As consequences of the architectural object, these concepts cannot therefore define it, though one can always correctly speak of the history, the program, and context of architecture in retrospect. In so doing, however, one is organizing one or another of the many texts conditioned by that object rather than observing any determining force acting upon it. Therefore no conclusion can be drawn from what is observed concerning what that object 'is'.

In theories of the idealized occupant, the architectural object, formerly and always insufficiently defined in any number of terms – aesthetics, program, type, context, political and social forces, etc. – is now redefined yet again, this time in terms of its representational qualities – its modes of meaning. Now, any theory of design that flows from the definition of the architectural object has in that definition a univocal, rational source of authority for architectural design processes. As I have outlined, this is a problem in itself, but it is even more conspicuously problematic when the theory functions in direct contradiction to its own stated goal – an architecture that embodies the conflicted ambivalence and multivocality intrinsic to its occupant. This goes to the very process of idealization, for no matter how thoroughly one thematizes the occupant, the result, as an idealization, will always remain within the phallogocentric conception of 'man' that the theory aspires to supersede. It does so at the very least in that it continues to valorize reason as able to comprehend the unreasonable – the accidental, the irrational, the mystical, and so forth.

Secondly, insofar as theory and design treats the idealization of the occupant as progressive, as moving from a prior, insufficient conception to a current, more elaborate one, those theories are inescapably teleological. Hence, they continue to treat the design process as a method of achieving solutions, albeit to evermore complex problems. As such, they remain implicitly devoted to a 'correct' architecture; though, because they propose to internalize the incorrect, they are no longer able to theorize 'the correct' as such.

Thirdly, theories in this form continue to respect the traditional terms of the relationship between architect and design object. In this relationship the architect, artist, and problem solver, is the source and sine qua non of the object, which itself remains merely the result, passively and completely determined by its creator. Yet, according to the very theorization of the occupant to which this work proposes to respond, this relationship is necessarily a mythology, an egocentrism of the most profound order.

Not only is this the case for all of the familiar analyses that have called into question the authority of the author over his or her work in general, but, in the case of architecture, additional factors disrupt and compromise this relationship. For example, if the architectural environment is truly one of the foremost scenes of resistance, of cultural and narcissistic investment, does this not imply that it is one of the foremost fields that contributes to the formation of the occupant's and therefore of the architect's sense of his or herself, a necessary consequence in both Freudian and Marxist thought? Can one think of the city, for example, without taking into consideration that to think as such already reflects the city, i.e., that the shape of thought is determined in part by the architectural milieu of the thinker? Are we not always already of the city before we are in the city, does not the city makes us as those who make it, before we make it?

This mythology has its most familiar and repressive consequence in the astonishing persistence of the false valorization of the intentions of the architect as the force which completely determines the content of the architectural object. Thus when Wittkower, for example, asserts in his work *Architectural Principles in the Age of Humanism*[4] that we should never read into architecture anything that was not intended by the architect, one is tempted merely to respond, 'why not?' But it is more important to note that it is not merely the morality of the principle under which such an invocation is made that is in question, but the assumption that underlies the principle itself.

The total content of the object is never determined by the architect's intentions. The genealogy of the architectural object, or of any object for that matter, does not determine its content, which always exceeds that genealogy. This does not mean, of course, that the architect exercises no control over the object, though it does mean that the terms, conditions, limitations, and conflicts of that control are far more complex than any theory can comprehend.

157

It is interesting to note how often the mythology of the intention of the architect functions to exteriorize as non-architectural potentially important events, and thus to repress them. Hence, the powerful and disturbing form of the leaning tower of Pisa is not seriously considered in architecture because it is held to be an accident, outside of the intentions of the architect. In fact, the entire system of accidents and coincidences, which characterize every building and every design is similarly theoretically excluded on the basis of this mythology to the detriment and impoverishment of architecture.

Finally, theories in this form remain within a tradition in which a theory of architecture consists of the application of current and general theoretical principles to the specific problem of architecture. Thus, architectural theory remains always in form a second order theory. It is always a special case application of general principles derived from other arenas of thought to the question of architecture, to the *problem* of the built environment. Though the details of the principles to be applied have, of course, changed through the centuries, nevertheless, this structure of architectural theory has remained the same.

For example, the work on representations of the ideal occupant is today conducted in terms of various discourses of cultural displacement or decentering since, in general, those discourses are constituted as internal interrogations of their respective discipline's own foundations. They are thus a locus of the development of strategies and tactics for conducting such interrogations and reconfiguring a discipline in response to the achieved insights. Now, if the proposition that problems at the level of architecture's foundation are the source of its growing irrelevance, then the references to those discourses and the attempt to apply their techniques are relevant and necessary to architecture as a discourse. However, we must distinguish between the relevance of that work to architectural discourse and its relevance to the processes and methods of architectural design.

Whether or not it can be said that any substantive relationships exist between any design and the writings with which it is purported to be associated is of little interest. It does not matter whether or not a project that claims to be 'deconstructive' can, by virtue of the excellence of some argument, have that claim verified or disproved, though the nature of the 'claim' as such, rather than its success, is important in as much as it can be said to have motivated those aspects of the project that are identified as displaced. Equally, it does not matter if an essay on architecture derives either its form or content from an understanding, or for that matter, from a misunderstanding of Heidegger. The work is neither canonized in the verification nor excommunicated in the contradiction. Therefore such arguments, though of interesting in their own right, are irrelevant to an architectural design theory.

Say, after reading Nietzsche's work on the revaluation of values, some architect designs an upside-down house to be constructed entirely in ice, contending that such constitutes a revaluation of architectural values. In terms of a theory of architectural design only three aspects of this situation are of interest: first, the fact that a particular choice, in this case a text by Nietzsche, motivated the design. Secondly, it is of interest how that motive was translated into a design process, which in this case was accomplished by illustrating the reversal of selected value pairs – up and down, permanent and impermanent – in an otherwise traditional design. Finally of interest is the terms by which the design is understood and evaluated. It is irrelevant whether or not it can be demonstrated that this design derives from a correct interpretation of Nietzsche's ideas. Such a demonstration can neither authorize nor indict the choice of motive, the process, nor the design.

In that sense *no architectural design has ever actualized the content of any theory as second order application*, this for reasons that flow both from the congenital deficiencies in definitions of the architectural object as well as from the problematic and complex relationship between the designer and the designed object. Thus architectural design is not and has never been a case of applied philosophy, applied science, or applied art, applied social or political theory, etc. Architectural design has never actualized any other body of ideas. The problem, therefore, is not that traditional architecture theory has always been a second-order theory, but that it is a second-order theory in form but never in fact.

For these and other reasons, the attempt in terms of design theory to respond to the destitution of architecture through a revised and more complex idealization of the occupant is futile. The process of conceptual idealization, i.e., the process of architectural theory as it has been historically constituted, itself is the process of repression, of destitution. It might be said that architectural theory itself, at least in its traditional form, is the source of an insufficient architecture!

Now, because it is physical, because it is functional, because it makes large demands on scarce resources, because it intrudes irresistibly and relentlessly into the public realm, architecture is necessarily and properly a domain of negotiation insofar as it addresses building. The physical, economic, moral, ethical, and political dimensions of architecture exist and are properly exercised, therefore, in the process of those negotiations. There can be little doubt, then, that a spectrum of rational and aesthetic theories of architectural negotiation are necessary. This spectrum of theory is the critical dimension of architecture. Furthermore, if it is true that architecture is metaphysically complete (the first of the two possibilities I suggested at the beginning of this essay), then it necessarily follows that negotiation theory, which is always rational in form, is the sole dimension in which architecture can and will develop.

However, if architecture is not closed in its metaphysical development but systematically stalled by a repressive hegemony of archaic design constraints such as the representation of the ideal occupant, then there is doubt that a rational theory of design processes, a theory that in essence prepares an architectural object to succeed in negotiations before those struggles begin, is of value. On the contrary, the indication is that such theories are resistance-producing.

From this point of view, what I have heretofore referred to as the spiritual and intellectual decline of architectural design is understood as nothing other than the result of a growing anticipation in the design process of the demands of the negotiation process. Moreover, this anticipation occurs not as an aspect of the decision-making process of the architect – he or she can exercise no choice in regard of that anticipation – but as a function of the decision making mechanism.

On the issue of design theory, then, we can summarize the nature of the flaws in that class of theories that propose to revise representations of the ideal occupant insofar as they remain within the form of a rational theory of architectural design. In short, they conflate new and important themes of negotiation, i.e., the political reconsideration of architectural representation and a consequent demand for the enfranchisement of difference, with the generation of design methods.

It seems we are confronted with a dilemma. If it is true that the growing irrelevance of architecture is the result of systematic repression, then it seems that the principal vector for the persistence and dissemination of that repression has been rational design theory. This is true even when theory in that form has taken upon itself the self-reflexive problem. As we have seen, rational discourse cannot give form to the necessary question 'what is (the form of) irrationality?' Irrationality and all of its conjugates – ambivalence, multivocality, simultaneity, the mystical and so forth – are collectively that which resist and exceed the rational form 'what is?' In short, there can be no prospect, in terms of a theory of design, of an 'improved discourse' or a 'more rigorous discourse,' whether such phrases mean 'more like philosophy,' 'more objective historiography,' 'more sensitive to the visual/aesthetic perception of the object,' 'more sociologically responsible' or whatever other criteria might be applied.

However, there cannot and will not be a simple abandoning of architectural design theory. Design theory is not an optional addendum to the design process, even for those architects who make claims of a 'purely intuitive' approach. Neither is it a separate but equal endeavor, as many hold – following Tafuri's attack on 'operative criticism.'

At the same time, it is not and has never been causative; no design has ever been faithful to the model of rational design theory. Rather, as I have suggested, at the point of design theory is the representation to the architect of the moral structure of the architectural world. This is confirmed in those correlates that name discourse's authority in the design process and thus its modes of repression, i.e., the true, the good, and the beautiful.

In an effort to resolve this dilemma, let us begin to pay theoretical attention to a logical necessity. If no practice has ever been faithful to the model of rational discourse, if every design exceeds its principles, and if this condition is not merely historical but constitutional, then what is at fault is neither the discourse nor the practice, but the model of the relationship between the two. The rationalist model is already irrational. Thus, strictly speaking, at the moment of design, architectural discourse is not and has never been theo-

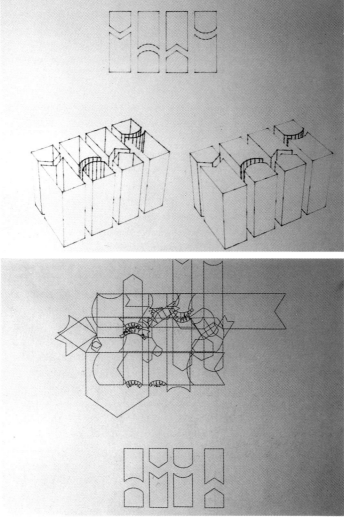

Figures 5, 6 Eisenman Architects, Frankfurt
Biocentrum, process drawing.

ry or history at all; once it moves to the question of design, it is nothing other than and nothing less than the morality of the design process, a gaining of permission for some forms, surfaces, and materials, a prohibition against others. In terms of design, it is therefore nothing other than and nothing less than the design process itself.

This condition, which in different words says that while the architect will always design for good reasons there are no good reasons for design, has, upon scrutiny of the history of design rationales, always persisted, from Palladio to Corb. What is proposed as different today is that we have come to a point where the ego correlates of design rationales, the good, the true, and the beautiful, are themselves suspected as sources of resistance. Those correlates do not exist as such but are merely the forms by which negotiation is always already anticipated by the architect in the design process.

Yet, in exploring the speculation that architectural irrelevance results from a stultification of the design process by the demands of negotiation, nothing is accomplished in merely illustrating the intention to conduct that exploration through deployment of an aesthetically contradictory vocabulary, i.e., the false, the bad, and the ugly. No new possibilities of meaning enter into design in that manner, since the dialectic of the decision-making process by which those characteristics enter design remains unchanged. They remained governed, albeit in opposition, by the true, the good, and the beautiful.

The goal for a design theory that explores the proposition in question must be to defer as long possible and/or dilute as thoroughly as possible the inevitable encroachment of the ego's demands of negotiation into the design process. At the moment of design there can exist no authentic authority. No ethical nor moral imperative, no priority of precedent, no cultural or aesthetic responsibility rightfully restrains the exploration into the possibilities of occupying material form. But design is always an ego process; it depends on the operation of authority through the architect and thus is always already conditioned by the constraints of negotiation.

Despite a veneer of authority, design theories are therefore only sources of motive, all of which are a priori inauthentic, and methods to translate those sources into design processes. In form, then, all design theories are and always have been *irreal*. The task now is to overcome the double bind, to develop design processes that dilute or defer the constraints of negotiation at the level of the traditional ego correlates, the sources of anticipation, while at the same time maintaining the function of a decision-making ego, which is to say the existence of the architect.

Currently, two classes of such design processes, which I term *absurd* and *surd*, hold out promise to accomplish this goal. To reiterate, the reason that these are promising is not that they are new classes of process, but that in retrospect all design processes throughout history fall into one or the other of these categories or some admixture of the two.

Both *absurd* and *surd* mean irrational, *absurd* in the sense of utterly senseless, illogical or untrue, *surd* in the sense of incapable of being spoken. *Absurd* has the etymological sense of being discordant to the ear; *surd* the sense of unavailable to the ear. The good, true, and beautiful voice of reason, the *logos*, is thus displaced differently in each of these two classes of processes.

In *absurd* processes, the operating principle is that, while the tradition of architectural logic is suspect in its authority, nevertheless the form of design logic can be maintained efficaciously if the sources of its motives and criteria for evaluation are displaced from the tradition of architectural decision-making. Thus pseudo-rational methods are maintained but the specific content, the sources of initial conditions and the criteria for testing progress in design, the process, is displaced from traditional architectural sources. For example, in the Eisenman Biocentrum project, the initial formal conditions were created by extruding forms drawn from biological symbols (figures 5, 6). These forms were then operated on with an amalgam of processes drawn from DNA replication and fractal geometry. Design progress was judged, at least initially, by the extent to which the formal manipulations analogized the borrowed processes and achieved new relationships intrinsic to those processes. As the design process proceeded, negotiation constraints were factored into the developing design.

Most of the criticism of this work has focused not on the resulting design but on the process used to generate it. Hence, this criticism continues to operate in obedience to the mythology that the genealogy of the object determines that object comprehensively. In other words, such criticism operates strictly as resistance.

From the point of view of *absurd* process theory, the choice of motive and method is irrelevant. Contrary to Eisenman's position, no argument can ever be made for a preference for biology and fractals over anything else, say portfolio management theory or morse code. The only issue is the extent to which the pseudo-rational process displaces the ego correlates of architectural process through a rigorously objective but non-architectural logic operating on select initial conditions.

In *surd* processes the focus is not on displacing architectural rationality in design, but on silencing it as much as possible so as to allow the entire self, rather than the rational architectural ego, to govern the design. The operating principle of *surd* processes derives from the fact that the architectural ego is but a reduced or narcissistic subset of the entire self of the architect. Thus the proposition is to construct processes that restore the architecturally disavowed aspects of the self to architectural design by suppressing the footholds for architectural rationality. The theme is objectification without rationalization under the assumption that rationalization – through geometry, for example – is but one process by which objectification can occur.

These processes typically begin either by choosing an external, non-architectural 'object' – a painting, a poem, a list of words, a way to behave or the like – and physicalizing the content of that source object. John Hejduk's work is a well-known example of such methods. Alternatively, initial objects can be 'prepared' in such as way as to remove all familiar architectural footholds (figure 7). The design process can be described as the construction of a specific ritual by which the architect objectifies *surd* material. These design process as well are carried to the point of addressing negotiation constraints as well.

It goes without saying that this short introduction does not constitute a thorough treatment of *surd* and *absurd* process theories. Nor have I discussed the very real problems these design theories pose for negotiation theory. For example, it is not yet clear how to evaluate the results of these processes. In a project in which Peter Eisenman and Jacques Derrida collaborated, for example, a project in which *absurd* processes were employed, the two of them concluded at the end of their work together that the result was, in both of their minds, truly beautiful. Now, does that mean successful? This conclusion becomes even more problematic when one takes into consideration that one of the themes in the collaboration was to destabilize Platonic thought as it persists in architecture. Has that been

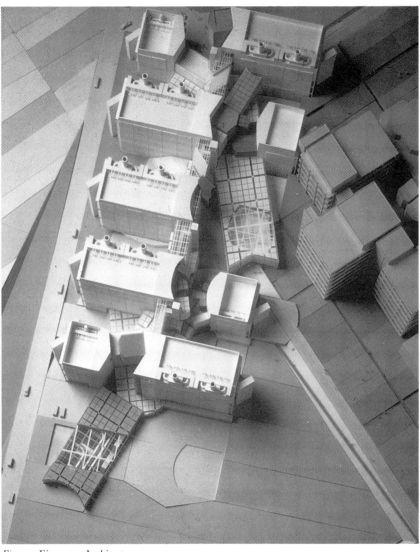

Figure 7 Eisenman Architects,
Frankfurt Biocentrum.

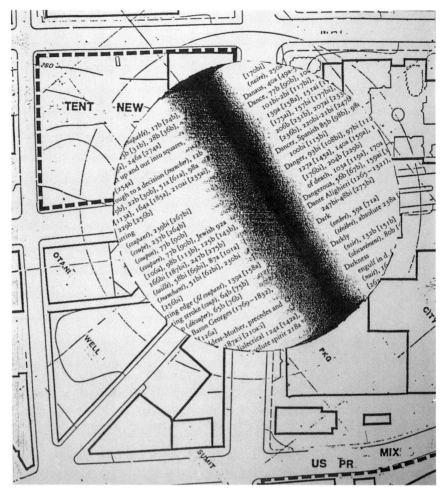

Figure 8 Daniel Libeskind/Jeffrey Kipnis,
Pre-pared Text.

accomplished when the project is pronounced a success in the most Platonic of terms?

Nor is there yet satisfying work on how to compare one of these projects to another, nor for that matter, very compelling work on why such efforts deserve to be realized despite the resistances that they will necessarily engender. Indeed, though I and others, including some of you, are at work on these questions, and though progress has been made on these issues it would be premature to declare those questions answered.

1 The following text was prepared as a talk and delivered at the CIAU conference in 1988. I never returned to edit, revise and polish it, so I am publishing here almost exactly as it was delivered. Since this text was written, my thinking on the questions of greatest interest to me such as architectural meaning, the form of architectural theory and the relationship between theory and design has changed so substantially that it would be impossible to revise this text to reflect those changes. Moreover, today, three years later, I find much about this text embarrassing, such as its immature arrogance of superior intentions, its naive and impertinent dismissal *en masse* of contemporary design, its inference of crisis, its logical antinomies, its broad generalizations and so forth. Indeed, if I continue this list, I might again lose my resolve to allow it to be published at all, not to mention in its original state! I do so, however, because whatever its conspicuous faults, I find on this belated reading a continued commitment to certain of its themes. Therefore, my only editorial gesture will be to request respectfully the reader's generosity.

2 G. W. Hegel, *Aesthetic*, for a complete English translation see, Hegel, *The Philosophy of Fine Art*, tr. F. P. B. Osmaston, 4 vols. (New York, 1975; reprint of 1920 ed.).

3 The most recent English translation of this work is, F. Nietzsche, *Daybreak; Thoughts on the Prejudices of Morality*, tr. R. J. Hollingdale (Cambridge, 1982).

4 R. Wittkower, *Architectural Principles in the Age of Humanism*, 3rd ed. (London, 1967).

Mark Linder is an Assistant Professor at the
Georgia Tech College of Architecture, and was
Visiting Assistant Professor at Rice University
School of Architecture in 1991. He is the editor
of the forthcoming critical monograph on the
work of Scogin Elam and Bray.

Architectural Theory
Is No Discipline

Mark Linder

My contention is that 'theory' – the attempt to decide architectural right and wrong on purely intellectual grounds – is precisely one of the roots of our mischief.
Sir Geoffery Scott, *The Architecture of Humanism*, 1924

One

Despite Geoffery Scott's attempted definition, the question 'What is architectural theory?' can be answered today only in a general and what seems, at first, a wholly trivial manner. The most we can say about contemporary architectural theory is that it can be called architectural theory. One is hard pressed to discern the definitive characteristics of such a discipline and equally taxed to draw the circle that delimits its boundaries. Nevertheless, during the last quarter-century, architects have had to face the expansive growth of a marginal discourse in architecture, which, for lack of a better name and in defiance of the multiplicity and specificity of its formulations, is called 'architectural theory'.

On the other hand, what we call 'architecture' is commonly understood as a distinct discipline. This is to say, it is a practice with agreed upon standards, techniques, and materials. It is commonly supposed that the discipline of architecture has limits that are perceptible – if not distinguishable – and that there exist terms of discourse that are outside of the normal constraints of architectural practice.

But architecture's limits prove elusive and theoretical attempts to understand architecture inevitably appeal to the authority of disciplines perceived to be more universal or nimble than architecture. Theorists attempt to explain architecture by invoking methods, terms, and concepts that seem only marginally architectural. Vitruvius appealed to the authorities of philosophy, myth, and the Emperor; Alberti adapted Neo-Platonic geometry and the achievements of perspective, and so on throughout history, from Palladio's harmonics to Alexander's set theory. Conversely, we are often confronted with descriptions of things, which are not architecture, as being architectural, for example, the architect of a peace treaty, the architecture of computers, even the architectonic of philosophy.

And what about architectural theory? As it is usually understood, architectural theory is not a theory that is architectural, but is an attempt to make architecture theoretical. But it seems that being theoretical means to borrow the 'discipline' of the scientist or the philosopher, and while this may be enlightening or potentially very sophisticated, it ignores the fact that architecture does not share all the features of philosophy or science. Thus it is that

I enter into an unlikely alliance with the humanist Scott, conceding not a distaste for the theoretical impulse, but for a particular and constrained definition of theory. But unlike Scott, who seeks to separate criticism from practice, I ask that they be joined emphatically. Architects could be architectural in their formulation of theory, rather than theoretical in their formulation of architecture. According to such a model, architectural theory would be understood as an activity with strong resemblances to the practice of architectural design. In other words, architectural theorists would ask what architects *do*, not what architecture is. The theorist would ask the same questions as the architect who designs a building. What is it for? Who is it for? How big is it? How long do we have to work on it?

Such a strategy is compelled by a desire to connect theory to the particulars of practice, in the hope that architectural theory would not struggle vainly to match up to science, philosophy or other specialized formulations of theory that, in the past, it has strived to imitate. A powerful model for this strategy is found in the work of the American pragmatists. The American pragmatists all strive to imagine – and to act as – intellectuals who do not separate doing and knowing, or imagining and thinking. Discontented with philosophy as a discipline, a system of thought, they wrestle with context and consequences, insisting that philosophy, like architecture, should be effective in shaping our world. Like the avantgarde, the pragmatists take philosophy into the streets.

John Dewey, the most famous of the pragmatists, spent most of his life trying to convince people that a separation between theory and practice is neither necessary nor fundamental, and strictly speaking, is not possible, either in theory or in practice.[1] Simply put, all theory is a form of practice just as all practice requires some form of theory.

> The problem of the relation of theory and practice is not a problem of theory alone; it is that, but it is also the most practical problem of life. For it is the question of how intelligence may inform action, and how action may bear the fruit of increased insight into meaning…[2]

Dewey moved away from attitudes that endorsed the construction of formal systems, and owed much to William James, whose Emersonian strategies endeavored to subvert the priority of rationality and the function of logic as objective objectives. More recently, Richard Rorty has redescribed this pragmatist approach as the 'transcendentalist point of view,'

> the attitude that there is no point in raising questions of truth, goodness, or beauty, because between ourselves and the thing judged there always intervenes mind, language, a perspective chosen among dozens, one description chosen out of thousands…in this sense, [it] is the justification of the intellectual who has no wish to be a scientist or a professional, who does not think that intellectual honesty requires…a 'disciplinary matrix.'[3]

We should not understand Rorty to be against theory. He believes that theory is best understood as a practical and therapeutic response to a problem, maintaining that 'anybody can get along without literary pretensions – without writing – if he [or she] is content simply to demonstrate how something falls into place in a previously established context.'[4] This attitude toward theory is critical of writers who imitate the methods of science and those who urge us toward professional standards, seeing both as restrictive, self-limiting and implicitly favoring the stability of the academy over the concerns of culture. It is suspicious of methods and systems, contending that no matter how impeccably we scrutinize our principles and no matter how communally we define our meanings we always run up against problems of individuality and the necessity of difference. It asks not for precisely coherent structures of meanings, but rather, wonders how the effort at precision will make any difference. That is, it asks the famous pragmatist question, 'What is the difference that makes a difference?'

Rorty imagines an alternative culture that embraces this pragmatist view.

> The high culture of an unfragmented world need not center around…anything more than anything else: neither poetry, nor social institutions, nor mysticism, nor depth psychology, nor novels, nor philosophy, nor physical science. It may be a culture which is transcendentalist through and through, whose center is everywhere and circumference nowhere.[5]

When Rorty writes of 'a culture which is transcendentalist through and through,' he is imagining a world where philosophical pragmatism and its allies have come to dominate the more entrenched modes of theoretical speculation, those that Dewey flatly called 'the classic philosophic tradition.'[6] This attitude links Rorty not only to Emerson, James, and Dewey, but to post-structuralist philosophers like Foucault and Derrida. They all have the sense that there is nothing 'out there' or 'deep down' to discover that will increase our wisdom or grant us greater freedom. Instead they believe that we have only what we make for ourselves, that we are imbedded not in a knowable reality, but in a comprehensible culture. Rorty calls this a 'post-Philosophical' culture, where pragmatism would join forces with other twentieth-century developments: a Heideggerian disavowal of the need for epistemology, a hermeneutic theory of interpretation derived from Gadamer, a 'therapeutic' existentialist attitude and, most recently, a deconstructive criticism in the manner of Derrida.[7] Both Rorty and Derrida have reasons to abandon prototypical modern projects such as analytic philosophy, and are supported in related fields by individuals like Harold Bloom with his swerve away from the New Criticism. They hope to reinvigorate lines of investigation that have been blocked by the severe regimen of philosophy's systematic traditions, which, they think, are rooted in Cartesian and Kantian frameworks. This dismissive attitude toward modern philosophy radically undermines the ideological claims of our humanist precursors and, as Cornel West and Richard Poirier have observed, throws us back on an Emersonian anti-ideology of self-reliance, a position that is as vulnerable as it is inspiring. On the other hand, the recent writings of Bloom and Poirier virtually canonize the texts of Emerson and the traditions of transcendentalism and pragmatism, which, according to Poirier,

> offer a way to think about literature and about life that seems…a crucial alternative to the dominant modernist and post-modernist ways of thinking [and] because they still remain insufficiently understood and assimilated, especially within the academic-journalistic practices of Anglo-American criticism in the past several decades, including what has been going on recently under mostly French provenance.[8]

West is less sanguine and warns of many weaknesses, yet ultimately he embraces Rorty's neo-pragmatism as a limited but 'useful springboard for a more engaged, even subversive…critical attitude.'[9] The value of this way of thinking, and its potential for application to the making of architecture and architectural theory, is a virtually unexplored territory, providing an untapped resource for a theory of architecture, which, like Rorty's philosophy, might be 'edifying' in its effort to 'generate new descriptions' of human activities and purposes realized in built form. To accept Rorty's notions is to be interested in building an operative, progressive culture, rather than constructing new conceptual systems for theory, or prescriptive methods for design. This attitude does not demand resolutions but, rather, offers revisions immersed in acts of making. It would enable architects to employ excluded and devalued approaches in an attempt to represent and empower otherwise 'unbuilt' cultures and institutions. It requires a cooperative and trusting attitude with the hope that we might progress together in a more or less eventful development, toward more appropriate, more assistant explanations of architecture, and in so doing, enable ourselves to create new and better social-cultural orders in the form of architecture.

Today, in our evolving cultural context, it becomes interesting and necessary not only to do architecture, but to speculate about architecture, that is, to do architectural theory or theoretical architecture. And further, if architects desire a culture that welcomes and facilitates change, growth, and transition, theoretical and speculative work will continue to be a necessary aspect of the architect's world.

Two

Theory, the pragmatists tell us, has consequences, as architecture too has consequences. It is the purpose of this essay, as theory, to explain the potential consequences of Rorty's post-Philosophical pragmatism upon architectural theory and, in turn, its consequences for architecture as practiced and understood today. Yet these purposes imply a task that can be only selective, since by its very definition, it is an approach that can be applied only partially and strategically to the activities of architects.

The architectural pragmatist asks a form of the question that Van Wyck Brooks, Colin Rowe, William James, Richard Rorty, and Harold Bloom all have asked, 'How is this building important *for us?*'[10] or 'What building would be better for us to build?' While the theorist might address the preceding questions, the architect labors under the consequences of their being asked. Architects would design buildings that might act in concert with the other arts – as well as 'theory' – helping to 'take us out of our old selves by the power of strangeness, to aid us in becoming new beings.'[11] Architects and architectural theorists might show us new ways to understand our task in the face of all the preconceptions and precedents that tug on our efforts to do architecture. They could offer readings – in the form of writings and buildings – of other theories, of buildings, and of the practice of making them.

The theorist also has the 'larger and broader' task 'to show how these practices [e.g., architecture and theory] link up with, or contrast with, other practices of the same group or other groups.'[12] As Bernard Tschumi has written (perhaps more symptomatically than critically), architects, theorists, and historians can no longer avoid consideration of 'the 'intertextuality' that makes architecture a highly complex human activity. The multiplicity of heterogeneous discourses, the constant interaction between movement, sensual experience, and conceptual acrobatics'[13] have forced the dispersal of the discipline and the questioning of architecture's perceived autonomy and limits. Like Rorty, Tschumi advocates a culture that obscures the lines that demarcate the disciplines and, instead, encourages interactions that the demands of specialization have excluded. Such a situation is not unlike the current splintering of departments within many universities that seems to be leading toward a community in which it is no longer meaningful to speak of 'interdisciplinary' work; rather, 'dedisciplinizing' scholarship flourishes,[14] and intellectuals compare and contrast practices within and across the entire culture.

Architectural research by these intellectuals would approach the historicizing of recent architecture with methods similar to those Carl Schorske has adopted.

> Where such an intuitive discernment of unities once served, we must now be willing to undertake the empirical pursuit of pluralities as a precondition to finding unitary patterns in culture.[15]

Pluralism has emerged as a key word to our understanding of contemporary and recent culture, if we are to judge by the frequency of its use in current theoretical and political discourse. Yet pluralism, despite its popularity as an ideal, is quite problematic, often serving as a tool to trivialize the significance of distinctions and differences or as a justification for the politics of consumption.

In an early essay, 'The Limits of Reductionism' (1961), Rorty deftly revised the 'traditional' conception of pluralism by redefining it as 'antireductionism.' Rorty's pluralist is someone who defends a 'cherished entity or concept' against devaluation by others, and unlike the traditional pluralist, does not engage in polemics that insist on the necessary virtues of 'richness and diversity.'[16] His pluralism is one that legitimates critical and contentious voices, while accusing the traditional pluralist of using reductive assumptions and arguments in the support of diversity.

We might call the antireductionist's approach 'theory-as-criticism.' The architectural theorist-as-critic, building upon revisionist histories, would attempt to expose the reductive, naively optimistic, exclusivist attitudes latent in contemporary architecture, emphasizing the indeterminacies of the architectural act, demonstrating the potentialities of alternative architectural vocabularies, and strengthening strategies that transgress the limits of architecture's professed autonomy as a discipline.

Three

Traditionally, architectural theory has tried to establish itself as a discipline with rules to determine the 'truth' of architecture, usually employing methods adapted from the traditions of philosophy or experimental science. Wishing to overrule the vagaries of beauty, taste, and style, architects instead proposed standards of truth, hoping to improve predictive capacity, as in science, and thus, to insure architectural success.[17] This theoretical preoccupation with the methodological establishment of truth is an impulse that Dewey characterized as driven by a vain, unrealizable goal. He called such efforts the

> quest for certainty…a quest for a peace which is assured, an object which is unqualified by risk and the shadow of fear which action casts… Quest for complete certainty can be fulfilled in pure knowing alone. Such is the verdict of our most enduring philosophic tradition.[18]

It is feasible to understand most architectural theory as needlessly struggling with the problems of epistemology – the theory of knowledge, including theories of truth – as much as, if not more than, with the traditions of aesthetic theory or the practice of building. Architects also are laboring under the constraints of various jargon-laden professional vocabularies and exclusive language games contrived from the systems of epistemology and investing in theories of truth, formulations that theory-as-criticism would not try to solve by proposing a new system, but would attempt to avoid. Rorty's critics would see themselves as doing no more than offering explanations of "how things hang together' – which, for the bookish intellectual of recent times, means seeing how all the various vocabularies of all the various epochs and cultures hang together.'[19] Of the strategies that are available to architecture and theory, one of the most obvious is the choice of vocabulary. We can choose among architectural vocabularies in much the same way we choose vocabularies when we write, and with similar consequences. If architecture resembles language in any significant way, it is because it has legible vocabularies, understandable as meaningful components, whether they are interchangeable within and outside of architecture (for example, Venturi's plea for literal signs, symbolism, and decoration) or, as Roger Scruton prefers, they are constrained within distinct categories called styles. Rorty stresses vocabulary choice; in a post-Philosophical culture, one chooses not between verifiable propositions, but among incommensurable vocabularies. The object is not to refute the arguments of your opponents, but to "problematize' the vocabulary"[20] that they use.

> You can argue only against a proposition, not against a vocabulary. Vocabularies get discarded after looking bad in comparison with other vocabularies, not as a result of an appeal to overarching metavocabularies in which criteria for vocabulary choice can be formulated.[21]

The architectural theorist, in Rorty's image, would resemble a 'culture critic' specializing in the issues that buildings involve, acting as 'the person who tells you how all the ways of making things hang together hang together.'[22] Architectural theorists would have

> no special 'problems' to solve, nor any special 'method' to apply…no particular disciplinary standards, [and] no collective self-image as a 'profession.'… They would be all-purpose intellectuals who were ready to offer a view on pretty much anything, in the hope of making it hang together with everything else.[23]

It does not particularly matter if we choose to do or to discuss, to do architectural theory (to show how vocabularies 'hang together' by employing a mediating vocabulary) or to do theoretical architecture (to modify an architectural vocabulary to 'hang together' in a different way, and requiring, as a consequence, yet another vocabulary to explain it). There would be no reason to separate the aims of theoretical architecture from the aims of architectural theory (which is better understood as a distinction between constituencies and vocabularies, not issues or purposes). If one refrains from such dichotomous distinctions and is willing to do architecture, and to discuss architecture, under those conditions architectural theory becomes not a discipline with 'architecture itself' as its object; rather, it becomes an activity of interpretation, persuasion, and communication within architecture.

Rorty provides a model for architectural theory that might avoid many of the versions of truth – especially truth as correspondence – which have driven architectural theory at least since Alberti. Theory-as-criticism, rather than authorizing arguments of truth, is more interested in criticizing, comparing and/or buttressing our beliefs and, because it does not rely on the 'philosophical' formulations that involve the 'problem' of reference, it does not endeavor to verify its correspondence with 'reality'. It would be the activity of 'talking about' architects, architecture, and theories of architecture, and would discard strategies that invest in the seemingly simple, but surprisingly problematic, intuitive concept of 'referring' to these matters.[24] We might think of architecture and architectural theory, as Rorty thinks of philosophy, defining them as edifying activities that utilize hermeneutic and narrative strategies in order to understand or explain other architecture and other theories of architecture.

These strategies would draw upon a pragmatist version of truth. Truth, in the pragmatist sense, is inseparable from meaning and value. The pragmatist conception of truth seeks

meaning in the consequences of action and belief, rather than in fixed statements, definitions, or rules. According to James, pragmatism is not a system, but a 'method'[25]; knowledge is not itself an end, but an implement of action with which we come to terms with our world. 'Theories thus become instruments, not answers to enigmas, in which we can rest. Pragmatism unstiffens all our theories, limbers them up and sets each one at work.'[26] The pragmatist 'turns away from abstraction and insufficiency, from verbal solutions, from bad a priori reasons, from fixed principles, closed systems, and pretended absolutes and origins. He turns toward concreteness and adequacy, toward facts, toward action and toward power.'[27]

James envisioned a philosophy that is continually evolving and assists involvement in a world full of chance events; he was not convinced that pragmatism would ensure a progressive intellectual evolution, or even one of a determined tendency. He saw philosophy as a ceaseless struggle to combat disorder, difficulties, and the perplexing problems that are continually emerging in the course of our lives. 'The truth of an idea is not a stagnant property inherent in it. Truth *happens* to an idea. It *becomes* true, it is *made* true by events.'[28] Jamesian pragmatism allows us to see language not as a system of atomistic words and true statements describing the world, but as a malleable, versatile instrument with which we can make ourselves at home.

Rorty adopts the Jamesian conception of truth, and revises it, describing it as a disturbingly ironic 'theory [that] says that truth is not the sort of thing one should expect to have a philosophically interesting theory about.'[29] For Rorty as for James, truth is not something to be discovered or defined; it is what we call statements that are persistently unproblematic and continually useful. Knowledge is thus more like a web of justified beliefs and habits than a traditionally defined epistemological system. In fact, Rorty wants to abandon epistemological projects altogether in his own writing but, in exchange, he does not attempt to 'avoid the 'hermeneutic circle' – the fact that we cannot understand the parts of a strange culture, practice, theory, language, or whatever, unless we know something about how the whole thing works, whereas we cannot get a grasp on how the whole works until we have some understanding of the parts.'[30] The 'hermeneutic circle' implies an unending repetition and an imperfect process, oscillating between here and there, then and now, establishing impermanent truths and ensuring the recreation of meaning. Hermeneutics, while an inventive and potentially poetic activity, always operates upon present frameworks and cultural formations; it inevitably 'employs materials provided by the culture of the day.'[31] It is thus therapeutic and self-avowedly parasitic upon the very systems that it wants to avoid. It does not replace them.

> 'Hermeneutics' is not the name for a discipline,… [it] is an expression of hope that the cultural space left by the demise of epistemology will not be filled…[32]

Hermeneutics, as proposed by Rorty, is a method of investigation that does not assume that all disciplines or vocabularies are commensurable, and asserts that certain discussions cannot produce strategies for rational agreement. For example, architects will never wholly agree with engineers about the technical strategies that most enhance the intentions of a design, and philosophers will not agree with scientists about how to seek truth. Diverse disciplines simply have not established, and need not have, standards of commensurability with which to reconcile each other's specific concerns.

174

For hermeneutics, to be rational is to be willing to refrain from…thinking that there is a special set of terms in which all contribution to the conversation should be put – and to be willing to pick up the jargon of the interlocutor rather than translating it into one's own.[33]

Rorty hopes that 'we shall look to our interlocutors rather than to our faculties' to justify our beliefs. 'Our certainty will be a matter of conversation between persons rather than a matter of interaction with non-human reality.'[34]

In a moment of metaphorical extension we might go so far as to say that architecture can be understood as a matter of conversation between buildings rather than an interaction with conceptual or material 'reality'; ideas do not represent objects, buildings do not embody meanings, and material is not an exemplification of form. Such an understanding would imply that the aim of architecture is to build an 'airtight case rather than an unshakable foundation.'[35] The architect, rather than 'building upon' her past work, criteria of truth or the principle 'elements' of architecture, would be deciding among buildings and vocabularies – whether inherited or invented – and thus would be defining herself as 'choosing objects to be compelled by.'[36] A conversant architecture would be an *assistant artifact*, rather than a referential object.

Four

Rorty describes two different types of conversation, which he calls 'normal' (commensurable) and 'abnormal' (incommensurable) discourse.

> Normal discourse (a generalization of Kuhn's 'normal science') is any discourse (scientific, political, theological, or whatever) which embodies agreed upon criteria for reaching agreement; abnormal discourse is any which lacks such criteria.[37]
>
> [Knowledge] is the product of normal discourse… The product of abnormal discourse can be anything from nonsense to intellectual revolution, and there is no discipline which describes it…[38]

Philosophy, architecture, and theory all have traditions, and have had periods of normality that have elevated consensus to the status of truth, often excluding abnormal practices. But those engaged in normal discourses should not see their abnormal counterparts as entirely unproductive, serving only to disrupt or discredit normal practices. In fact, abnormal practices operate to call attention to the inconsistencies or weaknesses of normal procedures, thus assisting their advance. Additionally, 'revolutionary' practices may be either normal or abnormal, in the first case providing new paradigmatic standards and methods, or in the other, advocating 'intentionally peripheral' practices that do not 'build for eternity', but build in order to interact in contemporary discourse, ultimately redirecting architectural 'conversation'. Normality need not be conservative, and abnormality need not be destructive. In this regard we might compare the early 'Architecture or Revolution' by Corbusier (normal) with the revolutions of the later Corbusier (abnormal) who was showing us how the vocabulary of his earlier white villas defined discursive limits that might be transgressed with revolutionary results. Or we might compare Robert Venturi to his employer Louis Kahn, the latter establishing an unquestionably original, yet normal, formalist paradigm for modern architecture, skillfully demonstrated, for example, in the Trenton Bath House (1953), a paradigm from which Venturi departed, toying with its strictures in a clever project like the Pearson house of 1957.

Rorty elaborates the categories of normal and abnormal discourse with a distinction between 'systematic' and 'edifying' philosophies, focusing on the work of Heidegger, Wittgenstein, and Dewey as models of edifying writers.

> I shall use 'edification' to stand for this project of finding new, better, more interesting, more fruitful ways of speaking. The attempt to edify…may consist in the hermeneutic activity of making connections between our own culture and some exotic culture or historical period, or between our own discipline and another discipline which seems to pursue incommensurable aims in an incommensurable vocabulary. But it may instead consist in the 'poetic' activity of thinking up such new aims, new words, or new disciplines, followed by, so to speak, the inverse of hermeneutics: the attempt to reinterpret our familiar surroundings in the unfamiliar terms of our new inventions.[39]

Rorty admires edifying philosophers, not because they offer knowledge, but because they are educators who give us 'a sense of the relativity of descriptive vocabularies to periods, traditions, and historical accidents.'[40]

> They have kept alive the historicist sense that this century's 'superstition' was the last century's triumph of reason, as well as the relativist sense that the latest vocabulary, borrowed from the latest scientific achievement, may not express privileged representations of essences, but be just another of the potential infinity of vocabularies in which the world can be described.[41]

Rorty's historicism, like his idea of philosophy, is reactive – or in the jargon of architecture, contextual – trying to remedy vacant and disused spaces in order to mend, not to reject or radically reconstruct, the fabric of our cities or our webs of meaning. A parasitic, therapeutic, reactive, and edifying discourse incorporates an Emersonian understanding of tradition, which needs to begin with accumulation and conformity, if only to then transform, interpret, and remake those very traditions into new origins, subverting accepted terms and meanings to new purposes and ideals. It is important to emphasize this reactive aspect in the case of architecture, particularly since the decline of the image of the architect as a visionary, whose projects are comprehensive and prescriptive projections for the future. It has become increasingly important to put forward self-descriptions for the architect that avoid heroics, yet still confirm his or her ability to project innovative proposals that, though reactive, will be influential, assisting social and cultural change.

Contemporary architects confront a peculiarly difficult relationship to their predecessors, at once acknowledging the limits of received styles and vocabularies, but also recognizing a need to continue them. They are wrestling with competing compulsions: to avoid simple historicism and, at the same time, to resist proposals that restore the twentieth century's wholesale repression of tradition. Architects cannot be satisfied to act like the revivalists of the nineteenth century or the rejectionists of the twentieth. We are in a period of pervasive revisionism, attempting to redefine architecture in a way that both perpetuates and renews its power.

Five

In an evocative metaphor that assimilates the various aspects of his position – and includes an implicit feminism – Rorty describes the systematic philosophies as a monumental 'Kantian' edifice upon which the parasitic, edifying 'Hegelian' philosophies grow like a great kudzu-vine, enveloping the building and gaining nourishment by rooting tendrils in the cracks of the building. This image presents the edifying project as one of criticism, cultivation, and deconstruction; the edifying philosopher sees the edifice as an object of constriction and authority that stands only on illusory foundations of truth, which constructive thinkers claim to have established. The edifying philosopher believes that

> the Kantian norm will in time become tedious, full of anomie and anomaly. The Kantian... escapes triviality, and achieves self-identity and self-conscious pride, only by the contrast between his mighty deeds and the mere words of the dialectician. He is no effete parasite, but one who does his share in the mighty time-binding work of building the edifice of human knowledge, human society, the City of Real Men. The non-Kantian knows that the edifice will itself one day be deconstructed, and the great deeds reinterpreted again, and again...– flowers could not sprout from the dialectical vine unless there were an edifice into whose chinks it could insert its tendrils... The Hegelian likes to think that there is not really a contrast between the vine and the edifice it covers – rather, the so called edifice is just accumulated dead wood, parts of the Great Vine itself, which were once fresh and flower-laden but now have come to lie in positions which suggest the outlines of a building.[42]

'Edifice' and 'edify' grow from the same Latin root, *aedis* (temple, dwelling, house), yet Rorty chooses to oppose them imagistically.[43] Traditionally, philosophers have invoked the image of architecture to describe the character and significance of their projects, just as architects have invoked the claims of philosophers to support and clarify their intellectual intentions. But Rorty's parable, as an architect might read it, highlights the ironies and complexities of this interdependence, and offers an image that challenges both architects and philosophers to reexamine their assumptions and motivations.

If architecture is to be edifying in Rorty's sense, architects must become more malleable in their understanding of the edificial. The resulting architecture would likely be abnormal, drawing its meaning from an hermeneutic interaction with the normal constructions around and within it. Like the novelists Richard Poirier admires, architects might build 'an environment...that thwarts any attempts to translate [it] into the terms of conventional environments.'[44] We find instructive and evocative examples of an edifying architecture in the historical accumulation of styles as at St. Etienne du Mont in Paris (as compared to framed relics or casual eclecticism), the 'organic architecture' of Wright (as compared to biomorphic imagery), the hands-on-design and craft of Scarpa (as compared to nostalgic craftsmanship), or the cannibalism of Frank Gehry's addition to his own house (as compared to simulated 'collisions'). All of these models employ notions of change, ingenuity, and temporality; none of them present us with timeless solutions to universal problems. Their greater force lies in juxtapositions and transitions, rather than structures or figures. This is not to say that either structural skeletons or figurative elements do not have an active role to play, but that they are treated as relatively inert, stable elements and materials, while the edifying architectural events happen in between.[45] This architecture finds power in the transitions and difficulties, the problems and paradoxes and, because they escape representation and containment, they are powerful only so long as we are actively remaking and spanning their missing connections. As Emerson wrote in 'Self-Reliance,' 'power ceases in the instant of repose; it resides in the transition from the past to a new state, in the shooting of a gulf, in the darting to an aim.'[46]

Just as the normal systems of structure, geometry or figuration provide the contextual background for edification, individual buildings are also edified by their normal or abnormal relationships with their larger context.

Pragmatists are supposed to treat everything as a matter of choice of context and nothing as a matter of intrinsic properties. They dissolve objects into functions, essences into momentary foci of attention, and knowing into success at reweaving a web of beliefs and desires into more supple and elegant folds.[47]

Such an approach implies that our buildings, like our vocabularies – whether systematic or edifying – 'are susceptible only to contextual definitions.'[48]

The importance of context leads to the observation that perhaps an urban metaphor is better than Rorty's image of the solitary, vine-covered edifice (as he begins to imply with his satirical quip about the City of Real Men). It is inconceivable that transcendentalist culture even could begin to find an adequate analogue in the individual building; the urban metaphor holds greater promise. The trope of the city provides a dynamic model for a discursive architecture. In the city we deal not with just Kantian buildings, but innumerable other structures, from the economic to the civic; the modern city, with its buried infrastructure and transitional neighborhoods, muddies the distinction between the 'vine' and the 'edifice' and instead resembles the final image that Rorty leaves us: a gnarled and tangled growth feeding and flowering upon its own remains. A 'Hegelian city of conversation' merits architectural exploration because it does not present us with a simple dichotomy of construction or destruction of truth and falsity, of object and context, or of practice and theory. If we accept the intellectual significance of efforts such as Rorty's and Dewey's to counteract the objectification of knowledge and experience, then the introduction of a new model for the city, which begins to transgress – without negating – the notion of the object, would be a very significant development indeed.

1 Dewey described an irresolvable paradox in his *Essays in Experimental Logic* (Chicago, 1916), p. 441: 'The paradox of theory and practice is that theory is with respect to all other modes of practice the most practical of all things, the more impartial and impersonal it is, the more truly practical it is.' Emerson offered this formulation on the first page of his first book, *Nature*, 'The most abstract truth is the most practical,' in *The Selected Works of Ralph Waldo Emerson*, ed. B. Atkinson (New York, 1968), p. 3.
2 J. Dewey, *The Quest for Certainty* (New York, 1960), p. 281.
3 R. Rorty, 'Professionalized Philosophy and Transcendentalist Culture,' *Consequences of Pragmatism* (Minneapolis, 1982), p. 67. Of course Rorty's transcendentalism is that of Emerson, not Kant.
4 R. Rorty, 'Philosophy as a Kind of Writing,' in *Consequences of Pragmatism*, p. 106.
5 R. Rorty, 'Professionalized Philosophy and Transcendentalist Culture,' in *Consequences of Pragmatism*, p. 70.
6 J. Dewey, *The Quest for Certainty*, p. 35.
7 'Pragmatists and Derridians are, indeed, natural allies. Their strategies supplement one another admirably. But there is no natural priority of one strategy over the other. It is not the case that we shall have rational grounds for rejecting realism only if we overcome the metaphysics of presence... If Derrida ever got his 'new logic', he would not be able to use it to out argue his opponents.' Rorty, 'Philosophy without Principles,' *Against Theory* (Berkeley, 1985), p. 135. Since writing *Philosophy and the Mirror of Nature* (Princeton, 1979), Rorty has clarified his sympathy toward deconstruction, and has explicitly clarified his reading of Derrida as a collaborator in the creation of a

post-philosophical culture (but not as the innovator of a new paradigm of rationality, as some fervent deconstructionists might claim).
8 R. Poirier, *The Renewal of Literature: Emersonian Reflections* (New York, 1987), p. 9.
9 C. West.,'The Politics of American Neo-Pragmatism,' in *Post-Analytic Philosophy* (New York, 1987), ed. J. Rajchman and C. West, p. 240.
10 Brooks wrote: '*What is important for us?*... The more personally we answer this question, it seems to me, the more likely we are to get a vital order from the anarchy of the present,' in 'On Creating a Usable Past,' *The Dial* 64, p. 341. Bloom wrote: 'The language of American criticism ought to be pragmatic and outrageous... American pragmatism, as Rorty advises, always asks of a text: what is it good for, what can I do with it, what can it do for me, what can I make it mean?' H. Bloom, *Agon* (Oxford, 1982), p. 19. '...on a pragmatic view there is no language *of criticism* but only of an individual critic, because again I agree with Rorty that a theory of strong misreading denies that there should be any common vocabulary in terms of which critics can argue with one another.' Ibid., p. 21. 'Rather than ask the question: what *is* a trope? I prefer to ask the pragmatic question: what is it that we want our tropes to do for us?' Ibid., p. 31. It is important to point out the distinction between *for us* and *for me*, for while the critic is always an individual the question is always, for the pragmatist, *for us*. For example, William James, in *Pragmatism*, 2nd ed. (Indianapolis, 1981), p. 37, explains that in order to know what is right we must ask: 'What would be better for us to believe[?]' Colin Rowe, comparing the benefits of the traditional versus the modern city, wrote: 'One might even feel constrained to digress and

ask which is the most useful model – for us.' *Collage City* (Cambridge, 1978), p. 90.

11 R. Rorty, *Philosophy and the Mirror of Nature*, p. 360.

12 R. Rorty, 'Habermas and Lyotard on Postmodernity,' *Praxis International* 4, 1, p. 36

13 B. Tschumi, 'Architecture and Limits III,' *Art Forum* 20 (September 1981), pp. 40-52.

14 See J. Rajchman, 'Philosophy in America,' in *Post-Analytic Philosophy*, p. xiii.

15 C. Schorske, *Fin-de-Siècle Vienna* (New York, 1980), p. xxii.

16 R. Rorty. 'The Limits of Reductionism,' in *Experience, Existence and The Good*, ed. I. C. Lieb (Carbondale, 1961), pp. 114-115. Robert Venturi's theoretical writings exhibit just the sort of pluralism that Rorty doesn't endorse, but Venturi's failings as a theoretician seem not to hamper his sophistication as an 'antireductionist pluralist' architect.

17 Perhaps the most obvious and literal consequences of the demand for truth in architecture are the persistent moral imperatives of structural and material honesty, the preference for buildings that do not 'lie' about the way they are supported or the way they are clad. We might even contend that architectural theory not only has accepted uncritically a notion of truth, but also a morality related to the Kantian claim of the individual's capacity for synthetic practical reasoning, leading to claims of 'the one right way' and 'what one ought to do.'

18 J. Dewey, *The Quest for Certainty*, p. 8.

19 R. Rorty, 'Introduction: Pragmatism and Philosophy,' in *Consequences of Pragmatism* p. xxxviii. The phrase 'hang together' is found sprinkled throughout pragmatist writings, but certainly was nothing more than a favorite turn of phrase until Rorty elevated it.

20 R. Rorty, 'Philosophy without Principles,' p. 135.

21 Ibid., pp. 135-136.

22 R. Rorty. 'Introduction: Pragmatism and Philosophy,' in *Consequences of Pragmatism*, p. xl.

23 Ibid., p. xxxix.

24 Rorty argues in favor of 'talking about' in a section of *Philosophy and the Mirror of Nature* entitled 'Reference,' pp. 284-295. "Talking about' is a common-sensical notion; 'reference' is a term of philosophical art.' The aim of Rorty's proposal can be furthered by understanding it as an elaboration of the distinction between a professor and a professional. Both titles derive from the same Latin root *profiteri* and thus the distinctions between them intermingle; yet as commonly understood there is a distinction to be made between their social roles: a professor is literally a 'speaker', and a professional is the taker of exclusive (ethical, technical or in its original sense, religious) 'vows'. Interestingly, the OED defines 'professor' as, among other things, 'one who makes open declaration of his sentiments or beliefs,' which brings James to mind. On the other hand, the OED cites meanings for 'professional' such as 'considered socially superior to a trade or handicraft' or 'skilled in the theoretic or scientific parts of a trade or occupation, as distinct from its merely mechanical parts,' recalling the image of the professional that Rorty attacks.

25 Although James introduces the term 'method,' it is important to remember that the pejorative cast it has acquired, the prevalent feeling today that methods are more cumbersome than liberating, was not present for James.

His description of pragmatism as a method was, in 1907, quite an extreme position for a philosopher to take, and one that implied none of the formulaic approaches that 'method' now implies.

26 W. James, *Pragmatism*, p. 28.

27 Ibid.

28 Ibid., p. 92.

29 R. Rorty, 'Introduction: Pragmatism and Philosophy,' p. xiii. (See also his disavowal of interest in Dewey's and James' 'metaphysical' works, *Experience and Nature* [New York, 1958] and *Essays in Radical Empiricism* [Cambridge, 1976] on pp. 213-214 of *Consequences of Pragmatism*.)

30 Ibid., p. 319. For Rorty, to 'be hermeneutic' means 'trying to show how the odd or paradoxical or offensive things [our opponents] say hang together with the rest of what they want to say, and how what they say looks when put in our own alternative idiom.' Ibid., p. 365.

31 Ibid., p. 366.

32 Ibid., p. 315.

33 Ibid., p. 318.

34 Ibid., pp. 156-157. There is a certain ironic pun in Rorty's opposition of 'faculties' and 'interlocutors' as well as an implication that academics are not the best conversational partners.

35 Ibid., p. 157.

36 Ibid., p. 160.

37 Ibid., p. 11.

38 Ibid., p. 320.

39 R. Rorty, *Philosophy and the Mirror of Nature*, p. 360.

40 Ibid., p. 362.

41 Ibid., p. 367.

42 R. Rorty, 'Philosophy as a Kind of Writing,' in *Consequences of Pragmatism*, pp. 107-108.

43 Rorty cursorily notes this irony in *Philosophy and the Mirror of Nature*. Explaining his notion of edification, he writes 'the activity is (despite the etymological relation between the two words) edifying without being constructive – at least if constructive means the sort of cooperation in…research programs which takes place in normal discourse.' p. 360.

44 R. Poirier, *A World Elsewhere: The Place of Style in American Literature* (Oxford, 1966), p. 7. An article by Richard Schiff, 'Art and Life: A Metaphoric Relationship' clearly develops very similar issues in *On Metaphor*, ed. S. Sacks (Chicago, 1979).

45 James was trying to do something similar in his critique of the classical empiricists (Locke, Berkeley, Hume, and Mill) whose associationist theories included only atomistic 'ideas' that were understood to be representations of isolated objects. James wanted to expand the empiricist theory to include not only the characteristics of an object, but the relations *between* them. Relations become real elements in our conceptions along with objects. This is to say that we should not only have a concept of distinct items such as 'house', 'door' and 'space', but also notions of 'if', 'but', 'at', or any such connector. In architecture this would include notions like poché, joint, transition, or inflection.

46 R. W. Emerson, 'Self-Reliance,' *The Selected Writings Of Ralph Waldo Emerson*, p. 158.

47 R. Rorty, 'Philosophy without Principles,' p. 134.

48 R. Rorty, *Philosophy and the Mirror of Nature*, p. 154.

Robert McAnulty teaches design and theory at the Parsons School of Design and Columbia University. He is a partner in a New York firm, Robertson and McAnulty Architects.

Body Troubles

Robert McAnulty

What are the consequences for architecture of the 'death of Man,' the revered subject of humanism? More importantly perhaps for architecture, what became of his body? All around us, everywhere we turn, the mechanisms of criticism are abuzz with talk of 'the post-structuralist body', 'body invaders', 'bodybuildings', and so on. Clearly the issue of rewriting the classical body is a hot topic these days. And an important topic for an architectural discourse whose very foundations, we have been taught to believe, rest on its relation to the human figure. Once 'man' has gone, and presumably taken his body along with him, what are we architects left with? Who do we serve? Where do we look for our formal models? Must we abandon ourselves to the 'procession of simulacra,' revelling in an apocalyptic fin-de-millennium free fall?[1] Must we resuscitate our fallen man phenomenologically or psychoanalytically so as to re-ground our 'destabilized' foundations? Or can we begin to imagine other ways of traversing the horns of this dilemma, routes which map the site of the body and multiply the possibilities for architectural action?

This paper is organized into four sections: the first three dealing with issues of body and architecture of Michel Foucault, Alberto Pérez-Gómez and Anthony Vidler respectively. Finally I will turn my attention briefly to the work of two of our contemporaries, Elizabeth Diller and Ricardo Scofidio, who are themselves attempting to rewrite the body in their projects.[2]

The numerous recent attempts to refocus attention on the body all share in their questioning of humanist theories of the subject. Such humanist theories have served indirectly to emphasize the hierarchical centrality of the human figure. Although they have been under attack for some time now, it is worth briefly recapitulating the issues at hand in architectural terms. We are all familiar with the famous drawing by Leonardo da Vinci of the Vitruvian Man, the male body standing upright with arms extended, inscribed within a circle and a square with the centers of both geometrical figures at the body's navel. Two formal issues are worth noting here. First, the body is presented frontally, as a statically balanced, symmetrical figure with well-defined limbs and orderly musculature, thus prompting an understanding of the human body as a figural unity: compositionally complete, confidently stable and hierarchically ordered. Second, a mathematical unity pervades the image in which both the natural figure (the body) and the geometrical figures (the circle and the square) share a point of origin in the body's navel. We find a body that is presented as embodying the harmonic order of a divinely inspired network of Euclidian geometry, thus empowering it in its claim to the pivotal position in an anthropocentric world.

The unified body of the Vitruvian image was taken as the model for classical architecture; buildings were to mimic the order, harmony, and proportions of the Vitruvian body. This mimetic relationship to the human figure dominated architecture through the sixteenth century and continues to have significant impact even today. As a graduate student I was assigned to read Geoffrey Scott's *Architecture of Humanism*, published in 1914. Nostalgically recalling a bygone era, Scott exhorted us that,

> The center of that architecture was the human body; its method, to transcribe in stone the body's favorite states; and the moods of the spirit took visible shape along its borders, power and laughter, strength and terror and calm.[3]

Scott's so-called architectural 'transcription' can be questioned in formal terms that inquire about the body's position relative to the building. If the body is to transcribe or project itself onto the building, then it must be operating at some distance from that which it is being projected upon. This distance is formalized in Euclidean geometry and perspectival models, which provide the conceptual framework for a relationship of division or alienation between the body/subject and its world/object. This dichotomy between subject and object is fundamental to a model of perception in which the body is seen as projecting its favorite *interior* 'states' onto the *exterior* world. The body is understood as necessarily being independent, complete and constituted prior to the world, a world that takes form only insofar as it is embodied. The terms underlying the very possibility of the body's figural self-sufficiency and its projection onto a presumably undifferentiated world are those which I would like to call into question.

Recent architectural discourse has grappled with questions about the centrality of the humanist subject, as raised by theoretical developments in other fields. In this country, Peter Eisenman has led the attack on anthropomorphism, describing it as a 'dangerous illusion' that has needed a 'reexamination [in all human endeavors] of the repressive effects of this illusion.' Eisenman prefers to couch his own reexamination in the language of psychoanalysis; yet, it is also clear that he has been influenced by the early writings of Michel Foucault.[4] Although Eisenman and other architectural theorists have typically focused on Foucault's critique of discursive structures and the appearance in history of discontinuities or 'ruptures', it is my sense that we would all benefit from a rereading of his seminal work on the body.

Foucault describes his research as an 'archeology of knowledge.' In the study of the history of such institutions as the prison, the clinic, and the school, the archeologist attends to the cultural play of discourse: discursive practices that constitute the channels in which we necessarily speak and think. Abandoning the kind of inquiry into the origin of subjectivity prior to its situation in a political field that marks the other disciplines, such an archeological approach avoids the shortcomings of histories of the body, which consider it biologically, psychologically, or historically. Such histories tend to overlook the fact that, '...the body is also directly involved in a political field; power relations have an immediate hold on it; they mark it, train it, force it to carry out its tasks, to perform ceremonies, to emit signs.'[5] Foucault considers the 'political technology of the body at some length in *Discipline and Punish*.[6] Focusing his inquiry on the systems of punishment that came to supplant public executions and torture, he formulates the model of a body that finds itself inscribed by its political situation. Foucault describes the formation of these newly subjected 'docile bodies' as follows:

> Through this technique of subjection a new object was being formed; slowly, it superseded the mechanical body – the body composed of solids and assigned movements, the image of which had for so long haunted those who dream of disciplinary perfection. This new object is the natural body, the bearer of forces and the seat of duration; it is the body susceptible to specified operations, which have their order, their stages, their internal conditions, their constituent elements... It is the body of exercise rather than speculative physics; a body manipulated by authority, rather than imbued with animal spirits; a body of useful training and not of rational mechanics...[7]

This newly formed natural body found its purest expression in the figure of the soldier. His body was instrumentally coded at the most minute levels. The articulation of his every gesture, from his marching posture to his penmanship was broken down into its component parts, each of which was assigned a duration and an order of appearance. The Vitruvian body, subject to metaphysical analysis, was replaced by the manipulable body, inscribed through training and control.

In *Discipline and Punish,* Foucault traces the change in disciplinary practices that accompanied the demise of sovereign power. The popular public executions and torture used prior to the eighteenth century allowed the power of the king to be publicly demonstrated through its marking of the body of the condemned. As political structures changed and were no longer associated solely with the figure of the sovereign, the nature of power changed as well. No longer perceived as the property of an individual or a dominant class, power came to be observable only by way of its exercise or activity. Consequently, Foucault argues that power must now be seen as 'investing' subjugated bodies within its structure, 'it is transmitted by them and through them, it exerts pressure upon them, just as they themselves, in their struggle against it, resist the grip it has on them.'[8] Such complete dispersion of the affects of power throughout political structures eliminates the necessity for an overt inscription of the condemned body wherein the exercise of power is observed directly in its graphic markings. The machine of Kafka's *The Penal Colony*,[9] which punishes the body of the condemned colonist by means of a system of vibrating needles inscribing such maxims as 'Honor Thy Superiors' is no longer necessary in a society that is itself inscribed by a network of socially accepted codes. Such overt inscription has been replaced by a system of constant surveillance that underwrites self-colonization. Foucault describes the insidious effect of surveillance as follows:

> He who is subjected to a field of visibility, and who knows it, assumes responsibility for the constraints of power; he makes them play spontaneously upon himself; *he inscribes in himself* the power relation in which he simultaneously plays both roles; he becomes the principle of his own subjection.[10]

The structures of power inevitably become so pervasive that the body monitors itself, inscribes on itself the disciplinary exercises to which it is exposed and subjected. Conformance to social codes or norms becomes a matter of self-discipline.

As I have already noted, the primary mechanism whereby disciplinary societies exercise power over bodies is surveillance. An architecture that facilitated visual observation was the natural outcome of the new disciplinary procedures for controlling bodies. The institutionalization of visual control was made manifest in an architecture that was

> ...no longer built to be seen (as with ostentatious palaces), or to observe the external space, but to permit an internal, articulated and detailed control – to render visible those who are inside it; in more general terms, an architecture that operates to transform individuals; to act on those it shelters, to provide a hold on their conduct, to carry the effects of power right to them, to make it possible to know them, to alter them.[11]

Although he traces the effects of this architecture of visibility in such institutions as schools, factories, and clinics, Foucault is especially interested in Jeremy Bentham's Panopticon as a 'compact model of the disciplinary mechanism.' Since his analysis of the formal characteristics of the Panopticon is by now well known among architectural theorists, its recapitulation is no longer necessary. Suffice it to say that for Foucault, architecture is clearly complicitous with the disciplinary structures of power. Rather than finding evidence of a divine harmony between an idealized body and its world in the circular, symmetrical form of the Panopticon, Foucault finds evidence of institutionalized subjection of the prisoner's pliable body. And the architect, caught within the intricate relations of power, subjects him/herself to the disciplinary procedures that confine practice to the socially inscribed norms of power.

By now I hope it is clear that Foucault has almost completely inverted the body-world problematic originally posed in the humanist model. In place of the autonomous figure shaping objects in its own image, Foucault inserts the figure of an individual fabricated by power. This new social body is formed from the exterior by its inscription within a network of complex and constantly changing cultural relationships and discursive practises. The web of power is always already active prior to the body, the social precedes the individual. Insofar as the body becomes autonomous and individuated at all, it is as the result of the actions of power. Although I find Foucault's critique of architecture's complicity with power to be somewhat rhetorical, it seems clear that his understanding of the body in terms of its *exteriority* (versus the interiority of humanism) and its position of engagement *within* the world (versus a position of perspectival distance) is one that contemporary architecture must confront, however uncomfortable such a confrontation may be. The body's struggle to inscribe the structures of social power requires a geometrical or relational model that is far more subtle than the Vitruvian circle. And although the ways in which architectural practice can proceed in its attempts to re-inscribe the body are not at all clear as yet, we should recognize our indebtedness to Foucault's insights before condemning his political impotence.

In recent architectural discourse, one response to the dilemma posed by Foucault's analysis has been what I consider to be a metaphysics of the mysterious, which, somewhat paradoxically, seems to draw its inspiration from existentialism. Insistently calling attention to the plight of the modern individual as estranged and isolated from any sense of community, much recent architectural theory seeks a means of redressing such alienation. For Alberto Pérez-Gómez, the abject condition of contemporary society has been caused for the most part by the growing importance of science and technology in our lives and the instrumentality that accompanies such growth. For architecture this instrumentality has

184

meant a loss of focus on what is understood to be fundamental to human experience: the body and its life-world. For this reason, in Pérez-Gómez' eyes, the body has fallen into disrepair and requires immediate attention if we are to find our way back to a 'meaningful reality'. As he has written in an article on the work of John Hejduk, entitled 'The Renovation of the Body,'[12] 'an authentic interest in architectural meaning in our times must be accompanied by a conscious or unconscious renovation of the body.'[13] Continuing on the theme of authenticity, he writes, 'Authentic architecture has always enabled man to come to terms with his mortality and transcend it.'[14] Pérez-Gómez goes on to argue that Hejduk's later work, in particular the Masque projects, is representative of such authenticity at work. These themes are also embodied in such modernist monuments as Le Corbusier's La Tourette, Aalto's Paimio Sanatorium, Mies' Barcelona Pavilion, and Gaudí's Sagrada Familia. What these works share, in the 'physiognomic' terms of the renovated body, is not at all clear from Pérez-Gómez' argument, but that is a subject for another time.

One thing these works apparently do share, in Pérez-Gómez' eyes, is a repudiation of what Foucault also refers to as the 'classical' tradition that came to supplant Renaissance theories of the cosmos in the eighteenth century. Alternatively, Pérez-Gómez valorizes what he terms the Homeric (preclassical) tradition, which does not distinguish between the body and its way of engaging the world. Sight, in this model, does not recognize the distinction between the subject who sees and the object seen, focusing rather on the immediacy of the act of seeing, which is necessarily prior to the body-world (subject-object) distinction. Pérez-Gómez believes that the continuity between the body and its lived world has been obscured by classical metaphysics and modern science, both founded on a Cartesian dualism that finds the body as unitary and distinct from the world.

By his own admission, Pérez-Gómez' proposed body renovation is heavily reliant on his reading of existential phenomenology, in particular, Heidegger and Merleau-Ponty. In this reading, the body and world must be understood as acting in concert, as a 'continuum'. Such a continuum reverses the hierarchical division of the rationalist, Cartesian model of the sciences:

> In spite of our rationalist prejudices, body and world remain mysteriously related. The world is endowed with meaning in the immediacy of perception, and it is given a physiognomy which derives from the projection of our body image on to it.[15]

In this model, the world achieves some measure of significance only insofar as it is embodied by the body's projection of its own image. The world as a projected, mimetic embodiment of the subject's interior is reminiscent of its humanist forebears and is subject to the same critiques. What is different in the phenomenological model is the site of the projection. Where for Renaissance theorists the body and world are formally linked in a divine naturalism based in geometry, for Pérez-Gómez, following Heidegger, the body finds the site for its projection onto the world in the figure of the 'clearing'.[16] This clearing is the place where a sort of primordial communion with nature occurs. It is the place where man 'dwells' in the recognition of his essentially non-instrumental unity with the world. This 'face-to-face' encounter must necessarily take place prior to any subsequent instrumentalization, any move to establish perspectival distance between the body and its objects, any formal projection of its image by the subject.

As we can imagine, the trick here is to find the site where the 'ground of being' reveals itself, where the body's continuity with the world is exposed. Pérez-Gómez describes the primordial experience of the clearing in the metaphysical-religious term: transcendence. In the experience of transcendence, the body somehow comes to terms with its own mortality, presumably by recognizing its essential identity with some aspect of nature that it sees as immortal. Authentic architecture facilitates transcendence by constructing places or clearings where the body 'dwells'. Unfortunately for all those seeking the transcendental experience, the modern world is dominated by inauthentic architecture that stands as evidence of the architect's growing interest in maintaining little more than 'efficient technological control'.

What then does all this have to do with Hejduk? How is he implicated in this argument? Not surprisingly, for Pérez-Gómez, Hejduk's work renovates the body and in doing so, it renovates architecture. His reading of Hejduk's work goes as follows:

> The participants in Hejduk's Masques are more like bodily skins than skins of buildings. They refer in a direct way to the body, but they are not anthropomorphic in the classical tradition. Rather they take on the qualities of the flesh, as described by Merleau-Ponty... The protagonists of the Masques have a mysterious emanation of being, a seductive power that can create dangerous illusions. Rather than representing that which is alive, pre-classical *daidala* allowed inanimate matter to become magically alive. Like Hejduk's architecture, they were *thaumata*, marvelously animated machines with brilliant suits of armour and scintillating eyes. This architecture is the mimesis of a transcendental emotion. It discloses the possible totality through the fragment.[17]

Hejduk's Masque projects abound with small-scale, totemic, solitary (typically upright), figures, each of which is frequently accompanied by a name for the construction, a name for its inhabitant and occasionally by a short, enigmatic text describing the inhabitant's history and his function within a fictional community or tribe. The figures are quite literally animal-like with scales, fins, and spikes. Since we understand the renovated body to be that body capable of experiencing transcendence, somehow that transcendence is to be achieved by the body's experience of these mysterious objects that seem alive, although not 'anthropomorphic in the classical tradition'. But, in the terms of Pérez-Gómez' argument, is it not true that the animism we ascribe to Hejduk's figures is directly attributable to the body's projection of its own image onto the world *subsequent* to the originary transcendental encounter? And isn't it the case that such animistic projection onto the world inevitably initiates a certain distance between the body and its objects, thus instrumentally undermining the sense of their essential continuity?

Whatever the answers to these questions may be, Pérez-Gómez identifies architecture's essential character with that of 'poetic naming,'

> Through poetic naming, the architecture attains an unfathomable concreteness. The word allows the architect to reveal the ground of the 'thing', of the products of *poesis*, and to attain archetypal meanings, thus the abstract becomes concrete and the figural is regained... Poetry speaks in images in order to let us dwell, states Heidegger.[18]

This, then, represents Pérez-Gómez' prescription for the renovation of the body. Future generations of architects, seeking authenticity, should turn their attention to the peculiarly personal task of poetic naming through the construction of enigmatic, animistic figures that allow the body to 'apprehend [its] place in the face of destiny'. This task is as 'rigorously introspective' as it is a-political, as self-absorbed as it is disconnected to its cultural situation, and as timeless and universal as it is a-historical. What starts as an attempt to outline a strategy for retrieving, resuscitating, and renovating the body in phenomenological terms becomes a prescriptive ideal with a very specific formal analogue. My sense is that the degeneration into animism marks the difficulty of translating the Heideggerian concept of dwelling, which is essentially non-volitional, into an architectural pragmatics, which is unavoidably instrumental.

A much more provocative attempt to reformulate the issue of the body in architectural terms comes from Anthony Vidler in a lecture entitled 'The Building in Pain'[19] (a play on the recently published *The Body in Pain* by Elaine Scarry[20]). Following a discussion of a 'gradual erosion of confidence' in the classical model of the unified body, Vidler raises the question, How does the perception that a building is a body manage to survive the various attacks on the classical model of the body? Has the notion that a building is a body disappeared? Has the body really disappeared? If not, how does it appear and what kind of presence might it have? These questions prefigure Vidler's response – no, the body has not disappeared, it continues to animate our experience of artifacts and buildings, although after Freud the body (and the self) has undergone some changes.

Like Pérez-Gómez, Vidler locates the beginning of what he is later to call the 'post-structuralist' body in existentialism. His lecture began with a recapitulation of Jean-Paul Sartre's questioning of the body in *Being and Nothingness*.[21] In Sartre's reformulation of the classic analogical model, the body is seen as a participant in an instrumental complex of tools awaiting action. The body comes to know itself only insofar as it is active in the instrumental world. It can never achieve sufficient distance from itself or its tools so as to be capable of understanding itself independent of its world. The body and the man-made object have a reciprocal relationship – each needs the other in order to recognize itself. And the body that is 'lived, not thought,' recognizes its contingency by virtue of its dependence on objects. The Sartre passage quoted by Vidler goes as follows:

> I live my body in danger as regards menacing machines for manageable instruments. My body is everywhere: the bomb which destroys my house also damages my body insofar as my house was already an indication of my body…my body always extends across the tool which it utilizes: it is at the end of the telescope which shows me the stars…it is my adaptation to those tools.[22]

This is a somewhat familiar critique of the humanist model: the dualistic model of the body-world relationship, which claims mimetic analogy as its formal operation, must be replaced by a 'post-structuralist' model whose initial insight recognizes a fundamental reciprocity (inter-relatedness) between body and world.

Having located in Sartre's work the possibility of rewriting the body in 'post-structuralist' terms, Vidler now returns to his initial questions. How can buildings be like bodies if the body has disappeared? Has the body really disappeared? If not, how does it manifest itself, how is it present in the objects of the world? This portion of Vidler's thesis relies heavily on Scarry. Sounding a note that has familiar overtones, Scarry argues that, '…artifacts are (in spite of their inertness) perhaps most accurately perceived as 'a making sentient of the external world.'[23] Such sentience is achieved by any man-made object as a projection of the human body. Scarry reformulates the phenomenon of projection in three different ways, each progressively more interior than the previous one. We move from

187

Robert McAnulty

bodily projections that are formally mimetic (lens, pumps), to the projection of bodily attributes (seeing, desiring), to the projection of an animistic sense of aliveness. Of animistic projection, she writes, "Aliveness' or 'awareness of aliveness' is in some very qualified sense projected out onto the object world.'[24] Here then we have the answer to the question of whether the body is really missing at all. Since all artifacts bear the mark of the bodies that made/projected them, then the preeminent status of the body in the very structure of perception is restored. Once again buildings can be like bodies.

How then, we must ask, do the exteriorized embodiments/projections of the so-called 'post-structuralist' body differ from those of the classical body? If in both cases, the formal model is projection, then we can only account for the differences between the forms projected by reformulating the interior conditions of the post-structuralist body. For this reformulation Vidler turns to Jacques Lacan. To briefly recount Lacan's famous essay on the 'mirror stage', he describes the moment an infant sees himself for the first time in the mirror and concomitantly identifies himself as a totality or integrated self. Prior to the mirror stage, the infant perceives himself only as 'morselated' or fragmented. Following the encounter with the mirror, this fragmentary condition is repressed in the unconscious. The subsequent unexpected reappearance of the repressed material returns through a pathological network of dreams and psychoses. The form of this repressed material is marked, in Lacan's words, 'by disjointed members and organs figured in exoscopy…'[25], which is presumably the formal character of 'morselation'. Vidler identifies the renewed contact with those experiences previously repressed or hidden from consciousness as the experience of the 'uncanny', about which he has written at length elsewhere.[26] To summarize the argument, we are led to understand that a building, as one of the man-made artifacts of the world, stands as the result of the projection of the body. Endowed with an animism that results from the exteriorization of the sentient qualities of the post-Freudian body, certain buildings cause us to lose our sense of grounding by revealing the presence of something that we had believed to be absent, but in fact had only been repressed.

Here again the language of animism has replaced that of anthropomorphism. Whereas Pérez-Gómez describes the animistic in Hejduk's work by reference to the 'marvelously animated machines with brilliant suits of armour,' Vidler cites the work of Alvaro Siza, Silvetti and Machado, and Coop Himmelblau. I have reason to believe that Vidler is unhappy with this portion of his lecture, so I won't dwell on his examples. Briefly, however, Coop Himmelblau's Red Angel Cafe is cited for its play on Melville's description of the wind in *Moby Dick* as being 'bodiless as object but not as agent.' Presumably Vidler reads the project's formal play of cutting and fragmentation as evidence of the 'animal-like' play of some bodiless agent (the mythic Red Angel), a presence that cannot be understood in the conventional terms of finite self-closure that characterize the body as a static, figural object. In Vidler's eyes, Siza's architecture school for Porta displays a similar animistic awareness in its fractional composition. It is not clear from Vidler's description of these projects how they serve to reveal the presence of some absent experience that has been repressed. Notwithstanding his detailed development of Scarry's thesis, Vidler's animistic readings of architectural projects are peculiarly limited in their scope. Since we come away from the lecture with a somewhat unsatisfying image of Coop Himmelblau's 'panther in the urban jungle' (whose formal counterpart turns out to be nothing more than a simple beam characterized as spinelike), we continue to wonder how the panther figures in our unconscious, how the animistic presence of its figural absence is representative of some presocial mirror stage. In deference to Vidler, perhaps we should assume that there is more analysis yet to come.

In noting the brevity of Vidler's account of the way in which animism or the body's animistic projection informs buildings, my reading is that he is less concerned with the 'post-structuralist' body in figural terms than he is with the psychological or psychoanalytic readings of the projects he has chosen to describe. Near the end of the lecture, his account shrewdly changes its focus from the question of the body's projection of its interior states to *our* body's experience of the products of such projection. In his description of our experience of such projects as the Red Angel Cafe, we are variously 'contorted, racked, cut, wounded, impaled, and dissected.' And the effect of all this pain is to make us lose our sense of 'grounding', to force us to question the apparent stability of our psychological foundations. In short, we experience the 'uncanny' and in so doing we initiate a movement wherein we will 'overcome the mirror stage' in our return to the 'stage before the mirror'. In summoning the experience of the 'uncanny', these buildings make possible our recognition that the apparent autonomy of consciousness and the unity of our bodies are never more than fictive social constructions. So far, so good we say, such a critique appears to be leading toward identifying the social inscription of the body in terms similar to Foucault's. But here we encounter a difficulty. For now, having described the frightening return of previously repressed materials, the so-called 'presence of absence', Vidler proceeds to speak of the importance of a *return* to a pre-mirror condition. The clever translation into spatial terms of the pre-mirror stage to the 'stage before the mirror' serves to mask the temporal condition in which the subject appears prior to the mirror rather than in front of it. This is precisely the sort of appeal to a primordial lost origin that characterized Pérez-Gómez' argument. We are to go back in search of the presocial body that is understood as being constituted prior to its experience of the world. Although this body is now described in formal terms that differ from those of the humanist figure, i.e., morselated versus whole, nonetheless we are once again faced with a model of a unified subject that precedes its object-making activities in the world. So once again, buildings can be like bodies because they are the exteriorized result of the body's projection of its interiorized condition, be they fragmented or otherwise. In spatial terms, this model regenerates the perspectival distance between the body and its objects that Heidegger and Sartre worked so hard to disperse.

Now isn't it curious that both Pérez-Gómez and Vidler arrive at the issue of animism in their search for the missing body? All the more curious because of the body's reactions to its own image projected animistically. For Pérez-Gómez, the body's experience of itself in the form of 'marvelously animated machines with brilliant suits of armour and scintillating eyes' is akin to an act of ritualized transcendence; its essence is revelatory and emancipatory. For Vidler, on the other hand, the experience is also revelatory, but this revelation is a frightening and uncomfortable one because it reveals to the body the instability of its egocentric unity. Whereas for Pérez-Gómez the body's concern for transcendence is natural and healthy, Vidler's body is in pain, its experience of its own animistic projections is necessary, but difficult.

Both, however, must be seen as reformulating the issue of the body and architecture in terms fundamentally unchanged from those of Geoffrey Scott. Both insist on a model that

189

Robert McAnulty

Figure 1 Diller and Scofidio, 'the with
Drawing room' installation at 65 Capp Street,
San Francisco, 1987.

finds the body as an interiorized subject projecting itself onto an exterior world. As such, both fail to answer the challenges posed by Foucault's formulation of the subject as pure exteriority, the product of the inscription of the relations of power in culture. And in failing to answer Foucault's critique, the psychoanalytic and phenomenological models fail us in two ways. First, in their unwillingness to propose an alternative to a model based on analogic projection, they fail to dislocate the preeminent position of the humanist subject within architectural discourse. Second, and perhaps more important, in their refusal to formulate the body-architecture question in *relational* terms, they fail to offer us the possibility of responding to it in anything other than *figural* terms. Having concluded that the body *figures* architecture, one finds little choice but to explore the languages of renovation or return; hardly the most fertile terrain in a culture whose *relational* structures remain to be mapped.

How does the work of Elizabeth Diller and Ricardo Scofidio manage to satisfy all the criticisms of the first three models? Very simply, it doesn't. I choose to focus on them because I find their work to be amongst the most aggressive and provocative being done in architecture today. This is not to posit it as a new formal model (although that has clearly already happened in the schools) or to suggest that a comprehensive new way of figuring the body is immanent in the work and susceptible to analysis. On the contrary, I bring their work to your attention in hopes of sparking a dialogue about the multiple possibilities for rewriting the body and about how we architects might best remain open to these possibilities.

To start with, we must get beyond Diller and Scofidio's own stated intentions. Due at least in part to the insatiable appetites of the media machinery, Diller and Scofidio have produced textual materials that do not always do justice to the projects themselves. One such text clearly locates Diller and Scofidio in the mainstream of body-world dualism:

> Leonardo da Vinci and Schlemmer constructed two fundamentally different models for the relationship between man and this world. As we slip further away from the model of Leonardo and past that of Schlemmer, into a time of revered artifice and spatial implosion, the relation of man to his world has become a subject of renewed interest. What could a new model of this relationship be? *Could there be one?* [27]

Only the final sentence suggests the possibility of moving beyond the self-projecting subject of humanism. Given the remarkably exploratory character of their projects, this inability to formulate the question in terms other than figural, those of a projected interiority, is testament to the success of the phenomenological and psychoanalytic models in suppressing the alternative possibilities for formulating (versus reformulating) the question. As long as the question is marked by figural terminology, our answers will be inevitably prefigured.

From the outset, I should note that although Diller and Scofidio have somewhat disingenuously attempted to unify their projects to date by identifying them as 'bodybuildings', I find the work lacking the unitary character of a 'body' of work. Hence, whether consciously or subconsciously, there is already a questioning of architecture's traditional insistence on identifying the body with the self-enclosed figure. My reading, prompted by Deleuze and Artaud, is that Diller and Scofidio are attempting to make themselves a 'body without organs'. Lacking a fixed hierarchy of ideas/organs organized by an internal logic of function and circulation, the projects indicate multiple directions for reformulating the

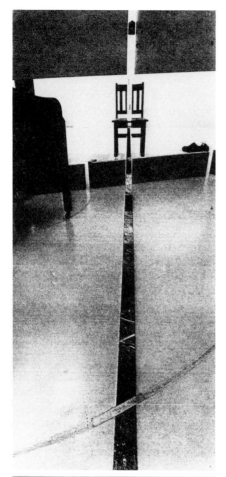

Figures 2, 3 Diller and Scofidio, 'the with Drawing room' installation at 65 Capp Street, San Francisco, 1987.

body; as such, these so-called 'probes' are intended to ignite our desire to engage the body anew. This body is not to be understood either as a corpse awaiting our autopsy, inert and static, nor as a figure to gaze upon, upright and complete. The readings of Diller and Scofidio work that follow attempt to map their body (of work) as a multiplicity of simultaneous trajectories sharing neither originary source, nor similar speed, nor parallel direction.[28] Such reading does not aspire to the synthetic completion or organic fullness of the historian's exegesis, but prefers instead to project possibilities for further investigatory work.

First, their writings notwithstanding, Diller and Scofidio's projects do not attempt to replace the Vitruvian figure with another figure. There is no attempt at renovation nor resuscitation here, no return to figural origins. By confining their focus to a limited number of peculiar *spatial* relationships, Diller and Scofidio shift attention from the figural presence of the body acting within a world of objects, to the conditions under which the body comes to embody certain social definitions. For instance, the remarkable emptiness of projects like the installations for Capp Street and Gallery Nature Morte is due to an unusual absence of figural bodies. This absence is not intended to nostalgically recall a time of figural presence, but to reveal the necessarily fictive identity of the body fabricated by social structures. Capp Street's floating 'dining room', less its floor (figure 1), the 'living room' cut by the reflected property line (figure 2), the 'bed room' with its hinged bed (figure 3), all speak to the absence of the bodies whose ritualized domesticity is inscribed in their workings. The domesticated body is no longer present in this project, replaced by Diller and Scofidio's concretization of the social practices that precede and prefigure the body. Here then we are not confined to the twin figures of figural 'presence' and 'presence of absence', which haunt Vidler's psychoanalytic readings of architecture. Instead Diller and Scofidio call to our attention a third possibility, that of the presence of something non-figural – the spatial structures that order our bodies. If this is so, then the effect of the emptiness to which I referred to earlier need not be frightening discomfort so much as startling disclosure. And by confining their attention to these non-figural structures, Diller and Scofidio resist the temptation to substitute some new 'postmodern' figure for the models written by Vitruvius, Leonardo, and Schlemmer. Alternatively, Diller and Scofidio actively engage the social practices that give form to our lives by cutting them open, laying them bare for our inspection, independent of our use. Their method is descriptive rather than prescriptive, culturally analytical rather than psychoanalytical.

Given the media's obsession with the bodily appendages, which appear in so many Diller and Scofidio projects, it may be difficult to find reason for my suggestion that the work be read as a spatial (versus figural) critique. But attention to such figures as the *Bride in Her Corset* and the *Automarionette* should be directed to their bondage rather than to their figural unity. The physicality of the human figure is the basis for the addition of the mechanisms of control. Reminiscent of Kleist's puppet figures, the apparatus of the *Automarionette* shapes the body's engagement with the world by limiting its sight (with a mask), its touch (with gloves), and its movement (with a system of counterweights) (figure 5). The *Bride*'s sexuality is held firmly in place (and protected) by her metal corset. In neither case does the body seem comfortable in its bondage (figure 4), that is, this is not an argument for some new form of biomechanical naturalism. These bodies are capable of action and reaction, but their movements are defined within a network of forces, both

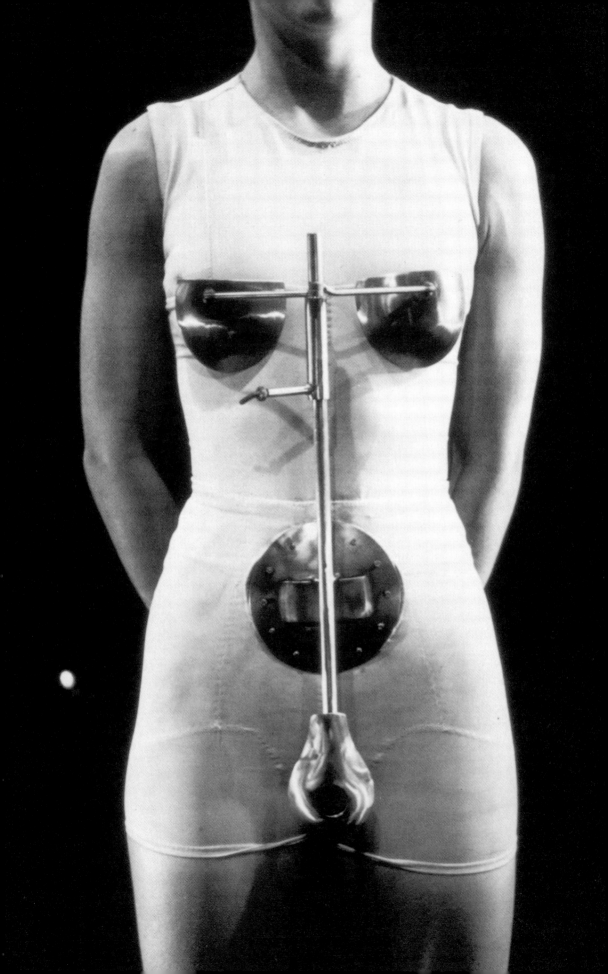

Figure 4 Diller and Scofidio, *The Bride's Armor,* from 'The Notary Rotary and his Hot Plate,' 1987.

Figure 5 Diller and Scofidio, *Automarionette,* from 'The Notary Rotary and his Hot Plate,' 1987.

195

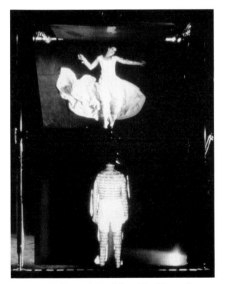

Figure 6 Diller and Scofidio, *The Chase,* from 'The Notary Rotary and his Hot Plate,' 1987.

Figure 7 Diller and Scofidio, *The Bachelor longs for his object of desire,* from 'The Notary Rotary and his Hot Plate,' 1987.

political and gravitational. And this network is important to us because it inscribes our bodies through our constructions, our spaces. Here again we are confronted with a model of space wherein the body's significance is not as a figural source of mimetic projection, but as site for the inscriptions of power.

Finally, we cannot fail to note the explicitly sexual character of Diller and Scofidio's body (of work), as opposed to the body's spiritualized asexuality in the models, which claim animism as their starting point. In their investigations of the social structures that assign sexual roles, Diller and Scofidio take on the issue the at level of gender difference. The performance apparatus for 'A Delay in Glass' (based on Duchamp's *Large Glass*) represents, in Diller and Scofidio's words, the 'irreconcilability between male and female.'[29] Despite tendencies to androgyny in the *Bachelor*, the classical sexual differences between male and female remain intact and unreconciled. The masks, the armor, the rope all are signs of a sexual struggle that resists easy conciliation. The stereotypical division of sexual roles, which is marked by the horizontal line in Duchamp's *Glass*, is dislocated from the vertical plane of the window to the horizontal plane of the floor (figures 6, 7). No longer pure and detached, this *Bride* is dominated by the same sexual energies as her suitor, yet their bodies are always separated by the social apparatus of the metallic door. The painful desire to reconcile, to become one, is only consummated virtually, in the reflection of the mirror mounted diagonally overhead. Neither the body of the *Bride* nor of the *Bachelor* can be understood independent of its sexuality, but the social roles inscribed by terms like masculinity and femininity are assigned by social conventions and institutions. Diller and Scofidio acknowledge architecture's complicity in prescribing sexual difference in the figure of the pivoting door, while simultaneously reflecting on the inscriptive power of convention through the figure of the mirror.

In the briefest outline this paper marks the beginnings of a map that reformulates the body in spatial (versus figural), inscriptive (versus projective), and sexual (versus animistic) terms. And as beginnings, it serves only to point the way for further exploration. One last thing should be said: we must be wary of all attempts to confine our mapping to areas already explored. No matter how cleverly the naturalistic terrain of humanism is newly refigured by phenomenology or psychoanalysis, we should not allow ourselves to be tricked into retracing our steps.

1 A. Kroker and D. Cook, *The Postmodern Scene* (New York, 1986), p. 12.
2 For a more extensive review of the work of Diller and Scofidio, see my essay in the Philadelphia Institute of Contemporary Art, *Investigations* 23 (Philadelphia, 1988), n.p.
3 G. Scott, *The Architecture of Humanism* (Gloucester, 1914), p. 177.
4 M. Foucault, *The Order of Things* (New York, 1970).
5 Ibid., p. 25.
6 M. Foucault, *Discipline and Punish*, tr. A. Sheridan (New York, 1979), passim.
7 Ibid., p. 155.
8 Ibid., p. 27.
9 F. Kafka, *The Penal Colony*, tr. W. and E. Muir (New York, 1961), pp. 191-230.
10 M. Foucault, *Discipline and Punish*, pp. 202-203. Emphasis added.
11 Ibid., p. 172.

12 A. Pérez-Gómez, 'The Renovation of the Body: John Hejduk and the Cultural Relevance of Theoretical Project,' *AA Files* 13, pp. 26-29.
13 Ibid., p. 27.
14 Ibid., p. 28.
15 Ibid., p. 26.
16 M. Heidegger, 'The Origin of the Work of Art,' in *Poetry, Language, Thought*, tr. A. Hofstadter (New York, 1971), p. 53.
17 A. Pérez-Gómez, 'The Renovation of the Body,' p. 26.
18 Ibid., p. 28.
19 A. Vidler, 'The Building in Pain: The Body and Architecture in Post-Urban Culture,' unpublished lecture delivered at the Cooper Union, Spring 1988. Since this paper was delivered in September of 1988, I understand that Vidler has taken steps to develop and refine the arguments presented in the lecture to which I refer herein.
20 E. Scarry, *The Body in Pain* (New York, 1985).

21 J.-P. Sartre, *Being and Nothingness* (New York, 1959).
22 Ibid., p. 428.
23 E. Scarry, *The Body in Pain*, p. 281.
24 Ibid., p. 286.
25 J. Lacan, 'The Mirror Stage,' *Écrits*, tr. A. Sheridan (New York, 1977), pp. 1-7.
26 A. Vidler, 'The Architecture of the Uncanny,' *Assemblage* 3, pp. 7-30.
27 Diller and Scofidio, unpublished teaching text.
28 I am indebted to G. Deleuze and F. Guattari, *A Thousand Plateaus*, tr. B. Massumi (Minneapolis, 1987) for this formulation.
29 Diller and Scofidio, unpublished teaching text.

Mark Rakatansky teaches design and theory at
the School of Architecture at the University of
Illinois at Chicago, where he is the Director of
the Committee on Physical Thought. He has
been a visiting critic at the Harvard University
Graduate School of Design and the University
of Florida at Gainesville. He is on the editorial
board of *Assemblage* and is the series editor of
*Theoretical Perspectives in Architectural
Criticism and History*, published by Yale
University Press.

Spatial Narratives

Mark Rakatansky

There is no mute architecture. All architects, all buildings 'tell stories' with varying degrees of consciousness. Architecture is permeated with narratives because it is constituted within a field of discourses and economies (formal, psychological, and ideological), to any one aspect of which it cannot be reduced, from any one of which it cannot be removed.

If we examine, for example, any type of domestic architecture we will find already inscribed *within* the architecture a complex array of mentalities and practices[1] concerning the relations between genders, between parents and children, between 'inside' and 'outside', between what is supposed to be 'public' and what is supposed to be 'private', between what is supposed to be seen, smelt, or heard and what is not, and so forth. The hierarchy and degree of definition of spaces, their relative size and location, and the sub-architectural apparatuses of each space (furniture, appliances, media devices) – all these are defined by and give definition to the social and psychological narratives that influence the behaviors (encouraged, allowed, discouraged, or forbidden) associated with each space. The elements of this field are polyvalent: each aspect will be influenced by mentalities and practices already established (perhaps already in decline) and newly emerging (perhaps not fully articulated) – and thus each will conflict with, reinforce, or ignore the others.[2]

Yet to speak of narrative strategies in architecture plunges one immediately into difficulty. Between those who would insist upon (or call for) the intrinsic nature of a 'non-rhetorical' architecture (claiming that a brick is just a brick, a wall just a wall, a room just a room, that stone and steel, metal studs and gypsum board can not or should not 'speak') and those all too eager to 'add meaning' to buildings through the 'telling of fables', there seems barely enough space to suggest another position.[3] The seemingly opposed positions of a 'non-rhetorical' architecture and a 'story-telling' architecture converge in their belief that rhetorical meaning does not reside in buildings other than in the most general sense, either as a 'timeless expression' of classical (or vernacular) ideals or as a 'zeitgeist expression'. Both of these positions posit that if architecture could tell a story, that story would need to be designed *into* the 'mute' and empty vessel of architecture as an *additive* feature.[4]

But rather than conceiving of narrative architecture as arising from an addition of a singular story-line, it would be critically more constructive to speak in the plural, of narratives – of exposing and reworking certain repressed narratives within the field of discourses and economies already at work in architecture.

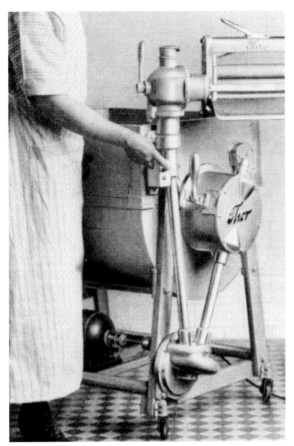

'The office building is a house of work   of
organization   of clarity   of economy.'
Ludwig Mies van der Rohe, 1923

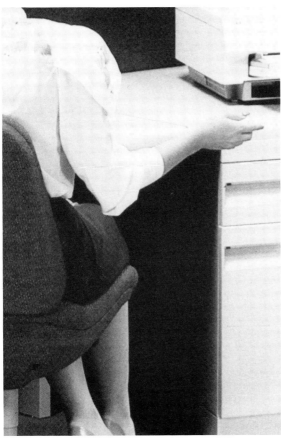

'If this wonderful new 'scientific
management' brings such results in
other businesses, why couldn't it do the
same in my business of home-making?'
Christine Frederick, 1926

Mark Rakatansky

One

Before proceeding further it will be necessary to address the so-called linear structures of both narrative and temporality, as these related issues inevitably arise as arguments that are supposed to keep narrative wholly distinct from architecture. There is still a tendency to conceive of narrative in terms of what was assumed to be the conventions operative in nineteenth-century realist fiction – a linear development from origin to end. And, thus, any strategy that opposes the 'naturalness' of these assumed conventions is thought to be 'anti-narrative.'

There are two problems with this view. On the one hand, recent literary theory has shown that the conventions of realism operate in much more complex and indeterminate ways than had been previously thought: beginnings do not constitute definitive origins, development is never seamlessly continuous (as transitions are inevitably disjunctive), endings do not provide definite closure.[5] And while it has been claimed that a book (unlike a building) can exert total control over its sequential unfolding, there isn't a definitive linear reading. Each time we reread a book we encounter aspects or relations between aspects that we remembered differently or not at all. Our attentions and inattentions are different with each passage through a book. The hegemonic claims of 'conventional' narrative are for naturalism and stability attempt to make these disjunctions, as Roland Barthes noted:

> …our society takes the greatest pains to conjure away the coding of the narrative situation: there is no counting the number of narrational devices which seek to naturalize the subsequent narrative by feigning to make it the outcome of some natural circumstance and thus, as it were, 'disinaugurating' it… The reluctance to declare its codes characterizes bourgeois society and the mass culture issuing from it: both demand signs which do not look like signs.[6]

On the other hand, 'anti-narratives' strategies (montage, meta-narrative, and so forth) always continue to narrate, can not avoid narrating – even as they problematize and resist certain conventional practices precisely in order to reveal the seams of narrative, to reveal how narrative is constructed from a discontinuous series of effects. 'Anti-narrative' strategies, in other words, are not non-narrative.

It is within this struggle, between the inability to narrate in a seamless and definitive manner and the inability not to narrate, that narrative is constituted. This is the way, as it were, that narrative narrates, within this field of disability and ability.

There has been a similar misunderstanding with regard to the temporal dimension of architecture. It is commonly claimed that temporality does not exist *within* architecture (the way it supposedly exists within – and thus makes possible – literary narrative), that buildings are 'frozen in time', that temporality exists only in the experience of a building through time. Given these claims, it is not surprising to find the current interest in 'processional' buildings and building complexes that appear to be the only architecture to develop a linear 'narrative' with a 'proper' beginning, middle, and end (Giuseppe Terragni's Danteum project, the Villa Lante, and the Sacra Monti are frequently cited examples). My previous comments regarding narrative extend to procession in architecture: that is, on the one hand, all so-called processional architecture operates in much more complex and indeterminate ways than is generally assumed,[7] and on the other hand, all architecture is processional (in other words, can not be non-processional).

When I say that all architecture is processional, I mean that whether a building maintains the conventional relationships between spatial units for a given institutional type or

202

attempts to disrupt such conventions, in both cases the subject will experience a procession through the various units of institutional space: from street to lobby, to stairs or elevators, to other lobbies or reception spaces or corridors or rooms, to other anterooms or other corridors or other rooms, and so forth. Even in the unlikely case that one's route through a building would differ each time, it would always be a sequence through a series of spaces. This is not merely an arbitrary procession along a 'neutral' continuum that has been characterized as 'public' on the one end and as 'private' on the other end.[8] We need only imagine a typical procession through the various spaces of a domicile, an office, or a governmental building to be aware not only how each space is deeply saturated with a complex field of social and psychological narratives, but also how the effects of these narratives accrue (not necessarily in a unified way) in the procession from space to space.

Thus one could argue that the most significant temporal dimension of architecture is not given by the physical experience of moving through a building, but rather by the temporality of institutional practices inscribed in architectural space. Our understanding of the (seemingly stable) types of institutional space (the domicile, the office, the school, the museum, and so forth), is such that, once we experience these types, we need not physically traverse a given building to have a sense of the temporal dimension of inhabitation likely to be found there. We know even before we enter a domicile in our culture, whether it is a suburban tract house or an 'open' loft, the forms of inhabitation that we can expect to find there: the processional ordering and temporal use of the spaces, and the temporal and spatial ordering of the institutional rituals that take place there. But perhaps it is in the relationship between these two temporalities (the temporality of physical procession and the temporality of institutional practices) that the temporal dimension of architecture is best described.

Two

Thus I will be arguing that *the ways in which human subjects are constituted and managed in institutional space* may provide one of the more productive themes for a narrative architecture.[9] In fact, all designed space functions as institutional space.[10] Institutions are the principal sites through which ideologies work, and thus, as in the case ideologies (and conventional narrative, as Barthes noted) it is in the interest of institutions to effect (or at least give the illusion of) stable conditions. And like narrative, both institutions and ideologies are constructs – they are neither natural, nor universal, nor timeless, but artificial structures created through shifting historical circumstances, discontinuous series of effects working within a field of ability and disability. The function of ideology, as Slavoj Zizek notes, 'is not to offer us a point of escape from our reality, but to offer us the social reality itself as an escape from some traumatic, real kernel.' It is the very inconsistency of the social field, the impossibility of its seamless constitution, its gaps and residues, that ideology has to mask, conceal, screen.[11] And it is in such gaps – at the level of the subject, the institutional program, the building, the site, and so forth – that certain critical architectural narratives might emerge.

The institutional program is one professional mask that architecture wears in the service of ideologies. Generally the ideological and social shifts that have affected architectural shifts in the built form of institutions (given rise to, been barriers to) have been given little attention by architectural historians and critics in favor of formal analyses. However, it is

203

difficult to comprehend the shift in western domestic space – from commonly unspecified spaces prior to the eighteenth century to the subsequent development of specialized rooms – unless this shift is read in relation to the history of domestic mentalities and practices: shifts in the concepts of family, gender, privacy, hygiene, the place of the child (and servants and non-family) in the house, the relationship of the family to the 'outside' society, relations between classes, as well as the partial transfer of education and moralization from the religious to the secular and familial domain.[12] Similarly, a number of developments in domestic, other institutional, and urban spaces beginning in the eighteenth century can be related to the 'need' of the State for the surveillance and management of social space (the policing of the social body) instigated by a 'concern' for hygiene. Beyond the official stated intentions, these hygienic programs involved the 'surveillance, analysis, intervention, and modification' of populations as a means of providing finer and more adequate control mechanisms, as well as the maintenance of bodies as usable labor.[13]

But there are also moments when seemingly contradictory ideologies coalesce. One such moment, as Foucault has pointed out, is that of the French Revolutionaries' embrace of Bentham's Panopticon project as an instrumental model for a 'transparent' society, which they linked with the Rousseauean vision of a totally unobstructed collective communication that would eradicate the darkness where injustice and unhappiness breeds.[14] Yet even in Rousseau it is already clear that this transparency is not to be equally distributed: Rousseau's desire for people to look freely into each other's hearts was not for him a matter of abolishing social differences, but merely a way to give the 'sense' of social fraternity in order to maintain the existing social order.[15] These contradictions within and between ideologies would become visible in the architectural form of the Panopticon, which is not specifically a prison (being equally useful for hospitals, factories, or schools) or even a building type. The Panopticon is a system of management, an instrument for the control of the visible and the invisible, of bodies, of power. The theme of instrumental transparency in architecture, which the Panopticon exemplifies, circulates around the problems of management, of the illumination of some darknesses and the preservation of other darknesses, of efficient communication and productive labor, and of the maintenance of the physical and moral 'health' of the 'social body'. This theme will return again and again: in the social hygiene movements, in the infiltration of Taylorism and Scientific Management in the work place and the home,[16] in many of the urban proposals and architectural polemics of the modern movement.[17] What is often constituted as, or presented under the guise of progressive reform or democratization or social health, harbors the technologies of management and surveillance either as its means or its ends.[18] A more recent manifestation of instrumental transparency can be found in the 'open office' system (which has been referred to as a 'managerial tool'), where a shift away from earlier forms of the spatial repressiveness of hierarchization and compartmentalization of the subject in the office environment would result in just other forms of hierarchization and compartmentalization, as well as an increased lack of privacy that came with an increased efficiency of institutional management and surveillance.[19]

Three

It should be clear, however, that architecture can not control behavior in some absolute manner. Architecture participates in the managing of subjects because its own structuring is not dissimilar, at many levels, to the structuring of the programs/institutions that it 'houses' in terms, for example, of the organization, hierarchization, and systematization of order, activities, behavior, movement, and visibility. One could examine how the obsessive rationality – obsessive to the point of irrationality – of both architecture and institution is woven through and through the space of, say, the office type: from the regularized architectonic systems of structure, to the hierarchical 'space-planning' of subjects (managers, staff, and visitors), to the standardized body registers of office practices (under the 'rigors' of ergonomic 'science'), right down to the compartmentalization of subjects and objects via various filing systems. These systems exemplify the capillary action of Foucault's 'microtechnologies of power,' the 'circulation of effects of power through progressively finer channels, gaining access to individuals themselves, to their bodies, their gestures and all their daily actions.'[20] It is in this manner that architecture functions both *as and under authority*. Architecture both structures and is structured by institutions.[21] It is a commonly held notion of our 'postmodern' time that different programs can inhabit the same space because programs are completely independent from architectural spatiality. But it is the similarity, not the disparity, between the structure of institutions, and between the structure of institutions and architecture, that allows this interchangeability of inhabitation and management.

205

From the preceding discussion it should also be clear that the play of ideologies in architectural form is so complex that it would be pointless to expect a unitary ideology to be reflected in a building (even at the moment it is actualized as a design project or in built form). The conceptual gaps and temporal lags between ideologies and built form are analogous to the gaps and lags between ideologies and 'material' conditions.[22] To trace this ideological drama one would need to examine how the object, in Manfredo Tafuri's words, 'reaches compromises with regard to the world and what conditions permit its existence' and thus what conditions govern its relationship to production and use.[23]

It would be equally pointless to imagine that any architectural project could be reduced, either in analysis or design, to a definitive map that could account for all the forces at play, to a totalizing diagram of formal, psychological, and social relations. The convergence of discourses and economies at the nexus of the subject, space, site, or program provides an opportunity not to resurrect an ultimate truth-value of 'Site' or 'Program', but to utilize each force against itself, against other forces, and against the entire project. The nostalgia of current 'contextualism' can be interrogated by architecturally utilizing past or present aspects of the context to simultaneously problematize the object by the site and the site by the object. The naive problem-solving of sixties' behaviorialism can be similarly interrogated by architecturally utilizing the program to question certain institutional practices. In all cases, any representation of these forces will always be one of many possible representations.

Four

Thus far I have been discussing some of the ways subjects are constituted and managed in institutional space. To demonstrate the deep pervasiveness of these structurings and mechanisms it will be necessary first to examine how they are involved in a kind of a repressed architectural unconscious, and second, how the examination of this architectural unconscious reveals certain gaps and inconsistencies within the social field from which critical

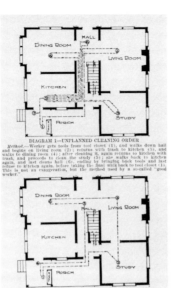

DIAGRAM 1—UNPLANNED CLEANING ORDER

Method.—Worker gets tools from tool closet (1), and walks down hall and begins on living room (2); returns with trash to kitchen (3), and walks to dining room (4); after cleaning it, again returns to kitchen with trash, and proceeds to clean the study (5); she walks back to kitchen again, and last cleans hall (6), ending by bringing back tools and last refuse to kitchen again, before taking the final walk back to tool closet (1). This is not an exaggeration, but the method used by a so-called "good worker."

DIAGRAM 2—PLANNED CLEANING ORDER

Method.—Worker gets tools from tool closet (1), and proceeds direct to study (2); from study through door to parlor (3); across parlor hallway to dining room (4); she then begins at upper end of hallway (5), and cleans its length back to the door opening on rear porch, carrying all waste and tools back directly to service porch (6). Note that this method eliminates *all* tracking to kitchen and results in about two-thirds less unnecessary steps and walking.

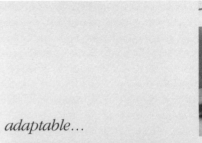

adaptable...

functional...

Starts and Stops Instantly at Your Touch

not studied the mechanism, tested it, used a little patience and followed well-worked-out rules for its operation.

I am quite sure that when somebody told your grandmother that finer, and more even, and perfect stitches could be taken in cloth with a needle set in a strange machine operated by a wheel and belt, than she could make by hand, that *she too, said that this new sewing machine "won't work"*—and it probably took some time for her to be convinced.

But you to-day know the perfection of sewing machine work, and

QUESTIONS ON HOUSEHOLD ENGINEERING

II

Plans and Methods for Daily Housework

1. Make out a schedule of your present plan of work. Study to see where it can be improved. Try the new schedule two weeks. Revise and try another two weeks, and report.
2. Time yourself for at least a week on the same task, as, washing dishes, peeling potatoes, making beds, or cleaning the bathroom. How long does it take? Do you find the time varying from day to day? Write down two complete "time-studies" on these tasks, showing the first record and the last.
3. "Standardize" some household task so that you can do it every day in an identical manner without much mental attention. Does this not make it seem less difficult?
4. What are your worst "interruptions"? Make a schedule which will take care of them as much as possible.
5. Do the same task with two different tools, and note the difference, or do the same task with two different methods, or do it under two different sets of conditions. Find out the way that seems the best and shortest for your particular case and report.

versatile…

flexible…

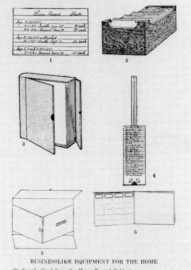

BUSINESSLIKE EQUIPMENT FOR THE HOME

(1) Sample Card from the Home Record Cabinet
(2) The Time and Worry Saving Home Record Cabinet
(3) A Vertical Letter File for Receipts
(4) A Tickler Which Reminds the Busy Housewife
(5) A Vertical Filing Envelope for Saving Large Clippings
(6) A Book of Handy Labels for Home Use

narratives and strategies might emerge.

The architectural project, like the social field, is never without some slippage, some gap, some residue that cannot be sheltered, institutionalized, concealed. In fact, one definition of architecture could be *the management of what can and cannot be 'concealed'*. One could speak, in this light, of many things that refuse to remain concealed: anomalous behaviors, sexuality, certain odors,[24] domestic violence (in the broadest sense), displaced social groups, and so on – as well as the social and institutional ideologies and mechanisms that attempt to manage the visibility of their own as well as others' practices. Yet it is because all that is supposed to be concealed refuses to remain concealed that it must be managed through the constant presentation of certain conventions of architectural order and propriety.[25]

The *unheimlich* is one word that has been used to refer to that which refuses to remain concealed. As several writers have noted, Sigmund Freud, in his essay 'The Uncanny,' puzzles over the strange confluence of meaning between two words that should have entirely opposite meanings: *heimlich* (the homey, the canny) and *unheimlich* (the unhomey, the uncanny). Freud, in the beginning of the essay, says that the '…German word *unheimlich* is obviously the opposite of *heimlich*, *heimisch*, meaning 'familiar', 'native', 'belonging to the home'; and we are tempted to conclude that what is 'uncanny' is frightening precisely because it is *not* known and familiar.' In the course of the essay what is revealed is another meaning of *heimlich*: "…concealed, kept from sight, so that others do not get to know about it…to behave *heimlich*, as though there were something to conceal…*heimlich* places (which good manners oblige us to conceal)'.' Thus, the 'uncanny is in reality nothing new or foreign, but something familiar and old-established in the mind which has been estranged only by the process of repression.' It is through this understanding that the force of Friedrich Schelling's definition of *unheimlich* as '…the name for everything that ought to have remained…hidden and secret and has become visible' becomes evident to Freud. The *unheimlich*, far from being the opposite and outside of the *heimlich*, *is* the *heimlich* – it is what is already inside, the homey that returns as the unhomey.[26]

Let me now go further with this already established elucidation. First, it is worth noting that it is not only in the German language that words related to the concept of home reveal an uncanny meaning. For example, the English verb 'to dwell' is derived from the Middle English *dwellen* (from the Old English *dwellan*), which means 'to lead astray, hinder,' and is akin to the Middle Dutch *dwellen,* which means 'to stun', and the Old High German *twellan* and the Old Norse, *dvelja*, which mean 'to delay, to deceive' – which in turn are all derived from the Indo-European base **dh(e)wel-*, which means 'to mislead, to deceive, to obscure, to make dull'[27]. And for the Sakalava, a tribe in Madagascar, among whom 'no one would refuse another entrance into his house *unless he were hoarding or hiding something*,' the word *mody*, which means 'at home' or 'heading home,' also means 'to pretend what one is not'.[28]

It is precisely the uncanny connotations of dwelling that Martin Heidegger repressed in favor of more *heimlich* ones (in his etymological 'derivations' from Old English and High German) in his late essay 'Building, Dwelling, Thinking.' It is interesting in this light to reconsider one of Heidegger's most famous statements: 'Language is at once the house of Being and the home of human beings.'[29] Heidegger claims that it is our highest 'summons' to try 'to bring dwelling to the fullest of its nature,'[30] but fails to acknowledge that this fullness includes both the *heimlich* and *unheimlich*. Such a failure of acknowledgement, Freud suggests, is what causes the *unheimlich* to return.

The *unheimlich* meanings of 'dwelling' suggest what is 'familiar and old-established' in architecture that returns in the uncanny. The very constitution of architecture reveals, in Zizek's words, a 'traumatic, real kernel.' I am referring to a condition that is not specific to recent times nor to western cultures but, as the anthropologist Peter J. Wilson notes, at the very least an aspect of all cultures that inhabit 'permanent' dwellings:

> When people adopted settlement and domestication as a permanent feature of their lives, they did not impinge directly on their drives of aggression and sexuality, but they did impinge directly on the *conditions of attention*. That is, they impeded their sensory ability to monitor, stimulate, and govern these drives. Living behind walls affects the various aspects of attention, and people so affected must respond. This occurs in part by specializing attention, by developing modes of surveillance, supervision, and inspection, and by evolving stratagems of evasion and display.[31]

Architecture constructs this evasion and at the same time is in constant flight from acknowledging its part in this construction. This evasion is the trauma of architecture, the 'antagonistic kernel' that always prevents the closure of the architectural field.[32] Thus it should not be so surprising to find language returns to us this uncanniness of inhabitation, this duplicity, this doubled concealment. And it should also not be surprising that the mechanisms and conventions masking the trauma of this uncanniness should themselves attempt to remain hidden and repressed so that they, like the ideologies they mask, appear natural, stable, unalterable.

I am suggesting that the constitution and management of subjects through the types, or rather stereotypes, of institutional space, that is, through the *compulsion to repeat* these stereotypes without examination, is one means by which the uncanny returns in architecture. In psychoanalytical terms, as Peter Brooks notes '…repetition is a way of remembering brought into play when recollection in the intellectual sense is blocked by repression and resistance.'[33] It is not the past as past that is recollected, that is, as 'something belonging to the past…in a bound state'[34]; what is repeated is repressed material brought into the present as an active force, as a defense against the direct examination of complex and potentially dangerous psychological relations. Architecture, for the most part, abandons itself to the unconscious repetition of stereotype – of the house, the office, the museum, the hospital, the library, and so forth – to such an extent that few architects think to re-examine the fundamental assumptions implicit within the conventional program. (As Freud says: 'The patient abandons himself to the compulsion to repeat, which is now replacing the impulse to remember.'[35]) The basic functions of institutional stereotypes, regardless of their varying configuration take from culture to culture or the formal shifts that may occur within a given culture through time, are as *mechanisms of management*, to reinforce 'proper' social and psychological relations, and as *mechanisms of defense*, to guard against potentially dangerous social and psychological relations, that is, all 'that ought to remain hidden and secret'. Architecture, according to Georges Bataille, is the expression of the very soul of society, but 'it is only the ideal soul of society, that which has the authority to command and prohibit, that is expressed in architectural compositions properly speaking. Thus great monuments are erected like dikes, opposing the logic and majesty of authority against all disturbing elements: it is in the form of cathedral or palace that Church or State speaks to the multitudes and imposes silence upon them.'[36]

The conservative cry within the architectural discipline to 'remember' and to repeat past formal, typological, and institutional models with the claim that these will shore us up, will make us safe and *heimlich*, is thus only the most vocal, *only the most apparent*, indication of this widespread compulsion to repeat. This architectural cry is similar to another current cry – to the 'Great Books' – a claim for connoisseurship as a defense against the critical examination of the classical canon. Such conscious cries for 'remembering' share with obsessional neurosis a 'forgetting' that 'consists mostly of a falling away of the links between various ideas, a failure to draw conclusions, an isolating of certain memories.'[37] This isolating of certain memories – literally in architecture an isolating of elements, institutional forms, 'typologies,' and styles of the past – seeks to bring back the past, to repeat what is 'remembered' as pleasurable, as *heimlich*. But, as Jacques Lacan observes, the object is not retrievable, what is recalled is never the object itself: 'The object is encountered and is structured along the path of repetition – to find the object again, to repeat the object. Except, it never is the same object which the subject encounters. In other words, he never ceases generating substitutive objects.'[38]

It is because the past is irretrievable (as only substitutive objects are generated in lieu of that past) and because, most importantly, truly conscious remembering requires a remembering not only of forms but of their repressed significance, that what is recalled in this repetition is repressed trauma.[39] Thus the most significant repetition that these conscious cries for 'remembering' mask is a behavioral repetition – *the resistance to critical analysis* as a mechanism of defense. As Freud states:

> The crux of the matter is that the mechanisms of defense against former dangers recur in analysis in the shape of *resistances* to cure. It follows that the ego treats recovery itself as a new danger… The patient now regards the analyst simply as an alien personality who makes disagreeable demands upon him and he behaves towards him exactly like a child who does not like a stranger and has no confidence in him. If the analyst tries to explain to the patient one of the distortions which his defence has produced and to correct it, he meets with a complete lack of comprehension and an imperviousness to valid arguments. We see then that there really *is* a resistance to the discovery of resistances and that the defense mechanisms…are resistances not only to the bringing of id-contents into consciousness but also to the whole process of analysis and so to cure.[40]

Five

Freud, in his discussion of defense mechanisms, states that they are 'in fact, infantilisms' that 'share the fate of so many institutions which struggle to maintain themselves when they have outlived their usefulness.' He continues this passage with a quote from Goethe's *Faust* summarizing the potential danger of both defense mechanisms and institutions. Reason becomes unreason, kindness torment.[41]

It is, of course, as impossible to escape the framework of institutions as it is to escape the framework of ideology. What is possible is an unending task – the development of abilities to perceive and examine the structuring of institutions, to reveal those conditions where reason becomes unreason, kindness torment. In opening our institutions up to questioning, we reveal their artificial, and therefore alterable, construct. Bertolt Brecht, whose work was based on revealing the changeable character of that which presents itself as familiar and immutable, has already noted the difficulty of breaking into the repetitive cycle of society:

For it seems impossible to alter what has long not been altered. We are always coming on things that are too obvious for us to bother to understand them. What men experience among themselves they think of as 'the' human experience. A child, living in a world of old men, learns how things work there… Even if he realizes that the arrangements made for him by 'Providence' are only what has been provided by society, he is bound to see society, that vast collection of beings like himself, as a whole that is greater than the sum of the parts and therefore not in any way to be influenced. Moreover, he would be used to things that could not be influenced; and who mistrusts what he is used to?[42]

Conventions, as representations of that which 'has long not been altered', are blocks both to awareness and to potential change. 'The past,' as Freud says, 'is the patient's armory out of which he fetches his weapons for defending himself against the progress of the analysis, weapons which we must wrest from him one by one.'[43] What are the means by which the defenses of the past might be wrest from the patient? To ignore them, to proceed as if they did not exist would, of course, be useless. However paradoxical it might at first appear, it is precisely by utilizing the compulsion to repeat against itself – by allowing it to display itself in its principal form (as a resistance to examination) – that progress is gained within the analysis: 'We render it harmless, and even make use of it, by according it the right to assert itself within certain limits…to display before us all the pathogenic impulses hidden in the depths of the patient's mind… Only when it has come to its height can one, with the patient's cooperation, discover the repressed instinctual trends which are feeding the resistance; and only by living them through in this way will the patient be convinced of their existence and their power.'[44] As Brooks observes:

> Repetition is both an obstacle to analysis – since the analysand must eventually be led to renunciation of the attempt to reproduce the past – and the principal dynamic of the cure, since only by way of its symbolic enactment in the present can the history of past desire, its objects and scenarios of fulfillment, be made known, become manifest in the present discourse… The narrative discourse – like the discourse of analysis – must restage the past history of desire as it exercises its pressure toward meaning in the present… At issue…is not so much the history of the past, or at least not the history of the past directly, as its present narrative discourse. This is a space of dialogue, struggle, construction.[45]

A restaging of the past history of desire as a construction requires a methodology that is able to distance itself enough from the past to perceive it as a construct – and therefore not just reproduce it. As Brecht suggests, such a methodology that would treat 'social situations as processes, and…regard nothing as existing except in so far as it changes, in other words is in disharmony with itself.'[46] But to create this distance it is necessary to denaturalize, to defamiliarize the past. For Brecht this involved a strategy he termed *Verfremdungseffekt,* most commonly translated as 'alienation effect': 'A representation that alienates is one which allows us to recognize its subject, but at the same time makes it seem unfamiliar,' in order to 'free socially-conditioned phenomena from that stamp of familiarity which protects them against our grasp today.'[47] As in the psychoanalytical model, this involves a two-fold process: a restaging, a working on the past (on what is repressing and what is repressed), and in this process a swerving, a distancing from any direct repetition in order to allow for analysis and the potential for a different construction. The point is not to reproduce the restrictive nostalgia of memory, but to develop the critical possibilities of counter-memory.[48]

attractive...

WEDNESDAY

6:00– 6:30	Rise and dress; start water heater
6:30– 7:00	Prepare breakfast
7:00– 7:30	BREAKFAST
7:30– 8:30	Wash dishes; inspect icebox; plan meals; start lunch
8:30– 9:00	Make beds; light cleaning
9:00–12:00	Ironing
12:00– 1:00	LUNCH
1:00– 2:00	Finish ironing; put away clothes
2:00– 3:00	Wash dishes; straighten kitchen
3:00– 4:00	*Rest period*
4:00– 5:00	Market; walk
5:30– 6:00	Prepare supper
6:00– 7:00	SUPPER
7:00– 7:30	Wash dishes

THURSDAY

6:00– 6:30	Rise and dress; start water heater
6:30– 7:00	Prepare breakfast
7:00– 7:30	BREAKFAST
7:30– 8:30	Wash dishes; straighten kitchen; plan meals
8:30– 9:00	Make beds
9:00–11:30	Bedrooms and closets cleaned
11:30–12:00	*Rest period*
12:00– 1:00	LUNCH
1:00– 2:00	Wash dishes; prepare vegetables toward supper
2:00– 3:30	Upstairs windows cleaned (Up and down stairs windows alternately each week)
3:30– 4:00	Silver polished
4:00– 5:30	*Rest period*
5:30– 6:00	Prepare supper
6:00– 7:00	SUPPER
7:00– 7:30	Wash dishes

FRIDAY

6:00– 6:30	Rise and dress; start heater
6:30– 7:00	Prepare breakfast
7:00– 7:30	BREAKFAST
7:30– 8:30	Wash dishes; straighten kitchen; plan meals

213

Earlier I suggested that it might be possible to pursue an architecture that would be critically productive in the sense of exposing, critiquing, problematizing, and reworking certain repressed narratives already at work in architecture. Rather than avoid sites of ideological and psychological saturation, such an architecture might draw out some of this saturation. This drawing out, this thematizing, is one method by which the obsessiveness and irrationality of the 'normal' and 'rational' may be revealed, may 'display before us all the pathogenic impulses' circulating around the repressed doubleness of inhabitation. One could characterize this inhabitation in the terms suggested by Wilson (in the developed modes and stratagems of surveillance, supervision, evasion, and display) or in the somewhat more general terms I suggested earlier: the organization, hierarchization, and systematization of institutional practices.

The architectural operations addressing these themes could occur not only in the traditional realms of the architect (spaces, walls, windows, doors, and so on), but also at the level of what I have called the 'sub-architectural'. It is at this level – of the office desk, or the filing system, or the household cabinet– that one might argue has at least as immediate, if not a more immediate impact in terms of the structuring of institutional ideologies, but it is at this level that architects mostly specify out of manufacturers' catalogues or leave others to select. Even given the task of designing, say, a reception desk, most architects would architecturally repress its obvious social and psychological aspects. Inscribed through and through with a libidinal and ideological economy, the reception desk is a site of institutional desire in the broadest of senses – as an apparatus of control, as a site that receives and keeps out, as an implicit participant and frame for the ubiquitous gender and class stereotyping of the 'receptionist' position. Architects are, of course, not inattentive to institutions; on the contrary, they custom design everything from spaces to furniture. It is just that their 'deepest' attention tends to reside in the *decorative* design of lobby spaces and executive desks, rather than designing these spaces and furnishings – or utilizing standardized objects – in a critical manner.

Six

The limits of these critical narrative strategies are when they become another conceit, another way for architects to feign interest in extra-formal issues. It is clearly of little value to make a casual reference to these themes in a project, or to use them to mask merely aesthetized objects. What becomes crucial is not the arbitrary or casual evocation of conceptually or politically current concerns but the critical act of selection, processing, and reworking – not to further mystify the object, nor to reduce the object to a diagram of social forces, but as a way to expose and examine the whole architectural enterprise. This, of course, includes the play of form through the architect, which is as much a theme to be explored and problematized as other psychological or social forces, and is thus subject to the same examinations and disjunctions within a narrative operation. In fact, the very act of architectural narration is not only not exempt from similar examinations and disjunctions, but requires that such techniques be turned on itself in order to expose the complexity and contingency of its own operations. There is, however, always a difficult balance between a discourse that fails to examine its own constitution and one that becomes self-consumed in privileging its own constitution, between, one might say, naive realism and unrelenting metafiction.

It only remains in this regard to suggest that the interventions that attempt to expose and problematize institutional narratives might also expose and problematize, rather than merely reproduce, the tedium of an absolutist rationality. In fact, it is from the gaps and slippages of that rationality that these interventions may emerge: 'Something that exceeds the thinkable and opens the possibility of 'thinking otherwise' bursts in through comical, incongruous, or paradoxical half-openings of discourse.'[49] As Brecht never tired of pointing out, this involves pleasure – the pleasure 'felt when the rules emerging from this life in society are treated as imperfect and provisional,'[50] the pleasure of 'the instability of every circumstance, the joke of contradiction and so forth: all these are ways of enjoying the liveliness of men, things and processes, and they heighten both our capacity for life and our pleasure in it.'[51]

However successful these narrative strategies may be at the level of the object, one still needs to acknowledge the limits of architectural practice to directly affect widespread social change, as well as the abilities of the hegemonic culture to absorb critical strategies. As Brecht has noted, 'Capitalism has the power instantly and continuously to transform into a drug the very venom that is spit in its face, and to revel in it.'[52] It is thus always necessary for critical strategies – and this includes the strategies that might emerge from the theoretical positions of this essay – to be constantly reevaluated and renewed.

Having stated certain critical limits of the architectural object I would nevertheless maintain the productiveness of an architectural narrative that is *constituted within and through these limits*. I would therefore disagree with the conclusions that Tafuri has drawn from his many years of analyzing the naiveté and bitter betrayals of avant-garde utopian dreams and progressive ideologies: 'To the deceptive attempts to give architecture an ideological dress, I shall always prefer the sincerity of those who have the courage to speak of that silent and outdated 'purity'; even if this, too, still harbors an ideological inspiration, pathetic in its anachronism.'[53] But what may be, for some, sincerity and courage, for others will be indifference, business as usual. At the risk of conveying, again in Tafuri's words, 'impotent and ineffectual myths, which so often serve as illusions that permit the survival of anachronistic 'hopes in design'.'[54] I would suggest that if we, with our lowered 'postmodern' expectations, can distinguish between direct political action and critical representations, we may be able to practice some means of both resistance and proposition within our work. In acknowledging the ineluctable rhetorical aspects of our discipline, we might critically examine within the limits of our practices (in ways that need not be, on the one hand, totalizing or utopian, nor on the other hand, conciliatory or reactionary) the complex relationships between architecture and social practices.

Regarding the illustrations: The office systems photographs appear courtesy of the Pleion Corporation. The other illustrations were taken from the following publications: C. Frederick, *The New Housekeeping: Efficiency Studies in Home Management* (Garden City, 1915), C. Frederick, *Household Engineering: Scientific Management in the Home* (Chicago, 1921); C. Frederick, *You and Your Laundry* (New York, 1922).

1 I am referring to mentalities and practices to avoid collapsing two related but distinct historiographic approaches. Regarding the former, see J. Le Goff, 'Mentalities: a history of ambiguities,' in *Constructing the Past: Essays in Historical Methodology*, ed. J. Le Goff and P. Nora (Cambridge, U.K., 1985), pp. 151-165. Regarding the latter, see M. Foucault, 'History of Systems of Thought' in Foucault, *Language, Counter-Memory, Practice*, ed. D. F. Bouchard (Ithaca, 1977), pp. 199-204 and his *The Archaeology of Knowledge* (New York, 1972). On the relations between the two approaches see L. Hunt, 'French History in the Last Twenty Years: The Rise and Fall of the *Annales* Paradigm, *Journal of Contemporary History*, Vol. 21 (1986), pp. 209-224 and P. Burke, *The French Historical Revolution: The Annales School 1929-89* (Stanford, 1990).

2 This multiplicity is further enlarged by several other constitutive elements. Whether a 'new' project or a renovation, the architectural work takes its place within a

productive…

CONTENTS

[xi]

physical site with its own field of discourses and economies. All these forces are 'filtered' and added to by the attentions and intentions (again at various levels of consciousness) of the architect, the succession of subjects who observe and inhabit the building, and the institutional programs under which they are managed.

For a discussion of the collision of forces under which architecture is constituted, and the concomitant 'collision' necessary in historiographic analysis, see M. Tafuri, 'The Historical Project,' in *The Sphere and the Labyrinth: Avant-Gardes and Architecture from Piranesi to the 1970s* (Cambridge, Mass., 1987), pp. 1-21.

3 The confusion that surrounds the term 'narrative architecture' is exemplified in the following attempt at a 'definition' by the editors of *Oz* (the journal of the College of Architecture and Design at Kansas State University) in their 1988 issue dedicated to this theme:

> Many architects have something to say in their architecture, a story to tell. There are a variety of means architects employ in expressing their own, or their clients values, thoughts, wishes, beliefs, and desires. They often communicate a unifying theme elaborated throughout the 'plot'. Some of the storytellers of our discipline choose to relate the entire story in a single building while others 'write' continuing sagas in which each building is a sequel to the last. Others, whether consciously or not, allude to earlier work by masters or to vital vernacular traditions. The architect's tale can be as captivating and powerful as the writer's. The best narratives give building added meaning and encourage people to become involved with and to cherish works of architecture. (p. 3)

4 The limit of these positions become apparent quickly if one considers, for example, the matter of the so-called appropriate character for a given institutional type (houses 'homey', museums 'stately', prisons 'foreboding'). Is this character supposed to be understood as an additive feature or as residing in the building?

5 See, for example, P. Brooks, *Reading for the Plot: Design and Intention in Narrative* (New York, 1984); F. Jameson, *The Political Unconscious: Narrative as a Socially Symbolic Act* (Ithaca, 1981); D. A. Miller, *Narrative and Its Discontents: Problems of Closure in the Traditional Novel* (Princeton, 1981); and E. W. Said, *Beginnings: Intention and Method* (Baltimore, 1975).

6 R. Barthes, 'Introduction to the Structural Analysis of Narratives,' *Image-Music-Text* (New York, 1977), p. 116. That certain postmodern practices seek to create signs that only look like signs is merely the flip side of the same coin, merely another attempt to posit a comforting separateness of 'coding' and 'narrative'.

In my use of 'hegemonic' here, I am referring not to a unitary power, but again to a diverse field of discourses and economies. As Ernesto Laclau and Chantal Mouffe (in their *Hegemony and Socialist Strategy: Towards a Radical Democratic Practice* [London, 1985], p. 142) have noted, 'the hegemonic formation…cannot be referred to the specific logic of a single social force. Every historical bloc – or hegemonic formation – is constructed through regularity in dispersion, and this dispersion includes a proliferation of very diverse elements… The problem of power cannot, therefore, be posed in terms of the search for *the* class or *the* dominant sector which constitutes the centre of a hegemonic formation, given that, by definition, such a centre will always elude us. But it is equally wrong to propose as an alternative, either pluralism or the total diffusion of power within the social, as this would blind the analysis to the presence of nodal points and to the partial concentrations of power existing in every

concrete social formation.'

7 So, for example, what is particularly interesting about Terragni's Danteum project is the numerous ways in which a strict linear narrative cannot be maintained, the ways in which gaps, slippages, breaks appear in the project, the ways in which Terragni's stated intentions (and the subject's experiences of the project) lose their linear grip, turn back on themselves, cross paths, dead end, and are subsumed by the problems of translation, not merely from book to building, but from intended (and non-intended) meaning to geometry, from metaphysical architecture to State architecture, and vice versa. Thus, understandably linear readings ('The progression from dense to framed to open – Inferno, Purgatory, Paradise – following a scheme of ascent to the most holy and sacred place leads finally to the room dedicated to the New Roman Empire' [T. Schumacher, *The Danteum* (Princeton, 1985) p. 32]) – also cannot be maintained. For example, the Paradise space can be read as more cagelike and less open (with its slitted walls, fields of glass columns and trellis) than the Purgatory space. And the room dedicated to the New Roman Empire, the Impero, is a narrow passage that gives no passage, a dead end that requires the visitor to double-back and pass through Paradise. One might also ask why Terragni releases his otherwise tight theatrical control in a number of locations: in the opening between Purgatory and Paradise, and in the arcades in Inferno and Purgatory that allow an avoidance of the direct thematic experience of those spaces.

8 It may be suggested that there is no such thing as pure 'public' or pure 'private' space, considering, for example, the degree to which the interventions of social values (from table manners to sexual manners) have shaped domestic practices.

9 I am using the term 'management' here in a similar manner as Foucault has used the terms 'power' or 'power relations', that is, to refer to *the entire range of its manifestations*, not solely the negative and repressive ones. His definition of the term 'subject', although brief, is also useful here: 'subject to someone else by control and dependence; and tied to his own identity by a conscience or self-knowledge.' (Foucault, 'The Subject and Power,' in *Art After Modernism: Rethinking Representation*, ed. B. Wallis [New York and Boston, 1984], p. 420).

10 For a discussion of how urban parks are involved in the constitution and management of subjects, see G. Cranz, *The Politics of Park Design* (Cambridge, Mass., 1982).

11 S. Zizek, *The Sublime Object of Ideology* (London, 1989), p. 45.

12 Cf. P. Ariès, *Centuries of Childhood: A Social History of Family Life* (New York, 1962). See also R. Evans, 'Figures, Doors and Passages,' *Architectural Design* (Autumn 1978), pp. 267-278 and his 'The Developed Surface: an Enquiry into the Brief Life of an Eighteenth-Century Drawing Technique,' *9H* 8 (1989), pp. 120-147.

13 M. Foucault, 'The Politics of Health in the Eighteenth Century,' in M. Foucault, *Power/Knowledge: Selected Interviews and Other Writings 1972-1977*, ed. C. Gordon (New York, 1980), pp. 166-182. Regarding the effects of hygienic movements on domestic and urban spaces see G. Teyssot, 'The Disease of the Domicile' in *Assemblage* 6 (1988), pp. 72-97. Regarding other institutional spaces, in addition to Foucault's studies of the clinic, the asylum, and the prison, see A. Vidler's essays on industry, hospitals, and prisons in *The Writing of the Walls: Architectural Theory in the Late Enlightenment* (Princeton, 1987) as well as his *Claude-Nicolas Ledoux: Architecture and Social Reform at the End of the Ancien Régime* (Cambridge, Mass., 1990). See also

R. Evans, *The Fabrication of Virtue: English Prison Architecture, 1750-1840* (Cambridge, U.K., 1982).

14 See M. Foucault's comments in 'The Eye of Power' in *Power/Knowledge*, pp. 146-165. Foucault refers to the discussion of the theme of social transparency in the writings of Rousseau by Jean Starobinski in *Jean-Jacques Rousseau: Transparency and Obstruction* (Chicago, 1988) and *The Invention of Liberty* (1964; Geneva/New York, reprint 1987), p. 100ff. Also J.-A. Miller's extensive reading of utilitarianism through the body of Bentham's work in 'Jeremy Bentham's Panoptic Device,' *October* 41 (1987), pp. 3-29.

15 J. Starobinski, *Jean-Jacques Rousseau*, pp. 92-101.

16 On the shifts in practices of the management of domestic space, see B. Ehrenreich and D. English, *For Her Own Good: 150 Years of Experts' Advice to Women* (Garden City, 1978); D. Hayden, *The Grand Domestic Revolution: A History of Feminist Designs for American Homes, Neighborhoods, and Cities* (Cambridge, Mass., 1981); and G. Wright, *Moralism and the Model Home: Domestic Architecture and Cultural Conflict in Chicago 1873-1913* (Chicago, 1980). For a discussion of the ways in which women's picture magazines played a mediating link between the social spheres of 'industrial production and…domestic reproduction,' reinforcing the scientific management lessons of order and efficiency, see S. Stein, 'The Graphic Ordering of Desire: Modernization of a Middle-Class Women's Magazine, 1914-1939,' *Heresies* 18 (1985), pp. 7-16.

For a discussion of Le Corbusier's embrace of and subsequent disillusionment with Taylorism see M. McLeod, 'Architecture or Revolution: Taylorism, Technocracy, and Social Change,' *Art Journal*: vol. 43, no. 2 (Summer 1983), pp. 132-147. Other aspects of Le Corbusier's work related to the themes of spatial management and instrumental transparency are discussed briefly in B. Brice Taylor, 'Technology, Society, and Social Control in Le Corbusier's Cité de Refuge, Paris, 1933,' *Oppositions* 15/16 (Winter-Spring 1979), pp. 169-186.

For an extensive reading of the work of Le Corbusier and Adolf Loos with regard to the construction of the subject in the domestic interior see B. Colomina, 'The Split Wall: Domestic Voyeurism' in B. Colomina, ed., *Sexuality and Space* (New York, 1991).

17 Laszlo Moholy-Nagy's comments (from his Bauhaus book, *Painting, Photography, Film)* contain a remarkable summary of these themes: 'Men still kill one another, they have not understood how they live, why they live; politicians fail to observe that the earth is an entity, yet television (Telehor) has been invented: the 'Far Seer' – tomorrow we shall be able to look into the hearts of our fellow-man, be everywhere and yet alone; illustrated books, newspapers, magazines are printed – in millions. The unambiguousness of the real, the truth in the everyday situation is there for all classes. *The hygiene of the optical, the health of the visible is slowly filtering through.*' L. Moholy-Nagy, *Painting, Photography, Film* (Cambridge, Mass., 1969), p. 38, emphasis in original text. (The first edition of this book was published in 1925; the second edition, from which this translation was made, was published two years later). Another example is Ludwig Mies van der Rohe's 1923 comments on office buildings (that appeared alongside his well-known statement 'Architecture is the will of the age conceived in spatial terms') in the first issue of the avant-garde publication *G*: 'The office building is a house of work of organization of clarity of economy. Bright, wide workrooms, *easy to oversee*, undivided except as the organism of the undertaking is divided. The maximum effect with the minimum expenditure of means.'

(from *Programs and Manifestoes on 20th-century Architecture*, tr. M. Bullock, ed. U. Conrads [Cambridge, Mass., 1970], p. 74; spacing in original, the emphasis is mine – although further emphasis could be given to the equation of office and house, as well as to the spatial aspects of work, organization, clarity, economy, and division).

18 As Foucault notes (in 'An Interview with Michel Foucault,' in *History of the Present* 1 [1985], p. 2.): 'As soon as a power infinitely less brutal and less extravagant, less visible and less ponderous than the big monarchical administration became necessary, greater latitudes for the participation in power and in the decision-making process were given to a certain social class. But at the same time and in order to compensate for it, a system of training was elaborated, essentially aimed at other social classes, but also at the new ruling class – for the bourgeoisie has in a way worked upon itself, it has developed its own type of individuals. I do not think that the two phenomena are contradictory: one was the price paid for the other. For a certain bourgeois liberalism to become possible at the level of institutions, it was necessary to have, at the level of what I call 'micro-powers,' a much stricter investment in bodies and behaviors. Discipline is the underside of democracy.'

19 This is not to suggest that transparency as such is repressive, even less to suggest that we return to earlier forms of cellular management.

20 M. Foucault, 'The Eye of Power,' p. 151-152.

21 As Denis Hollier notes (in his *Against Architecture: The Writings of Georges Bataille* [Cambridge, Mass., 1989], p. 33): 'There is consequently no way to describe a system without resorting to the vocabulary of architecture… Architecture under these conditions is the archistructure, the system of systems. The keystone of systematicity in general, it organizes the concord of languages and guarantees universal legibility. The temple of meaning, it dominates and totalizes signifying productions, forcing them all to come down to the same thing, to confirm its noologic system. Architecture is a compulsory loan burdening all of ideology, mortgaging all its differences from the outset.' For a further discussion of architectural metaphor in philosophical thought, see M. Wigley, 'The Production of Babel, the Translation of Architecture,' in *Assemblage* 8 (1989), pp. 7-19.

For a discussion of the structuring and counter-structuring of architecture and culture see C. Ingraham, 'Lines and Linearity: Problems in Architectural Theory,' in A. Kahn, ed., *Drawing/Building/Text* (New York, 1991).

22 By temporal lag between ideologies and built form I am referring to the time between the height of the 'open classroom' pedagogical movement and the appearances of the first built examples, and to the degree to which these built examples may even have assisted in the movement's decline. As George Duby notes (in 'Ideologies in Social History,' in J. Le Goff and P. Nora, *Constructing the Past: Essays in Historical Methodology*, pp. 158-159) ideologies indicate changes in 'the lived reality of social organisation…slowly and reluctantly, because they are by nature conservative. They are the locus of a process of adaptation, but this is sometimes very slow and always remains partial. Moreover, in a subtle dialectical process, the weight of ideological representations is sometimes such as to hold back the development of material and political structures…'

23 M. Tafuri, 'The Historical Project,' p. 17.

24 For a discussion of the historical shifts in cultural practices related to various odors, see A. Corbin, *The Foul and the Fragrant: Odor and the French Social Imagination* (Cambridge, Mass., 1986) and N. Elias, *The Civilizing*

Process: The Development of Manners (New York, 1978).

25 For a discussion of the relationships of propriety, property, and the proper name see C. Ingraham, 'The Faults of Architecture: Troping the Proper' in *Assemblage* 7 (1988), pp. 7-13.

26 All the quotations in this paragraph are from Sigmund Freud, 'The 'Uncanny'' in Freud, *On Creativity and the Unconscious* (New York, 1958), pp. 122-161.

For two other discussions on the uncanny in architecture see A. Vidler, 'The Architecture of the Uncanny: The Unhomely Houses of the Romantic Sublime,' in *Assemblage* 3 (1987), pp. 7-29 and M. Wigley, 'Postmortem Architecture: The Taste of Derrida,' *Perspecta* 23 (1987), pp. 156-172.

27 *The Compact Edition of the Oxford English Dictionary* (New York, 1971) and the *Webster's New World Dictionary* (New York, 1978). I would like to thank James F. Gramata for pointing out this etymology to me.

28 G. Feeley-Harnik, 'The Sakalava House (Madagascar),' *Anthropos* 75 (1980), p. 580, quoted in P. J. Wilson, *The Domestication of the Human Species* (New Haven, 1988), p. 98. Emphasis in original text.

29 M. Heidegger, 'Letter on Humanism' in Heidegger, *Basic Writings* (New York, 1977), p. 239.

30 M. Heidegger, 'Building, Dwelling, Thinking' in Heidegger, *Poetry, Language, Thought* (New York, 1971), pp. 145-161.

31 P. J. Wilson, *The Domestication of the Human Species*, p. 182. Emphasis in original.

32 S. Zizek (in *The Sublime Object of Ideology*, pp. 162-164; emphasis in original) is using the term 'the Real' in the Lacanian sense, that is, not to refer to an 'transcendent positive entity', but an entity, like the Freudian example of the primal parricide, which 'although it does not exist (in the sense of 'really existing,' taking place in reality), has a series of properties – it exercises a certain structural causality, it can produce a series of effects in the symbolic reality of subjects.' In fact it is only in a series of effects that this entity is present, but 'always in a distorted, displaced way… Laclau and Mouffe (in *Hegemony and Socialist Strategy*) were the first to develop this logic of the Real in its relevance for the the social-ideological field in their concept of *antagonism*: antagonism is precisely such an impossible kernel…only to be constructed retroactively, from a series of its effects, as the traumatic point which escapes them; it prevents a closure of the social field.'

It would be pointless, as Zizek has noted regarding the primal parricide, to search for the 'traces' of the built *unheimlich* in 'prehistoric reality, but it must none the less be presupposed if we want to account for the present state of things.' In addition, we should not expect that architecture would need to continually and blatantly enunciate its *unheimlich* side (as it does in the rare example, say, of the panoptic prison) for its effects to be felt. In other words, direct suppression is not the only or principal means of control, as Jacques Lacan notes (in J. Lacan, 'Television' in *October* 40 [1987], pp. 31-32; emphasis in original): 'Freud didn't say that repression *comes from* suppression: that (to paint a picture) castration is due to what Daddy brandished over his brat playing with his wee-wee: 'We'll cut it off, no kidding, if you do it again." That this enunciation is repressed and masked not only does not take away from its pervasive power, it assures it.

33 P. Brooks, 'Psychoanalytic constructions and narrative meanings,' in *Paragraph* 7 (1986), p. 57.

34 S. Freud, *Beyond the Pleasure Principle* (New York, 1959), pp. 12, 30.

35 S. Freud, 'Further Recommendations in the Technique of Psychoanalysis: Recollection, Repetition and Working Through' in Freud, *Therapy and Technique* (New York, 1963), p. 161.

36 D. Hollier, *Against Architecture*, pp. 46-47. Bataille continues: 'It is, in fact, obvious that monuments inspire social prudence and often even real fear. The taking of the Bastille is symbolic of this state of things: it is hard to explain this crowd movement other than by the animosity of the people against the monuments that are their real masters.' Hollier commenting on this passage says (pp. 49, 55): '[Architecture's] job…is to serve society to defend itself against that which is its basis only because of its threat… Architecture functions as the fantasy that man identifies with to escape his desire (to escape it is to control it). Man is confined: *conformed* within himself.'

37 S. Freud, 'Recollection, Repetition and Working Through,' p. 159.

38 J. Lacan, *The Seminar of Jacques Lacan: Book II, The Ego in Freud's Theory and in the Technique of Psychoanalysis 1954-1955*, ed. J.-A. Miller (New York, 1988), p. 100.

39 As Joan Copjec notes (in '*India Song/Son nom de Venise dans Calcutta desert*: The Compulsion to Repeat' in *October* 17 [1981], pp. 42-43): 'The compulsion to repeat is definitely not, according to psychoanalysis…an attempt to return to a previous state of satisfaction; rather it is the return to a trauma, which is conceived, psychoanalytically as it is medicosurgically, as a wound, a break in the protective skin which triggers catastrophe, misfortune through the whole of the organism.'

40 S. Freud, 'Analysis Terminable and Interminable' in Freud, *Therapy and Technique* (New York, 1963), pp. 256-258.

41 Ibid., pp. 255-256. Freud continues: 'The adult ego with its greater strength continues to defend itself against dangers which no longer exist in reality and even finds itself impelled to seek out real situations which may serve as a substitute for the original danger, so as to be able to justify its clinging to its habitual modes of reaction. Thus the defensive mechanisms produce an ever-growing alienation from the external world and a permanent enfeeblement of the ego and we can readily understand how they pave the way for and precipitate the outbreak of neurosis.'

42 B. Brecht, 'A Short Organum for the Theatre,' in *Brecht on Theatre*, ed. J. Willett (New York, 1964), p. 192.

43 S. Freud, 'Recollection, Repetition and Working Through,' p. 161.

44 Ibid., pp. 164-165.

45 P. Brooks, 'Psychoanalytic Constructions and Narrative Meanings,' pp. 57, 62, 67.

46 B. Brecht, 'A Short Organum for the Theatre,' p. 193.

47 Ibid., p. 192.

48 On the concept of counter-memory see F. Nietzsche, 'History in the Service and Disservice of Life' in Nietzsche, *Unmodern Observations*, ed. W. Arrowsmith (New Haven, 1990), pp. 87-145 and M. Foucault, 'Nietzsche, Genealogy, History,' in *Language, Counter-Memory, Practice* (Ithaca, 1977), pp. 139-164. It is also interesting in this regard to note Jacques Derrida comments on architecture and 'memory' (in 'Jacques Derrida in Discussion with Christopher Norris,' *Deconstruction in Architecture II [Architectural Design Profile 74*, London, 1989], p. 73, emphasis in original):

> Now as for architecture, I think that *Deconstruction* comes about – let us carry on using this word to save time – when you have deconstructed some architectural philosophy, some architectural assumptions – for instance, the hegemony of

the aesthetic, of beauty, the hegemony of usefulness, of functionality, of living, of dwelling. But then you have to *reinscribe* these motifs in the work. You can't (or you shouldn't) simply dismiss those values of dwelling, functionality, beauty and so on. You have to construct, so to speak, a new space and a new form, to shape a new way of building in which those motifs are reinscribed, having meanwhile lost their hegemony. The inventiveness of powerful architects consists I think in this reinscription, the economy of this reinscription, which also involves some respect for tradition, for memory. Deconstruction is not simply forgetting the past. What has dominated theology or architecture or anything else is still there, in some way, and the inscriptions, the let's say, *archive* of these deconstructed structures, the archive should be as readable as possible, as legible as we can make it.

49 This is Michel de Certeau's characterization of the method of investigation of Foucault. De Certeau, *Heterologies: Discourse on the Other* (Minneapolis, 1986), p. 194.
50 B. Brecht, 'A Short Organum for the Theatre,' p. 205.
51 B. Brecht, 'Appendices to the Short Organum,' in *Brecht on Theatre*, p. 277. Theodor Adorno's critique of Brecht, even given (to use Jameson's apt expression [in *Aesthetics and Politics* (London, 1977), p. 209]) 'its partiality,' would not be the first nor the last to comment on the distance between theory and practice, and the difficult relationship between direct social content and ambiguity, in the work of Brecht. I would suggest that, although on the one hand, the danger

of social content in an aesthetic work that lacks a degree of ambiguity is overly simplistic didacticism; on the other hand, the danger of ambiguity from without, rather than from within, specificity of content is easy and empty seduction (as witnessed by the success of such politically questionable artists as Joseph Beuys and Anselm Kiefer). Closer examination of Adorno's position reveals, again in Jameson's words (in *Late Marxism: Adorno, or, The Persistence of the Dialectic* [New York, 1990], p. 223), a 'subtle appreciation of his great adversary, Brecht,' even in the aggressively critical essay 'Commitment' (in *Aesthetics and Politics*, pp. 177-195), but particularly in the more balanced *Aesthetic Theory*: 'Still it is Brecht in large measure to whom we owe the growth in the self-consciousness of the art work, for when it is viewed as an element of political praxis its resistance to ideological mystification becomes that much stronger.' (New York, 1984, p. 344.)

52 B. Brecht, 'Rauschgift,' in *Gesammelte Werke*, vol. VIII (Frankfurt, 1967), p. 593, quoted in Y.-A. Bois' essay (on the work of the artist Hans Haacke) 'The Antidote' in *October* 39 (Winter 1986), p. 143. Bois continues: 'This recuperative power undoubtedly complicates Haacke's preparation of the antidote. His strategy is to convey his awareness of this in the work itself.'
53 M. Tafuri, *Architecture and Utopia: Design and Capitalist Development* (Cambridge, Mass., 1976), p. ix. Also see his *The Sphere and the Labyrinth*.
54 M. Tafuri, *Architecture and Utopia*, p. 182.

Robert Segrest is Chair of the Department
of Architecture at Iowa State University.

Frank Lloyd Wright
at the Midway
Chicago, 1893

Robert Segrest

Strategies in
Architectural Thinking

...raw red
dead white
bad blue paint.

Another 'World's Fair' effect.

Frank Lloyd Wright, *An Autobiography*

White mythology – metaphysics has erased within itself the fabulous scene that has produced it, the scene that nevertheless remains active and stirring, inscribed in white ink, an invisible design covered over in the palimpsest.

Jacques Derrida, 'White Mythology'

Geography

The fairs – the mythic spaces of the American imperial landscape, marked points of ideological intensity in a polychrome frame of power and its effects, and, in closer view, themselves complex machines, architectures – reproduced the figurations of nationhood and recirculated the narratives of white mythologies. As maps of dislocation these texts installed the great dualities, and, as maps of consolidation, these hegemonic fusions instilled the necessities of power relations (between genders, among classes, races, and bodies). They were the machines for the distillation and purification of a 'culture', plotters that situated the technologies of power and the object of fascination and fantasy in the vastness of an external geometry of the slightly possible and the might-have-been.

The fairs were as sand castles – so many grains of Truth in a momentary yet momentous artifice.

Chicago

At Chicago, Frederick Jackson Turner had announced the end of the American frontier, the end of the Edenic quest. The continental geography had been encompassed and regulated. There was no longer any possible Providence outside the margins of occupation. Rather, the ideal had to be confirmed, delineated within what already was; the managers had to become alchemists, had to turn the base metal blackness of the American city to celestial white. In this utopia, power had to be providential and pervasive.

The Fair was thus an ideological machine, an economy of symbols configured in the geometries of difference and distance. As a lived experience, the phenomenon was spectacle and simulation and fantasy. As a political architecture, the Fair was a typology of containment and display, the 'space of constructed visibility'. As a theorem of American history, the Fair was an instrument of legitimacy, a reregistering of the political and social landscape. The white machine was, finally, a master writing machine, an excursive device that wrote fiction as it furiously tried to erase the realities of its own production. This other (red) text – always under erasure – is the discourse of what follows.

The agents of this fabrication, the managers, are the necessary economists of the utopian agenda. They, secretly, are the agents of exchange, the accountants who crisscross the ledger seeking the impossible unity between the debits of now and the assets of otherwise. Across the ledger, within the white field, the accountant secretes trails of red ink and, in this residue of loss, is that other text – the blood-lines of distorted and dismembered genealogies, the discontinuous flows of carnival speech. Under his gaze, in his travels, the itinerant builds a pathology, a complex of lesions, which mark a different geography, a cartography of problematics.

(In this geography, follow the itinerants. The evidence of their legerdemain is the marks of crossing and conflict and sacrifice, the detritus of clumsy magicians. Blood is hard to erase.)

Metaphors

> So you see why theatrics of faceless masks: every effect is a mark and, as there is no cause, there is no face. These masks do not mask any lost origin (a hardly more refined notion of cause), they become conductors of one another without it being possible to cite the order of their appearance, without a law of concatenation, and hence according to anonymous uniquenesses.[1]

In the utopia, the issue is the insistence of metaphor, the necessity of timely completions and definitive origins. Metaphors make it work. Concealed in the smooth white body of architecture (the one and the same), the complex of clasps, claws, tongues, and hinges mechanize an apparition (the desire of whiteness is to be none and the same). The white houses – all theaters – invite the infection of time, seek the self-conscious abstractions that history affords the priests who, being magicians also, conceal the machines and present the body – smooth, glassy – as it always, was and now, in an effacement, must be. Wires, pulleys, the unseemly license of metaphor, are erased from the glossies (the knowing but unknowing text). The white masks, so much paste and paper, render the illusion of last beginnings and mark time. These templates – mask, temple – are the ordinances of the metaphorical display of the Fair.

But the device of deception – the concealment of the production metaphor within good form – is a red herring. It stinks and cannot be missed. (Columbo must be the detective here.) The space of misconception is the interruption of the chase – the odorous marks of dead fish that stop time in its tracks and send the day's allegories on a few wild-goose chases. In Gide's retelling, Theseus ceases to seek the minotaur when he and his band are overcome by the drug-pots that Daedalus has secreted in the garden. The logic of the metaphor is reflected into the paradox of the Lyotardian paralogism. No way out, no way in, and no sense. Only the machines.

(Inside the red zones are many red herring houses, the prop rooms of priests. Smoke them out.)

On the surfaces of white architecture, the litter of machines (if we look closely) and the broken testaments of classicism (the testimonies of priests) are the surreal evidence of many investigations, the ruined maps of frustrated detectives. A mirror architecture – another machine – gathers intelligence, subverts the lying metaphor, is a gathering place, a joint, i.e., the bookie's joint – 'an outside book-maker's paraphernalia of list-frame, umbrella, etc., some of which are jointed together in movable pieces.' (OED)

The bookie plays the numbers, makes the odds. The joint is an apparatus of production, consumption, and recording situated on the body of the socius. The bookie pricks desire and violates the metaphorical succession.

(In the red zones are the bookies' houses – jack-built and jury-rigged. Look there too.)

In the essential configuration of modernism, Descartes' *cogito*, the joint is the enigmatic link in the construction of causality, the device of analytic and referential thought. The joint – the conjunction – casts metaphors onto the metonymical field and conjures theory and equation. But the conjunction is also a violation, a cleaving of the unity, a parasite on the continuum. The joint, the disjunctive bar, is a looking machine for the magician and the voyeur, from Galileo to Hitchcock. The joint is a writing machine, unstable at the moment of its synchronicity, leaving tracks. The joint is a machine of decomposition. In Peter Greenaway's film *Zoo*, two brothers (twins) construct an apparatus for their own experimental (cinematic) death – a template (a temple altar) on which their bodies, after lethal injections, will be traced by the grinding, secreting of snails and their deterioration recorded coldly and systematically by a camera. The apparatus, a complex of joints – gears, rods, chains of actions and reactions – works (for looking, for writing, for composing, and decomposing). The gazing, the knifing, scratching, sliming, gnawing of the surface of the body, changes its materiality and makes textures and tattoos. The machines – in violation – gather intelligence and make *diagrams,* the effects of machines.

(In the red zones are the workshops of cartographers. Find them.)

Theory

The red city – the city of another architecture – is a coincidence, which is not to say that it is accidental, but rather that like some texts and some science it is a moving field of possibilities (local logics, floating crap games) lettered with the armatures of uncertain production and the surfaces of a particular present. The red city is also speculation and a mask of uninvited and unwanted guests.

The agency of theory, the law, renders the illegitimacy of such a concept. Theory unmasks, installs the paradigm, consoles in the assurance of good form and certain opposition. Yet the ideological necessity of the city (theory, metaphor, image) follows antithetically on its absence. Derrida paraphrases the 'American' philosopher Rousseau:

> Political decentralization, dispersion and decentering of sovereignty calls paradoxically for the existence of a capital, a center of usurpation and substitution. In opposition to the autarchic cities of Antiquity, which were their own centers and conversed in the living voice, the modern capital is always a monopoly of writing.[2]

Theory ('a monopoly of writing') is the binary switch of American urbanism; but to withhold a theory of urbanism is to expose again the subversive textuality not of Rousseau's

225

primitive speech, but of a different urbanism that is parasitic to the dominion of the authorized: a social field of problematic, apparatus, and the machine.

> Death, masks, makeup, all are part of the festival that subverts the order of the city, its smooth regulation by the dialecticism and the science of being. Plato, as we shall see, is not long in identifying writing with festivity. And play. A certain festival, a certain game.[3]

This other textuality is the radical litany of the carnival. The carnival is a play on things as they are: political figuration, bodily transformation, kitsch. The carnival is reflected (mythified again) in the Midway – the crucial life support system for the flaccid body of the White City – but it is less a domain or an architecture (the Midway is the self-conscious apparatus of inclusion/exclusion of the utopian figure; a sanctioned combat zone, a red-light district for the fetishes of the hegemony) and more the multiple diagrams – flows and blockages – of the red zone.

The architecture of the zone is engendered and generates; it is traversed and traverses. There are no structures (theories, temples, masks that represent origins and confirm archetypes). It is eccentric, left out, broken in. The condition, the site; is a problematic – a disruption, an intensity; the apparatus – the mechanical, the material – reflects meaning, does not seek it. The object is cinematic and glossy (red).

gloss
1. a word inserted between the lines or in the margins as an explanatory or critical equivalent (a parasite)
2. a comment, interpretation, explanation often used in the sinister sense (a virus)
3. a layer of glowing matter (film)
4. a superficial lustre (the movies).

Glossy architecture is the architecture of the fun-house: reflexive and reflective. Behind the mirrors, the machines; in the mirrors, the resistance of the mirror people; but on the mirrors, scratches – H's and chicken's feet; through the mirrors, passage; before the mirrors, Narcissus.

Gloss
Coppola's film *The Conversation* is enveloped in, as it is infolded around, a murder. The possibility of an intentional, violent death is represented as an intensity: an alignment of disparate chains of information, the consolidation of broken images (membranes, blood, members), and the localization of an event (the murder room). But it is an intensity that does not ever take form; rather, it engenders other instances in the field.

In *The Acoustic Mirror*, Kaja Silverman follows Coppola's Harry Kaul as he obsessively tries to decipher the intentions/confessions of his targets and, simultaneously, but on a different net, constructs the lineage of his own psyche.[4] Kaul – in the end woven as Ahab to the body of his mother – destroys the architectonic of his surroundings ('normal architecture') just as he builds a different architecture that is not of form and materials, but of partial intelligence ('smart buildings'). With an array of devices, he searches for meaning only to face at each turn the altered replay of what already was. Deflected, Kaul's obsession is finally wholly contained within the complex of the apparatus – bugging, cinematic, psychic – which situate him, define him, in the film.

With his machines Kaul – the bugging apparatus – lives by traces; he recognizes masks by 'evidence'. The city (nominally San Francisco) is a field of disassociations and of innuendo. There is no truth here, no center, only the tracking back and forth of the surveillance camera across the charades of human activity, only the silence of small machines, only bits of lived experience.

Though he desires mastery, there is no final control. Though he desires to know (self and circumstance), there is no final knowledge. Within the space of the film Kaul's body, like his psyche, is a glossy membrane fixed by the flow and resistance of artificial fields just as its own devices – hearing and memory – generate other fields to locate and fix other membranes. The voyeur is an exile; the detective, a criminal.

Exiles

The red zones are the non-places of exiles: tracks in the desert, the scorched landing zones of UFOs, stains in concrete, the contraptions of sacrifices. The exile is the medium of exchange, an aberration, and a condition of normalcy. The red zones are asylums, both refuge and prison. The issue is insanity and difference and contamination.

The exile is isolated, caught in the flicker of the camera eye, in the beam of the gaze. Seen or seeing, s/he becomes sacrifice and a purifying architecture. Lot's wife sneaks a peak at the black city and becomes a field marker for utopia. Eurydice is looked at by the sonorous, amorous Orpheus and becomes an apparition, a way station on the path to Hades. In Alex Cox's *Repo Man,* an exiled, glossy car, fleeing repossession, vaporizes the curious and the pernicious. Exile is a process and a construction, a ritual of the purifying narrative.

Frank Lloyd Wright is only a character here (a fiction, a mark, a cypher) in this scene (an invisible man, an exile). Take him if you will after Derrida as the over determined *pharmakos* (wizard, magician, poisoner, but also scapegoat).

> At Athens they led out two men to be purifications for the city; it was at the Thargelia, one was for the men and the other for the women (Harpocration). In general, the *pharmakoi* were put to death. But that, it seems was not the essential end of the operation. Death occurred most often as a secondary effect of an energetic fustigation aimed first at the genital organs. Once the *pharmakoi* were cut off from the space of the city, the blows were designed to chase away or draw out the evil from their bodies.
>
> The city's body *proper* thus reconstitutes its unity, closes around the security of its inner courts, gives back to itself the word that links itself within the confines of the agora, by violently excluding from its territory the representative of an external or (an) aggression.[5]

The *pharmakos* is both paradox and parasite, the outside constituted as inside, a kind of emissary and another kind of writing. And if we take the reconstituting word as 'theory', he is also the *alter ego* of the *theor,* the bearer of the word, the messenger of the oracle, the recorder of spectacles.

Wright, the demiurge, puts things into texts, texts into things. In the moment of the Transportation Building, he is expelled, as an outsider. After, he carries the image of the Fair as an uncertain, disquieting metaphor.

The Woman's Building

> It is all about fathers and sons, about bastards unaided by any public assistance, about glorious, legitimate sons, about inheritance, sperm, sterility. Nothing is said of the mother, but this will

227

not be held against us. And if one looks hard enough as in those pictures in which a second picture faintly can be made out, one might be able to discern her unstable form, drawn upside down in the foliage, at the back of the garden. In the garden of Adonis, *eis donidos kepous* (Plato, 276*b*).[6]

At the back of the garden is the Woman's Building. Designed by Sophia G. Hayden from Boston and under the stewardship of Bertha Palmer, it is a signal, ambiguous achievement of the Fair. Contained within it are the icons of the 'woman questions' and the lineage of a newly conceived history of feminism. Programmed in and around it are events that consider the changing status of women in America. Intentionally, it is a reflection of prominence and the instrument of rational discourse.

Unintentionally, the Woman's Building is also a gate. Behind it is the labyrinth of the Midway marked (unwittingly?) by a columnar spiral on which movement, energized by electricity, is dissipated by gravity. Ariadne stands at the entrance, the guardian of morality, the purveyor of white, but also the possibility of corruption and deception. Alice – child, playing – passes into the Midway and, by doing so, abrogates representation.

> [The representation of power] never establishes any connection between power and sex that is not negative: rejection, exclusion, refusal, blockage, concealment, or mask. Where sex and pleasure are concerned, power can 'do' nothing but say no to them; what it produces, if anything, is absences and gaps; it overlooks elements, introduces discontinuities, separates what is joined, and marks off boundaries. Its effects take the form of limit and lack.[7]

The Woman's Building is an allegory of womanhood built in the image of reflection and passage, in the figures of metaphor and metonymy. As a kind of prismatic leak from the coherence, the theoretical unity of the White City, it is an oxymoron, a problematic. The minor science of the Midway, a field of problematics, is encoded in the androgynous and android women of the Fair, in the cypher at the back of the garden. Later in Fritz Lang's *Metropolis,* another science fiction, the city of capital and the underground of machines are again linked by the manifold woman (Maria is at once virgin, vamp, and robot).

In each case, the fair and the film, the problematical nature of a feminist architecture – that it *is* problematic, not theoretical – is attested. Alice, the woman of 1893, Ariadne, and Maria are affective figures in an interstitial space that is reflective and transitory. The feminine architecture is not architecture at all. Feminism undermines as it occupies. Perhaps, an architecture of problematics: 'sections, ablations, adjunctions, projections'.

Kathy Aker describes the space of the woman/exile:

> My room is the room no one else in the world wants. My bedroom is a large white hexagon in the left front corner of the hotel. It has no clear outside or inside or any architectural regularity. Long white pipes form part of its ceiling. Two of its sides, which two is always changing, are open. My bedroom's function is also unclear. Its only furniture is two barber's chairs and a toilet. It's a gathering place for men.[8]

The Midway

The dialectic of Lent and the Carnival is the allegorical surface of the Fair. The Midway is the *alter ego* of the White City; the market place – the polychromed space of vulgar behavior, of confidence men and prostitutes, 'cannibals', new machines, of the exotic, the grotesque, the simulated, and the sublime – is set off from, is supplement to the agora – the space of conceit and display.

Plato's derision is the projection of Rabelais: democracy in the image of the carnivalesque, the boundary where authority, legitimacy, hierarchy, and order are contested by the chain of excesses and the challenge of kitsch. The Midway Plaisance is the trace of democratic pleasure, but it is also the archetype of the capital exploitation of misogynist and colonialist fantasies.

In the Midway the metaphorical shell of the White City dissolves in a panoply of machines and bodies. But awe and male pleasure are again the instruments of the ideological intent of the Fair, and, unlike Bakhtin's conception of the Rabelaisian carnivalesque, the Midway is not an enclave subject to its own laws. It is the space of controlled play and determined aspect. The *flaneur* is transmogrified into a voyeur, the paradigmatic composition into the special effects of Daedalus. And like the White City the Midway restores the illusions of cultural unity as it displaces and degrades difference.

(In the labyrinth, the chiasma of alterity and states, Ariadne's red line marks the dalliance of Theseus and the corruption of the gift.)

The Zoogyroscope

At the center of the Midway in the shadow of the Ferris wheel, on a site designated for the diorama of the Destruction of Pompeii is a small building, unique in its anonymity, pretentious in the overbearing of its name: Zoopraxigraphical Hall. It is not on the official map of the Exposition.

Inside is a small machine – zoogyroscope – and in projection are sequences of bodies in motion. The machine and the image produce an interval and an effect, curious on this site, not of the representation of destruction, but rather of the destruction of traditional representation.

Unlike the architecture of the White City, Eadweard Muybridge's house – his factory of desire – has no master name, no founding metaphor; it exists rather in apostrophe, in a succession of intervals – architectural, historic, programmatic, psychological, cinematic. It is absent to the point of production; it collapses in the gravity of the instant. It – architecture – is only the instant.

The geometry of the interval, the form of its architecture, is the film, a kind of surface coded with *poché*, inverse, which is not the surface of the device (for example, the *construzione legittima* of classical perspective, the surface of symptom, of effect). Rather, it is the surface of affect; not that which has already been inscribed, but the infinite possibility of writing. The film is also the illusion of difference constructed in a fiction of reason, the permeable membrane of the body and the projected image.

Muybridge's building maps the instant of a new social field that is heterotopic and problematic, an architecture of displacements.

Postscript

Some years later, Wright designs the Midway Gardens. In the *Autobiography* the story of its prostitution, the turning into kitsch, is intertwined with the blood of the Taliesin murders. In each, there is the text of the *pharmakos* and the trace of the carnival. In the interval – kitsch, madness – architecture is exposed and becomes its other self. But there is erasure and mythification; the White City closes around itself and is reconstituted. A drive-in laundry replaces Xanadu.

1 J.-F. Lyotard, 'For a Pseudo-Theory,' *Yale French Studies* 52 (1975), pp. 126-127.
2 J. Derrida, 'From/Of the Supplement to the Source,' *Of Grammatology*, tr. G. C. Spivak (Baltimore, 1976), p. 302.
3 Ibid.
4 K. Silverman, *The Acoustic Mirror: The Female Voice in Psychoanalysis and Cinema* (Bloomington, 1988), pp. 87-89.
5 J. Derrida, 'Plato's Pharmacy,' *Dissemination*, tr. B. Johnson (Chicago, 1981), pp. 130-132, 133.
6 Ibid. p. 143.

7 M. Foucault, *The History of Sexuality, Volume 1: An Introduction* (New York, 1989), p. 80.
8 K. Aker, *Blood and Guts in High School* (New York, 1978), p. 36.

Jennifer Bloomer has infused the preparation of this essay with an indispensable critical dimension. Again, I am indebted. Thanks also to Robert Cheatham for his provocative response to the original paper given at the conference.

230

Dr. John Whiteman was the first Director
of the Chicago Institute for Architecture
and Urbanism from 1987 to 1990. He was
appointed Director of the Mackintosh School
of Art in Glasgow in 1991.

Do You See What I Mean?

Refractions of the Art Object in the Self-images of Ontology

John Whiteman

Strategies in
Architectural Thinking

This paper is written as both prospect and foil to a philosophy of art.

It is the implicit structure thought that determines the nature of the things we make, over and above their overt and deliberated content. A finished product both disappoints and exceeds conscious intention.

When thought is applied to production there is transposed into the structure of the consequent artifact a strange likeness of thought itself. Subsequently, because thought cannot attend to itself directly (except in risking infinite recursion, escalation, delay, or avoidance), the theory of art, which however masked, is always a theory of the production of art, is perpetually problematized in a continuous denial that the world of our artifice bears the inscription of the logos in/by which it is formed.

Yet, the images at work behind certain dominant or recurrent models of ontology, those often used to control production, are continually exhausted in the application of thought. Ubiquitously and constantly the implicit images of thought become detectable, even self-evident in the world that thought produces. Indeed, if not treated overtly and reflexively in the construction of sense and product both, then embarrassingly so. Always the pictures that thought holds of itself are painted on the surfaces of sense and its objects. The presence of such images interrupts the direct line of control that thought may presume to exercise over the production of its objects.[1]

In the consequent image of chronic incoherence, the concept of an (art) object may be continually refracted from the ontologies in which such images serve.

Realism: The Image of the Object in Ontological Models

A dominant tendency in models of ontology is to define the objects of our attention externally, and to be concerned solely with problems of their identity and definition. In resisting the apparently endless demands on sense aroused by the play of an object within the fields of its significance, ontological models tend to treat objects only as symbolically inert entities. The last vestige of this resistance is the inability of an ontological model to disassociate the apparatus for the definition of its objects from metaphors of the structural conditions necessary for their apprehension. It is as though the definition of the object in an ontology cannot be finalized as the end of a course of inquiry without initiating, or rather forcing the acknowledgement of the shifting revisions of a play of meaning in which a human subject is inevitably placed and involved.[2] Otherwise put, the optical metaphors that pervade analytical philosophy must be taken as a tell-tale sign in themselves. But of what it is not clear.

The realist conception of the object, which is symptomatic of the project of applied science in production, is here rejected as insufficient to serve as the concept of an art object. This rejection is based on the observation that a realist ontology will not let its objects themselves serve as symbols. A realist ontology must necessarily, if reluctantly, use symbols to define its objects. Such symbolic definitions most commonly invoke direct analogies of correspondence or mapping between the logos of the symbol and the structure of the world as claimed. By supplementing the act of denotation with idealized or 'proto'-pictures, realist ontologies identify the world and its objects by analogical correspondence.[3] Yet it is denied that the objects of a realist ontology are themselves symbolic, and it is resisted that their identity and definition should be determined by their association with other objects (which themselves could only be understood within the shifting movements of symbolism). Objects in a realist's ontology are therefore posited as simples, devoid of internal structure. In such pristine elementarity their identity is divorced from the conditions of their significance; that is, from their position and play within a matrix of signs and signification. The objects of a realist's ontology 'are merely what they are', or so the intention goes.[4]

Specifically excluded in a realist ontology is the possibility that an object with particular internal compositions may receive its very definition from a play in signification, from the way it possesses meaning by the techniques of reference or by intension. The techniques of reference and intension do not necessarily and always involve morphological analogies and idealizations of correspondence, but may function instead through acts of assignment or denotation in which no indexical link or analogical correspondence between sign and signifier is necessarily maintained.

Yet the object in a realist ontology finds its definition only within such an implied and idealized morphology, for realism must, however belatedly, return a picture of the world. The realist's object cannot therefore indicate simultaneously the determination of its being and the structure of its placement within a context without putting the realist's picture of the world at risk. Since art objects are always set within the wider formal culture of the city or the landscape, and since their individual configurations also reverberate with(in) other media and traditions of sense making, no art (in a self-conscious tradition of form-making, at least) can be fully accounted by a realist ontology.

Rejection of the Artwork as an Autonomous Field of (Re)Presentation

Neither can the art work be accounted effectively as a fully internalized field of play, as presenting a properly circumscribed, self contained, and complete context or composition within the play and configuration of which are presented all the preconditions for situations, events, and subjectivities through the composition's own immediately self-evident movement and structure.[5]

While such a description of the object is indeed more sympathetic to the project of art than, say, the realist's ontology rejected above, it is an incorrect or rather a radically incomplete description of how the artwork functions. To stress the autonomous nature of the art work is indeed a description sympathetic to the ways of art, placing an emphasis on the internal nature of composition, stressing how the artwork emerges as an intensification (in Lukacs' words) or condensation (in Roman Jakobson's words) of its beginnings and its yearnings.

It is further true that, within the process of creating a silvered web of definition and contrast internal to itself, the artwork creates the illusion of a space all its own in which familiar things and their spacings may be reset, achieving novel definitions and an altered status from that which is taken to be real or ordinary. The ordinary world is refracted and re-formed in the recoiling face of art.[6]

It is not true, however, that all the sense and feeling of a work is so self-contained, even though the force of that sense and feeling apparently relies exclusively on the material and the spacings of the work itself. Else the artwork can only be mistakenly described as a structure akin to a joke, a trick, or a deception.[7] But it is not clear how the senses of a work can, on the one hand, be so singular, concrete, restricted, and compelling, so internalized, and yet, on the other, so duplicitous, abstract, connective, and fleeting, so external to the work itself. It is almost as though an artwork invites the intellect to take one side of an apparent contradiction: the artwork cannot be understood to cohere as an object, and yet object it seems so definitely to be.

In the charge of 'Contradiction!' mainly in an intimation that the strength of the charge is false, that it is in excess of the logic that apparently founds it and gives it validity as a charge, we hear not the reasoned distinction between sense and nonsense, but instead the exasperation of an immature logic in its inability to master the object of its attention.

This situation arises because a work of art may seem at first to deliberately obfuscate its own relations and setting to the culture. It may do this in a number of ways, all of which may be understood as techniques of indirection: by transfiguring the ordinary or what may be taken to be real within the several systems of representation operating within a culture at a particular time; by obfuscating the links by which its material, its configurations, its meanings, and its significance may be traced to their source or origin, employing modes of reference in which the links between material, meaning, and significance are especially difficult to follow.

A work of art betrays rather than displays its meanings. In its reluctance, in the impossibility of its being direct in sense-making, the artwork opens the space and opportunity for the real to be reworked. Indeed, so compelling may be its (re)vision, that 'Art may (appear to) cause revision to strike anywhere.'[8]

Furthermore, we will be at a loss to know if the revisions that art may work upon us are real. We cannot tell if art gives either truth or falsehood.[9] It may well be that the loser in the exchange between reason and art is (the narrow conception of a realist's) truth rather than (the supposed indeterminacies of) art. This is so, because an artwork potentially removes the grounds upon which it can be judged. The work of art is prophetic, in the secular sense of the word, in that the structure of value, by which it may be judged, is irrevocably altered by the creation of the work itself. The threat of art lies in the fact that no ordinal system of value, by which an independent assessment of the work can be made, may survive in temporal continuity the interruptions created by the very work itself. This is both the promise and the danger of the work of art.

Realist and Irrealist Alike

Symptomatically, the conception of the object as an autonomous field of reflection may be readily opposed in a dialectic to the objects posited by the realist or scientific ontology. The former conception stresses the internal nature of art objects (their composition or configuration), the latter their external nature (or the independent definition of their identity). Both stress the autonomy of objects, and in this lies their idealization. But, while the realist ontology reaches for an object without further symbolic meaning, the conception of the artwork as autonomous reaches for an object saturated with symbolic meaning that cannot be traced to its origins or to its cultural setting.[10] Their mutual emphasis on the autonomy of the artwork and their signal difference with respect to the issue of meaning is the system of similarity and difference that constructs the mutually reinforcing economy of the two conceptions.

The two conceptions maintain and reinforce one another. They are but two sides of the same coin, and do little to resolve the same contradictions or idealizations upon which each is based. To subscribe to one is to implicitly believe the other. I suspect that in Lukacs' formulation of the artwork, for example, an autonomous, internal investigation of the art object allows him both to appreciate the intricacies and nuances of the individual piece and also to continue thinking of it as an ideological construct from the perspective of realism.[11] This subtle but schizophrenic gesture of appreciation and dismissal allows a continuation of the strict project of scientific realism, but with a simultaneous continuation of the classical and conservative gesture in which art is constructed as significant, but irrelevant.[12]

The critical difficulty of any autonomous conception of the art object is its failure to provide a pragmatic account of the significance of art as both knowledge and practice. The knowledge that art brings is severed from an account of how that knowledge is produced. In such a mutual economy of accounts,[13] theory and practice are insulated one from another, keeping their respective distances and differences.

To point to this difficulty is not necessarily to imply that it can be resolved once and for all. Not all problems demand an answer; some demand that they be inhabited without deliberated resolution. Perhaps, as De Man and others have suggested, it is unthinkable that historically situated agents should be able to change the material conditions of their existence, even (especially) by the most radical of intellectual strategies, by translating thought into action through a sustained effort of ideological critique.

Yet surely this issue is at least undecided, if not undecidable. For, historically, without the link to action both within and on the circuits of our subjectivity, the artwork has inevitably been set up as either something purely symbolic or else purely ideological (in the strong pejorative sense of the word), or both. The possibility of art as knowledge and its intimate involvement in the creation of our own subjectivity is denied.[14] Yet the effect of art as such is readily admitted or implied by the extraordinary valuations that we as a culture place upon its objects.

An Ontology of Art without Images of Apprehension

Rejecting the symbolically mute conception of the object implied by a realist ontology, denying also the irrealist view of the artwork as an autonomous field saturated with untraceable meaning, the artwork may be conceived subsequently as a problematic or troubled field. The artwork, then, must be defined as a real but constantly revisable working space. Indeed, the same would have to be true of the world in which the artwork is placed and in which it signifies, and may be said to represent.

The artwork is the space of an intersection in which several differentiated modes of representation are conjoined under the yoke of a single work or reconfiguration. A new world of experience is contingently founded.[15]

Within the space of the work itself the conflicting representations do not originate in an equal, undifferentiated status. The contemporary work specifically reworks or supplants current (and dying) strategies of representation by forming a new relation between itself and previous representational strategies that have become pathological, in the sense that they may be thought to constitute common sense (i.e., in that their rhetorical gambits go unnoticed so that we naturalize them, mistaking them for or rather constituting them as reality itself).

The artwork is a concatenation of representations referring not to some essential real world, but instead to other representations by which the world has previously been, is currently, and may in the future be, constituted.[16]

A work of art is not, therefore, easily differentiated from its subject matter, for the latter is also constituted through a symbolic system. Thus, in art, neither the painting being painted, nor the building being drawn, nor even ultimately the subject(s) for whom the object is made, can be considered as things whose definition is not given by a play of signification. None can be considered objects whose essence or nature lies outside the gambits of symbolic strategy.

Such a formulation of the artwork reconfigures many of the central dilemmas in the contemporary philosophy of art. For example, obviated is the duality in the relation between interpretation and its object, in which artworks are treated either as mere illustrations of a theory that purports to explain them, or else as possessing an idealized and mystical objecthood that lies beyond all explanation (i.e., anagogy).

Lost also is the need for essentialist or idealist statements concerning artworks, since the work can be treated within the technique and metaphoricity of its several intersecting representations. Thus, for example, the contemporary fashionable images of multiplicity, contamination, and disruption need no longer be treated in their currently idealized, foundational, and imagistic way, as automatic assumptions of qualities to be desired in a contemporary work (i.e., overtly presented as illustration).[17]

And yet, in such a conception of the artwork, there is overtly preserved the link between the logic of the artwork and a philosophy of (artistic) action, conceived as a problem of reworking the space of the intersection of representations as a cognition. The problem of making a thing, such as a painting or a building, is conceived then as a dyadic link between its physical objecthood and the pattern of thought that guides or determines (in the sense of giving a dominant inclination to the interpretation of) its existence and appearance in the world. The relation between thought and thing is not treated within the instrumental conception of production whereby things are produced under the direct guidance or tutelage of thought. (As if the things made do not 'speak back'.) Instead, dominant and operative idealizations in the formation of ideas are exhumed for the images upon which they rely, images of sight and light that we blindly build in the operation of our desire in built form. These images, once recognized and made evident, show what they hide or gloss over: that art already contains logic, and thus evades any more restricted system of thought that can be brought to bear upon it.

Finally, the fallacies of the insult 'Formalism!' are exposed, in that the artwork under this new definition must indeed be configured formally within the intersections of the representations with which it deals. Yet the result cannot only be considered on such self-contained grounds of internal coherence. Even though it cannot necessarily be formulated a priori, a condition of internal coherence must be satisfied to produce conviction in the senses of the work. But internal coherence by itself is not sufficient to determine the work as a work.[18] Instead an artwork must equivocate its own objecthood in such a way that it is at once a thing, appearing as hard, concrete, and present, but also a mere void, suspended in the web of relations in which it plays.

The principal difficulty to be encountered both practically and intellectually in working out an artwork under such a conception of itself is this: how is it possible to reconstruct the subject of the work[19] at the same time as countenancing the predicative/metaphorical structures upon which the sense of the work is based? The artwork must therefore self-consciously configure its object within the strictures of the ordinary, but cannot do this without at once reformulating the ordinary and also the self-same common sense extant within a culture that may be thought to guide the formation of its objects.

(Re)reading the Ordinary

The common sense that we generate to guide our actions in making things (like paintings and buildings) tends to collapse into a form of realism and to determine our objects in such a way that it reveals less about our immediate purposes and intentions for which our things are made than it does about itself. That is to say, when we paint, sculpt, or build, we create and confirm an image of the world that was already implicit in the hidden model of our own thinking. Thus, instead of reading the world made in the direct terms of desires met and intentions satisfied, the world of our artifice can be read symptomatically as a reflection of images and desires either suppressed, hidden, or unrecognized. This 'backward' reading shows not just that the things we make are conditioned by ontological models of what we are prepared to let a thing be, but also that the world we make simultaneously and inevitably forms an inscription of the (self-imposed) conditions of our subjectivity. With art we underwrite our own subjectivity. Yet subjectivity is something that we also make: and it is made in reciprocal reference to the objects by which we create the realms of our life, objects such as paintings, sculptures, and buildings.

1 The idea that the medium of thought is not transparent to thought itself is indeed an old one. *Inter alia*, it can be found in Plato, and was, for example, a central preoccupation of the poet Stéphane Mallarmé. Yet, knowing this history, the temptation to idealize thought in such a way that it is abstracted from the medium in which it is posited remains ever present within the culture. It is this chronic condition that gives rise to a permanent temptation to historicize one's current situation, claiming it to be 'new', saying that the contemporary is predicated on the passing away of previous conditions. This belief opens the widest channel for the persistence of our culture's strongest pathologies.
2 By using the word 'involved' I do not mean to transfer the legitimacy of architectural appreciation to an idealized conception of the subject. As the word 'involved' itself may be used to suggest, such a subject may not survive

its (re)-placement.
3 The issue of how pictures may work in the fixing of an ontology is indeed a complex one. The picture may serve in an hierarchical relay of signs from word to image to thing in order to identify 'what we are talking about'. (See, for example, the description of the imagination given in G. W. F. Hegel, *Encyclopaedia: Philosophy of Mind* [Oxford, 1971], section 455 et seq, pp. 207-213.) Or, more subtly it may, as in Wittgenstein's (celebrated, but later rejected) picture theory of sentences fix the sense of a proposition by being a picture of a world or state of affairs that the proposition itself has posited. (See L. Wittgenstein, *Tractatus Logico-Philosophicus*, tr. C. K. Ogden [London, 1922], remark #2.033 et seq.) The nuances of this issue are much more subtle than I may seem to be implying here. They do not, however, radically alter the proposition that I am making,

namely that in a realist ontology (often confirmed as an ontology by the supplement of the picture or image) the definition of an object is implicitly claimed to be independent of its placement and play in fields of significance.

4 It is Wittgenstein who first notices that, in the name of simplicity, the logical atomism common to most ontological models requires the elimination of the internal structure of its constituent elements, its objects. See D. Pears' account of Wittgenstein's understanding of objects in the *Tractatus*, in 'The Basic Realism of the Tractatus' in *The False Prison: A Study of the Development of Wittgenstein's Philosophy* (Oxford, 1987), pp. 89-114. Wittgenstein's later appreciation of this issue is much altered by his rejection of elemental simplicity; the revision being prompted in part by the difficulty of color predicates. See L. Wittgenstein, *Philosophical Remarks* (Chicago, 1975), remark #83.

5 See, for example, Lukacs' conception of the art object as an autonomous field of reflection in which the contradictions inherent in the depiction of reality are 'so resolved' that the work of art provides 'an inseparable sense of integrity.' From G. Lukacs, 'Art and Objective Truth' in *Writer And Critic*, tr. A. Kahn (London, 1978), pp. 25-60, extracts and synopses here presented are from pp. 34-35.

6 This conception of the relation of art to objective truth may be understood as a form of irrealism, although not in the strict sense that Nelson Goodman uses the word; more in the sense belied by the humor of Oscar Wilde, when he says that art can 'make and unmake many worlds' and can 'draw the moon from heaven with a scarlet thread.' See O. Wilde, 'The Decay Of Lying,' *The Artist As Critic: The Critical Writings Of Oscar Wilde*, ed. R. Ellman (Chicago, 1968), pp. 306-307.

7 Which conception has, of course, a long and venerable tradition, beginning perhaps with Plato. What such a conception misunderstands is the ability of the human being to countenance two realities simultaneously, and to hold them contingently against each other. In this sense art and logic seem indistinct to me, for in art as 'in a proposition a world is as it were put together experimentally.' L. Wittgenstein, *Notebooks 1914-1916*, eds. G. H. von Wright and G. E. M. Anscombe, tr. G. E. M. Anscombe (Oxford, 1961), see the entry for 29 September 1914.

8 To transform and misuse Quine's famous remark. It is important to remember that art is not so much a suspension of belief as it is a contingent suspension of values.

9 See the brief account of truth and the imitation of truth in the rhetoric of the Greek Muse given by A. Bergren in 'The Mouseion (Museum/Muse I am) of Venice, CA.' Paper presented at a conference on The Texts and Textures of Urban Memory, held at Southern California Institute of Architecture, on 18 March 1988, p. 3. I am making a slightly different point here in that I am not only interested in the question of truth and its imitation as a limitation on the understanding as I am (and no doubt Ann Bergren also) interested in the implications engendered by this realization. A central tenet flowing from the realization that truth and its imitation form a restricted circuit in the understanding, is that truth too is a fabrication and that, as such, there are

many, possibly conflicting truths to be told of the same object or indeed about 'the' world. On this see, 'Rightness of Rendering,' the final chapter of N. Goodman's *Ways of Worldmaking* (Cambridge, 1978), pp. 109-140. Some may say that to pursue the question like this (i.e., in this analytical vein) is to commit philosophy's mistake once again, to paradoxically attempt to fix up philosophy by extending its range, making it do what it currently cannot. If this be so, then I see no way out of it and understand the situation to be philosophy's fate – something that just has to be worked out to the point of its exhaustion.

10 Again the symptom of irrealism.

11 In the sense that an ideology may be blinding and absolutely prohibitive of rational action.

12 Lukacs refers to scientific realism as 'objective truth', the techniques for which are not (presumably) to be found in the present. Notice how conservative and radical may implicitly believe the same thing about 'The World' (so called) in their mutual emphasis and reliance on realism.

13 Accounts of the individual artwork, that is.

14 Relevant is Raymond Williams' determined if finally unsubstantiated attempt to reformulate the concept of ideology within Marxism by removing what he takes to be the absurdity of a totalizing conception of ideology in which the possibilities of action are denied by the very social reasoning that an individual possesses.

15 Note that, while I intend to valorize an ambiguous quality of openness in the individual work of art, I intend also to ascribe more determinate senses to the work than is normally associated with such a position. I do not subscribe to the play of pure chance in a work, seeing such gestures not as the radical intention they are often claimed to be, but instead as the inadvertent betrayal of a hidden faith in an excessive determinism. Artistic reason is allowed no middle course between a rigid determinism and mere chance. Lost are more subtle appreciations of artistic gesture. See, for an example of the object of my criticism, the thesis put forward by U. Eco, *The Open Work*, tr. A. Cancogni (Cambridge, 1989).

16 The reader might be tempted to see this statement as synonymous with the contemporary redescription of reality as a textual phenomenon. While accepting the basic idea behind such a redescription (that things find their identity in a play of significance), I do not feel that the extension of the term 'text' is sufficient to catch the radical difficulties of variation in sign systems and their media.

17 There is, of course, no small irony in the idealization and imagism of the philosophically described properties of contamination and disruption in the artwork, since idealization and imagism, as unacknowledged techniques in the automatic assumption of these qualities, reinstate all of the difficulties that the authentic work of art might pit itself against.

18 Think, for example, of Alberti's tests for the finalization of a composition as being indicators or symptoms that 'something else' is wrong with the painting, not merely that it is 'formally' incorrect.

19 *Double sens entendre.*

239

Mark Wigley is an architect who teaches
at Princeton University and writes on the
strategic role of architectural discourse,
focusing on the question of ornament.

The Translation
of Architecture
The Production
of Babel

Mark Wigley

Strategies in
Architectural Thinking

How then to translate deconstruction in architectural discourse? Perhaps it is too late to ask this preliminary question. What is left to translate? Or, more important, what is always left by translation? Not just left behind, but left specifically for architecture. What remains of deconstruction for architecture? What are the remains that can be located only in architecture, the last resting place of deconstruction? The question of translation is, after all, a question of survival. Can deconstruction survive architecture?

One

It is now over twenty years since Derrida's first books were published. Suddenly his work has started to surface in architectural discourse. This appears to be the last discourse to invoke the name of Derrida. Its reading seems the most distant from the original texts, the final addition to a colossal stack of readings. An addition that marks in some way the beginning of the end of deconstruction, its limit if not its closure.

After such a long delay – a hesitation whose strategic necessity must be examined – there is such a haste to read Derrida in architecture. But it is a reading that seems at once obvious and suspect. Suspect in its very obviousness. Deconstruction is understood to be unproblematically architectural. There seems to be no translation, just a metaphoric transfer, a straightforward application of theory from outside architecture to the practical domain of the architectural object. The hesitation does not seem to have been produced by some kind of internal resistance on the part of that object. On the contrary, there is no evidence of work, no task for the translator, no translation. Just a literal application, a transliteration. Architecture is understood as a representation of deconstruction, the material representation of an abstract idea. The reception of Derrida's work seems to follow the classical teleology from idea to material form, from initial theory to final practice, from presence to representation. Architecture, the most material of the discourses, seems the most detached from the original work, the most suspect of the applications, the last application, the representational ornament that cannot influence the tradition it is added to, a veneer masking as much as it reveals of the structure beneath. The last layer, just an addition, no translation. Yet.

But how to translate? Deconstruction is no more than a subversion of the architectural logic of addition that sets in play a certain thought of translation. One cannot simply consider translation outside and above either deconstruction or architecture. The question immediately becomes complicated. There is no hygienic starting point, no superior logic to apply. There are no principles to be found in some domain that governs both deconstructive discourse and architectural discourse. Nevertheless, certain exchanges are already occurring between them. Architecture, translation, and deconstruction are already bound together, already defining an economy whose pathological symptoms can be studied. It is a matter of identifying the logic of translation that is already in operation. Since there is no safe place to begin, one can only enter the economy and trace its convoluted geometry in order to describe this scene of translation.

This can be done by locating that moment in each discourse where the other is made thematic, where the other comes to the surface. The line of argument that surfaces there can then be folded back on the rest of the discourse to locate other layers of relationships. These hidden layers are not simply below the surface. They are within the surface itself, knotted together to form the surface. To locate them involves slippage along fault lines rather than excavation. As there are no principles above or below the convoluted folds of this surface, it is a matter of following some circular line of inquiry, of circulating within the economy, within the surface itself.

Two

Translation surfaces in deconstructive discourse when Derrida, following Walter Benjamin's *The Task of the Translator*, argues that translation is not the transference, reproduction, or image of an original. The original only survives in translation. The translation constitutes the original it is added to. The original calls for a translation that establishes a nostalgia for the innocence and the life it never had. To answer this call, the translation abuses the original, transforming it.

> And for the notion of translation, we would have to substitute a notion of transformation: a regulated transformation of one language by another, of one text by another. We never will have, and in fact never have had, a 'transport' of pure signifieds from one language to another, or within one and the same language, that the signifying instrument would leave virgin and untouched.[1]

There is some kind of gap in the original that the translation is called in to cover over. The original is not some organic whole, a unity. It is already corrupted, already fissured. The translation is not simply a departure from the original, as the original is already exiled from itself. Language is necessarily impure. Always divided, it remains foreign to itself. It is the translation that produces the myth of purity and, in so doing, subordinates itself as impure. In constructing the original as original, the translation constructs itself as secondary, exiled. The supplementary translation, which appears as a violation of the purity of the work, is actually the possibility of that very purity. Its violence to the original is a violent fidelity, a violence called for by the original precisely to construct itself as pure. The abuse of the text is called for by an abuse already within the text. Translation exploits the conflict within the original to present the original as unified.

Consequently, in translation, the text neither lives nor dies, it neither has its original life-giving intention revived (presentation) nor is it substituted by a dead sign (representation). Rather, it just lives on, it survives. This survival is organized by a contract that ensures that translation is neither completed nor completely frustrated.[2] The contract is the necessarily unfulfilled promise of translation. It defines a scene of incomplete translation, an incompletion that binds the languages of the original and translation together in a strange knot, a double bind. This constitutional bond is neither a social contract nor a transcendental contract above both languages. Neither cultural nor acultural, it is other than cultural without being outside culture. The negotiable social contracts within which language operates presuppose this non-negotiable contract that makes language possible, establishing the difference between languages while making certain exchanges between them possible.

This translation contract is not independent of the languages whose economy it organizes. It is inscribed within both languages. Not only is the original already corrupt, already divided, but translation is occurring across those divisions. The gap between languages passes through each language. Because language is always already divided, inhabited by the other, and constantly negotiating with it, translation is possible.[3] The translation within a language makes possible translation outside it. Which is to say, one language is not simply outside the other. Translation occurs across a gap folded within rather than between each language. It is precisely these folds that constitute language. The contract is no more than the geometry of these folds, the organization of the gaps.

Consequently, any translation between architecture and deconstruction does not occur between the texts of architectural discourse and those of philosophical discourse.[4] Rather, it occupies and organizes both discourses. Within each there is an architectural translation of philosophy and a philosophical translation of architecture. To translate deconstruction in architectural discourse is not, therefore, to faithfully recover some original undivided sense of deconstruction.[5] Rather, it is one of the abuses of the texts signed by Derrida that constitutes them as originals. To translate deconstruction in architectural discourse is to examine the gaps in deconstructive writing that demand an architectural translation in order to constitute those texts as deconstructive. The architectural translation of deconstruction is literally the production of deconstruction. This production must be organized by the terms of a contract between architecture and philosophy that is inscribed within the structure of both in a way that defines a unique scene of translation.

Three

A preliminary sketch of this scene can be drawn by developing Heidegger's account of the relationship between architecture and philosophy. Heidegger examines the way in which philosophy describes itself as architecture. Kant's *Critique of Pure Reason*, for example, describes metaphysics as an 'edifice' erected on secure foundations laid on the most stable ground. Kant criticizes previous philosophers for their tendency to 'complete its speculative structures as speedily as may be, and only afterwards to enquire whether these foundations are reliable.'[6] The edifice of metaphysics has fallen apart and is 'in ruins' because it has been erected on 'groundless assertions' unquestioningly inherited from the philosophical tradition. To restore a secure foundation, the critique starts the 'thorough preparation of the ground'[7] with the 'clearing, as it were, and levelling of what has hitherto been wasteground.'[8] The edifice of metaphysics is understood as a grounded structure.

Heidegger argues that Kant's attempt to lay the foundations is the necessary task of all metaphysics. The question of metaphysics has always been that of the ground (*grund*) on which things stand even though it has been explicitly formulated in these terms only in the modern period inaugurated by Descartes. Metaphysics is no more than the attempt to locate the ground. Its history is that of a succession of different names *(logos, ratio, arche... etc.)* for the ground. Each of them designates 'Being', which is understood as presence. Metaphysics is the identification of the ground as 'supporting presence' for an edifice. It searches for 'that upon which everything rests, what is always there for every being as its support.'[9] For Heidegger, metaphysics is no more than the determination of ground-as-support.

Metaphysics is the question of what the ground will withstand, of what can stand on the ground. The motif of the edifice, the grounded structure, is that of standing up. Philosophy is the construction of propositions that stand up. The ability of its constructs to stand is determined by the condition of the ground, its supporting presence. Heidegger repeatedly identifies presence with standing. The 'fundamental' question of metaphysics (why there are beings rather than nothing) asks of a being 'on what does it stand?'[10] Standing up through construction makes visible the condition of the ground.

But, in Heidegger's reading, construction does not simply make visible a ground that precedes it. The kind of ground clearing Kant attempts does not simply precede the construction of the edifice. The ground is not simply independent of the edifice. The edifice is not simply added to the ground, it is not simply an addition. For Heidegger, a building does not stand on a ground that preceded it and on which it depends. Rather, it is the erection of the building that establishes the fundamental condition of the ground. Its structure makes the ground possible.[11] The ground is constituted rather than revealed by that which appears to be added to it. To locate the ground is necessarily to construct an edifice.

Consequently, philosophy's successive relayings of the foundation do not preserve a single, defined edifice.[12] Rather, it is a matter of abandoning the traditional structure by removing its foundation.[13] The form of the edifice changes as the ground changes. Having cleared the ground, Kant must reassess its load-bearing capacity and 'lay down the complete architectonic plan' of a new philosophy in order to 'build upon this foundation.'[14] The edifice must be redesigned. Relaying the foundations establishes the possibility of a different edifice. For Heidegger, the laying of the foundation is the 'projection of the intrinsic possibility of metaphysics'[15] through an interrogation of the condition of the ground. This interrogation is the projection of a plan, the tracing of an outline, the drawing, the designing of an edifice, the drawing of the design out of the ground. Interrogating the condition of the ground defines certain architectonic limits, certain structural constraints within which the philosopher must work as a designer. The philosopher is an architect, endlessly attempting to produce a grounded structure.

In these terms, the history of philosophy is that of a series of substitutions for structure. Every reference to structure is a reference to an edifice erected on a ground, an edifice from which the ground cannot simply be removed. The motif of the edifice is that of a structure whose free play is constrained by the ground. The play of representations is limited, controlled, by presence: 'The concept of centered structure is in fact the concept of a play based on a fundamental ground, a play constituted on the basis of a fundamental immobility and a reassuring certitude, which itself is beyond the reach of play.'[16] Philosophy is the attempt to restrain the free play of representation by establishing the architectonic limits provided by the ground. It searches for the most stable ground in order to exercise the greatest control over representation.

244

The metaphor of grounded structure designates the fundamental project of metaphysics to identify a universal language that controls representation in the name of presence, a *logos*. Derrida traces the way that metaphysics maintains its logocentric protocol of presence/presentation/representation with an account of language that privileges speech over writing. While speech is promoted as presentation of pure thought, writing is subordinated as representation of speech. The role of architecture in this hierarchy can be identified by recalling Heidegger's identification of the original sense of the word *logos* as 'gathering' in a way that lets things stand, the standing of construction. A link between structure and presence organizes traditional accounts of language. The means by which language is grounded is always identified with structure. Speech is identified with structure, which makes visible the condition of the ground it is bonded to. Phonetic writing, as the representation of speech, is identified with ornament that represents the structure it is added to. If writing ceases to be phonetic, if it loses its bond with speech, it becomes representation detached from pure presence, like an ornament that refers away from the structure it is attached to. The protocol of metaphysics, sustained by the account of language as thought/speech/phonetic writing/nonphonetic writing, is established by the architectural motif of ground/structure/ornament.

Metaphysics is dependent on an architectural logic of support. Architecture is the figure of the addition, the structural layer, one element supported by another. Metaphysics' determination of the ground-as-support presupposes a vertical hierarchy from ground through structure to ornament. The idea of support, of structure, is dependent on a certain view of architecture that defines a range of relationships from fundamental (foundational) to supplementary (ornamental). With each additional layer, the bond is weaker. The structure is bonded to the ground more securely than the ornament is bonded to the structure. But as the distance from the ground becomes greater, the threat to the overall structure diminishes. The vertical hierarchy is a mechanism of control that makes available the thought of the ground-as-support, which is metaphysics.

Structure makes present the ground. Structure is grounding, submission to the authority of presence. Ornament either represents the grounding of structure or deviates from the line of support, detaching itself from the ground in order to represent that which is other than the structure. Philosophy attempts to tame ornament in the name of the ground, to control representation in the name of presence. The philosophical economy turns on the status of ornament. It is the structure/ornament relationship that enables us to think of support, and thereby, to think of the ground.

Four

The strategic importance of this architectural metaphor emerges when Heidegger examines the status of art. Metaphysics' determination of ground-as-support also determines art as merely a representative 'addition' to a utilitarian object, a 'superstructure' added to the 'substructure', which, in turn, is added to the ground. The architectural metaphor organizes this relationship: 'It seems almost as though the thingly element in the art work is like the substructure into and upon which the other, authentic element is built.'[17] The material object is the 'support' to which the artwork is added, the presentation of the ground to which the artwork is added as a representation.

But it is not just the internal structure of the art object that is understood in these architectural terms, it is also the status of art as a discourse. Heidegger notes that metaphysics treats art itself as a superstructure added to the substructure of philosophy. Metaphysics understands itself as a grounded structure to which is attached the representational ornament of art. It subordinates the arts, and therefore architecture, by employing the vertical hierarchy dependent on a certain understanding of architecture. Art is subordinated by being located furthest from the ground. Architecture, then, plays a curious strategic role. It is able to pass between philosophy and art in a unique way. It is involved in a kind of translation. The metaphor circulates between and within the two systems, complicating them as it folds back on itself. A convoluted economy is sustained by the description of architecture as ornamented structure, which enables art to be subordinated to philosophy even while philosophy describes itself as architecture. Philosophy describes itself in terms of the very thing that it subordinates.

Heidegger argues that art is actually 'foundational' to the philosophical tradition that subordinates it to the level of ornament. This convolution is doubled in the case of architecture itself. Metaphysics organizes itself, around an account of the object as grounded structure. It projects an account of architecture outside itself, which it then appeals to as an outside authority. It literally produces an architecture. As Derrida argues, in reading the architectural metaphor in Kant's aesthetics, 'Philosophy, which in this book has to think art through – art in general and fine art – as a part of its field or of its edifice, is here *representing itself* as part of its part, philosophy as an art of architecture. It re-presents itself, it *detaches itself*, detaches from itself a proxy, a part of itself beside itself in order to think the whole, to saturate or heal over the whole that suffers from detachment.'[18] It does so to cover up some kind of gap, some internal division. Metaphysics produces the architectural object as the paradigm of ground-as-support in order to veil its own lack of support, its ungrounded condition. Philosophy represents itself as architecture, it translates itself as architecture, producing itself in the translation. The limits of philosophy are established by the metaphorical status of architecture.

Philosophy draws an edifice, rather than draws on an edifice. It produces an architecture of grounded structure that it then uses for support, leaning on it, resting within it. The edifice is constructed to make theory possible, then subordinated as a metaphor in order to defer to some higher, non-material truth. Architecture is constructed as a material reality in order to liberate some higher domain. As material, it is but metaphor. The most material condition is used to establish the most ideal order, which is then bound to reject it as merely material. The status of material oscillates. The metaphor of the ground, the bedrock, the base, the fundamental, inverts to become base in the sense of degraded, material, less than ideal. The vertical hierarchy inverts itself. In this inversion, architecture flips from privileged origin to gratuitous supplement, foundation to ornament.

Philosophy treats its architectural motif as but a metaphor that can and should be discarded as superfluous. The figure of the grounded structure is but an illustration, a useful metaphor that illustrates the nature of metaphysics, but outlives its usefulness and must be abandoned from the final form of metaphysics, a representation to be separated from the fundamental presentation, a kind of scaffolding to be discarded when the project is complete, a frame that traces the outline of the building, a trace that lacks substance, but is structurally necessary, an open frame that is the possibility of a closed structure to which it then becomes an unnecessary appendage. Scaffolding is that piece of structure that

becomes ornamental. When philosophy reflects upon its own completion, it defines architecture as metaphorical. Metaphysics is the determination of architecture as metaphor.

But can architecture be so simply discarded? The use of the figure of structure 'is only
metaphorical', it will be said. Certainly. But metaphor is never innocent. It orients research
and fixes results. When the spatial model is hit upon, when it functions, critical reflection
rests within it.'[19] The very attempt to abandon metaphors involves metaphors. Even the
concept that the metaphorical can be detached from the fundamental is itself metaphorical.
Metaphysics grounds itself in the metaphors it claims to have abandoned. Metaphor 'is the
essential weight which anchors discourse in metaphysics'[20] rather than a superfluous ornament. Metaphor is fundamental. The metaphor of the grounded structure in particular
cannot be discarded in order to reveal the ground itself. The 'fundamental' is itself an
architectural metaphor so architecture cannot be abandoned in favor of the fundamental.

> Thus, the criteria for a classification of philosophical metaphors are borrowed from a derivative
> philosophical discourse… They are metaphorical, resisting every meta-metaphorics, the values
> of concept, foundation, and theory… What is fundamental corresponds to the desire for a firm
> and ultimate ground, a terrain to build on, the earth as the support for an artificial structure.[21]

Philosophy can only define a part of itself as non-metaphorical by employing the architectural metaphor. This metaphor organizes the status of metaphor. In so doing, it organizes
the tradition of philosophy that claims to be able to discard it. Architectural figures cannot
be detached from philosophical discourse. The architectural metaphor is not simply one
metaphor among others. More than the metaphor of foundation, it is the foundational
metaphor. It is therefore not simply a metaphor.

The architectural motif is bound to philosophy. The bond is contractual, not in the
sense of an agreement signed by two parties, but a logical knot of which the two parties are
but a side effect. More than the terms of exchange within and between these discourses, it
produces each discourse as a discourse. The translation contract between architecture and
philosophy works both ways. Each constructs the other as an origin from which they are
detached. Each identifies the other as other. The other is constructed as a privileged origin
that must then be discarded. In each there is this moment of inversion.

This primal contract, which is neither a contingent cultural artifact nor an atemporal
acultural principle, establishes the possibility of a social contract that separates architecture
and philosophy and constitutes them as discourses. The eventual status of architecture as a
discipline began to be negotiated by the first texts of architectural theory, which drew on
the canons of the philosophical tradition to identify the proper concern of the newly constituted figure of the architect with drawing *(disegno)* that mediates between the idea and
the building, the formal and the material, the soul and the body, the theoretical and the
practical. Architecture – architectural drawing – is neither simply a mechanical art bound
to the bodily realm of utility, nor a liberal art operating in the realm of ideas, but is their
reconciliation, the bridge between the two. Architectural theory thus constructs architecture as a bridge between the dominant oppositions of metaphysics and constitutes itself by
exploiting the contractual possibility already written into the philosophical tradition
wherein it describes itself as architecture.

It is not simply that architecture has some familiar unambiguous material reality that is
drawn upon by philosophy. Rather, philosophy draws an architecture, presents a certain

understanding, a theory, of architecture. The terms of the contract are the prohibition of a different description of the architectural object, or rather, the dissimulation of the object. To describe the privileged role of architecture in philosophy is not to identify architecture as the origin from which philosophy derives, but rather to show that the condition effected when philosophy infects itself from outside, by drawing on architecture, is internal to architecture itself. Architecture is cut from within, and philosophy unwittingly appeals to architecture precisely for this internal torment.

The concern here is to locate certain discursive practices repressed within the pathological mechanisms of this economy, to trace the impact of another account of architecture hidden within the tradition. Deconstruction is not outside the tradition. It achieves its force precisely by inhabiting the tradition, and thereby operating in terms of the contract. The question is, what relationship does deconstruction assume with the account of architecture repressed by that tradition?

The translation of deconstruction in architecture does not simply occur across the philosophy/architecture divide. It is occurring within each discourse. It is not a matter of simply generating a new description of the architectural object in architectural discourse but rather of locating the account of architecture already operative within deconstructive writing. It is the difference between this account and that of traditional philosophy that marks the precise nature of deconstruction's inhabitation of philosophy. The limits of deconstruction are established by the account of architecture it unwittingly produces.

Five

As architecture is bound up into language,[22] this account can be located precisely in the discussion of translation itself. Inasmuch as deconstruction tampers with the philosophical ideal of translation, it tampers with the philosophical ideal of architecture.

Derrida's account of translation is organized around an architectural figure: the Tower of Babel. The failure of the tower marks the necessity for translation, the multiplicity of languages, the free play of representation, which is to say the necessity for controlling representation. The collapse marks the necessity for a certain construction. The figure of the tower acts as the strategic intersection of philosophy, architecture, deconstruction, and translation.

The tower is the figure of philosophy because the dream of philosophy is that of translatability.[23] Philosophy is the ideal of translation. But the univocal language of the builders of the tower is not the language of philosophy, it is an imposed order, a violent imposition of a single language.[24] The necessity of philosophy is defined in the collapse rather than in the project itself. As the desire for translation produced by the incompletion of the tower is never completely frustrated, the edifice is never simply demolished. The building project of philosophy continues, but its completion is forever deferred.

The tower is also the figure of deconstruction. Since deconstruction inhabits philosophy, subverting it from within, it also inhabits the figure of the tower. It is lodged in the tower, transforming the representation of its construction. Inasmuch as philosophy is the ideal of translation, deconstruction is the subversion of translation.[25] That subversion is found within the conditions for philosophy, the incompletion of the tower: 'The deconstruction of the Tower of Babel, moreover, gives a good idea of what deconstruction is: an unfinished edifice whose half-completed structures are visible, letting one guess at the scaffolding behind them.'[26] Deconstruction identifies the inability of philosophy to establish the stable ground, the deferral of the origin that prevents the completion of the edifice, by locating the untranslatable, that which lies between the original and the translation.

But the tower is also the figure of architecture. The necessity of translation is the failure of building that demands a supplementation by architecture. Just as it is the precondition for philosophy, understood as building (presentation), translation also marks the necessity for architecture (representation), but as a representation that speaks of the essence of building, an architecture that represents the ground in its absence: 'If the tower had been completed there would be no architecture. Only the incompletion of the tower makes it possible for architecture as well as the multitude of languages to have a history.'[27] The possibility of architecture is bound up with the forever incomplete project of philosophy. Philosophy requires the account of building as grounded and architecture as detached precisely because of this incompletion. Structural failure produces the need for a supplement, the need for a building/architecture distinction, the need for architecture. Architecture is the translation of building that represents building to itself as complete, secure, undivided.

249

Since the tower is the figure of deconstruction, architecture, and translation, the question shifts from identifying the common ground between them, the identity, to locating the difference. The once discrete domains become entangled to the extent that the task becomes to identify the convoluted mechanism of translation that produces the sense of separate identities. This mechanism must be embedded in the scene of translation that bears on the status of structure.

Translation between the discourses is made possible by a breakdown in the sense of structure that is the currency within them. Derrida argues that the incompletion of the tower is the very structure of the tower. The tower is deconstructed by establishing that 'the structure of the original is marked by the requirement to be translated'[28] and that it 'in no way suffers from not being satisfied, at least it does not suffer in so far as it is the very structure of the work.'[29] There is a gap in the structure that cannot be filled, a gap that can only be covered over. The tower is always already marked by a flaw inasmuch as it is a tower. This is a displacement of the traditional idea of structure. Structure is no longer simply grounding. It is no longer a vertical hierarchy, but a convoluted line. The structure is no longer simply standing on the ground. The building stands on an abyss.

This argument follows Heidegger's attempt to dismantle the edifice of metaphysics in order to reveal the condition of the ground on which it stood. In doing so, he raises the possibility that the ground *(grund)* might actually be a concealed 'abyss' *(abgrund)* such that metaphysics is constructed in ignorance of the instability of the terrain on which it is erected: 'we move over this ground as over a flimsily covered abyss.'[30] Metaphysics becomes the veiling of the ground rather than the interrogation of it.

Heidegger's later work developed this possibility into a principle. He argues that philosophy has been in a state of 'groundlessness' ever since the translation of the ancient Greek terms into the language of metaphysics. This translation substituted the original sense of ground with that of the sense of ground-as-support, ground as supporting presence to which the world is added.[31] For Heidegger, metaphysics is groundless precisely because it determines the ground as support. The original sense of *logos* has been lost. With metaphysics, the origin is seen as a stable ground rather than an abyss. The 'modern' crisis, the 'groundlessness' of the age of technology, is produced by philosophy's ancient determination of the ground as support for a structure to which representations are added.[32] The crisis of representation is produced by the very attempt to remove representations in order to reveal the supporting presence of the ground. Man is alienated from the ground precisely by thinking of it as secure.

Because of the very familiarity of the principle of ground-as-support, 'we misjudge most readily and persistently the deceitful form of its violence.'[33] Metaphysics conceals this violence. The architectural motif of the grounded structure is articulated in a way that effects this concealment. The vertical hierarchy is a mechanism of control that veils its own violence.

Heidegger attempts to subvert this mechanism by rereading the status of the architectural motif. He argues that the thought of architecture as a simple addition to building actually makes possible the thought of the naked ground as support. Undermining the division between building and architecture displaces the traditional sense of the ground: 'But the nature of the erecting of buildings cannot be understood adequately in terms either of architecture or of engineering construction, nor in terms of a mere combination of the two.'[34] The thought of that which is neither building nor architecture makes possible the original ground that precedes the ground-as-support. The linear logic of addition is confused. The building is not simply added to the ground, the ornament is not simply added to the structure, art is not simply added to philosophy. The vertical hierarchy of ground/structure/ornament is convoluted. The architectural motif undermines itself.

But while certain Heideggerian moves subvert the logic of addition by displacing the traditional account of architecture, Heidegger ultimately contradicts that possibility, confirming the traditional logic by looking for a stable structure. Derrida argues that Heidegger is unable to abandon the tradition of ground-as-support. Indeed, he retains it in the very account of translation he uses to identify its emergence.

> At the very moment when Heidegger is denouncing translation into Latin Words, at the moment when, at any rate, he declares Greek speech to be lost, he also makes use of a 'metaphor.' Of at least one metaphor, that of the foundation and the ground. The ground of the Greek experience is, he says, lacking in this 'translation.' What I have just too hastily called 'metaphor' concentrates all the difficulties to come: does one speak 'metaphorically' of the ground for just anything?[35]

The thought of ground-as-support is not just produced by a mistranslation. It is itself no more than a certain account of translation. Translation is understood as presentation of the ground, and mistranslation is understood as loss of support, detachment from ground. The collapse of the tower establishes the necessity of translation as one of reconstruction, edification.[36] Heidegger's account of translation undermines itself when dealing with the translation of the original ground into the idea of the edifice. Heidegger appears to employ an account of translation similar to Derrida's inasmuch as he argues that the violation of the original ground is already there in the Greek original. But then he attempts to go beneath this sense to erase the violation, and, in so doing, restores a traditional account of translation.[37] He rebuilds the edifice he appears to have undermined.

Six

Derrida departs from Heidegger precisely by following him. He takes the Heideggerian line further until it folds back on itself, transforming itself. 'Deconstruction' is a 'translation' of two of Heidegger's terms: *Destruktion,* meaning 'not a destruction but precisely a destructuring that dismantles the structural layers in the system,' and *Abbau,* meaning 'to take apart an edifice in order to see how it is constituted or deconstituted.'[38] Derrida follows Heidegger's argument that this 'destructuring' or 'unbuilding' disturbs a tradition by inhabiting its structure in a way that exploits its metaphoric resources against itself.

> The movements of deconstruction do not destroy structures from the outside. They are not possible and effective, nor can they take accurate aim, except by inhabiting those structures. Inhabiting them *in a certain way,* because one always inhabits, and all the more when one does not suspect it. Operating necessarily from the inside, borrowing all the strategic and economic resources of subversion from the old structure, borrowing them structurally...[39]

The concern here is with the way deconstruction inhabits the structure of the edifice, that is, the structure of structure. Deconstruction is neither unbuilding nor demolition. Rather, it is the 'soliciting' of the edifice of metaphysics, the soliciting of structure 'in the sense that *sollicitare,* in old Latin means to shake as a whole, to make tremble in entirety.'[40] Solicitation is a form of interrogation that shakes structure in order to identify structural weaknesses, weaknesses that are structural.

Derrida destabilizes the edifice by arguing that its fundamental condition, its structural possibility, is the concealment of an abyss. The edifice of metaphysics claims to be stable because it is founded on the bedrock exposed when all the sedimentary layers have been removed. Deconstruction destabilizes metaphysics by locating in the bedrock the fractures that undermine its structure. The threat to metaphysics is underground. The subversion of presence is an underground operation. Deconstruction subverts the edifice it inhabits by demonstrating that the ground on which it is erected is insecure: 'the terrain is slippery and shifting, mined and undermined. And this ground is, by essence, an underground.'[41] But the fissures in the ground that crack the structure are not flaws that can be repaired. There is no more stable ground to be found. There is no unflawed bedrock.

Consequently, deconstruction appears to locate in metaphysics the fatal flaw that causes its collapse. It appears to be a form of analysis that dismantles or demolishes structures. It appears to be an undoing of construction. It is in this sense that it is most obviously architectural. But this obvious sense misses the force of deconstruction. Deconstruction is not simply architectural. Rather, it is a displacement of traditional thought about architecture.

> Now the concept of de-construction itself resembles an architectural metaphor. It is often said to have a negative attitude. Something has been constructed, a philosophical system, a tradition, a culture, and along comes a de-constructor and destroys it stone by stone, analyses the structure and dissolves it. Often enough this is the case. One looks at a system – Platonic/Hegelian – and examines how it was built, which keystone, which angle of vision supports the authority of the system. It seems to me, however, that this is not the essence of deconstruction. It is not simply the technique of an architect who knows how to de-construct what has been constructed, but a probing which touches upon the technique itself, upon the authority of the architectural metaphor and thereby constitutes its own architectural rhetoric. De-construction is not simply – as its name seems to indicate – the technique of a reversed construction when it is able to conceive for itself the idea of construction. One could say that there is nothing more architectural than de-construction, but also nothing less architectural.[42]

Deconstruction leads to a complete rethinking of the supplemental relationship that is organized by the architectural motif of ground/structure/ornament. To disrupt meta-

251

physics in this way is to disrupt the status of architecture. But it is not to simply abandon the traditional architectonic. Rather, it demonstrates that each of its divisions are radically convoluted. Each distinction is made possible by that which is neither one nor the other. The architectural logic of addition is subverted by demonstrating that it is made possible by precisely that which frustrates it.

This subversion of structure does not lead to a new structure. Flaws are identified in the structure but do not lead to its collapse. On the contrary, they are the very source of its strength. Derrida identifies the constitutional force of the weakness of a structure, that is, the strength of a certain weakness. Rather than abandoning a structure because its weakness has been found (which would be to remain in complicity with the ideal of a grounded structure), Derrida displaces the architectural motif. Structure becomes 'erected by its very ruin, held up by what never stops eating away at its foundations.'[43] Deconstruction is a form of interrogation that shakes structure in order to identify structural flaws, flaws that are structural. It is not the demolition of particular structures. It displaces the concept of structure itself by locating that which is neither support nor collapse.

> Structure is perceived through the incidence of menace, at the moment when imminent danger concentrates our vision on the keystone of an institution, the stone which encapsulates both the possibility and the fragility of its existence. Structure then can be *methodically* threatened in order to be comprehended more clearly and to reveal not only its supports but also that secret place in which it is neither construction nor ruin but lability. This operation is called (from the Latin) *soliciting*.[44]

The edifice is erected by concealing the abyss on which it stands. This repression produces the appearance of solid ground. The structure does not simply collapse because it is erected on, and fractured by, an abyss. Far from causing its collapse, the fracturing of the ground is the very possibility of the edifice. Derrida identifies the 'structural necessity' of the abyss:

> And we shall see that this abyss is not a happy or unhappy accident. An entire theory of the structural necessity of the abyss will be gradually constituted in our reading; the indefinite process of supplementarity has always already *infiltrated* presence... Representation *in the abyss* of presence is not an accident of presence; the desire of presence is, on the contrary, born from the abyss (the indefinite multiplication) of representation, from the representation of the representation, etc.[45]

The abyss is not simply the fracturing of the ground under the edifice. It is the internal fracturing of the edifice, the convolution of the distinction between building and architecture, structure and ornament, presentation and representation. Architecture always already inhabits and underpins the building it is supposedly attached to. It is this convolution that makes possible the thought of a ground that precedes the edifice, a thought that subordinates architecture as merely an addition. Architecture makes possible its own subordination to building.

Deconstruction is concerned with the untranslatable, the remainder that belongs neither to the original nor to the translation, but nevertheless resides within both. Deconstruction marks the structural necessity of a certain failure of translation. That is to say, the structural necessity of architecture. Architecture becomes the possibility of building rather than a simple addition to it. Inasmuch as translation is neither completed nor completely frustrated, the edifice of metaphysics is neither building nor architecture, neither presentation of the ground nor detachment from it, but the uncanny effacement of the distinction between them, the distinction that is at once the contractual possibility of architectural discourse and the means by which to repress the threat posed by that discourse. Deconstruction traces architecture's subversion of building, a subversion that cannot be resisted because architecture is the structural possibility of building. Building always harbors the secret of its constitutional violation by architecture. Deconstruction is the location of that violation. It locates ornament within the structure itself, not by integrating it in some classical synthetic gesture, but, on the contrary, by locating ornament's violation of structure, a violation that cannot be exorcised, a constitutional violation that can only be repressed.

Seven

Such a gesture does not constitute a method, a critique, an analysis or a source of legitimation.[46] It is not strategic. It has no prescribed aim, which is not to say that it is aimless. It moves very precisely, but not to some end. It is not a project. It is neither an application of something nor an addition to something. It is, at best, a strange structural condition, an event. It is a displacement of structure that cannot be evaluated in traditional terms because it frustrates the logic of grounding or testing. It is precisely that which is necessary to structure but evades structural analysis (and all analysis is structural); it is the breakdown in structure that is the possibility of structure.

The repression of certain constitutional enigmas is the basis of the social contract which organizes the overt discourse. Rather than offering a new account of the architectural object, deconstruction unearths the repressive mechanisms by which that figure of architecture operates. Hidden within the traditional architectural figure is another. The architectural motif is required by philosophy not simply because it is a paradigm of stable structure; it is also required precisely for its instability.

For this reason, to translate deconstruction in architecture is not to simply transform the condition of the architectural object. As metaphysics is the definition of architecture as metaphor, the disruption of architecture's metaphoric condition is a disruption of metaphysics. But this is not to say that this disruption occurs outside the realm of objects. The teleologies of theory/practice, ideal/material, etc. do not disappear. Rather, there is a series of non-linear exchanges within and between these domains, which problematize, but do not abandon, the difference. It is thereby possible to operate within the traditional description of architecture as the representation of structure in order to produce objects which make these enigmas thematic.

Such gestures are neither simply theoretical, nor simply practical. They are neither a new way of reading familiar architecture, nor the means of producing a new architecture. Objects are already bisected into theory and practice. To translate deconstruction in architecture does not lead simply to a formal reconfiguration of the object. Rather, it calls into question the condition of the object, its objecthood. It problematizes the condition of the object without simply abandoning it. This is a concern with theoretical objects, objects whose theoretical status and objecthood are problematic, slippery objects that make thematic the theoretical condition of objects and the objecthood of theory.

Such gestures do not simply inhabit the prescribed domains of philosophy and architecture. While philosophical discourse and architectural discourse depend on an explicit account of architecture, they have no unique claim on that account. The translation contract on which those discourses are based underpin a multiplicity of cultural exchanges. The concern becomes the strategic play of the architectural motif in these exchanges. This cultural production of architecture does not take the form specified in architectural discourse; architecture does not occupy the domain allotted to it. Rather than the object of a specific discourse, architecture is a series of discursive mechanisms whose operation has to be traced in ways that are unfamiliar to architectural discourse.

Consequently, the status of the translation of deconstruction in architecture needs to be rethought. A more aggressive reading is required, an architectural transformation of deconstruction that draws on the gaps in deconstruction that demand such an abuse, sites that already operate with a kind of architectural violence. There is a need for a strong reading which locates that which deconstruction cannot handle of architecture.

Possibilities emerge within architectural discourse that go beyond the displacement of architecture implicit in deconstructive writing. To locate these possibilities is to (re)produce deconstruction by transforming it. Such a transformation must operate on the hesitation deconstruction has about architecture, a hesitation that surfaces precisely within its most confident claims about architecture.

Derrida writes:

> The 'Tower of Babel' does not merely figure the irreducible multiplicity of tongues; it exhibits an incompletion, the impossibility of finishing, of totalizing, of saturating, of completing something on the order of edification, architectural construction, system and architectonics. What the multiplicity of idioms actually limits is not only a 'true' translation, a transparent and adequate interexpression, it is also a structural order, a coherence of construct. There is then (let us translate) something like an internal limit to formalization, an incompleteness of the constructure. It would be easy and up to a certain point justified to see there the translation of a system in deconstruction.[47]

This passage culminates symptomatically in a sentence that performs the classical philosophical gesture. Architecture is at once given constitutive power and has that power frustrated by returning its status to mere metaphor. Here the tower, the figure of translation, is itself understood as a translation, the architectural translation of deconstruction. Which, in Derridean terms, is to say a figure that does not simply represent deconstruction, but is its possibility. But an inquiry needs to focus on why an architectural reading of deconstruction is 'easy' and what is the 'certain point' beyond which it becomes unjustified, improper. A patient reading needs to force the convoluted surface of deconstructive writing and expose the architectural motif within it.

But perhaps even such an abusive reading of Derrida is insufficient. Inasmuch as deconstruction is abused in architectural discourse, its theory of translation, which is to say its theory of abuse, needs to be rethought. Because of architecture's unique relationship to translation, it cannot simply translate deconstruction. It is so implicated in the economy of translation that it threatens deconstruction. There is an implicit identity between the untranslatable remainder located by deconstruction and that part of architecture that causes deconstruction to hesitate – the architecture it resists. Consequently, deconstruction does not simply survive architecture.

1 J. Derrida, *Positions*, tr. A. Bass (Chicago, 1981), p. 20.
2 'A text lives only if it lives *on [sur-vit]*, and it lives *on* only if it is *at once* translatable *and* untranslatable… Totally translatable, it disappears as a text, as writing, as a body of language *[langue]*. Totally untranslatable, even within what is believed to be one language, it dies immediately. Thus triumphant translation is neither the life nor the death of the text, only or already its living *on,* its life after life, its life after death.' J. Derrida, 'Living On: Border Lines,' tr. J. Hulbert, in *Deconstruction and Criticism* (New York, 1979), p. 102.
3 Cf. J. Derrida, 'Me – Psychoanalysis: An Introduction to 'The Shell and the Kernel' by N. Abraham,' tr. R. Klein, in *Diacritics* (Spring 1979).
4 Deconstruction is considered here in the context of philosophy. While Derrida repeatedly argues that deconstruction is not philosophy, he also notes that it is not non-philosophy either. To simply claim that deconstruction is not philosophy is to maintain philosophy by appealing to its own definition of its other. It is to participate in the dominant reading of Derrida that resists the force of deconstruction. That force is produced by identifying the complicity of the apparently non-philosophical within the philosophical tradition. Deconstruction occupies the texts of philosophy in order to identify a non-philosophical site within them. Deconstruction cannot be considered outside the texts of philosophy it inhabits, even as a foreigner.
5 'For if the difficulties of translation can be anticipated… one should not begin by naively believing that the word 'deconstruction' corresponds in French to some clear and univocal signification. There is already in 'my' language a serious ('somber') problem of translation between what here or there can be envisaged for the word, and the usage itself, the reserves of the word.' J. Derrida, 'Letter to a Japanese Friend,' *Derrida and Différance*, eds. D. Wood and R. Bernasconi (Coventry, 1985), p. 1.
6 E. Kant, *Critique of Pure Reason,* tr. N. K. Smith (London, 1929), p. 47.
7 Ibid., p. 608.
8 Ibid., p. 14.
9 Ibid., p. 219.
10 M. Heidegger, *An Introduction to Metaphysics,* tr. J. Macquarrie and E. Robinson (New York, 1962), p. 2.
11 Cf. the Greek temple in 'The Origin of the Work of Art': 'Truth happens in the temple's standing where it is. This does not mean that something is correctly represented and rendered there, but that what is as a whole is brought into unconcealedness and held therein.' M. Heidegger, 'The Origin of the Work of Art,' tr. A. Hofstadter, in *Poetry, Language, Thought* (New York, 1971), p. 56. The edifice is neither a representation of the ground, nor even a presentation, but is the production of the world.
12 'It is precisely the idea that it is a matter of providing a foundation for an edifice already constructed that must be avoided.' M. Heidegger, *Kant and the Problem of Metaphysics,* tr. J. S. Churchill (Bloomington, 1962), p. 4.
13 'The foundation of traditional metaphysics is shaken and the edifice…begins to totter.' Ibid., p. 129.
14 E. Kant, *Critique of Pure Reason,* p. 60.
15 M. Heidegger, *Kant and the Problem of Metaphysics,* p. 5.
16 J. Derrida, 'Structure, Sign and Play in the Discourse of the Human Sciences,' tr. A. Bass, in *Writing and Difference* (Chicago, 1978), p. 279.
17 M. Heidegger, 'The Origin of the Work of Art,' p. 19.
18 J. Derrida, 'Parergon,' tr. G. Bennington, A. Bass, and I. McCleod, in *Truth in Painting* (Chicago, 1987), p. 40.
19 J. Derrida, 'Force and Signification,' *Writing and Difference,* tr. A. Bass (Chicago, 1978), p. 17.
20 Ibid., p. 27.
21 J. Derrida, 'White Mythology: Metaphor in the Text of Philosophy,' tr. A. Bass, in *Margins of Philosophy* (Chicago 1982), p. 224.
22 Not in the sense of the structuralist concern for architecture as a kind of language, a system of objects to which language theory can be applied, but as the possibility of thought about language.
23 'With this problem of translation we will thus be dealing with nothing less than the problem of the very passage into philosophy.' J. Derrida, *Dissemination,* tr. B. Johnson (Chicago, 1981), p. 72.
24 'Had their enterprise succeeded, the universal tongue would have been a particular language imposed by violence, by force. It would not have been a universal language – for example in the Leibnizian sense – a transparent language to which everyone would have access.' J. Derrida, *The Ear of the Other,* ed. C. V. McDonald, tr. A. Ronell (New York, 1985), p. 101. On the violent imposition of language, cf J. Derrida, 'Languages and the Institutions of Philosophy,' *Recherche et semiotique/ Semiotic Inquiry* 4, no. 2 (1984), pp. 91-154.
25 'And the question of deconstruction is also through and through *the* question of translation…' J. Derrida, 'Letter to a Japanese Friend,' p. 6.
26 J. Derrida, *The Ear of the Other,* p. 102.
27 J. Derrida, 'Architecture Where the Desire May Live,' *Domus* 671 (1986), p. 25.
28 J. Derrida, 'Des Tours de Babel,' *Difference in Translation,* ed. J. F. Graham, tr. J. F. Graham (Ithaca, 1985), p. 184.
29 Ibid., p. 182.
30 M. Heidegger, *An Introduction to Metaphysics,* p. 93.
31 This degenerate translation is based on a degeneration that already occurred within the original Greek, requiring a return to a more primordial origin: 'But with this Latin translation the original meaning of the Greek word is destroyed. This is true not only of the Latin translation of *this* word but of all other Roman translations of the Greek philosophical language. What happened in this translation from the Greek into the Latin is not accidental and harmless; it marks the first stage in the process by which we cut ourselves off and alienated ourselves from the original essence of Greek philosophy… But it should be said in passing that even within Greek philosophy a narrowing of the word set in forthwith, although the original meaning did not vanish from the experience, knowledge, and orientation of Greek philosophy.' M. Heidegger, *An Introduction to Metaphysics,* p. 13.
32 'The perfection of technology is only the echo of the claim to the…completeness of the foundation…. Thus, the characteristic domination of the principle of ground then determines the essence of our modern technological age.' M. Heidegger, 'The Principle of Ground,' tr. K. Hoeller, in *Man and World* 7 (1974), p. 213.
33 Ibid., p. 204.
34 M. Heidegger, 'Building, Dwelling, Thinking,' *Poetry, Language, Thought,* p. 159.
35 J. Derrida, 'Restitutions of the Truth in Painting,' *The Truth in Painting,* p. 290.
36 Note how Derrida argues that the university is 'built' on the ideal of translation (J. Derrida, 'Living On: Border Lines,' pp. 93-94) in the same way that he argues that it is 'built' on the ideal of ground-as-support (J. Derrida, 'The University in the Eyes of Reason,' *Diacritics* [Fall 1983], pp. 11-20).
37 '*Beneath* the seemingly literal and thus faithful translation

there is concealed…a translation without a corresponding, equally authentic experience of what they say. The rootlessness of Western thought begins with this translation.' M. Heidegger, 'The Origin of the Work of Art,' p. 23 (emphasis added). 'We are not merely taking refuge in a more literal translation of a Greek word. We are reminding ourselves of what, unexperienced and unthought, *underlies* our familiar and therefore outworn essence of truth…' Ibid., p. 52 (emphasis added).

38 J. Derrida, 'Roundtable on Autobiography,' tr. P. Kamuf in *The Ear of the Other*, p. 86. Of the word 'deconstruction': 'Among other things I wished to translate and adapt to my own ends the Heideggerian word *Destruktion* or *Abbau*. Each signified in this context an operation bearing on the structure or traditional architecture of the fundamental concepts of ontology or of western metaphysics.' J. Derrida, 'Letter to a Japanese Friend,' p. 1.

39 J. Derrida, *Of Grammatology*, tr. G. C. Spivak

(Baltimore, 1976), p. 24.

40 J. Derrida, 'Differance,' *Margins of Philosophy*, p. 21.

41 J. Derrida, *Limited Inc*. (Baltimore, 1977), p. 168.

42 J. Derrida, 'Architecture Where the Desire May Live,' p. 18.

43 J. Derrida, 'Fors,' tr. B. Johnson, in *The Georgia Review* 31, no. 1 (1977), p. 40.

44 J. Derrida, 'Force and Signification,' p. 6.

45 J. Derrida, *Of Grammatology*, p. 163.

46 'In spite of appearances, deconstruction is neither an *analysis* nor a *critique* and its translation would have to take that into consideration. It is not an analysis in particular because the dismantling of a structure is not a regression toward a *simple* element, towards an *indissoluble origin*. These values, like that of analysis, are themselves philosophemes subject to deconstruction.' J. Derrida, 'Letter to a Japanese Friend,' p. 4.

47 J. Derrida, 'Des Tours de Babel,' p. 165.